CW01649565

PEEL IN CARICATURE

The 'Political Sketches' of John Doyle ('H.B.')

edited by Richard A Gaunt

ABOUT THE CONTRIBUTORS

Dr Richard A Gaunt is Associate Professor in Modern British History at the University of Nottingham and a Fellow of the Royal Historical Society. He has edited the diaries of the fourth Duke of Newcastle in two volumes (2003, 2006) and written widely on British political and electoral history between c.1780 and 1850. His study of *Sir Robert Peel. The Life and Legacy* was published in 2010 (London and New York). Dr Gaunt became a Life Member of the Peel Society in 1994.

Professor Fintan Cullen is Professor of Art History at the University of Nottingham. His main research area is the art and representation of Ireland from the eighteenth century to the twentieth century. Before coming to Nottingham in 1994, he worked as a Lecturer at Trinity College Dublin and at Staffordshire University as well as spending time as a curatorial assistant at the National Gallery of Ireland. As a graduate student at Yale he worked as an intern in the Department of Prints and Drawings at the Yale Centre for British Art. His many publications include *The Irish Face: Redefining the Irish Portrait* (2004) and *Ireland on Show: Art, Union and Nationhood* (Farnham, 2012).

COPYRIGHT NOTICE

© Richard A Gaunt, Fintan Cullen and The Peel Society 2014
All rights reserved. No part of this publication may be reproduced, stored or introduced into a retrieval system or transmitted in any form by any means (electronic, mechanical, photocopy, recording or otherwise) without permission from the publishers.

Whilst every care has been taken to ensure the accuracy of the information contained in this publication, the authors and the Peel Society cannot accept any responsibility for any error or omission.

ISBN: 978-0-9521878-9-9 (13 digit)
0-9521878-9-2 (10 digit)

Designed and printed by:
4word Ltd, Bristol
2014

The Peel Society gratefully acknowledges financial assistance towards the cost of publication provided by:

The University of Nottingham
UNITED KINGDOM · CHINA · MALAYSIA

Arts & Humanities Research Council

CONTENTS

The plates:

THE PEEL SOCIETY

Chairman – Norman Biggs   The Peel Society is a Registered Charity No. 509865

Patrons: H.M. Lord-Lieutenant and Custos Rotulorum of Staffordshire * The Rt Hon David Cameron, M.P. * The Rt. Hon The Earl Peel, G.C.V.O. D.L. * The Rt Hon The Earl Ferrers * The Rt. Hon The Lord Briggs of Lewes, F.B.A. * The Rt Hon Lord Hurd of Westwell, C.H., C.B.E. * The Rt Hon Sir John Major, K.G., C.H. * The Rt Hon Tony Blair * The Rt Hon Gordon Brown, M.P. * Christopher Pincher, M.P. * The Chief Constable of Staffordshire * Lady Lightbown * County Cllr Brian Jenkins

Sir Robert Peel was born in 1788 into the world of Joshua Reynolds, of stage coaches and highwaymen, and died in 1850 in the age of Darwin, of *Punch*, railway excursions, trade unions and income tax.

He was M.P. for Tamworth, twice Home Secretary and Prime Minister. When he died in 1850, he was a hero of the working classes as a result of the Repeal of the Corn Laws, which brought cheap bread to the urban masses. He reformed the Criminal Justice system, founded the Police force and was instrumental in the establishment of modern business practices.

He lived at Drayton Manor in Staffordshire and was squire of Drayton, bringing up a family of seven children with his beloved wife, Lady Julia. Here he housed part of his large collection of old masters, which is now in the National Gallery.

Since 1979, the Society has created a major collection of Peel memorabilia, which is on show at Middleton Hall, B77 4NW; this is open most Sundays from Easter to the end of September and on Bank Holidays. Private visits can be arranged by contact through the society's web site **www.thepeelsociety.org.uk**.

The Peel Society has celebrated a number of major anniversaries associated with Peel's life and achievements such as The Tamworth Manifesto (1834) and the Repeal of the Corn Laws (1846). These celebrations have attracted well known politicians and academics to Tamworth to give their opinions about Peel's heritage.

The Society promotes its aims by exhibitions, lectures and excursions to sites associated with the life and times of Sir Robert Peel. It has also visited a number of parliaments and assemblies such as the EU in Strasbourg, Peel committee room in the House of Commons, the Dial and the Senate in Dublin, Tynwald in the Isle of Man, The Welsh Assembly in Cardiff, The Scottish Parliament in Edinburgh and Stormont in Northern Ireland.

The objectives of the Society are to encourage the study of the life, works and times of Sir Robert Peel and to preserve the memorials, associations, manuscripts, letters, books etc. of the Peel Family and of the Police and to bring these items together for display in a "Peel Museum". Membership of the Society is open to all persons interested in these objectives.

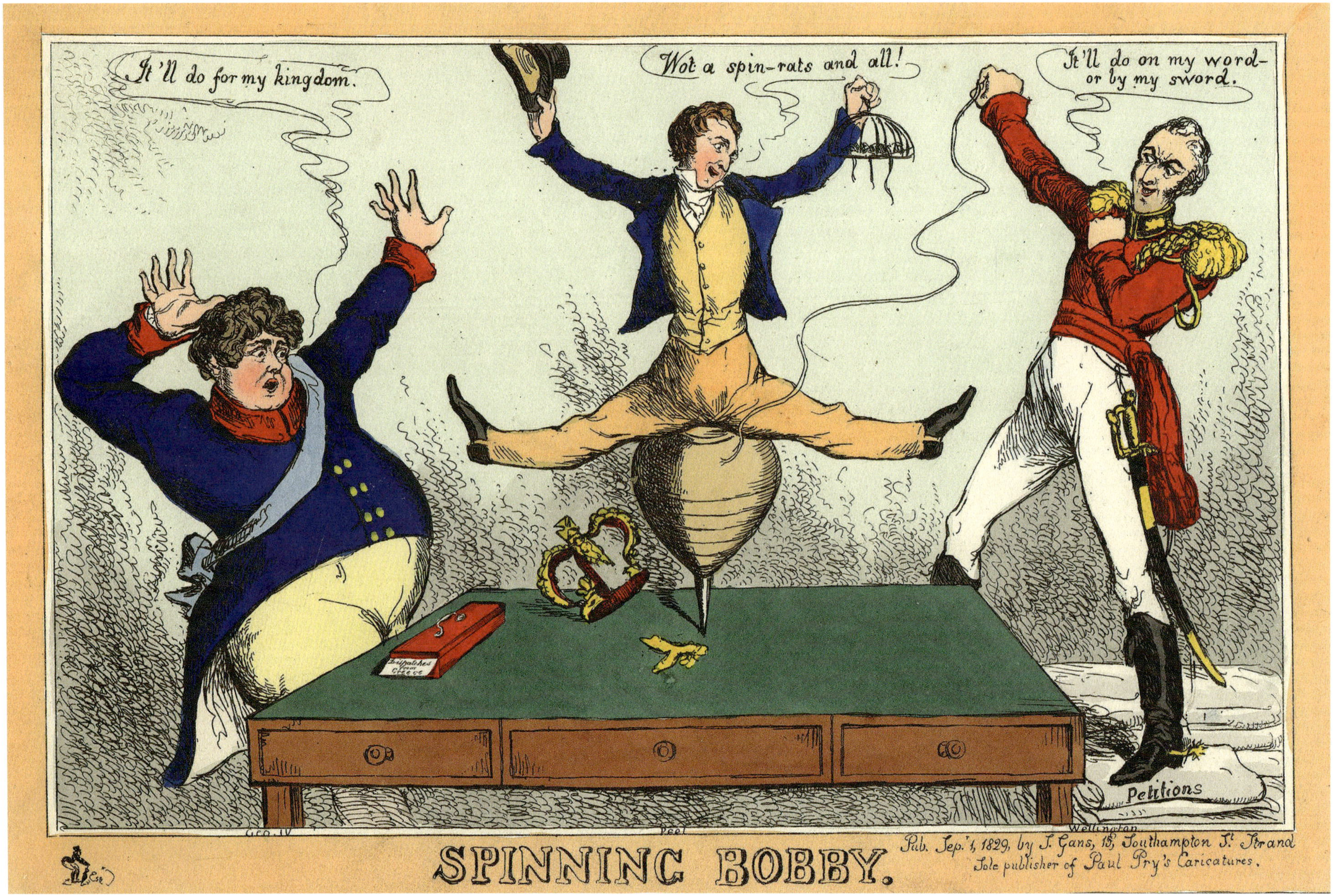

FIG. 1: William Heath, *The Spinning Bobby* (1 September 1829), © The Trustees of the British Museum

Peel in Caricature: The Historical Context

Richard A Gaunt

In October 1829, a paragraph appeared in the newspapers under the title 'Ministerial Occupation':

> Yesterday afternoon the Right Hon Home Secretary amused himself for some time with viewing the caricatures at a shop in Henrietta Street, Covent Garden. At some of them he laughed heartily; but the one that attracted most attention was a picture entitled 'Spinning Bobby' that represents the most illustrious Personage in the kingdom [George IV] at one end of a table, and a person very like the Duke of Wellington at the other end of it. There is a top on the table spinning way right merrily, and seated on it, with legs in an extended and regularly fly-away condition, a Right Hon Gentleman, very similar in appearance to the Home Secretary previously to the late Mr Canning's Administration [Peel]. 'At what a rate I *spin*'. Mr Peel also laughed at this picture a little. The personages seated at the table appear to be most heartily enjoying the little Orange-looking gentleman's spinning.

A letter from Peel to his wife, Julia, confirms that the incident was correct in all but one particular:

> We sometimes complain of our movements being noticed by the newspapers but the paragraph shows a more than ordinary attention to them. It is all quite true. I did stop as I was coming from Sir Thomas Lawrence's and I did laugh, not at the caricature which it mentioned there but at one called 'Peeling a Charley' in which I am represented stripping one of the old watchmen of his great-coat.[1]

The episode is illuminating for a number of reasons. In the first place, it confirms what contemporaries (and subsequent historians) were sometimes at pains to deny – that Peel had a healthy sense of humour, not least respecting himself.[2] The fact that it was only six months since Peel had been universally castigated in caricatures as a 'rat', a 'Jesuit' and a 'turn-coat' for having passed Catholic Emancipation, after two decades of persistent hostility to the measure (hence his nickname as Protestant or 'Orange' Peel), was a testament to the various purposes to which caricature could be turned and its fickle approach to the individual politicians whom it satirised. Peel's new Metropolitan Police Force, which replaced the system of 'watchmen' first instituted under Charles II – the so-called 'Charleys' – provided the subject for good-humoured observation in 'Peeling a Charley', much as the connotations of Peel's turn-coat or 'spinning' qualities – reinforced by his ancestry as the son of a Lancashire cotton and calico manufacturer who had utilised new technologies such as the 'Spinning Jenny' – had been the nub of the joke in 'Spinning Bobby'.

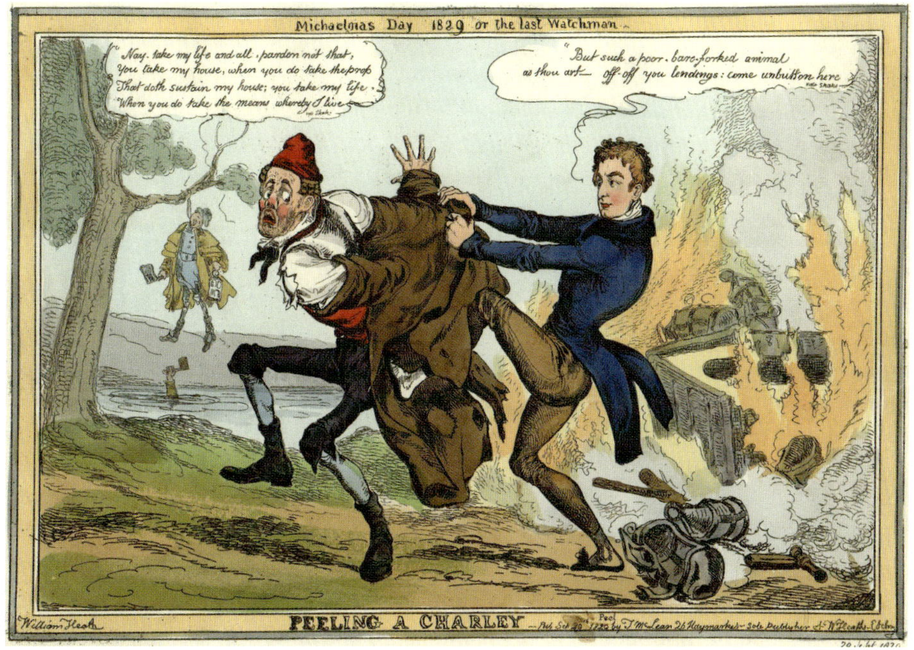

FIG. 2: William Heath, *Peeling a Charley* (29 September 1829), © The Trustees of the British Museum

The 'Golden Age' of Caricature

Caricatures were a mainstay of British political life in the 'age of Peel'. From their introduction into England as a subject of polite amusement, during the eighteenth century, this new and subversive art form was pioneered by a variety of amateur artists – notably George Townshend and Henry Bunbury – before reaching new heights of popularity, ubiquity and commercial success under the master craftsmen of the so-called 'golden age' of caricature (1760–1830), James Gillray, Thomas Rowlandson and George Cruikshank. Caricatures were overwhelmingly metropolitan in their focus – produced and marketed in a range of fashionable caricature shops and print sellers in the City of London and the West End. This signified both the principal audience and focus of caricatures.

Print sellers' windows of the sort which Peel stopped by on his way through Covent Garden offered a crucial (and enticing) means of marketing, advertising and – to those who could not afford to purchase them – 'consuming' the latest products of the caricaturists. The shop-window was both inclusive, in that it invited 'window shoppers' to partake in these productions, and 'exclusive', in that many caricature shops charged admission to view exhibitions of their latest works and were conscious of the need to turn interest into hard cash, either through selling copies of prints or lending portfolio albums for hire as a form of evening entertainment. It is an irony that one of the consequences of the introduction of the 'Bobbies' onto the streets of London was an increasing tendency to disperse large crowds of spectators from congregating outside print shop windows, because they were considered a 'public nuisance'.[3]

The caricaturists themselves came to their craft for a variety of reasons; a number were highly-trained artists and engravers who had been disappointed at their lack of patronage and frustrated by their attempts to gain acceptance in the world of 'high' art, by admission into institutions such as the Royal Academy. It is especially piquant that, in the episode above, Peel should have been on his way home from the studio of Sir Thomas Lawrence, President of the Royal Academy and the leading portraitist of his day. The most renowned caricatures reflected the artistic and technical training of their creators; they were produced by etching the image into copper plates, from which impressions (or prints) were taken. These could be sold monochrome or in colour, the latter often being 'sub-contracted' to colourists for completion. Because copper plates could wear out after a relatively small number of impressions – a fact which was sometimes obscured by heavier colouring – the number of prints from a single plate does not seem to have exceeded 2000–3000, though many caricatures had much smaller 'runs', which added to their exclusivity. The introduction of steel plates increased the durability and 'life-span' of caricatures, during the 1820s. However, the emergence of new reproductive methods – notably lithography (impressions taken from pencil or crayon on marble or stone) and wood-cuts (which allowed text and images to be reproduced together at a much more economical rate) – challenged the older methods of production. Likewise, at a time when newspapers were considered expensive, because of taxation, caricatures were a 'high-end' commodity, marketing at, on average, from six-pence to a shilling uncoloured and double for colour. Much as with stamps, coins, medals and other artefacts, caricatures were highly collectable, with individual prints being gathered together in large portfolios, appearing in de-luxe editions and albums and making their way onto a variety of surfaces, including handkerchiefs, fans, fire-screens, ceramics and the walls of newly designated 'print rooms'. Like Charles James Fox and George IV before him, Peel was an avid collector of caricatures, numbering some 3000 examples amongst his collection.[4]

Caricatures relied for their effectiveness on a central conceit: whilst the person being satirised was exaggerated in some way (usually through distorting their physical attributes), the individual had to be recognisable enough to be identified by the audience, who thereby shared in the joke. Practically speaking, the lack of direct identification of the subject of a caricature was a useful defence against potential legal action – directly implicating a person, especially in a scurrilous or even blasphemous print, exposed the artist and their publisher to potential prosecution, even if the chances of securing a conviction were low. Using puns, such as 'Spinning Bobby' and 'Orange Peel', colour-association – Peel literally coloured Orange or wearing it – and inserting words, whether as captions, speech-bubbles, quotations or the like, helped to make the association clear but also created different layers of meaning. The more educated or knowledgeable the viewer/reader, the more the meanings, allusions and humour of caricatures could be penetrated or understood. This was particularly true of caricatures relating to specific political episodes or events, which were often immediate and ephemeral. It was even more apparent where caricatures employed Biblical, classical or textual allusions or parodied 'high art' itself. Like newspapers, the events of the day, once topical, soon became matters of history. This meant that, even in their own day, caricatures required a high degree of 'visual literacy' – an ability to penetrate the different layers of meaning which they encompassed. Audiences might 'get' the caricature on a surface level but those with a deeper and more sophisticated knowledge would be able to go deeper and gain more from what was on view. As historians are increasingly coming to acknowledge, this makes caricatures not only sophisticated artistic productions, in respect of their technical attributes and qualities, but important sources of information about the events to which they relate.[5]

With the death of James Gillray in 1815 and the movement of George Cruikshank from hard-edged political satire into book illustration – most famously, as the illustrator for Charles Dickens – the tradition of the single-sheet caricature appeared to be in decline. However, it enjoyed a new resurgence under the entrepreneurial publisher and print-seller, Thomas McLean (1788–1875), of the Haymarket. Between 1825 and 1830, McLean published the work of William Heath, the artist whose work Peel stopped and laughed at in Covent Garden. Heath worked under the pseudonym of 'Paul Pry', a character immortalised on stage by the actor John Liston; he sported a top hat, spectacles and – frequently misplaced – umbrella, and was perpetually interfering in other people's affairs.[6] Heath's most famous series, published at the time of the Catholic Emancipation crisis, was a series of coaching prints imitating London characters: Peel appeared as *The Cad* [or Conductor] *to the Man Wot Drives the*

Sovereign. The series inspired a host of imitators – an important reminder that caricature was indebted to the creative ideas (and commercial success) of its competitors and rivals. McLean began to issue stern textual reminders of which were 'genuine' as opposed to fake or imitative prints, whilst devices such as embossing with small oval or lozenge-shaped stamps indicated consumers were receiving the 'genuine article'. These devices became increasingly important with the commercial success of Heath's successor, 'H.B.'[7]

John Doyle: The artist formerly known as 'H.B.'

In 1835, *The Times* described the appearance of 'H.B.'s *Political Sketch*, number 414, as 'singular evidence of the extraordinary fertility, as almost every one of the 400 and odd is a proof of the originality, of that genius which has left him without a rival except Gillray amongst his predecessors in this department of political satire'. Elsewhere, it called him 'the prince of caricaturists' and 'that very clever humourist in outline'.[8] Subsequent commentators have, likewise, crowned 'H.B.' the 'father' or 'king' of political caricature in this period.[9]

'H.B.' was, in fact, John Doyle (1797–1868), the eldest of two sons born to James Doyle, a silk-mercer, of Dublin. The Doyles claimed a long and noble ancestry – the family could trace its origins to various branches of 'D'Ouilly', 'D'Oyly', 'D'Oel' and 'Doyle' antecedents originating from Pont d'Oilly near Rouen in Normandy. In 1333, Alexander D'Oyley, the grandson of Sir John Doyley of Stoke Doyley, was granted lands in County Wexford, Ireland, by King Edward III of England, for his role in the invasion of Ireland. The family's coat of arms were emblazoned with 'Fortitudine Vincit' ('He conquers by fortitude') under a crown and stag. However, 'not until the seventeenth century does it become possible to trace [Doyle's] line of descent without a break'. At the Glorious Revolution of 1688, the Doyles were dispossessed of their lands in favour of the Duke of York and, by 1762, the family's remaining property at Barracurra (Tipperary) had been abandoned. Richard Doyle, John's grandfather, went to Dublin, where he became a silk merchant. His son James (born c.1755) was Doyle's father.[10]

John Doyle exhibited precocious talents as an artist, which were nurtured through his early training in Dublin. He learned drawing from the Italian landscape painter Gaspare Gabrielli (fl. 1803–1833) and studied art in the drawing school of the Dublin Society (later, the Royal Dublin Society) as a miniature painter under John Comerford.[11] Here he acquired great 'skill at exact and unforced delineation of likenesses and expressions' and 'rigorously developed his powers of exact observation…in a way which was to prove of great value to him in his later career as a portrait caricaturist'.[12] As such, though

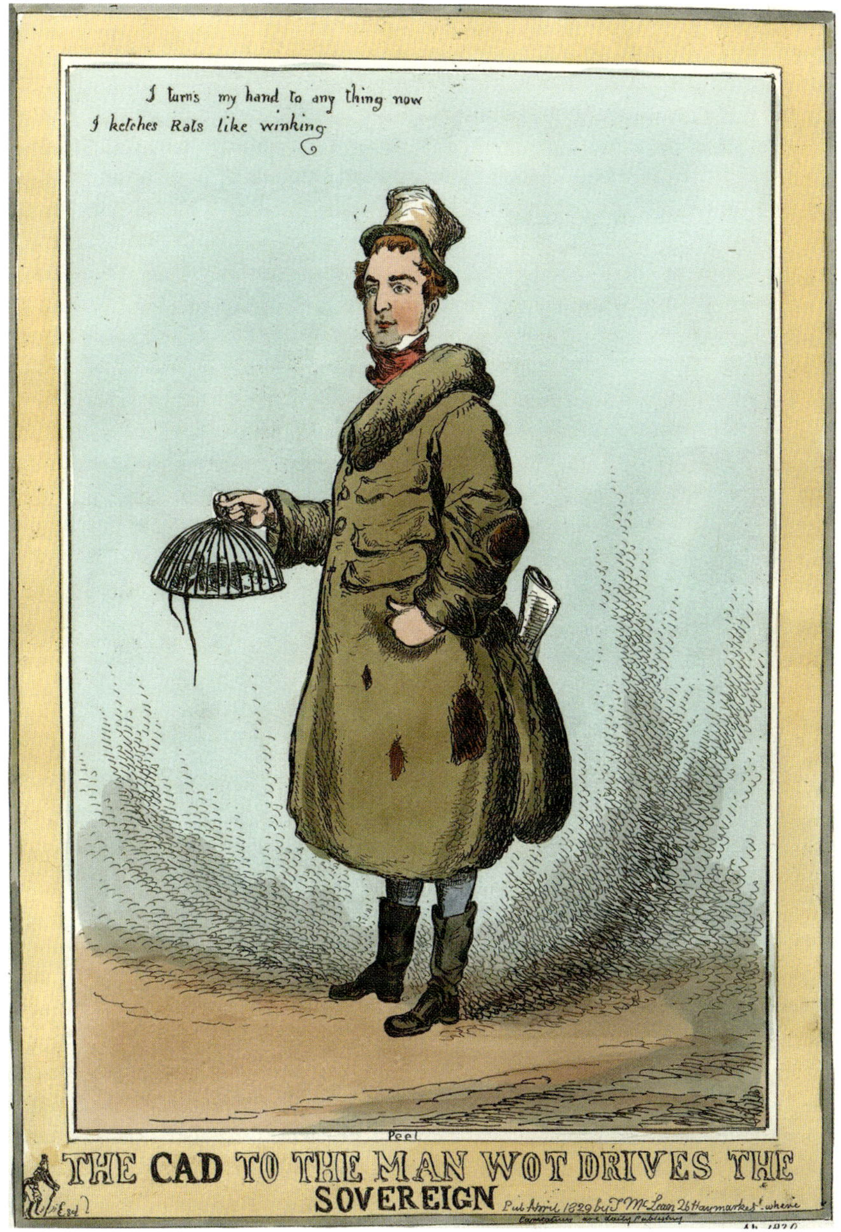

FIG. 3: William Heath, *The Cad to the Man Wot Drives the Sovereign* (April 1829)
© The Trustees of the British Museum

Doyle was never a member of the Royal Academy, he was wrong to disclaim any connection 'whatever with any artistic society'.[13]

Doyle developed particular skill as an equestrian artist, producing pictures 'of a very pleasing, well finished, slightly stylised nature'.[14] He enjoyed foxhunting and this brought him the patronage of high-ranking members of the Anglo-Irish elite, including Judge Mayne, Sir Edward Kerrison, the Lord Lieutenant (Lord Talbot) and the Marquis of Sligo. Though Peel served as Chief Secretary to the Lord Lieutenant of Ireland, at this period, no connection with Doyle has, so far, emerged. From 1814–1821, Doyle exhibited some twenty equestrian portraits and portraits of horsemen at the Hibernian Society of Artists (1814) and in the Dublin Society's house in Hawkins Street (1815, 1817, 1819) and the Royal Arcade (1821).[15]

By 1822, Doyle had left Dublin for England. According to family legend, he brought with him a painting by Van Dyck of William Howard, 1st Viscount Stafford (a victim of the 'Popish Plot' of 1679), some seventeenth-century family plate with the Doyle arms embossed on it and a sixteenth-century medical mortar.[16] He also brought with him a new wife: Marianna Conan, the daughter of James Conan of Dublin.

Over the course of the next thirteen years, Doyle and his growing family changed London address four times: from 60 Berners Street (1825) to 14 Manning's Place, Lambeth (1827) to 23 Euston Crescent (1830) and 5 Brill Terrace, Somers Town, North London (1835). He also exhibited at the annual exhibitions of the Royal Academy in 1825–1827, 1830–1831 and 1835; invariably, these were portraits of unidentified 'gentlemen' and 'ladies'. His greatest successes were his multi-plate series *The Life of the Race Horse* (1822) and his first Royal Academy exhibit, *Turning out the Stag* (1825). Other work was in keeping with Doyle's developing expertise – coaching scenes, hunting scenes, race meetings and royal portraits – including *The Duke of York on his cob*, *The Duke of Wellington on his charger*, *George IV sketched at Ascot* (1828), *Princess Victoria in her pony phaeton* (1829) and *William IV and party riding on the Downs near Brighton* (1832).[17]

In 1827, Doyle first turned his hand to the art-form, and series, which was to establish his contemporary fame. Supplying some lithographic sketches to McLean, the enterprising publisher hit upon the idea of a regular, serialised, production, taking the form of numbered *Political Sketches*. These began to appear regularly (at a rate of three or four at a time), throughout the parliamentary season, from 1829, priced at two shillings each.[18] Though the output began to decline during the later-1840s, they continued until March 1851, having reached number 917.[19] Initially, the designs 'were simply drawn on stone; but a tint was soon adopted, of various delicate colours, with the white paper used as lights. Some have yellow borders. To please some of "H.B."s admirers, hand-colouring was employed'.[20]

Who, how and at what point the device of masking the identity of the artist under the initials 'H.B.' came about is still not clear. The device – a monogram or cypher – consisted of two capital Is (one above the other) next to two capital Ds, the combined effect of which was to form the 'H.B.' (I being a common denominator for the letter J). Anyone who cared to examine the initials closely, and thought seriously about Doyle's public acclaim as a lithographer, might have uncovered 'H.B.'s identity.[21] The fact that his anonymity was maintained for upwards of a decade, in the close-knit political world of late-Georgian and early-Victorian London, is remarkable. Lord Nugent speculated in 1832 that Harry Barnard of the Guards was 'H.B.' because 'he drew capitally'; months later, Thomas Moore stated that he had breakfasted with 'H.B.': Doyle and Moore certainly knew one another, but whether Moore actually knew Doyle *was* 'H.B.' is another matter.[22] In 1842, in the correspondence in which Doyle disclosed his identity as 'H.B.' to Peel, he commented that he preserved the pseudonym 'not from any affectation of secrecy' but the better to preserve 'my personal independence'. By Doyle's own account, 'the only friends in my confidence were [two men] on the liberal side' – one was a peer 'who had known me from boyhood' and both had held 'high offices under the late Government [i.e. the Whig ministry of 1835–1841]'.[23]

In the meantime, 'many and free were the conjectures as to the authorship of the sketches. The name of professional artists and of possible amateurs were suggested and withdrawn, but the author preserved his disguise'.[24] As time progressed, Doyle's desire to preserve his *incognito* became more pronounced. In 1874, Robert Buss noted, with more than a hint of incredulity, 'the drawings were called for in a mysterious hackney-coach, mysteriously deposited in a mysterious lithographic printing-office, and as mysteriously printed, and mysteriously stored until the right day for publication'.[25] In the *Dictionary of National Biography,* Austin Dobson stated that Doyle disclaimed authorship of the painting *The Reform Bill receiving the King's Assent by Royal Commission* (1836), engraved by Walker and Reynolds, for fear of being discovered. Likewise, Doyle's series of *Equestrian Sketches* (published by McLean in 1839), though putatively anonymous, offered further clues to 'H.B.'s identity. Doyle himself was not above poking fun at his own expense – producing a *Political Sketch* called *'H.B.' Discovered* which showed him at work in his studio.[26]

In 1948, Daria Hambourg speculated that Doyle's desire for anonymity was the consequence of his acute self-consciousness at being the ex-patriot descendant of a dispossessed Catholic family:

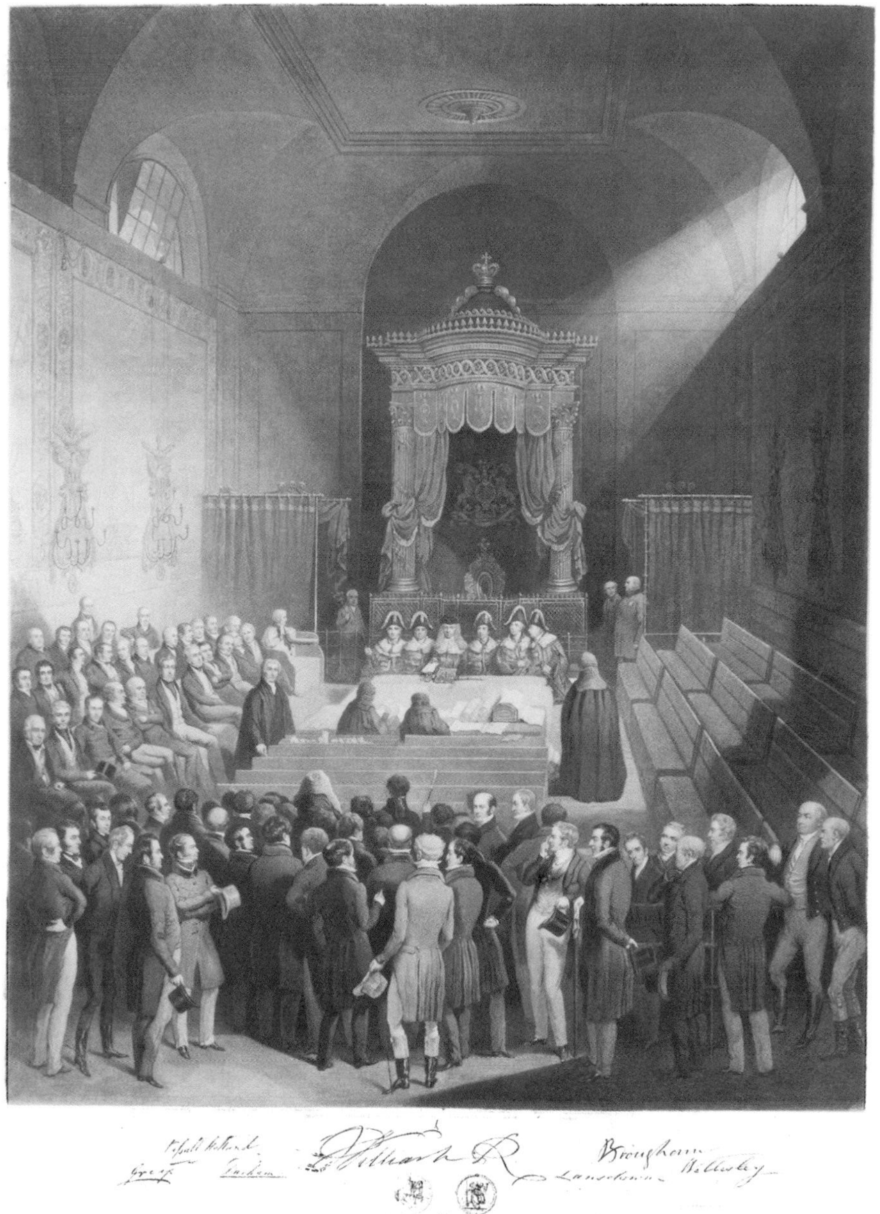

FIG. 4: *The Reform Bill receiving the King's Assent by Royal Commission, 7 June 1832* (Samuel Walker) © National Portrait Gallery, London

> Publicity with its attendant claims would have violated the sanctuary of their inmost family circle. This triumph of family pride over artistic vanity was carried to such lengths that the work of 'H.B.' was never discussed in John Doyle's household and there is no reference to it in the [published] journal which [his son] Richard kept as a boy.[27]

Within the family, Doyle was known affectionately, but rather pointedly, as 'Lord John', the 'Governor General' (or 'Guv'), the 'Commander in Chief', and 'J.D.'; nevertheless, the wisdom of maintaining a guarded detachment was not lost on his children. When Doyle's youngest son, Charles, ventured into political caricature, in 1856, his brother Richard advised him 'to adopt some sign to put in the corner of your pictures so that people will begin to learn your identity though they don't know your name'.[28]

Anonymity raised the twin spectres of imitation and misattribution. Doyle was known to have a host of imitators, including 'Philo HB', 'h.B.', 'H.H.' [Henry Heath], 'B.H' [Bob Hamerton] and the like.[29] Some were clearly skilful: in 1835, *The Times* dismissed one production as 'a personification of all that is stupid and tasteless'; in fact, the *Political Sketch* in question, *Dancing Jim Crow* was genuine – and forms part of the Peel Society Collection (catalogue, No. 57). By contrast, the newspaper accepted as genuine a letter claiming to come from 'H.B.', which it thought proved the writer to be 'as great a wag in writing as in sketching'.[30]

More recently, David Blayney Brown has suggested that John Doyle was the original artist of *Samuel Rogers at his Breakfast Table*, a picture which is largely known from the engraving by Charles Mottram (1807–1876). The subject matter was one of the famous 'breakfasts' of literary figures held at the home of the poet Samuel Rogers (1763–1855) in Stoke Newington. Blayney Brown had discovered two proof impressions, 'one bearing not only Mottram's signature but also the early – indeed contemporary – pencil inscription *Painted by John Doyle*'. He also discovered the date '1815…in the underline on one of the proofs'. Because the painting in question included Lord Byron (who died in 1824), Blayney Brown dated the picture to c.1823, thereby suggesting it was a contemporary rather than historical group-portrait.

In fact, new evidence from the Conan Doyle archive in Lausanne casts considerable doubt on this attribution and dating. In a volume of letters from Richard Doyle to Charles Doyle (two of Doyle's younger sons), dating from the 1850s, Richard Doyle tells his brother:

> [Our eldest brother] James is going to Sam Rogers's to breakfast, with Mr [John] Hullah[31] some morning, to talk to him about a companion picture to the Reynolds dinner party, of a breakfast of poets at Rogers's, Scott, Byron, Moore, Campbell, &c. McLean is anxious to have it engraved, if done.

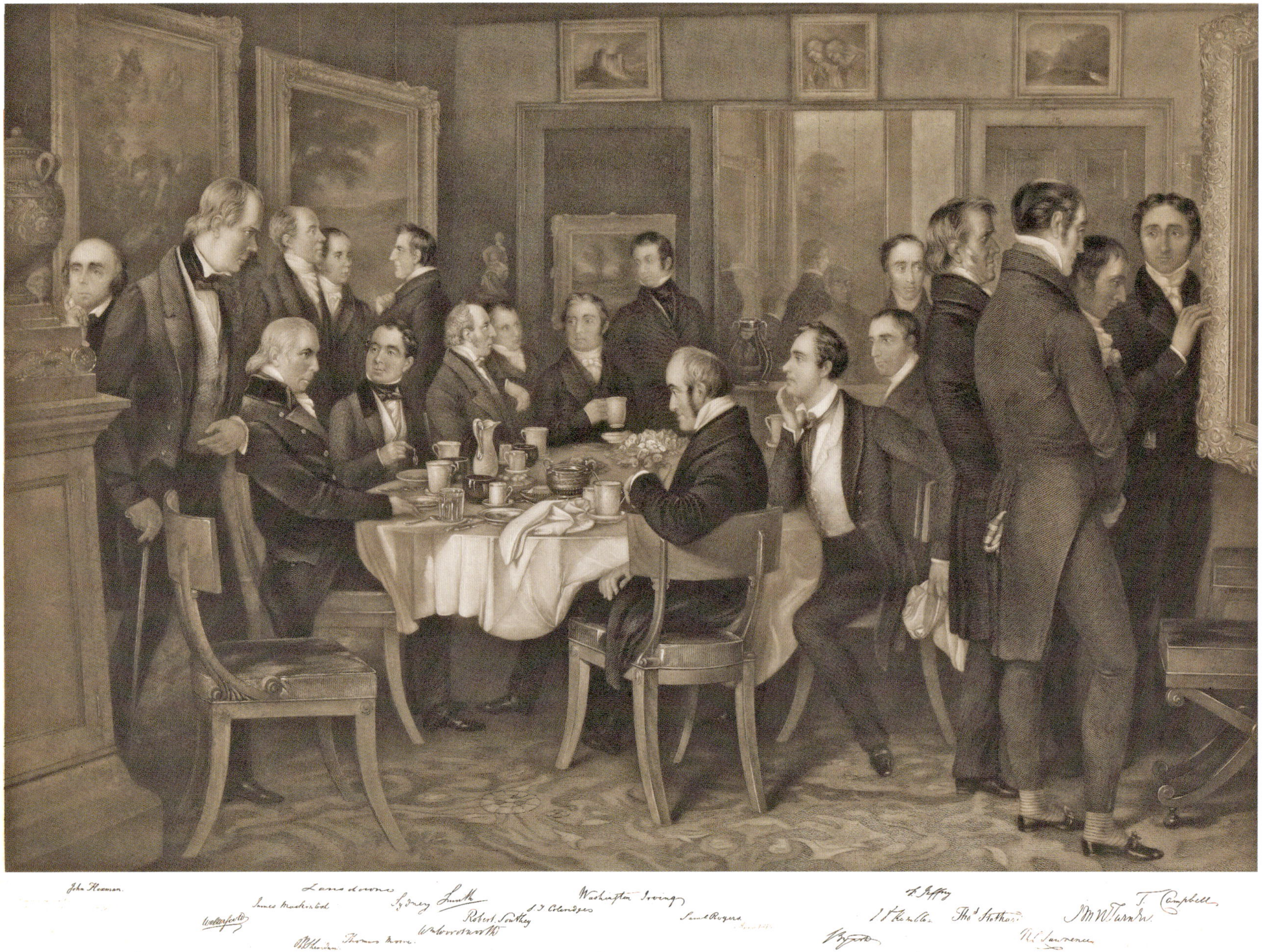

FIG. 5: *Samuel Rogers at his Breakfast Table* (circa 1823), engraved by Charles Mottram after John Doyle (1797–1868) © Tate, London 2014

The letters no longer survive in the original, having been typed up by Arthur Conan Doyle (the son of Charles Doyle and grandson of 'H.B.') at some point before his death in 1930. However, internal evidence suggests that the letter was written sometime after a fete was held at the Fulham home of Benjamin Lumley (1811–1875), the manager of Her Majesty's Theatre, at which Charles Dickens was also in attendance. This took place on 19 June 1850. If James Doyle commenced work on the picture in 1851, then 1815 may be a mis-dating of the year 1851. Alternatively, as a historical portrait, it is possible that 1815 refers to the date at which the scene is supposed to have occurred. In any case, there is enough evidence to question Blayney Brown's belief that 'there is no reason to doubt the ascription of the original design to John Doyle'.

Further letters confirm that the commission was the brain-child of James Doyle rather than his father: 'James went with Hullah to breakfast with old Sam Rogers the Poet, on Saturday preliminary to making a sketch of his room for the companion picture to the "Reynolds dinner" of a Rogers breakfast with portraits of all the "poicks" [poets]'. Elsewhere, Charles Doyle is told that 'The Rogers breakfast gets on very well, and is getting near finish'.[32]

James William Edmund Doyle (22 October 1822–3 December 1892) is probably the least recognised of John Doyle's sons. He is principally remembered as the writer and illustrator of *A Chronicle of England, BC55–AD1485* (1864) which included some 81 plates engraved and printed in colour. His *Historical Baronage of England...from 1066 to 1885*, a massive three volume work (1885–1886), with a thousand line illustrations, took thirteen years labour and proved to be a financial failure, although it is still an authoritative textbook of the College of Arms. According to Richard Doyle, James was selected by Queen Victoria and Prince Albert to paint the two Walter Scott subjects on the walls of the Royal Summer House at Buckingham Palace, whilst his pencil drawing of Cardinal Newman (dating from 1852) was later lithographed. Within the family, James, a 'tall, rather stooping figure' with a 'long black beard, discreet behaviour and pensive expression' was known as 'The Priest', so seriously did he take the family's Roman Catholicism.[33]

However, the most telling evidence of James' authorship of the picture is provided by his earlier representation of *A Literary Party at Sir Joshua Reynolds* which, as the letters quoted above demonstrate, acted as a prototype for the Samuel Rogers companion-piece.[34] Why the signature of John Doyle should appear on proof impressions is still unclear – whether James was known as 'John' within the family, or whether his father did in fact assist his son in the production, cannot yet be determined. What is clear is that, not for the first time, father and son may have been confused.[35]

The *Political Sketches* critiqued

In January 1838, in a review of 'H.B.'s work, the author observed that 'it is not our province to say who "H.B." is – even the author of the "Great Metropolis" does not profess to know – our business is with his character as an artist'.[36] Similar sentiments had been made by the artist Benjamin Haydon, seven years earlier: 'Whoever "H.B." is, he is a man of great genius. He has an instinct for expression, and a power of drawing, without academic cant I never saw before, but evidently an amateur from the delicacy of his touch, or timidity rather'.[37]

These comments are characteristic of contemporary attitudes towards the *Political Sketches*. It was common for critics to highlight the 'untaught' nature of Doyle's work – in 1878, Samuel Redgrave described the drawings as 'stiff and formal, wanting in vigour and abandon'.[38] A number of commentators remarked that, by comparison with his predecessors, Doyle was not really a caricaturist at all – 'the whole effect is humorous, and highly laughable, without the slightest approach to caricature'.[39] The most serious criticism of this nature was made by the Hon Grantley Berkeley, who claimed to have provided 'H.B.' with an idea for one of his subjects:

> Caricature underwent a complete change...It became cold, almost classical, elegant, clever, but never funny... We have portfolios of his works in most country houses, as a provocative to cheerfulness, but the figures seem ghosts, and the wit of the design, if it ever had any, must have evaporated when the subject became obsolete. He closes the long line of pictorial humourists who worked for the shop-windows.[40]

The charge of lack of imagination was one which *The Times* occasionally indulged in and could be levelled with asperity by critics keen to castigate 'H.B.'s 'sterility of invention'.[41] By contrast, Graham Everitt, in the first major study of English caricature to be published, proclaimed 'H.B.' 'a graphic satirist...of genuine originality...he possessed a taste for satiric art, and had essayed several subjects of political character which he treated in a style and manner differing altogether from the medium in which satirical pictures had hitherto been treated'. Earlier, Robert Buss observed that 'H.B.'s work initiated 'a new epoch in caricature, not only in style, method of execution, invention, but by a certain elegance or gentlemanly feeling infused into his caricatures'.[42]

The reason for such conflicting opinions over Doyle's originality and status as a caricaturist can be found in the form and tone of the *Political Sketches* themselves. Doyle introduced new methods of pictorial satire, by eschewing the old focus on exaggeration – the attribute which, for many commentators, was the essence of 'caricature' – and replacing it with a mixture of good-natured humour, discipline and restraint. 'Even at [their] most critical', Robert Wark notes, the prints retain 'an air of decorum and good taste'.[43] 'In composition, "H.B." was timid, contenting himself with as few figures as possible, just sufficient to tell the story [Robert Buss observed]. He avoids elaboration, complexity of tints, and depth of effect, keeping his backgrounds simple, and the entire design light and grey'. Buss concluded that 'there is scarcely one which could not be placed before the victim himself, so devoid are they of scurrility or venomous feeling'. Another contemporary reviewer noted that 'H.B.' was 'a reformer of caricatures' whose 'satire pricks, it never wounds. Though sharp, he is without poison'.[44] As late as 1945, Peter Quennell observed (with evident distaste), that Doyle enjoys the 'somewhat doubtful credit of having "led English satiric art into a path of reticence and good breeding which it had never trodden before"'.[45]

The element of 'restraint' in 'H.B.'s work has often been remarked.[46] So too have the amazingly lifelike portraits which dominated the *Political Sketches*.[47] The quality of the portraits becomes explicable, once one recalls Doyle's early training in Dublin and proven expertise in this branch of the arts. As Dorothy George concluded, Doyle was 'a natural portraitist who made himself into a graphic satirist'.[48] Indeed, one of the reasons why Doyle transferred from a promising career in portraiture – witnessed by his Royal Academy exhibits – to working on the lithographic stone may be the 'unfortunate defect' in his health, which incapacitated him 'from painting much in oil'. As he told Peel in 1842, this had 'been an obstacle to my attempting with a fair chance of success to attain eminence in that class of Portrait painting which would have suited my taste and my capacity'.[49] Only a few survivals of Doyle's expertise in 'formal' portraiture survive; notably, an unfinished portrait in oils of the sculptor Christopher Moore (1790–1863).[50]

It was commonly remarked that the *Political Sketches* provided both 'the truest and the cheapest' portraits of political personalities to be found in the period 1830–1850. Amongst these, Doyle's portrayals of Peel were singled out for special praise – 'the sketches of "H.B"...exhibit, with surprising fidelity, the man as he is daily seen during the sitting of Parliament in the House of Commons, or walking between Whitehall and St Stephens'.[51] Doyle's skilful, accurate representations of his 'sitters' was based on a prodigious memory and his frequent visits to the lobbies and galleries of the Houses of Parliament.[52] Doyle's favourite history painter was Horace Vernet (1789–1863), who painted huge canvases from memory 'with extraordinary accuracy'.[53] It was for this reason that Doyle later assured Peel that he did not 'require a sitting in the ordinary sense of the term. It must – with me – be mainly a work of memory'.[54]

It was Doyle's capacity for capturing 'those little foibles and gestures that their contemporaries knew so well' and for 'showing great men as they actually appeared rather than as they would have liked to be seen' which explains much

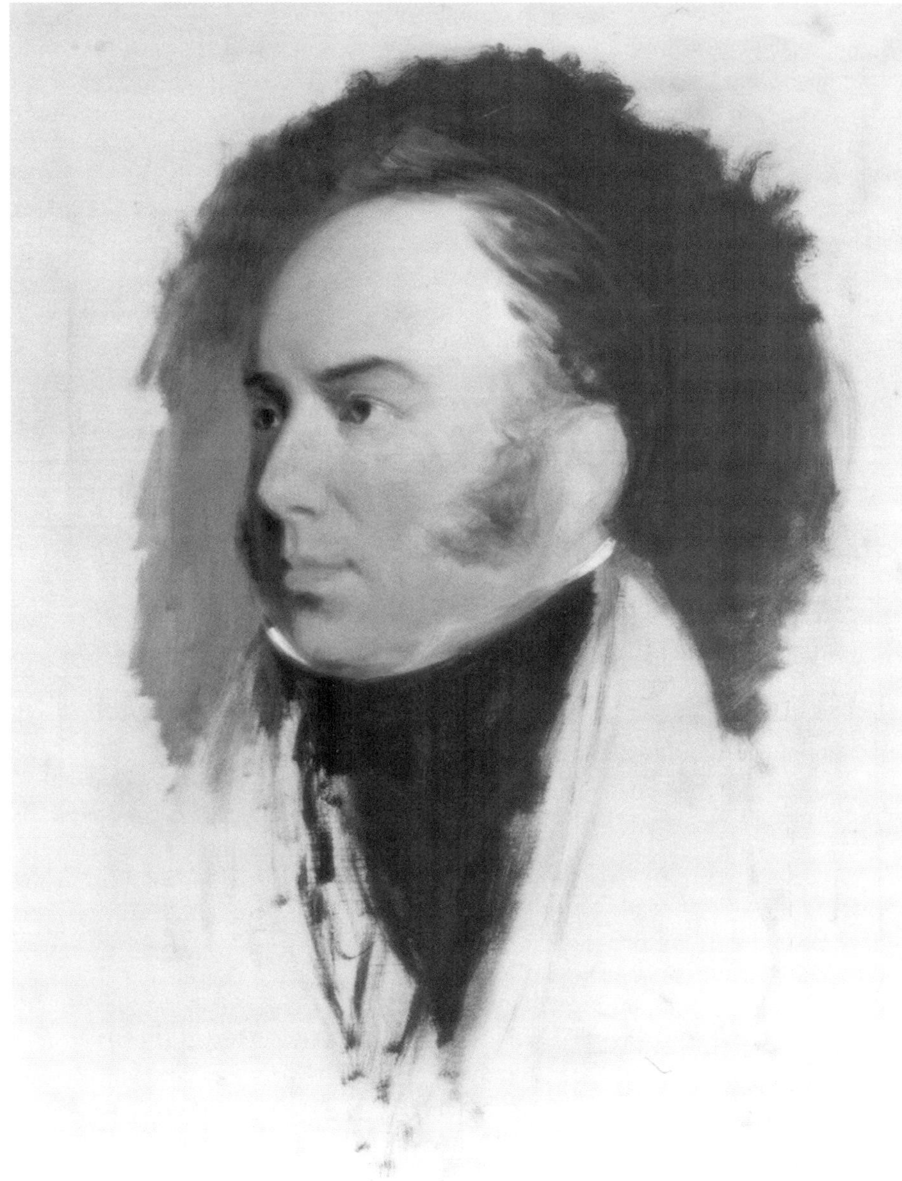

FIG. 6: John Doyle, portrait of Christopher Moore, © National Gallery of Ireland (NGI 144)

of the success of the *Political Sketches*.[55] Even critics apt to be harsh in other respects were moved to state that 'in the art of producing a likeness ['H.B.'] has never been excelled, and we much doubt if he has ever been equalled'.[56]

At the same time, whilst critics acknowledged that the relatively new technique of lithography was well-turned to capturing the subtle nuances of expression and attitude which were the defining characteristic of 'H.B's portraits, the observation was usually combined with an unflattering comparison with his predecessors, who worked in copperplate:

> The fatal facility of the lithographic stone gave a temptation to hurried and careless execution, which the sterner discipline of the copperplate would have repressed. 'H.B.' would have been a greater artist had he worked on the same material and with the same tools as Gillray or Cruikshank; but we should probably not have possessed so complete a gallery of portraits, comprising all the men of note who took part in political affairs.[57]

If accuracy of political portraiture was one outstanding characteristic of the *Political Sketches*, another was Doyle's recurring 'compositional method' of transposing 'a current political event into the context of a well-known literary or artistic incident, sometimes with devastating satiric effect – providing the reader knew the allusion'.[58] The sources for these allusions (often called 'travesties' or 'parodies') were unusually wide-ranging: Shakespeare, *Don Quixote*, myth, folklore and legend, contemporary painting – including work by Haydon, Wilkie, Stothard, Reynolds and Landseer – and sculptures as well as Biblical and classical references. Doyle had a deep knowledge of history and the arts, both contemporary and historical, and 'an acute sense for current and past artistic models which he transformed cleverly to suit his purposes'.[59]

Critics have been divided as to whether this technique of 'appropriation' and 'parody' represents originality or not. Doyle told Peel in 1842 that, 'where it was not intended merely to amuse by some harmless jest', his method was to direct attention 'to the furtherance of some intelligible public object, that by such means as would *by fair analogy* be considered legitimate in political warfare'.[60] However, for a contemporary critic, this smacked of plagiarism: 'if he is the cause of mirth in others, it is only because others have first caused mirth in him. He is the sketcher only – not the inventor of his scenes. He gives birth to ancient jokes'. Later scholars have been more appreciative, seeing in Doyle's 'clever' use of visual parody a clear debt to Gillray, 'though his designs have a sober correctness far removed from Gillray's robust exuberance'.[61]

Another way in which Doyle built on existing satirical models was in his characterisation of 'John Bull', the visual representation of 'Englishness' since the eighteenth century, which had been steadily transformed at the hands of successive graphic satirists. According to G M Trevelyan, 'H.B.'s John Bull is 'perhaps the last entirely satisfactory appearance of that symbolic personage in art'. Doyle portrays him as 'a sensible country gentlemen or gentleman farmer, very portly and partly bald'. He is 'stout, sensible, and good-natured with a vast waistcoat, broad-brimmed hat and shoes'.[62]

Today, the *Political Sketches* are acclaimed as 'a document of political and afterwards historical value'. This element was appreciated in their own day, *The Times* describing them as 'fresh illustrations of modern history' and 'H.B.' as a 'pictorial historiographer' who had performed the invaluable service of rescuing 'from oblivion scenes [which] otherwise would in a few years be too dull for narrative'.[63]

John Doyle and His Family

It was frequently assumed that the *Political Sketches* made John Doyle a rich man. In 1838, an anonymous reviewer stated that 'H.B.'s caricatures were 'admirably fitted for commercial success' whilst, much later, Robert Buss remarked that it was to be hoped that the artist had amassed a 'fortune equal in value to the great reputation he had achieved, and the money his works had brought to his publisher'.[64] That this was not the case was evidently part of the reason why Doyle disclosed his identity as 'H.B.' to Peel in January 1842. 'I might perhaps have occupied some of the best years of my life more profitably and, though my publisher has been much the larger gainer, I am not dissatisfied', he remarked.[65]

The family's circumstances changed markedly with the death of Doyle's wife, Marianna Conan, in 1832, shortly after the birth of their final child, Charles. Sometime after this, Marianna's brother Michael and his wife Anne moved in with the family. Michael Conan was an artist, a music and art critic and worked at one period as the drama critic for *The Morning Herald*. He was an expert on the Old Masters and an authority on the Medieval Renaissance. Later, he became Paris correspondent for *The Art Journal* edited by Marcus Huish. Conan was a positive influence on the family – 'an endearing character with the light-hearted Irish twinkle in his eye, a fund of stories and a talent for spiking his reviews with clever words and phrases'.[66] He took the Doyle children to concerts, balls and the opera and encouraged them to think critically and enjoy the delights of the London season. The Conans were no less proud of their lineage than the Doyles; Michael Conan traced his ancestry from the Dukes of Brittany. When his nephew Charles became father to a son, on 22 May 1859, Conan gave the baby a copy of *Arthur de Bretagne*. The boy was named Arthur Conan Doyle and Conan became the baby's godfather.[67]

In addition to James, whose work has already been referenced, John and Marianna Doyle had four sons and two daughters. Their third son, Henry Edward Doyle (1827–17 February 1892), was the only one of the children to be born in Dublin, where he later undertook art training. Though he briefly followed his father into satirical illustration (for *Punch* in 1844 and *Fun* in 1867–1869), Henry Doyle was principally known for his strong Catholicism and attachment to Ireland: he published an *Illustrated History of Ireland* in 1868. In 1862, Doyle was commissioned by Cardinal Nicholas Patrick Stephen Wiseman (1802–1865) – a close family friend – to represent the Papal States at the International Exhibition, being awarded the Pio Nono (the Order of Pope Pius IX) in recognition.[68] Two years later, he completed ten frescos for the Chapel of the Dominican Convent at Cabra near Dublin, featuring the chief saints of the Dominican order, and ceiling paintings of figures from the Old Testament. He also painted murals of the Last Judgement for the Roman Catholic cathedral at Lancaster.[69] Having served as Art Superintendent to the Dublin exhibition of 1865 and as Honorary Secretary to the National Portrait Gallery (1865–1869), he became the second Director of the National Gallery of Ireland on 22 March 1869, retaining the post until his death. During his incumbency, Doyle extended the gallery's collection of oil paintings (including many of Irish origin) and acquired seventeenth century Dutch and Flemish works, after the fashion of Sir Robert Peel. In 1884, he founded the National, Historical and Portrait Gallery, with nearly 150 portraits. Henry's own portraits – of his brother Richard and of John Ruskin – are now part of the Gallery's collection, whilst that of his father, reproduced on the back of this book, is in the National Portrait Gallery.[70] Doyle was a Member of the Royal Hibernian Academy (1874), a Companion of the Bath (1880) and married Jane Ball, the daughter of the Justice of Common Pleas. The secret of Henry Doyle's success was clearly his connections with various influential Catholics; around 1851, Richard Doyle told his brother Charles that Henry was being introduced to 'a great many Catholic families, who are likely to be permanent friends'. Undoubtedly, their support and patronage were pivotal in the development of Henry Doyle's career.[71]

By contrast, Charles Altamont Doyle (1832–10 October 1893), the youngest of the children, had a far less prosperous life.[72] In 1849, he left the family home to become Assistant Surveyor (architect) to Robert Mathieson in the Office of Works in Edinburgh. He retained this position – and virtually the same salary (which never exceeded £250 per annum) – until 1876. Charles was a gifted designer and artist who hankered after the recognition and lifestyle achieved by his elder brothers. John Doyle greatly admired his son's architectural designs and did what he could to advance his career, whilst Arthur Conan Doyle felt that his father was 'a great and original artist…far the greatest, in my opinion, of the family'.[73] Though Charles designed the fountain for the courtyard of Holyrood Palace, Edinburgh, and a window in Glasgow Cathedral, as well as exhibiting six times at the Royal Scottish Academy (1862–1887), sustained success eluded him. Charles gradually succumbed to alcoholism and depression, exacerbated by what appears to be epilepsy. 'My father's life was full of the tragedy of unfulfilled powers and of undeveloped gifts', Arthur Conan Doyle later observed. Charles Doyle moved through a succession of hospitals and asylums, including Fordoun House, Montrose Royal Lunatic Asylum (the unfortunately named *Sunnyside*), Edinburgh Royal Infirmary and Crichton Royal Institution near Dumfries. The family's care and upbringing was left to the formidable woman whom Charles had married in 1855 – Mary Foley (1838–1921) – known as 'The Ma'am' within the family. Of ten children, seven (two sons and five daughters) survived. Late in life, Charles provided some of the first illustrations for his son's 'Sherlock Holmes' adventures, portraying him in a manner which looked uncannily like Charles himself – 'a tall man, long-bearded and elegant…a man of sensitive genius…unworldly and unpractical'.[74]

Two of John Doyle's children died before reaching adulthood. Francis (or Frank) was widely regarded as exhibiting the most artistic talent within the family. Until now, historians have been unable to say precisely when he died.[75] However, Doyle's letters to James – afterwards Sir James – Emerson Tennent (1804–1868) chart Frank's final struggle and death from consumption – the contemporary term for tuberculosis. On 6 June 1843, John Doyle told him:

> Poor Frank's state can scarcely be worse. He grows weaker each succeeding day: and although those more urgent symptoms which the medical men seemed ten days ago to anticipate almost hourly, have not yet become manifest, yet nothing has appeared, to offer the slightest hope of ultimate recovery. This is rather [a] severe trial for me, but my mind is now resigned [to] it.

Frank died on 9 June 1843: he was 13. 'At length the unequal struggle is over – It ceased at a little after 5 o'clock yesterday afternoon', Doyle informed Tennent:

> Prepared as I was for this event and inured as I have been to the contemplation of a greater calamity, I yet feel it very bitterly. The character of the Boy – his amiable disposition and faultless temper – made him a special favourite with us all, and it will be long 'ere his loss ceases to be deeply felt by every member of my family. I shall endeavour to rally my spirits and resume my usual habits as soon as possible and hope then to see you often.[76]

Less than a year passed before further tragedy visited the household. On 4 April 1844, Doyle informed Tennent that his daughter Adele (or Adelaide) had also died of consumption: 'It occurred at 4 o'clock on Tuesday morning [2 April 1844]'.[77]

Doyle's correspondence with Peel thus came in the midst of a decade of personal turmoil for the man who was 'H.B.'. To outward appearances, the family remained a respectable, moderately well-to-do household. By 1840, they had settled at 17 Cambridge Terrace, Hyde Park – at what is now the east end of Sussex Gardens. The house was four-storied, with a music room, drawing room and dining room, complete with a resplendent (and somewhat famous) dining table, around which the luminaries of the artistic and political worlds were entertained by successive generations of Doyles. The list includes the likes of Southey, Macaulay, Rogers, Disraeli, Thackeray,[78] Ruskin, Coleridge, Wordsworth, Rossetti, Samuel Lover, Landseer, Constable, Count d'Orsay, William Holman Hunt, Millais, Wilkie, Leech, Sir Richard Owen, Newman, De Quincey and Dickens.[79] The table passed down the family from John Doyle to his son Richard and from him to his nephew Arthur.[80] Conan Doyle described the family as 'fairly well-to-do, thanks to my grandfather's talents…they lived up [to] their income, however, and it became necessary to find places for the boys'.[81]

It was in this context that Doyle wrote to Peel seeking new employment, after nearly fifteen years of labour as 'H.B.'. Doyle's interest in various 'public improvements' then underway in London, including the development of Trafalgar Square, Hyde Park and Kensington Gardens, led him to offer his services. The correspondence – which is reproduced in full in the Appendix – remained largely one-sided – Peel did not respond favourably to the original purpose of the letters (Doyle's wish to produce a portrait of Peel) nor to the subsequent solicitation for an office or agency under the crown.

As a result, Doyle's hopes remained focused on the artistic training and development of his sons. Pre-eminent amongst them was Richard Doyle, the famous 'Dicky Doyle', who became one of *Punch* magazine's earliest and most renowned illustrators. Richard (18 September 1824–11 December 1883) was Doyle's second son. He was immortalised through his pioneering and creative imagining of 'fairyland', in a host of mid-Victorian publications, as well as in his role as illustrator for, amongst others, William Makepeace Thackeray. His fame was enhanced by the posthumous publication of an illustrated journal, kept during the year 1840, which showed the origins of his later fame.[82] This was due, in no small measure, to the strict – not to say severe – habits instilled within him by John Doyle.

As more than one commentator has observed, the Doyle children were involved in a constant battle 'with one another for the approval of their father'.[83] This took its adolescent form in the weekly Sunday shows held at Cambridge Terrace, where the children would take it in turns to show their father (and one another) the results of their week's labours. Dick's *Journal* illustrates one of these occasions, showing John Doyle looking on with what has been described as 'a non-committal expression'. Elsewhere, Richard wrote of how he was 'tortured with the fear that Papa will think [my work] little when finished'.[84]

On reading his brother's account of life at Cambridge Terrace, Charles Doyle responded in kind, confirming the sociable but orderly nature of the family's routine:

> On Sunday the Day was observed by all the children…going to the Mass, celebrated at the French Chapel at 8 o'clock a.m. This in winter meant going from Cambridge Terrace, up Edgeware Road – down George Street a couple of miles – often in the dark, and getting home to Breakfast at 10 – The after day was spent in perfect quiet till 8 in the Evening when the camphor [*sic*] lamp and mole candles were lit in the drawing room, and guests began to arrive, often comprising the most distinguished literary and artistic men of London and foreigners…Most delicious music was discoursed by Annette on the piano and James on the [violoncello] till about 10 when the supper tray was laid – generally just cold meats and salad, followed by punch – We boys all retired when this appeared – but upstairs in bed I have often listened to indications of most delightful conversation till 1 or 2.[85]

Both Richard's *Journal* and James' *Chronicle of England* began life as exercises in the close recording and truthful observation of subject matter, produced for the benefit of (and after the fashion of) their father.[86] Though the children had a tutor – Mr Street – and a dancing and fencing master, James Harbour, Doyle did not believe in formal art training. Instead, he instructed Richard, in particular, 'to make a record of all reviews, ceremonies and processions', 'to write to him notes and accounts of what he saw, and to illustrate his stories by sketches', faithfully relating the impressions he had derived from a 'painfully large number of history books', in an effort to enhance his ability to reproduce accurately from memory.[87] Outings to the opera, to concerts and the zoo, to exhibitions, galleries and the studios of painters and sculptors, were all treated as sources from which to train his sons' productive and reproductive capacities. A collection of illustrated letters from Richard, Henry and Charles Doyle to their father, during the 1840s,[88] confirms the regular habits of observation and reproduction to which this gave rise:

> In their walks they should always try to remember one or more figures they had seen, and immediately on their return home, make the best drawing they could in pen and ink; also to frequent the National Gallery or other important picture exhibitions, remaining in front of any one picture that might attract their attention until they had fairly mastered the subject, and then to make the best recollection of it in pencil or colour as they felt inclined.[89]

At the same time, Doyle's sons were fined sixpence for each day they didn't visit Hyde Park for health reasons – an injunction which received additional force after the deaths of Francis and Adelaide.[90]

All of this had the effect of making Richard Doyle 'precociously successful as a pictorial satirist'; something to which John Doyle referred in his correspondence with Peel, amongst others.[91] However, because Richard had been trained to follow his father's method, his own work 'resembled his father's in being linear and calligraphic'.[92] Through the intervention of his uncle, Michael Conan, Richard Doyle began working for Mark Lemon on the staff of *Punch*, at a salary of £800 per annum. His first 'Big Cut' or 'Cartoon', which was published on 16 March 1844, featured (appropriately enough) Sir Robert Peel.

The cartoon shows clear signs of Dicky Doyle's ancestry, even though the print itself was (in a typically 'H.B.' fashion) anonymous, identifiable only by a small 'dicky' bird, underneath which was a diminutive letter D. The subject matter of 'The Modern Sisyphus' was, nevertheless, strictly in the artistic tradition of John Doyle by clothing contemporary political affairs (Peel's attempt to ameliorate Ireland) in classical analogy – the story of Sisyphus, who was condemned for ever to roll a stone to the top of a mountain, only for it to fall down again. In a pre-sentiment of Dicky Doyle's later pre-occupation, the scene also features a series of 'furies' or imp-like devils (in the shape of the Whig Lord John Russell and the Irish Richard Shiel), together with the more angelic-looking Queen Victoria, acting as observers of the scene.

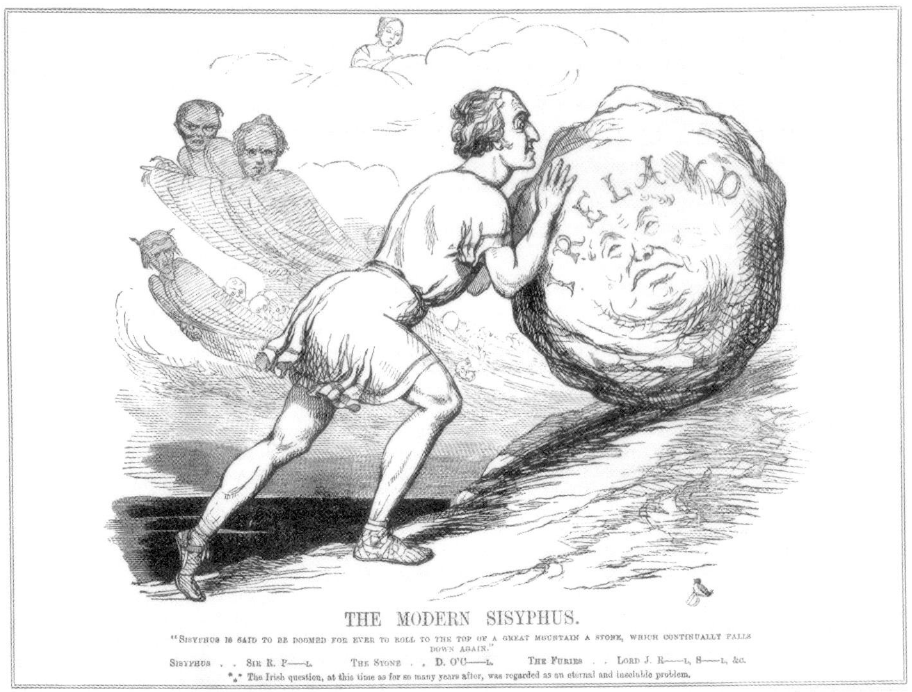

FIG. 7: Richard Doyle, *The Modern Sisyphus* from *Cartoons from 'Punch'*, Volume I (1906)

In 1851, following the resumption of the Catholic hierarchy in England, and the legislative attempt by the Whig government to counter the use of non-Anglican 'Ecclesiastical Titles', Dicky Doyle resigned from *Punch*.[93] He did so because of his principled opposition to the anti-Catholic feeling demonstrated by the magazine, most especially in its visual attacks on the Pope. Historians have noted that Dicky was a 'small, shy artist, who felt himself, as an Irish Catholic, to be an object of suspicion to some of his colleagues'.[94] However, Dicky was also acting in conformity with his father's strict Catholicism. On 23 May 1851, John Doyle told Emerson Tennent that he was 'sorry to learn that you have been suffering from the prevailing epidemic [of anti-Catholic feeling] and regret the consequences: but these things can't be helped. I hear the debate [on the Ecclesiastical Titles Bill] is not likely to be postponed'.[95]

John Doyle maintained his loyalty to the Catholic faith with a perseverance which amounted, in the opinion of one writer, to 'intransigence':

> it was not so much a question of religious mysticism as of militant conservatism, and an untiring devotion to the family beliefs. The sufferings they had entailed may have seemed to justify them in some mysterious way. In fact his fidelity to the rites of his chosen religion was symbolic of his desire to keep his family traditions and history as much alive in London as they had been in Ireland.[96]

Such firm beliefs must have made it hard for the family to mix with those of less settled convictions; Doyle's life in London revolved around close acquaintance with a community of distinguished Anglo-Irishmen and exiles from Ireland, though he himself only returned to Ireland occasionally.[97]

In 1842, Doyle told Peel that the abiding political issue of his early life had been the achievement of Catholic Emancipation, which made him side naturally with its strongest (Whig) supporters. However, after the achievement of that measure (at Peel and Wellington's hands), he had determined that the 'Catholics were bound in honor [*sic*], if not in conscience, to abstain from all attacks upon the temporalities of that Establishment. I could not therefore without strong disapprobation, and some shame, view the subsequent proceedings of the Catholic party, both in and out of Parliament – under the misguidance of Mr [Daniel] O'Connell'.

This rather calls into question G M Trevelyan's description of Doyle as having 'no party attachments and no personal adulations or feuds'; at the very least, he was 'a mild Conservative'.[98] In terms of political influence, Doyle's obituarist believed that 'H.B.' 'played with the pencil a part similar to that of Junius [the eighteenth century satirist] with the pen' and was 'attached to the highest and purest ameliorative conservative principles of policy' though he never 'made his services to the men of that party a source of remuneration'. Likewise, Arthur Conan Doyle said that his grandfather 'exerted, I am told, quite an influence upon politics'.[99] Some of these claims appear hard to substantiate, beyond the 'very liberal patronage bestowed upon' the *Political Sketches* by 'the Nobility, Gentry, and Subscribers' who bought them.[100] Doyle told Peel in 1842 that his prints had been 'an agent of some little influence' and that they were 'governed by a certain steadiness of moral and political principle'. This line was taken up by *The Times*, in 1844:

> It would be difficult to assign to the silent moral of the pencil its exact position in political instruction...Everyone who has ever seen the 'Political Sketches' of 'H.B.' will readily acknowledge that there is at least a possibility, through the instrumentality of the pencil, as well as through that of the pen, of carrying forward praise or blame beyond mere personalities, and of making it pass on through the individual into an approbation or exposure of general policy or conduct...It conveys a general lesson of praise or censure, but it is through the medium of particularising individual conduct. It is an expression of public opinion, but it is one which limits itself to vindicating the past, and ignores the future to be inferred from the retributive justice which it exacts for what is gone.[101]

If it is hard to estimate Doyle's precise influence on the public sphere, what remains beyond doubt is the impact which he exerted in the privacy of Cambridge Terrace. Doyle's influence over his sons' lives extended into adulthood as each, in their own ways, continued to seek his approval.[102] A measure of their success is the fact that, 'With John Doyle the family makes its entry into English history by the front door; he and four of his descendants, including his grandson Arthur Conan Doyle, appear in the *Dictionary of National Biography*'.[103]

Doyle after 'H.B.': the final years (1851–1868)

The lightning success of Richard 'Dicky' Doyle, during the mid-1840s, marked a moment of transition in the life of John Doyle. Though Doyle's reputation and good name stood high, following the exposure of his identity as 'H.B.', the momentum had clearly passed to the next generation.[104]

'H.B.'s last published *Political Sketch* (March 1851) was, appropriately enough, related to a subject on which he was passionate: the rights of Catholics. It showed Lord John Russell in the guise of Hudibras, setting out on his crusade against Mummeries. Around the same time, Lord Brougham commented that '"H.B." had not been doing him lately, upon which Thackeray said, "Sir, he has left it to his son"'.[105] In fact, Doyle had not completely abandoned the field to his son, but worked on a series of *Political Sketches* during the General Election of 1852. These remained unpublished. Dicky Doyle told his brother Charles that 'things are not brilliant as yet, but they have not been well "put about", and especially it was unfortunate they were not well over the country before the Elections. One of them representing the Derby Minister in the character of a thimble-rig party is admirable – equal to anything the "Guv" has ever done'.[106]

However, turning prospects into realities remained a continuing problem, for Doyle and his sons. In spite of their enduring historical fame, the sense of disappointment and frustration entertained by successive generations of Doyles, during their lifetimes, provides a common reference point in considerations of their lives. For J H Pollen, writing in 1885, it was 'hard to avoid the feeling that Richard Doyle's later life was tinged with a slight sadness'. Likewise, James Doyle was known to have harboured a profound sense of disappointment at his lack of artistic recognition, whilst Charles Doyle has been described as 'an imaginative man unable to cope with banishment at an early age from the close knit London home of the Doyles to a humdrum job'.[107] Something of the sense of domestic despair from which John Doyle suffered, from the mid-1840s, is symbolised in Dicky's illustrations of Charles Dickens' *The Cricket on the Heath*, which featured a man (acknowledged to be John Doyle) sat, head in hands, surrounded by agonies.[108]

Doyle re-entered the public fray in 1850, when he published *A Letter to Lord John Russell on the future location of The National Gallery and Royal Academy*. The pamphlet picked up some of the interests which Doyle had revealed in his earlier correspondence with Peel, by demonstrating 'that very serious objections exist to Trafalgar Square as a permanent site for the National Gallery...whether the question be examined on the grounds of convenience, economy, or fitness'.[109] According to Dicky, the letter resulted in a number of Royal Academicians, 'affected by "dad's" pamphlet even to kindness', sending tickets to a private view of the Vernon Gallery.[110]

However, what Doyle continued to hold out for – in vain – was a public office of some description which would enable him to execute his ideas for public works, parks and gardens. A letter from Richard Doyle to his brother Charles, in August 1853, reveals the repeated rebuffs which John Doyle experienced – as well as Dicky's attempts to intercede on his behalf:

> the most notable instance is the interview a short time ago between the Guv'nor and Sir William Molesworth, which I brought about at the latter's office, and which was of as unsatisfactory a notion as it could well be. I wrote to Lady Molesworth [Andalusia Grant Carstairs] the same day to tell her as much, and she wrote back in a kindish tone (mine was curt and 'offended') saying that 'she feared as much', that 'Sir W's sense of duty! was such

that unless he saw the necessity', etc, – also that 'Ministers had been a very short time in office, and had not yet had time, etc', – likewise 'we must wait till next session, etc'. The upshot of the whole being that nothing is to be hoped for in the Board of Works while Sir W is at the head, and that we have only to look to my Lord Aberdeen [the Prime Minister], who Lady M thinks will offer [the] Gov' something whenever he has the power. Of course it either may, or may not suit.[111]

A fresh opportunity presented itself when Dicky refused to contribute illustrations to a hostile new Conservative newspaper, *The Press*, with which Disraeli was involved. 'It is quite true that considerable temptations[112] were held out to induce me to do so [he told Aberdeen] but my reasons for refusing being come to from a sense of duty, having confidence in your Lordship's government, and feeling it impossible for me to take part in attacks against that portion of it with which your Lordship is more especially identified'. Having seen a letter from Aberdeen to Lady Molesworth which expressed a wish, on the Prime Minister's part, 'to serve me' in some way, as an expression of thanks for his forbearance, Dicky now took the opportunity to solicit a position for his father:

> Lord Carlisle, then at the head of the Woods and Forests, expressed his opinion that an office, the duties of which would include a personal superintendence of the Parks etc with a view to their improvement in matters of taste and detail, would be most desirable...Lord Seymour, who succeeded him, I believe did not take the same view with regard to such an office being wanted...The result has been that my Father has been for years in expectation, and uncertainty, acting under the advice of friends, among whom I may mention Sir Robert Inglis, Sir Richard Mayne, and Mr B Hawes, the Deputy Secretary at War, as most conversant with his qualifications and the steps he has taken in the matter...my Father, although he has most earnestly advocated the appointment of an office such as I have described, on Public grounds, personally only desires such a one as, being in accordance with his tastes, and connected with pursuits he has studied much, will enable him to be of real advantage to the Public.[113]

Aberdeen's response was discouraging. Having confirmed what Dicky already knew to be true – Sir William Molesworth's opposition to the creation of such an office – the Prime Minister concluded, 'I know not how far it might be possible to create it with his support; but without it, I could not venture to make the attempt'. In spite of renewed applications on Dicky's part, some months later, the matter seems to have quietly dropped.[114]

As the 1850s unfolded, John Doyle gradually entered a life of quiet, secluded retirement, during which he 'took comfort in his religion' and rode occasionally in Hyde Park, 'visiting art galleries' and taking in exhibitions by French artists including Paul Gavarni (1804–1866) and Eugène Delacroix (1798–1863). Arthur Conan Doyle remembered his grandfather 'in his old age, [as] a very handsome and dignified man with features of the strong Anglo-Irish Duke of Wellington stamp'.[115] According to Richard Mullen, 'During the Crimean War, Doyle invented a tent with better ventilation for which service he received a prize of £300 from the War Office. Ever patriotic, Doyle used the money to develop waterproof boots for the soldiers'.[116] By 1864, he had moved from Cambridge Terrace to 54 Clifton Gardens, Maida Hill (now Maida Vale) with Dicky and Annette, neither of whom ever married. It was here, on 2 January 1868, that John Doyle died at the age of 70. He was buried at West Norwood cemetery.[117]

Doyle's obituary in *The Art Journal* described him as a:

> tall, graceful figure, and by a noble cast of features...unfailingly pre-possessing. An innate amiability of the most winning kind was united in him with an unaffected self-respect, on which no levity could trespass. There were few men to whose sound sense and assured taste an appeal could be more safely made. He was one whom to know, even but little, was insensibly to esteem; to know much, to love much. In a word, he was from the hands of nature a rare gentleman.

If Doyle did not live long enough to witness the fame of his grandson as a novelist, writer and adventurer, then he was also spared the family rift which resulted from Arthur Conan Doyle's disavowal of his Catholicism, at the start of his medical career. The combined force of James, Richard and Annette Doyle attempted in vain to dissuade their nephew from this course of action. Late in life, Richard Doyle continued to recommend Arthur to such wealthy Catholic patrons as the Bishop of Portsmouth and the Duke of Norfolk, without thanks. 'To this aloof, Doyle circle [one of Conan Doyle's biographers commented], ageing and childless, all that [mattered] in life was the Catholic Church. Their ancestors had given up everything for it. Material possessions were ephemeral; the Faith was real'.[118]

Such an attitude can only have been reinforced by the straitened circumstances in which John Doyle found himself at the end of his life. Only months before his death, J R Herbert wrote to Doyle's old friend, Sir James Emerson Tennent, relaying his disappointment 'that your kind exertions [to secure a government pension for Doyle] had been without result'. Herbert remarked that an 'opportunity... for repairing that omission' had presented itself with the death of Edward Hodges Baily, a member of the Royal Academy, who had been in receipt of an official pension worth £1000 per annum. Correspondence after Doyle's death suggests that Lord Derby – the Conservative Prime Minister in whose gift the pension lay – had 'promised this year' [i.e. 1868] to do something for Doyle. Given this, Herbert renewed the appeal for assistance on behalf of Doyle's heirs:

Might, were a memorial signed by the same persons, [we] place that little pension at the service of Miss [Annette] Doyle. I throw out this suggestion because I know that poor Doyle's means were so very limited, and that his daughter is left with next to nothing. I am sure that you had such an affectionate regard for that talented man that you will, if you see a likely-hood [*sic*] of bringing this help about, gladly lend a helping hand towards it.[119]

At the time of his death, 'H.B.'s work languished in obscurity; a sale of Doyle's effects, held by Christie's, had to be cancelled for lack of interest. Nevertheless, in 1880, four of Doyle's drawings were acquired for a thousand guineas, and three more were sold (for a similar sum), twelve years after that.[120] The gradual acquisition and cataloguing of the *Political Sketches* and Doyle's preparatory drawings, by the British Museum, from the late-nineteenth century, opened up the means for greater engagement with Doyle's work. However, as with caricature studies more generally, this was not kept pace with at the level of academic scholarship. Only one selection from the *Political Sketches* appeared in print throughout the whole of the twentieth century – G M Trevelyan's *The Seven Years of William IV* (1952) – and another sixty years have passed between that book and the current volume. As the Peel Society's recent acquisition of nearly 150 hand-coloured *Political Sketches* demonstrates, Doyle's work as 'H.B.' is still highly collectable. Nevertheless, by comparison with the likes of Gillray, Cruikshank and Rowlandson (in the eighteenth century) and Tenniel and Leech (in the later-nineteenth century), John Doyle remains one of the least well-known and least well-appreciated of pictorial satirists.

REFERENCES

1 [Place of publication is London unless stated]. Norman Gash, *Mr Secretary Peel. The Life of Sir Robert Peel to 1830* (Harlow, 1961), pp.506–507.

2 According to M D George, caricatures of Peel belied his usual image, showing him as 'handsome, and likeable, with none of the stiff moroseness of which contemporaries complained': *Catalogue of Political and Personal Satires, Preserved in the Department of Prints and Drawings in the British Museum,* Volume XI (1954), xxvii.

3 See, in particular, Diana Donald, *The Age of Caricature: Satirical Prints in the Reign of George III* (1996); Vic Gatrell, *City of Laughter: Sex and Satire in Eighteenth Century London* (2006); and Brian Maidment, *Comedy, Caricature and the Social Order, 1820–1850* (Manchester, 2013); cf. *The Times,* 14 June 1832, for one case involving a 'public nuisance'.

4 The Peel caricature collection is now held by The Morgan Library and Museum, New York.

5 For a recent exploration, see Ian Haywood, *Romanticism and Caricature* (Cambridge, 2013).

6 Doyle paid homage to this character when he told a correspondent that he possessed 'a foible to which like Paul Pry – I am very prone to, to wit, forgetting my umbrella!': British Library Additional Manuscripts, 39954, f.253, John Doyle to Mrs Owen, 31 May [after 1852]. For Paul Pry, see David Vincent, *I Hope I Don't Intrude. Privacy and its Dilemmas since 1800* (forthcoming), which explores the origins of modern debates about privacy through the prism of Pry.

7 Thomas McLean stated that 'spurious copies, and imitations of style and signature, much inferior to the celebrated Originals, are in circulation. None of "H.B."s productions can be warranted genuine unless they possess the sole Publisher's Name and Address, 26 Haymarket, at the bottom of each plate': *A Key to the Political Sketches of "H.B.", Nos. 1 to 164, Arranged as Published, up to 7th November, 1831* (1831).

8 *The Times,* 9 October 1835; 4 November 1836; 16 May 1835.

9 Arthur Conan Doyle, *Memories and Adventures* (1924), p.7; John Dickson Carr, *The Life of Sir Arthur Conan Doyle* (1949), p.13.

10 Pierre Nordon, *Conan Doyle* (1966), pp.3–4; see Adrian Conan Doyle, *Sir Arthur Conan Doyle Centenary 1859–1959* (New York, 1959), family tree facing p.29 (including a picture of James Doyle, John Doyle's father).

11 J D Herbert, *Irish Varieties for the Last Fifty Years: Written from Recollections* (1836), p.56, which names Doyle as a product of the Dublin Society's Drawing Academy.

12 David Blayney Brown, 'New Light on "H.B." An Early Work by John Doyle', *Print Quarterly,* 22/1 (March 1985), 49; Rodney Engen, Michael Heseltine and Lionel Lambourne, *Richard Doyle and his Family* (1983), p.19.

13 John Doyle, *A Letter to Lord John Russell, on the Future Location of The National Gallery and Royal Academy* (1850), p.21. Doyle claimed that, in this respect, he had 'neither obligations to acknowledge…nor resentments for real or supposed wrongs to gratify'.

14 Sally Mitchell, *The Dictionary of British Equestrian Artists* (Woodbridge, 1985), p.199.

15 Richard Mullen, 'Polite Points of Wit', *Country Life,* 173 (2 June 1983), 1496; Walter G Strickland, *A Dictionary of Irish Artists* (1913), Volume I, 297–298; *The Art Journal* (March 1868), 75; Helen Andrews, 'John Doyle', *The Dictionary of Irish Biography* [online edition].

16 Nordon, *Conan Doyle*, p.5; Dickson Carr, *Conan Doyle*, p.14.

17 Algernon Graves, *The Royal Academy of Arts. A Complete Dictionary of Contributors and their work from its foundation in 1769 to 1904* (1970 edition), Volume I, 366; Freeman O'Donoghue, *Catalogue of Engraved British Portraits Preserved in the Department of Prints and Drawings in the British Museum*, Volume II (1910), 315; Charles Lane, *British Racing Prints 1700–1940* (1990), pp.99–100.

18 'Everybody who has a couple of shillings to spare should procure a copy': *The Times*, 13 August 1836.

19 M Dorothy George, *Hogarth to Cruikshank: Social Change in Graphic Satire* (1967), p.220. There were about a dozen *Political Sketches* in 1848 and 1849 and none in 1850.

20 Robert William Buss, *English Graphic Satire and its relation to different styles of Painting, Sculpture, and Engraving* (Privately printed, 1874), p.157; the British Museum holds many of Doyle's original designs and rough sketches in pencil or chalk: *Catalogue of Drawings by British Artists and Artists of Foreign origin working in Great Britain, Preserved in the Department of Prints and Drawings in the British Museum,* Volume II (1900), 44–96.

21 Attested to in 'A View of the Present State of Lithography in England', *Library of the Fine Arts, or, Repertory of Painting, Sculpture, Architecture, and Engraving* (1831–1832), Volume II, 212.

22 *The Diary of Benjamin Robert Haydon, Volume III (1825–1832)*, ed. W B Pope (Harvard, 1963), 638; Fintan Cullen, 'Visual parody and political commentary: John Doyle and Daniel O'Connell' in *Irish Elites in the Nineteenth Century,* ed. Ciaran O'Neill (Dublin, 2013), p.233.

23 See Appendix.

24 J H Pollen, 'Introduction', *A Journal Kept by Richard Doyle in the Year 1840* (1885), v.

25 Buss, *English Graphic Satire,* p.154.

26 O'Donoghue, *Catalogue,* Volume I (1908), 112; *The Times,* 2 April 1839.

27 Daria Hambourg, *Richard Doyle. His Life and Work* (1948), pp.9–10; cf. Engen, Heseltine and Lambourne, *Richard Doyle and His Family,* p.13.

28 Bibliotheque Cantonale et Universitaire, Lausanne, Conan Doyle Letter Book inscribed *The Letters of Richard 'Dicky' Doyle to Charles and Annette Doyle, 1850–1860* [hereafter CDLB], pp.14, 36 and 87, where Richard congratulates his brother on having '"broke out" in the comic character of the Scotch H.B.'. I am indebted to Laura Saggiorato for providing me with access to this material.

29 Graham Everitt, *English Caricaturists and Graphic Humorists of the Nineteenth Century* (1886), p.276; George, *Catalogue,* Volume XI, xlvii.

30 *The Times*, 4 November 1836; 27 December 1834. On 'Jim Crow' see Tom Scriven, 'The Jim Crow Craze in London's Press and Streets, 1836–1839', *Journal of Victorian Culture* (forthcoming, 2014).

31 John Hullah (1812–1884) was a musician and composer.

32 CDLB, pp.100, 124, 46; *The Letters of Charles Dickens, Volume Six 1850–1852,* ed. Graham Storey, Kathleen Tillotson and Nina Burgis (Oxford, 1988), 113 n.1; Blayney Brown, 'An Early Work'. Lumley's fetes were much remarked upon by contemporaries: see *The Morning Chronicle,* 7 July 1851 and Benjamin Lumley, *Reminiscences of the Opera* (1864), pp.323–324.

33 *The Athenaeum* (31 December 1892), 921 for James' obituary; Nordon, *Conan Doyle,* p.7; CDLB, p.66; there is a picture of James Doyle in Dickson Carr, *Conan Doyle,* facing p.17.

34 The picture is reproduced in *Arthur Conan Doyle Centenary*, p.32.

35 i.e. Michael Baker's belief that John Doyle spent his honeymoon at Arundel as the guest of the Duke of Norfolk: *The Doyle Diary* (1978), p.xi; in fact, the person in question was James Doyle: Rodney Engen, *Richard Doyle* (Stroud, 1983), p.127; Nordon, *Conan Doyle,* p.6; Rosemary Mitchell, 'James Doyle' in *The Oxford Dictionary of National Biography* (hereafter *Oxford DNB*) [online edition, 2004].

36 'The Caricatures of H.B.', *The London and Westminster Review* (January 1838), 289; James Grant, *The Great Metropolis* (2 Vols, 1838).

37 *Haydon* ed. Pope, 572 (29 October 1831).

38 Samuel Redgrave, *A Dictionary of Artists of the English School: Painters, Sculptors, Architects, Engravers and Ornamentists: With Notices of their Lives and Work* (New Edition, 1878), p.130.

39 *The Times,* 16 May 1838; 17 April 1841; John Paget, *Paradoxes and Puzzles Historical, Judicial and Literary* (Edinburgh, 1874), pp.461–462; Everitt, *English Caricaturists,* p.239; Buss, *English Graphic Satire,* p.154; G M Trevelyan, *The Seven Years of William IV. A Reign Cartooned by John Doyle* (1952), p.3; M Dorothy George, *English Political Caricature. A Study of Opinion and Propaganda, 1793–1832* (2 Vols, Oxford, 1959), Volume II, 257.

40 Grantley F Berkeley, *My Life and Recollections,* Volume IV (1866), 139–140.

41 *The Times,* 3 November 1842; 'The Caricatures of H.B.', 290; Engen, Heseltine and Lambourne, *Richard Doyle and His Family,* p.8

42 Everitt, *English Caricaturists*, pp.238–239; Buss, *English Graphic Satire,* p.154; *The Times,* 19 June 1835; 6 April 1837; 11 April 1840.

43 Robert R Wark, *Charles Doyle's Fairyland* (San Marino, California, 1980), p.5.

44 Buss, *English Graphic Satire,* pp.155–156; 'The Caricatures of H.B.', 292. Arthur Conan Doyle put the same point more crisply: 'My grandfather was a gentleman, drawing gentlemen for gentlemen, and the satire lay in the wit of the picture and not in the misdrawing of faces': *Memories and Adventures,* p.7.

45 Peter Quennell writing in *The Cornhill Magazine*, 963 (1945), taking issue with Austin Dobson's conclusion about Doyle in *The Dictionary of National Biography* (hereafter *DNB*); Quennell's comments are echoed in H L Mallalieu, *The Dictionary of British Watercolour Artists up to 1920* (Woodbridge, 1976), p.86.

46 Including by George Charles Williamson in *The Catholic Encyclopedia* (1913); Engen, *Richard Doyle*, p.14; and Kenneth Baker in *Oxford DNB*.

47 Hambourg, *Richard Doyle*, p.13; Trevelyan, *Seven Years*, p.3.

48 M D George, *Catalogue*, Volume XI, xlvi.

49 See Appendix; Austin Dobson (in the *DNB*) remarked that Doyle's 'success as a portrait-painter was not commensurate with his deserts'.

50 Moore reciprocated with a marble bust of Doyle, completed in 1849 and exhibited at the Royal Academy in 1850. This took its place against the wall of the drawing room in the family's London home. It has been described by Pierre Nordon as revealing a 'calm but masterful patrician': Nordon, *Conan Doyle*, p.6; Dickson Carr, *Conan Doyle*, p.44. The bust (National Gallery of Ireland, Catalogue Number 8298) is reproduced in *Arthur Conan Doyle Centenary*, p.30.

51 'The Caricatures of H.B.', 292.

52 Public Record Office of Northern Ireland [hereafter PRONI], D2922/B/10/4, Doyle to Tennent, 30 March 1843; D2922/B/10/13, Doyle to Tennent, 'Thursday'; both refer to Doyle's attendance in the lobbies and galleries. Doyle's obituary in *The Art Journal* (March 1868), 75, referred to him as 'a quiet, silent, unsuspected frequenter of the lobby and gallery', whilst George, *English Political Caricature*, Volume II, 234, says Doyle 'haunted Parliament in search of copy'.

53 Nordon, *Doyle*, p.9; Engen, Heseltine and Lambourne, *Richard Doyle and His Family*, p.14.

54 See Appendix.

55 Mullen, 'Polite Points of Wit', 1496; cf. Engen, Heseltine and Lambourne, *Richard Doyle and His Family*, p.7; Everitt, *English Caricaturists*, pp.240, 275; the same point is made (with more qualification) in Buss, *English Graphic Satire*, p.156.

56 Paget, *Paradoxes*, pp.461–462. *The Times*, 26 March 1836, noted 'an accuracy amounting to identification'.

57 Paget, *Paradoxes*, p.462; cf. Miles L Chappell and James N McCord Jnr, 'John Doyle, Daniel O'Connell, "The Great Liberator", and Rubens: The Appropriate and Appropriation in Political Caricature', *Southeast College Art Conference Review*, 11/2 (Spring 1987), 127; Everitt, *English Caricaturists*, p.274 is unusually severe on this point.

58 Engen, Heseltine and Lambourne, *Richard Doyle and His Family*, p.19.

59 Chappell and McCord, 'Appropriation', 127; cf. George, *English Political Caricature*, Volume II, 258.

60 My italics: see Appendix. For more discussion on this point, see Fintan Cullen's essay below.

61 'The Caricatures of H.B.', 291; M D George, *Catalogue*, Volume XI, xlvii.

62 Trevelyan, *Seven Years*, p.5; George, *English Political Caricature*, Volume II, 258; George, *Catalogue*, Volume XI, xiv. A comparison between 'H.B.' and Gillray was also made in *The Times*, 21 March 1835.

63 Nordon, *Conan Doyle*, p.5; *The Times*, 24 December 1838; 18 March 1843. George, *English Political Caricature*, Volume II, 234, refers to their 'documentary character different in kind from the caricatures of his contemporaries'.

64 'The Caricatures of H.B.', 289.

65 See Appendix.

66 Engen, Heseltine and Lambourne, *Richard Doyle and His Family*, p.14.

67 Nordon, *Conan Doyle*, p.14; *Arthur Conan Doyle Centenary*, p.13; a picture of Michael Conan appears in Dickson Carr, *Conan Doyle*, facing p.17. Arthur Conan Doyle described his godfather as 'a man of distinction, an intellectual Irishman of the type which originally founded the Sinn Fein movement' and a 'dear old volcanic Irishman': *Memories and Adventures*, p.21.

68 See CDLB, pp.50, 107, 128; PRONI, D2922/B/10/27, Tennent to Doyle, undated; D2922/B/10/29, Doyle to Tennent, 3 April 1865; regarding co-operation with Cardinal Manning on his projected (but never completed) biography of Wiseman.

69 One contemporary publisher described Henry as 'an extremely careful and painstaking artist': *The Brothers Dalziel. A Record of Work, 1840–1890* (1901), p.308.

70 A picture of Henry is reproduced in *Arthur Conan Doyle Centenary*, p.33.

71 CDLB, p.107.

72 The best study of Charles Doyle remains Baker, *The Doyle Diary*, which reproduces his 1889 diary (other volumes are held privately).

73 CDLB, pp.4–5, 111; Conan Doyle, *Memories and Adventures*, p.11.

74 Conan Doyle, *Memories and Adventures*, p.30; a picture of Charles Doyle appears in *Arthur Conan Doyle Centenary*, p.30.

75 E.g. Engen, *Richard Doyle*, p.35.

76 PRONI, D2922/B/10/10–11. By 25 June 1843, Doyle could report that he had 'in a great degree recovered my usual tranquillity of mind', helped (in no small measure) by a family 'blessed with an elasticity of spirit which nothing can long depress': D2922/B/10/12.

77 PRONI, D2922/B/10/14. The family left London in consequence, taking a house at 1 Belle-View Place, Richmond, for a fortnight: D2922/B/10/15, 10 April 1844.

78 Violet Hopkins Warner, 'Thackeray and Richard Doyle, the "Wayward artist" of *The Newcomes*', *Harvard Library Bulletin* (April 1978), 193, says that John Doyle helped arrange a connection between Thackeray and *The Morning Chronicle*.

79 Richard Doyle introduced Dickens to his father at Lumley's fete on 19 June 1850: 'They got on very well together, did "Pa" and Boz [Dickens' early pseudonym], and the whole thing was voted successful': CDLB, p.106; *The Letters of Charles Dickens, Volume Six,* 113 n.1. For later correspondence, see *The Letters of Charles Dickens, Volume Seven 1853–1855,* ed. Graham Storey, Kathleen Tillotson and Angus Easson (Oxford, 1993), 719.

80 Baker, *The Doyle Diary*, p.xi; *Arthur Conan Doyle Centenary,* p.31 reproduces a picture of the dining table (with silver plaques denoting the names of famous men who were entertained at it) and a letter from Samuel Rogers to John Doyle discussing their mutual friend Sir Walter Scott.

81 Conan Doyle, *Memories and Adventures,* p.8.

82 The journal was sold to the British Museum for £200 in 1885, largely in an effort to realise financial capital for Richard's sister Annette (James Doyle negotiated the purchase). Dick's estate at death was valued at £1500: *Oxford DNB*.

83 Hambourg, *Richard Doyle,* p.10; cf. Hopkins Warner, 'Thackeray and Richard Doyle', 194.

84 *Richard Doyle's Journal*, ed. Christopher Wheeler (1980), pp.51, 143 (25 April, 23 November 1840); Nordon, *Conan Doyle,* p.9.

85 Baker, *The Doyle Diary,* p.15.

86 *The Athenaeum* (31 December 1892), 921; Austin Dobson, 'John Doyle', *DNB*; Penelope M Fitzgerald, 'Notes on the Fairy Pictures of Richard Doyle', *World Review* (December 1950), 67.

87 Hambourg, *Richard Doyle,* p.12; Pollen, 'Introduction', vii; Engen, Lambourne and Heseltine, *Richard Doyle and His Family,* pp.14, 29.

88 The letters (51 from Richard, 25 from Henry and 3 from Charles) are held by The Morgan Library and Museum, New York.

89 *The Brothers Dalziel*, p.56.

90 Engen, *Richard Doyle*, p.27. Doyle's concern for the health of his surviving daughter, Annette, emerges from PRONI, D2922/B/10/21, Doyle to Tennent, 9 August 1852 – 'I hope to get her a little more country air before the autumn is over'. Also see CDLB, p.64. In both instances, Annette was sent to friends (the Jacksons) at Hampstead.

91 E.g. PRONI, D2922/B/10/18, Doyle to Tennent, 18 July 1845, which references the very 'flattering things' which Prince Albert and Queen Victoria had said about one of Dicky's 'whimsical but extraordinary' works. Given the date, this may be *A Grand Historical Allegorical Classical and Comic Procession of Remarkable Personages Ancient and Modern*, representing a christening procession for the Prince of Wales, based upon an earlier representation of the procession for the christening of the Princess Royal in 1840: Engen, Heseltine and Lambourne, *Richard Doyle and His Family*, p.68.

92 Hopkins Warner, 'Thackeray and Richard Doyle', 196.

93 Though not before providing it with the iconic cover illustration for the magazine which continued to be used from 1849–1956: 'Richard Doyle' in *World Encyclopaedia of Cartoons*, ed. D M Horn (1980).

94 *The Letters of Charles Dickens*, *Volume Six*, 78 n.1; for the wider issue, see Eleanor McNees, '*Punch* and the Pope: Three decades of anti-Catholic caricature', *Victorian Periodicals Review,* 37/1 (2004), 18–45.

95 PRONI, D2922/B/10/20.

96 Nordon, *Conan Doyle,* p.6.

97 CDLB, p.54 notes a trip during the 1850s. Doyle was not above placing a bet on a Sunday. The wager (which was witnessed by Michael Conan and Francis Moore) was that there would be no Anglo-French war; the sum involved was a sovereign: *Richard Doyle's Journal,* p.120 (5 October 1840).

98 Trevelyan, *Seven Years*, p.4; Mullen, 'Polite Points of Wit', 1497.

99 *The Art Journal* (March 1868), 75; Conan Doyle, *Memories and Adventures,* p.7.

100 McLean, *A Key to the "Political Sketches" of "H.B.", Nos. 1 to 164*.

101 *The Times,* 18 May 1844. The newspaper had not always held a consistent line on the subject. Earlier, it had described 'H.B.' as 'a sort of "chartered wag", [who] sometimes aims a sly blow at his friends'; elsewhere as 'the most impartial as well as the best of caricaturists': 12 April 1838; 4 December 1834.

102 Engen, *Richard Doyle,* p.139.

103 Nordon, *Conan Doyle,* p.4; successive Doyle entries can also be found in, amongst others, Mark Bryant and Simon Heneage, *Dictionary of British Cartoonists and Caricaturists 1730–1980* (Aldershot, 1994), pp.63–65 and Rodney K Engen, *Dictionary of Victorian Wood Engravers* (Cambridge, 1985), pp.76–77.

104 Sir Duffus Hardy, Keeper of the Records, told James Doyle in 1875 that he held 'a very distinguished name and, as a son of so eminent a man as your father, you enjoy a great advantage over most people': Nordon, *Conan Doyle,* p.6 n.1.

105 CDLB, p.105; Brougham told Dicky that 'he had had the pleasure of being introduced to my father by Charley Phillipps': *ibid*., p.102.

106 CDLB, p.14. Though Rodney Engen used this (undated) letter, he dated its contents to the General Election of 1855. In fact, contextual evidence from the letter – notably, Charles Gavan Duffy's return for New Ross, Craven's unsuccessful candidacy for Dublin County

and the election riots at Limerick and Belfast – prove that the contents relate to the 1852 contest: Engen, *Richard Doyle,* pp.139–140; *The Times,* 8, 16, 22 July 1852. Reference to the 'Thimble-Rig' shows Doyle reverting to proven methods: see catalogue, No. 32.

107 Pollen, 'Introduction', xv; *The Athenaeum* (31 December 1892), 921; Engen, Heseltine and Lambourne, *Richard Doyle and His Family,* p.8.

108 The illustration is reproduced in Engen, *Richard Doyle*, pp.63–64. More positively, Richard Doyle's 'The Enchanted Tree' (exhibited at the Royal Academy in June 1868) was produced in memory of his father; *ibid*., p.139.

109 John Doyle, *A Letter to Lord John Russell on the future location of* The National Gallery *and Royal Academy* (20 June 1850), p.15.

110 CDLB, p.106.

111 CDLB, pp.56–57; also see p.18. Sir William Molesworth (1810–1855) was First Commissioner of Works (1853–1855) in Aberdeen's Whig-Peelite cabinet (1852–1855). He was a noted Radical M.P.

112 Dicky told Charles that he was offered £800 a year to work for *The Press*: CDLB, p.68.

113 British Library, Additional Manuscripts, 43253, ff.38–41, Richard Doyle to Aberdeen, 27 April [1854]. Benjamin Hawes (1797–1862) was Deputy Secretary at War until 1857. Viscount Morpeth (1802–1864) succeeded the Earl of Lincoln as First Commissioner of Woods and Forests (1846–1850); he was succeeded by Lord Seymour (1804–1885); in 1851, the post was abolished and replaced by that of First Commissioner of Works. Doyle was friends with Robert Inglis (1786–1855) and Richard Mayne (1796–1868). Mayne was one of the two commissioners of Metropolitan Police appointed by Peel in 1829. Doyle had worked with Mayne to ensure the safe movement of the crowds in Hyde Park during the Great Exhibition: CDLB, pp.51, 130.

114 British Library Additional Manuscripts, 43253, f.67, Aberdeen to Richard Doyle, 4 May 1854; 43254, ff.23–25, Doyle to Aberdeen and reply, 17 and 21 August 1854; *ibid.,* ff.105–107, Doyle to Aberdeen, 19 September 1854 (enclosing a letter from Lewis A Jones to Mr Monsell Eyre M.P., 21 August 1854).

115 'John Doyle' in *The Dictionary of Irish Biography* [online edition]; Conan Doyle, *Memories and Adventures,* p.7; British Library, Additional Manuscripts, 39577, ff.49–50, John Doyle to Thomas Cubitt, 12 December 1848, inviting him to visit.

116 Mullen, 'Polite Points of Wit', 1497.

117 Charles Doyle feared that his father had died as the result of making a journey to see him in Edinburgh, which had been conducted in inclement weather: Dickson Carr, *Conan Doyle*, p.19.

118 Dickson Carr, *Conan Doyle,* p.44; Nordon, *Conan Doyle,* p.30. By contrast, Conan Doyle seems to have accepted his Uncle Henry's offer to act as a referee: Dickson Carr, *Conan Doyle,* p.48.

119 PRONI, D2922/B/10/31–32, J R Herbert to Emerson Tennent, 24 May 1867, 20 February 1868. John Doyle's estate was valued at £450: *Oxford DNB*. Also see n.82 above.

120 Nordon, *Conan Doyle,* p.5; Engen, *Richard Doyle,* p.139.

Appendix: The Peel-Doyle Correspondence

British Library Additional Manuscripts
Vol. 40497, ff.116–17, Doyle, 17 Cambridge Terrace, Hyde Park, to Peel, 11 Dec. 1841
Private

Sir

In casting aside an incognito which I have endeavoured to maintain for ten years & upwards, & openly addressing you as the author of HB's Political Sketches, feeling while I do so, not less sensibly aware of your exalted station than of my own singular though humble position, I am impelled by reasons which – when explained will I trust be accepted by you as some apology for a step at once so bold & so contrary to my habitual reserve.

Those reasons Sir, relate partly to my authorship & partly to certain public improvements in which I believe you take a warm interest, & regarding which I have formed some strong opinions. – But the more immediate cause of my now addressing you is as follows.

Happening to be in the House of Commons the evening you gave notice of your motion of Want of Confidence in the late Government, the occasion struck me – both for General Situation & concentrated political interest – as affording the best subject for a historical portrait, that had come within my experience – and I have no doubt that such a portrait – if fairly executed – would be very acceptable to a large portion of the Public, in the form of an Engraving. I have already made a study [see Fintan Cullen's essay, Fig. 3], with a view to this attempt & should feel proud of its successful accomplishment. But this portrait, in its' mode of treatment – being essentially different from the slight & unpretending sketches which I have heretofore ventured upon, I cannot with satisfaction to myself or with a reasonable chance of success, proceed without, Sir, your sanction & in some degree, kind aid. I do not require a sitting in the ordinary sense of the term. It must – with me – be mainly a work of memory. The interview which would be necessary for a satisfactory explanation of the other objects to which I have alluded, & which form the primary cause of this communication, would I hope enable me to work out the detail of my first impression.

The honor of this interview, I now respectfully solicit, at such time as may be least inconvenient to yourself. I have no reason to flatter myself Sir, that you have ever viewed the humble performances of HB with that favour which it has been his fortune to receive so generally from the political world, but I do trust that you will give the Author credit for the possession of sufficient discretion & delicacy, to at once assure you that he would not seek any thing at your hands, the granting of which he conceived would, in the slightest degree, be inconsistent with your high sense of public duty. I trust too, Sir, that you will appreciate the motive which made him prefer thus frankly addressing you, to the more formal mode of a personal introduction.

I have the honor to be
Sir,
Your most respectful Humble Servant
John Doyle

Ibid., f.118, Peel, Whitehall, to Doyle, 12 Dec. [1841]
To be copied

Sir

I very much regret that I am under such Engagements with respect to sitting for my portrait – and also with regard to the occupation of my time in public business, I am unable to accede to your request – and must therefore ask you to Communicate to me in writing the purport of what you wish to convey to me personally, I assure you that I am very sensible of the great merit of those performances of which you can with just pride claim the authorship.

I am &c
Your obedient
RP

Ibid., f.119, Doyle, 17 Cambridge Terrace, to Peel, 17 Dec. [1841]

Sir

I beg respectfully to apologise for not sooner complying with your request that I would state in writing the purport of what I wished to have communicated to you personally: the delay having been occasioned by indisposition which rendered the necessary application very painful to me. In a few days however I trust to be able to make the attempt, with better success. I beg at the same time to observe that the subject to which the statement alluded to refers, is not of an urgent nature, and should probably have been postponed by me to a later period, but for the Circumstance of the portrait, which to be seasonable, must be speedily produced, and which I had, from an indisposition to intrude upon time, that I knew must be pressed upon by matters of the very highest importance – delayed as long as possible, consistent with the object I had in view.

I beg Sir, most respectfully to thank you for the kind terms in which you are pleased to express yourself regarding that authorship which I have acknowledged, and to assure you that such approbation is most gratifying to me.

I have the honor to be
Sir
Your most obedient Humble Servant
John Doyle

Vol. 40500, ff.312–24, Doyle, 17 Cambridge Terrace, Hyde Park to Peel, 22 Jan. 1842

Sir

As the chief subjects connected with the public improvements upon which I wished to lay my thoughts before you, are not likely – from the financial state of the country – to engage for some time to come, the serious attention of Government, and as – from the near approach of the meeting of Parliament – more weighty matters must press upon your consideration, I feel it alike due to you, and the importance of the subjects themselves to postpone my communication regarding them to a more seasonable period meanwhile I shall have the opportunity of more carefully maturing my ideas, and be enabled thereby to submit them to you in a more satisfactory shape than I at present could.

I may however – without entering into details – be permitted Sir, to name the subjects to which these remarks more particularly apply. The first is a project for the erection of a new National Gallery – its proposed site &c – assuming from the increasing wants of the Royal Academy, and the growing disapprobation of the present Edifice, as a depository for the national pictures, that the subject will at no distant day – Earnestly engage public attention. My second, relates to the north bank of the Thames – between Westminster and Waterloo Bridges, and is designed with the double view of Embellishing that part of the river, and remedying the serious and Encreasing [*sic*] evil arising from the accumulation of deposit, caused by the projecting Terrace of the new Houses of Parliament.

Two other subjects, of comparatively trifling importance but which do not present the same difficulties in design nor obstacles to execution, I note – for the sake of convenience – in the form of the annexed memorandum. The other accompanying paper was written in anticipation of my being able at an earlier period to lay the first-named subjects fully before you, and is in substance what I should probably have said, had I been favored [*sic*] with a personal opportunity. As it relates only to myself privately, and is of no immediate consequence, I beg Sir, that you will lay it aside, until it shall suit your entire convenience to peruse it.

I have the honor to be
Sir
With the deepest respect
Your obedient humble Servant
John Doyle

[Memorandum] January 1842

Labouring Sir, under the disadvantage of claiming your attention without a personal introduction I hope I may be pardoned if I make some reference to my past conduct in regard to the authorship which I have avowed, not with the view of wanting any undue favour, but – by establishing a just estimate of my character – bespeak for the suggestions which will be found in the annexed paper, such notice as upon a patient consideration, they may be thought to merit.

To any one who has honoured the Sketches of "HB" with continued observation, I trust it will be unnecessary to say, that from the first, they have been governed by a certain steadiness of moral & political principle. Although commenced in sport, I soon became convinced from the extent of their sale & the importance attached to them in political circles, that I possessed in my hands an agent of some little influence. This influence, such as it was, I resolved should not be turned to any unworthy purpose by me, but that scrupulously avoiding all indelicacy, private scandal, and party bitterness, it should – where it was not intended merely to amuse by some harmless jest – be directed to the furtherance of some intelligible public object, that by such means as would by fair analogy be considered legitimate in political warfare. How far I have adhered to these principles it is for others to judge, I will only say, and can say it with perfect truth, that I never wilfully violated them. This, where the line between right & wrong was strongly marked, would be a poor boast, but in instances – and they were many – where the distinction was not obvious, that in the course of so extended a period, including seasons of such violent party strife, exposed to importunity, the temptation of immediate pecuniary profit, and the incitement to licence in the very nature of the thing itself, that I have deviated so little, is matter not only of agreeable reflection to myself, but a fact upon which I trust I may without presumption lay some claim to personal confidence, particularly when addressing one who is so capable of appreciating the difficulties of such a position, and who himself took so pre-eminently leading a part in the great transactions and stirring scenes, which these sketches may be said, humorously to record & illustrate.

With regard to my political opinions, they may in a great degree, be traced in the Sketches themselves. As however they may seem to have undergone some change, I beg your permission Sir, briefly to allude to them – When I commenced what I may call my political Career, the Catholic question was the one which most occupied the attention of the Country and divided parties. Being an Irishman & a Roman catholic, I was naturally an ardent supporter of that measure, and regarded the Whig party who had identified itself with the cause as specially entitled to my respect & Even gratitude. I had formed too, some strong opinions upon what I conceived to be the undue magnitude of the Irish Church establishment. But upon the relief Bill being passed, I felt that the Catholics were bound in honor [*sic*], if not in conscience, to abstain from all attacks upon the temporalities of that Establishment. I could not therefore without strong disapprobation and some shame, view the subsequent proceedings of the Catholic party, both in & out of Parliament – under the misguidance of Mr O'Connell, – though in this opinion I had the pain to differ from some near friends & relatives whom I know to be men of high principle. Then upon the question of Reform, I found myself again at variance with old & esteemed friends. I was a reformer as the term used to be understood, and certainly thought the so-called Tory party resisted too long those ameliorations in the representation which time had rendered expedient. I could not however approve of the new & sweeping measure of their adversaries. It appeared to me to be as imprudent as it was unnecessary, and that no amount of probable or possible good to be derived from it, justified the means by which alone it could be carried. From that time my mite of influence has been opposed to popular innovation. Throughout however I have preserved my personal independence, and it was that I might the better do so, & not from any affectation of secrecy that I maintained to the best of my ability, a strict incognito. The only friends in my confidence were on the liberal side – two in number – one a peer who had known me from boyhood, and both holding high offices under the late Government – while neither any member of the conservative party – with one unwilling exception & that at a comparatively recent period – I never held the slightest personal intercourse. Although in its ranks were comprised some early and kind friends, and though I was constantly honoured – as I was indeed by all parties – by the most copious & confidential correspondence. And I trust I may obtain implicit credit when I assure you Sir that you are the first Gentleman connected with public life to whom, as such, I have ever voluntarily committed my secret. I am quite aware that my name has, from imprudence somewhere, transpired, and been for some time associated with those sketches by those who have taken any interest in the matter. Still presumably – from the seclusion in which I lived – I was unknown. I feel now however placed in new circumstances and that even this degree of privacy, I cannot maintain long. New duties devolve upon me – the duties of a Father to a grown-up daughter [Annette; another daughter, Adelaide, died young] – and those oblige me to mix more with the world than I have done. It would I own be very irksome to me to be identified in society with these sketches, but as a thing passed. The battle too in which I fought as an humble auxiliary being fairly won, I feel no longer the excitement which I felt, when the contest was doubtful and great interests at stake. I may occasionally throw a tiny shot, but I feel that virtually "HB's" "occupation is gone". If in looking back upon his career I see no cause for triumph, neither have I much to regret. – If on the one hand I have not made any personal friends, I have been assured on the other – and the assurance coming from such a quarter that alluded to was the more grateful to me, – that I had not in my assumed character, made a personal Enemy: while public opinion on the whole has been very kind to me. With the pecuniary results – although I might perhaps have occupied some of the best years of my life more profitably and though my publisher has been much the larger gainer, I am not dissatisfied. They have enabled me to bring up so far respectably – a pretty large family, but no more. My sons however – five in number – from 8 to 18 years of age [James William Edmund, Richard, Henry Edward, Francis and Charles] – all shewing [*sic*] the strongest taste for the arts, and the three eldest evincing the most unequivocal promise, I have reason to look forward with more confidence than fear to the future. One of them – the second [Richard, 'Dicky' Doyle, of *Punch* fame] – who possesses with a most ready pencil, a singularly original fancy, has already tried his strength in two little publications, which have attracted very gratifying notice. With some of their performances indeed I feel assured Sir, from your high appreciation of finished art, you would in a season of relaxation be pleased, as the spontaneous productions of Boys not uncultivated certainly, but uncontrolled by Education. To foster and direct this native talent will occupy much of my future attention, but being in my 43d year, I still feel young enough to raise up an honourable reputation upon some new foundation. An unfortunate defect in my health which incapacitates me from painting much in oil, has hitherto been an obstacle to my attempting with a fair chance of success to attain eminence in that class of Portrait painting which would have suited my taste and my capacity. But in matters such as those to which I am about to solicit your attention I have always taken the liveliest interest and feel a deep rooted conviction that I possess some capabilities to be useful. While the occupation from its' involving more of personal activity is more suited to my constitution. It may naturally be enquired whether I have given any practical evidence of possessing this kind of talent? I can refer to one. In the second competition for the Nelson Testimonial, I sent in a design, at the particular request of my friend Mr More O'Ferrall then at the Treasury Board – he being pleased with the opinions & ideas which I expressed in a conversation which we had together upon the Subject. That my design did not attract any special notice I am not surprised from the haste with which the drawing was executed & from an accident which injured it in going in, but this is not all. The subject involved two considerations – the Testimonial itself and the disposal of the ground. With regard to the first I have no right to set up any claim, as my design differed essentially from the one adopted, I will trespass however so far upon your indulgence as to state the principle upon which I mainly differed from Mr Railton. It struck me forceably [*sic*] that even were a column surrounded by a Figure the best thing in the abstract – which I believe is very doubtful – the close proximity of the [Duke of] York Column was a fatal objection to it. It seems to me to provoke criticism and even ridicule. Had an object of great altitude been desirable I should have preferred an Obelisk: – but I was opposed to both. My aim was – keeping the primary object in view – to design something which instead of crushing the already diminutive proportions of the National Gallery would have harmonised with and aided its general Effect. With the particulars of my design as far as concerns the Testimonial itself I shall not trouble you Sir, but merely say that it was a colossal group in Bronze with water as an accessory. It is upon the second consideration – namely the laying out of the ground – that I claim some character, My plan was in its main feature precisely similar to that which is now being carried into Effect, being designed some months before Mr [Charles] Barry's was made or I believe thought of, and being the only one among about a hundred competitors, which involved the same principle. What makes my coincidence of opinion with Barry the more remarkable is, that the description which I sent in with my drawing – and which Mr O'Ferrall can attest as he in consequence of the way in which I was pressed at the moment for time, was kind enough to assist me in writing it, was in an important part, not only the same in Effect, but in precise words. With the view of aiding the building before referred to, I proposed instead of raising, to lower the ground forming the centre of Trafalgar square, and to obtain thereby an artificial base or terrace to the National gallery "of <u>from 8 to 10 feet</u>". In some points of detail my plan differed from Mr Barry's, and in these points I must frankly say that I still prefer my own. I would have had a grand flight of steps in the centre, – the breadth of the portico & which from Charing Cross, would have the Effect of being incorporated with – & descending from it. While Mr Barry's steps are at the angles of the square and have no apparent connexion with the Building but my object is not to point out where I dissent from Mr Barry, but to shew [*sic*] that I anticipated an eminent architect in a not unimportant plan of public improvement, for which I believe he has obtained some credit.

In these preliminary observations Sir, I regret – from my want of habit in this kind of correspondence – that I have been unable to express what I wished to say with more brevity. Being personally unknown to you I could hardly in justice to myself avoid some reference to those circumstances of my life to which I have alluded. But in those references, I beg most distinctly to disavow on the part either of myself or my family, having any indirect or unworthy object in view. It has been my anxious Endeavor [*sic*] to impress upon my sons a lesson which I have learnt myself – that it is not to individual patronage, but to their own well-directed talents, & the community, that they must look for any solid & permanent prosperity. For myself, having long felt a deep interest in the progress of Public Works, and feeling also a deep faith in my own capacity for their practical consideration, I ask no favour but such as can be conceded to me on public grounds. If I did not feel this confidence – a confidence which in other matters forms no part of my character, & in this, I hope will not be associated with presumption – you Sir, are the best person to whose scrutiny I would submit my pretentions.

I have the honor to be –
With deep respect –
Sir
Your obedient humble Servant
<u>John Doyle</u>

[Memorandum]
Public Improvements.
Kensington Gardens –
Hyde Park –

Kensington Gardens – Recent operations regarding cutting and planting, conducted with more zeal than judgement, defective taste in parts of the latter. How these defects may in some measure be corrected.

Hyde Park. – Circular Basin. How it might, by the erection of a well-designed fountain – that species of Embellishment in which our metropolis is so singularly destitute – be converted from an unsightly object, as it now is, to something very ornamental: the natural situation and existing facilities being alike favourable to such an improvement.

As a satisfactory explanation of his views in detail, could be only given on the spot, the Writer would be most happy to meet any gentleman of intelligence in matters of taste, whom Sir Robert Peel or Lord Lincoln [First Commissioner of Woods and Forests] might be pleased to appoint.

J.D.
Jan. 22nd 1842.

Editorial Notes

Richard More O'Ferrall (1797–1880) – Irish politician.

William Railton (1800–1877) – English architect best known for winning the competition to design a memorial to Lord Nelson in Trafalgar Square (Nelson's Column). This was erected in 1843.

Charles Barry's plans for Trafalgar Square (1838) incorporated an upper terrace next to the National Gallery with a lower level square (to accommodate Nelson's column and fountains) linked by steps.

Robert Peel, John Doyle and Visual Parody

Fintan Cullen

In July 1831, the pro-Reform MP Thomas Babington Macaulay wrote to his sister of how, when visiting 10 Downing Street in London to see the Whig Prime Minister, Earl Grey, he was asked to wait in a drawing room. Macaulay idled away his time by turning over 'two large portfolios of political caricatures. Earl Grey's own face', Macaulay writes, 'was in every print. I was very much diverted. I had seen some of them before. But many were new to me, and their merit is extraordinary. They were the caricatures of that remarkable artist who calls himself "H.B."'[1]

While Macaulay refers to Lord Grey, many of the prints that he may have leafed through in what he referred to as the 'splendid drawing-room' overlooking St James's Park would have included images of Robert Peel. Whilst he was not in power until later in the decade, by 1831, Peel was already featuring extensively in 'H.B.'s caricatures or political sketches. This chapter will examine just a few of those images of the 1830s and 1840s. In one such image, part of the Peel Society collection (catalogue, No. 8), we find Peel and Grey together as they attempt to influence John Bull (who had been used by visual satirists for generations as the personification of England). In the print, dating from March 1831, Peel is on the left encouraging John Bull to stay with the old while Grey stands to the right with an array of new lamps.[2]

'H.B.' was the pseudonym of John Doyle (1797–1868), an Irish-born artist who, by the 1830s, was the most important producer of visual political satires in London. Given that Peel was one of the most illustrious political success stories of the first half of the nineteenth century, an examination of Doyle's political satires gives us a useful insight into how visual satire played a part in the exclusive world of Westminster and parliamentary London at that time.

Doyle's political sketches were not cheap and were largely seen and enjoyed by the genteel who could afford them.[3] In the mid-1830s, a single print cost 2 shillings, which was about three times the price of a newspaper and, as Doyle's prints tended to appear in pairs or in sets of three or four, sales must have been limited to an elite few. While the representation of Peel in *New Lamps for Old* is straightforward and relatively benign, a genre of visual satire that Doyle perfected during this period was the use of compositional and thematic borrowings from topical paintings or well-established stories. Throughout the 1830s, Doyle frequently used contemporary paintings by artists such as Edwin Landseer (1802–1873) which had recently been on display at the Royal Academy of Arts. Their annual summer exhibitions were held at Somerset House on the Strand in central London until 1836 and subsequently at the National Gallery in Trafalgar Square. There was no attempt at plagiarism here, as Doyle always acknowledged his sources and made it very clear from where he had taken them. Fully grasped as they were by the politically aware, people like Peel, Grey, and Macaulay, Doyle's political parodies were also regularly discussed in *The Times*.

To demonstrate Doyle's borrowings and his use of high art parody, let us look at one example from the 1830s. In his lithograph of 15 August 1838 *None but the Brave deserve the fair* (Fig. 1), Doyle advises us on the sheet itself that 'Mr E. Landseer's admired picture [is here] seen in a new point of view' (his emphasis).[4] The painting in question carries the same name and is

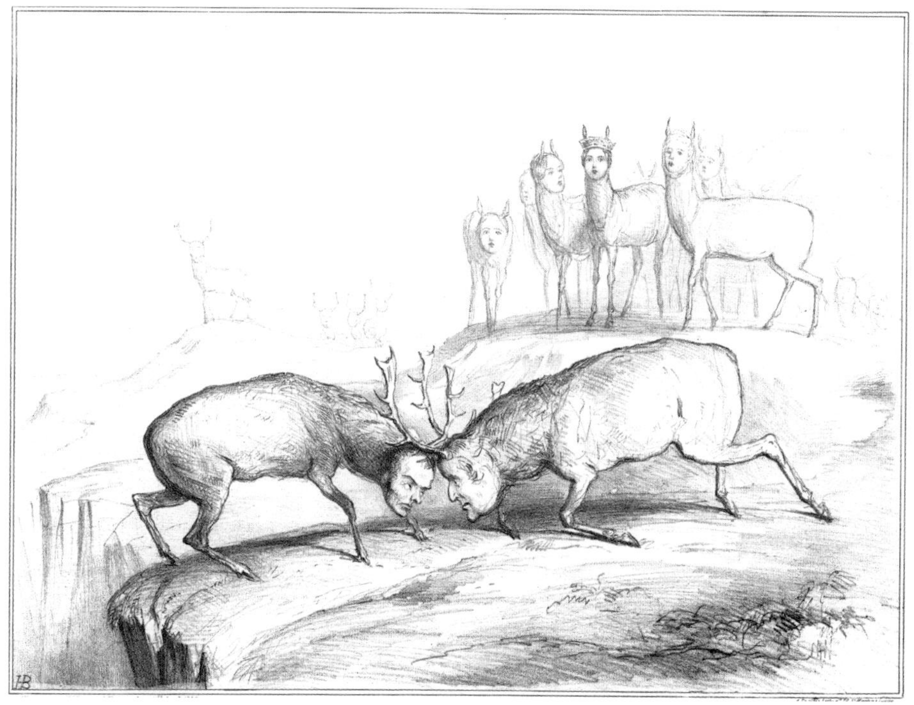

FIG. 1: 'H.B.', *None but the Brave deserve the Fair. Mr E. Landseer's admired picture seen in a new point of view*, lithograph, 1838 (The Tabley Collection and the British Cartoon Archive, University of Kent, www.cartooons.ac.uk)

now in a private collection but, in 1838, it had already been exhibited at the Royal Academy in London.[5] In Landseer's painting, set in a Scottish Highland mountain top, a pair of stags, an older one on the right with his back to us, battles with a young buck who is being pushed precariously near to the cliff edge. A large collection of hinds or female deer look on, threatening clouds loom above while, in the background on a far ridge, an even older stag stands silhouetted against the sky. In Doyle's print, the focus is directly on the fighting stags, which carry the faces of Peel as the older animal (on the right) with his Whig opponent, Lord John Russell, as the young buck (on the left). As Home Secretary at the time that the print was produced, Russell 'still had the best of it' as Thomas McLean (Doyle's publisher) suggested in his 1841 account of 'H.B.'s *Political Sketches*. McLean's point was that, on a rise above the fighting stags, Russell was 'obtaining the smiles of the fair spectators in the background' which have been denied to his rival, Robert Peel.[6] Clearly marked out wearing a crown is the young Queen Victoria who had only recently ascended to the throne, surrounded by her ladies in waiting. Off to the far left, the old stag of Landseer's painting is replaced by a resemblance to the aged Duke of Wellington, a former Tory Prime Minister.

By 1838, the year of Doyle's lithograph parody of the Landseer painting, *The Times* was carrying regular announcements of 'H.B.' prints, offering descriptions of the individual *Political Sketches* (as they were called) and comments on the artist's 'unrivalled' 'richness of whim' and his 'display of imagination'. According to the newspaper, 'H.B.' could convey a meaning which was 'serious' in such a way as to make one 'smile freely' but also 'reflect'.[7] Writing in a similar vein in the *Westminster Review* in 1840, William Makepeace Thackeray was of the opinion that,

> You never hear any laughter at 'H.B.'; his pictures are a great deal too genteel for that – polite points of wit, which strike one as exceedingly clever and pretty, and cause one to smile in a quiet, gentlemanly-like kind of way.[8]

The fame or renown of paintings such as the Landseer oil would have been such that members of the political elite, either Tory or Whig, would have got the joke. Indeed, it is important to note that Landseer's *None but the brave deserve the fair* appeared in engraved form by no less a figure than the artist's brother, Thomas Landseer, in the same year that it was exhibited at the Royal Academy and was parodied by John Doyle. The engraving acted as a frontispiece to William Scrope's *The Art of Deer-Stalking* (Fig. 2), and it is this version that may well have been a more immediate source for Doyle, as in it Thomas Landseer has focused quite deliberately on the battle of the stags.[9] The need for recognition of the original source was important, as it greatly increased the humour value as well as the visual power of the satire. Although many black and white versions of 'H.B.'s *None but the brave*... were produced, hand-coloured versions do exist and doubtless cost more. As a very versatile and speedy technique for print production, by the mid-1830s, lithography had become a popular medium. It allowed for a linear clarity which suited Doyle's talent. At the time of his death in 1868, the *Art Journal* could claim that the cartoonist had 'haunted parliament in search of copy, a quiet, silent unsuspected frequenter of the lobby and gallery.' And it is for these 'quiet', mildly humorous political prints that he is best remembered today.[10]

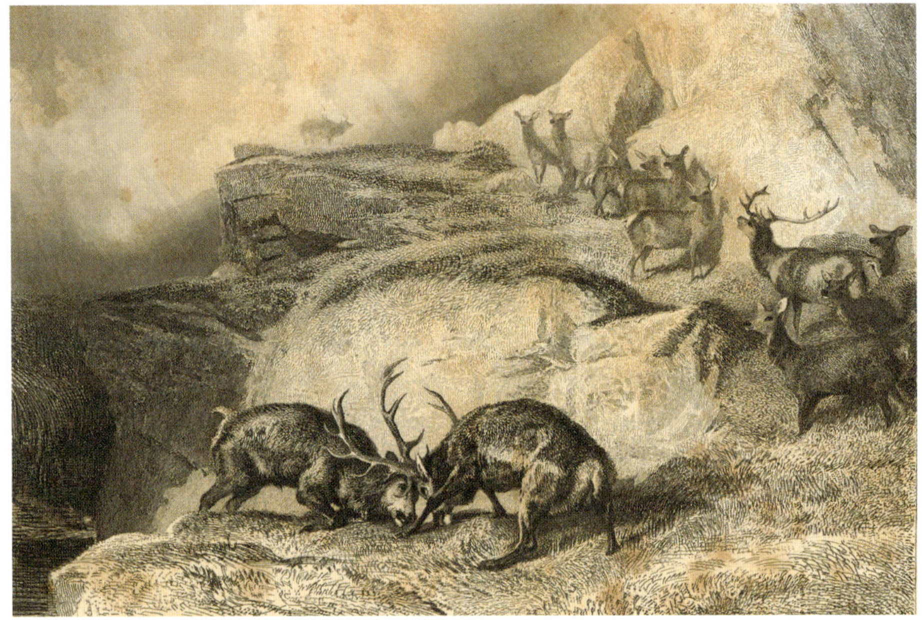

FIG. 2: Thomas Landseer © The British Library Board. William Scrope, *The Art of Deer-Stalking* (London, 1838), frontispiece entitled 'Forest Joust' (Ref/W3/0955)

An ink drawing of Peel in the British Museum taken from the life, while observing the politician in Westminster, exemplifies Doyle's speedy technique (Fig. 3).[11] The thinly drawn lines were easily transferred to the lithographic stone and prints could be made in large numbers. As was noted earlier, Doyle's political satires were produced in groups and sold in volumes and, as such, they can be seen as comparable to a periodical of visual images and enjoyed wide dissemination. It must also be emphasised that Peel featured in a large number of the 900 or so *Sketches* that the artist published between the late 1820s and 1851.

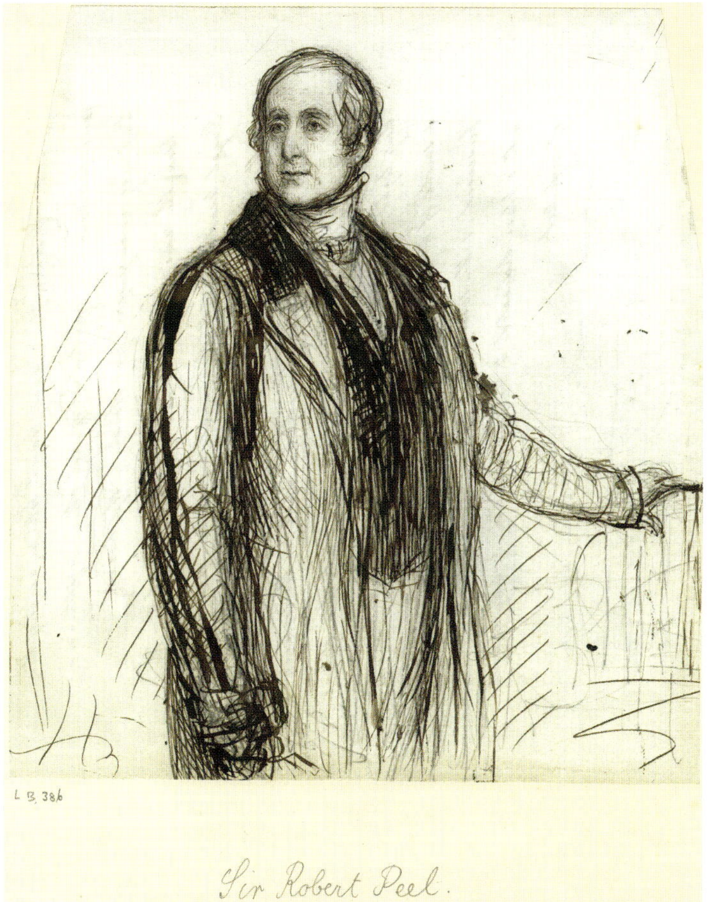

FIG. 3: 'H.B.', *Robert Peel*, pen and brown ink over graphite, early-1840s © The Trustees of the British Museum

How did Peel feature in Doyle's cartoons? On the whole, Doyle's representation of Peel is rarely negative. Using this brown ink drawing and comparing it with the numerous representations of Peel as he appeared in the *Political Sketches* throughout the 1830s and 1840s (the focal point for this volume), we can see that Peel's features are never caricatured. Such a comparison can be made with another Landseer parody dating from 1846, *Stag at Bay* (catalogue, No. 143), which appeared only a few years after the ink drawing in the British Museum. Based on the animal artist's similarly titled *Stag at Bay,* which featured in that year's Royal Academy exhibition, in the Doyle print, Peel is being pursued by hounds in the guise of fellow Conservatives, Benjamin Disraeli and Lord George Bentinck but Peel's face, although here showing alarm, is clearly unmistakeably that of the statesman. The bird flying in top right is Lord John Russell who would take over from Peel as Prime Minister after June 1846.[12]

One could say that the Peel of *Stag at Bay* is sympathetic and even empathetic yet, when Doyle resorts to more critically-tuned visual allusions, as in *The Frogs and King Stork* of a few years earlier (1842), the depiction of Peel is not at all aggressive (Fig. 4).[13] While shown as a powerful bird with a menacing beak, Peel as Prime Minister, according to McLean's interpretation, is in fact not promoting any particular political interests but a safe 'middle of the road' attitude to the general good.[14] Instead of parodying a contemporary painting, in this print Doyle uses a well-known Aesop fable; the frogs were sent

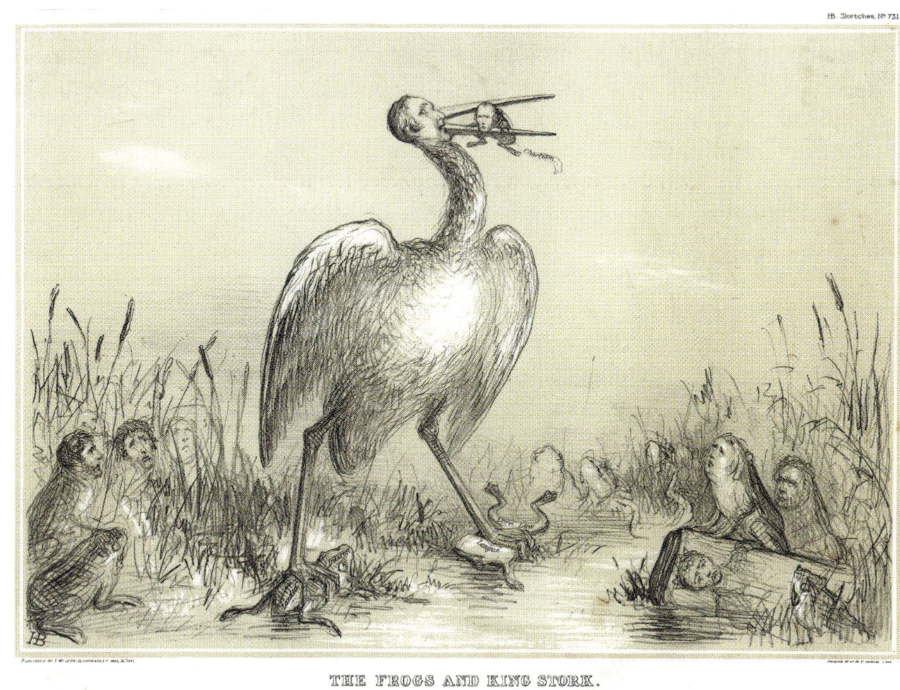

FIG. 4: 'H.B.', *The Frogs and King Stork*, lithograph, 1842 (The Tabley Collection and the British Cartoon Archive, University of Kent, www.cartoons.ac.uk)

a stork by Zeus as their king after being disillusioned with an inanimate log. Not surprisingly, the stork eats them all up: the moral being 'better no rule than cruel rule'. Despite such a didactic message, the print itself is demonstratively entertaining. The inert log is inscribed with the face of the opposition Whig Lord John Russell, who has been discarded by his party in the person of the radical Thomas Wakley (M.P. for Finsbury from 1835–52). To demonstrate Peel's supposedly non-partisan approach, one foot of the stork treads on the landed interest (who were against Peel's Corn Law reforms) whilst another foot treads on the supporters of the Corn Bill. At the same time, the bird swallows radical Chartism in the person of John Arthur Roebuck, the M.P. for Bath. The frogs behind the stork represent other radical M.P.s who will be gobbled up in time.[15]

The implication of all these parodies of the 1830s and 1840s, some referring to Landseer paintings and others to Aesop and familiar tales, is that humour is to be extracted from high politics. 'H.B.'s visual technique of using a well-known painting or a fairy tale and inserting familiar resemblances of equally well-known politicians was openly referred to at the time as a 'parody' or a 'facsimile'. Thomas McLean wrote of prints such as *None but the Brave…* that only those 'who are acquainted with the original can fully appreciate the merit of the parody.'[16] According to the *Oxford English Dictionary's* definition of 'parody', imitation is usually accompanied by ridicule, but that was not Doyle's style. In a letter to Peel, written in 1842, Doyle revealed his identity, which prior to this had been masked by the fact that all his prints carried the monogram 'H.B.'. Doyle confessed that his sketches were 'an agent of some little influence', wrote of how he had 'scrupulously avoid[ed] all indelicacy, private scandal, and party bitterness' and argued that the work 'should … amuse [and] be directed to the furtherance of some intelligible public object, and that by such means as would by fair analogy be considered legitimate in political warfare.'[17]

By the late 1830s and into the 1840s, the appearance of parody was not of course limited to Doyle's satires, it was appearing in poetry and prose as well as in images. Contemporaneous with the publication of Doyle's *None but the Brave…*, *Fraser's Magazine* carried verse parodies of Robert Burns that made fun of the various administrations of the 1830s, especially that led by Lord Melbourne during the early years of Queen Victoria's reign.[18] Not surprisingly, Thackeray was at the forefront of the use of parody in the London periodicals of the day. For a couple of years in the late 1830s, and in direct relevance to the world of art exhibitions and art reviews that would have been visited and read by the politicians satirised in Doyle's prints, Thackeray published in *Fraser's Magazine* a number of lengthy reviews styling himself as Michael Angelo Titmarsh, writing to the farcically-named Parisian art critic Anatole Victor Isidor Hyacinthe Achille Hercule de Bricabrac. In many ways, Thackeray's Titmarsh pieces are more biting satire than gentle parodies. In his review of the 1838 Royal Academy exhibition, for example, Thackeray made fun of Landseer who had exhibited, amongst other paintings, *None but the Brave deserve the Fair*. In his review, Thackeray refers to the animal painter as 'Edwin, Earl of Landseer', who 'can paint all manner of birds and beasts as nobody else can. To tell you a secret', he informs Bricabrac:

> I do not think he understands how to paint the great beast, man, quite so well, or, at least, to do what is the highest quality of an artist, to place a soul under the ribs as he draws them. They are, if you like, the most dexterous pictures that ever were painted, but not great pictures.[19]

Although Doyle saw his *Political Sketches*, as he said in his letter to Peel, as potential political weapons, it could be said that his great tool was really visual irony. His ironic stance is evident in the way that his print, *None but the Brave…*, uses the original work as a contributing part of the parody. He does not attack the original painting by Landseer nor does he really attack the people being satirised. And yet it was an art form that had clear elitist connotations. Doyle's audience was expected to grasp quickly the artistic or literary allusions and such an expectation limited its appeal to a well-educated clientele. Given the renown of his visual and literary sources, the celebrity of his political actors and the frequency with which publications like *The Times* praised Doyle's productions, the *Political Sketches* offer a triangular connection between the public art exhibition or the popular tale, the commercially orientated print-market and the printed word in newspapers such as *The Times*. The newspaper informed the political elite of the art and literature that could be seen and read yet it also informed that same, relatively limited, audience of the pictorial satires derived from such art and literature. These satires featured their own political activities and ambitions but, most of all, their faces.

REFERENCES

1 *The Letters of Thomas Babington Macaulay*, 6 vols., ed. Thomas Pinney (Cambridge, 1974–1981), Volume II, 64, 8 July 1831, Macaulay to his sister Hannah.

2 *Political Sketches of 'H.B.'*, No. 113, *New Lamps for Old*, 8 March 1831. Peel says to John Bull: 'Take my advice and keep your old lamp such as it is…Any trifling little repairs it may require I shall be most happy to do for you not that I have any wish to get the job…I would not upon my honor, have such a thing suspected for all the world!' For John Bull,

see Reva Wolf, 'John Bull, Liberty, and Wit: How England Became Caricature', in *The Efflorescence of Caricature, 1759–1838*, ed. Todd Porterfield (Farnham, 2011), pp.49–60.

3 For more on Doyle and his political satires of the period, see Fintan Cullen, 'Visual parody and political commentary: John Doyle and Daniel O'Connell', in *Irish elites in the nineteenth century*, ed. Ciaran O'Neill (Dublin, 2013), pp.233–247.

4 *Political Sketches of 'H.B.',* No. 553.

5 For the original painting see Richard Ormond, *Sir Edwin Landseer* (Philadelphia, 1981), p.169 and Richard Ormond, *The Monarch of the Glen: Landseer in the Highlands* (Edinburgh, 2005), pp.106, 110.

6 Thomas McLean, *An Illustrative Key to the Political Sketches of 'H.B.'* (1841), pp.390–1.

7 *The Times,* 27 Jan. 1835; 21 Mar. 1835; 16 May 1835.

8 W.M. Thackeray writing in *The Westminster Review*, 34 (June 1840), 7.

9 McLean, *An Illustrative Key* (1841), pp.390–1; William Scrope, *The Art of Deer-Stalking* (1838), frontispiece; also see Ormond, *Sir Edwin Landseer,* p.169.

10 *Art Journal,* 75 (March 1868), 47.

11 British Museum, Department of Prints and Drawings, 1882, 1209.688; also see Cullen, 'Visual parody', pp.239–40.

12 *Political Sketches of 'H.B.',* No. 868 (26 June 1846); the oil was exhibited at the Royal Academy in 1846, see Ormond, *The Monarch of the Glen,* pp.113–114, 141.

13 *Political Sketches of 'H.B.',* No. 731.

14 Thomas McLean, *An Illustrative Key to the Political Sketches of 'H.B.'* (1844), p.134.

15 Ibid.

16 McLean, *An Illustrative Key* (1841), p.258.

17 See Appendix above.

18 *Fraser's Magazine*, XII (1835); ibid., XVII (1838).

19 *Fraser's Magazine*, XVII (1838), 761.

Catalogue of the Peel Society Collection of prints by John Doyle

(‘H.B.’)

EDITORIAL NOTE ON THE PLATES AND DESCRIPTIONS

The *Political Sketches* of 'H.B.' (John Doyle) did not lack for contemporary description. Not only did *The Times* newspaper note the production of new sketches in the series on a periodic basis but Thomas McLean, the enterprising publisher who marketed them, ensured the audience's ready familiarity with the characters featured in them by producing, on a regular basis, 'keys' to the series. Each folio volume of 100 'sketches' (marketed for the clientele which collected them as library specimens, of the type represented in the Peel Society collection) contained a contents page listing the number, title and personalities represented in individual sketches. McLean also marketed the contents pages separately in small stand-alone booklets which commemorated the achievement of each centenary. See *A Key to the Political Sketches of 'H.B.' Nos. 1 to 200* (Arranged as Published, up to June, 1832); *idem., …Nos. 201 to 300* (n.d.), *idem., ..Nos. 301 to 400* (Arranged as Published, up to July 1835); *idem., … Nos. 401–500* (Arranged as Published, up to Sept. 1st, 1838). More detailed catalogues, containing descriptions of the content and allusions represented in the sketches (as well as a key to the individuals featured in them) were later issued in two substantial volumes: Thomas McLean, *An Illustrative Key to the Political Sketches of 'H.B.'* (1841, 1844). I have relied upon the latter for the vast majority of the descriptions of H.B.'s work published from 1833–1844. A further *Key*, covering *Sketches* Nos. 801–887, was published in 1847.

In most cases, whilst I have allowed McLean's text to stand for itself, I have taken the opportunity of revising or editing out such passages as appeared to be either expressive of the personal political views of the author or which, in a modern age, appear more questionable. A good example is the reference to (then well-known) classical subjects with the prefatory comment, 'as every schoolboy knows'. I have also taken the opportunity to add such contextual information or detail as necessary to render the original descriptions more accessible to the modern reader. For the sketches after No. 801, I have written entirely new descriptions, relying for the identification of individuals on the catalogue of Doyle's drawings published by the British Museum in 1900.

In 1882, the British Museum acquired 411 drawings by John Doyle. The vast majority of these consisted of early versions and workings-out of individual *Political Sketches*, together with a number of separate character studies and portraits (for one example, see Fig. 3 in Fintan Cullen's essay). This collection, quite separate from the *Political Sketches* themselves, was catalogued by Laurence Binyon (1869–1943), later famous as the author of the haunting war poem 'For the Fallen' but then working as an assistant in the Department of Prints and Drawings at the British Museum, in his *Catalogue of Drawings by British Artists and Artists of Foreign Origin working in Great Britain, Preserved in the Department of Prints and Drawings in the British Museum*, II (1900), 44–96.

For the *Political Sketches* published before 1832, the standard modern authority is the doyenne of British caricature studies, Mary Dorothy George. I have relied upon her descriptions of 'H.B.'s work in M D George, ed., *Catalogue of Political and Personal Satires, Preserved in the Department of Prints and Drawings in the British Museum,* Volume XI, [covering the period 1828–1832] (1954).

The images themselves have, in the vast majority of instances, been cropped of their borders to provide the clearest and largest possible image. However, all of the boundary text contained in those borders (as titles, sub-titles etc.) has been reproduced in the catalogue descriptions. A number of examples of un-cropped versions can be found later in the catalogue and, separately, as Figs. 1 and 4 in Fintan Cullen's essay.

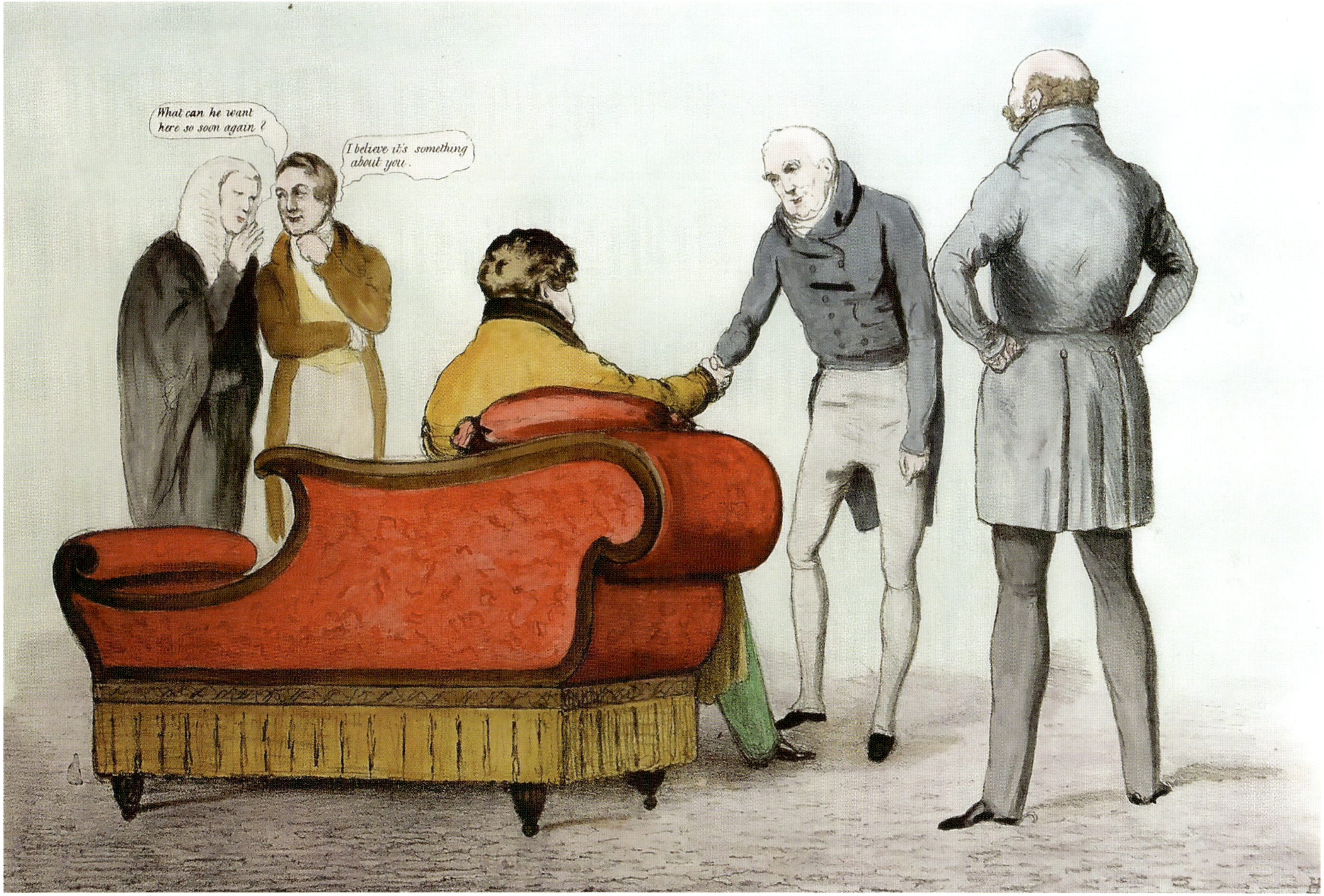

[1] ***No. 9, 'The Mysterious Visit'*** George IV, seated on a sofa and almost in back view, shakes hands with Eldon (right) while the Duke of Cumberland, on the extreme right and in back view, seems to superintend the interview. At a little distance (left), Lyndhurst, in wig and gown, and Peel whisper together; the Lord Chancellor (Lyndhurst) asks: 'What can he want here so soon again?' Peel: 'I believe it's something about you.' The possible dismissal of the Ministry with Eldon reinstated as Lord Chancellor is implied.

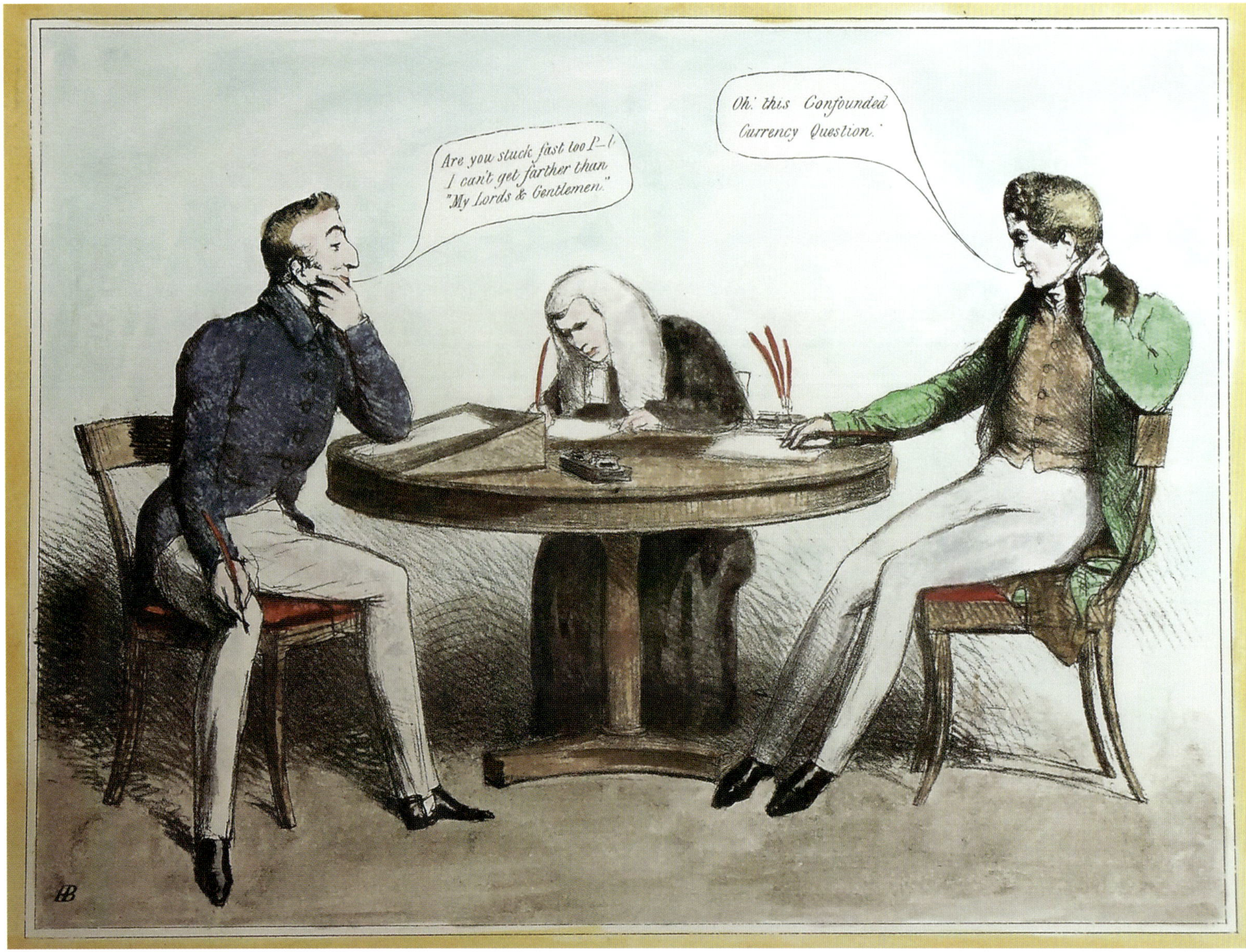

[2] ***No. 43, 'Writing the K___g's Speech' (published Feb. 1830)*** Wellington (left) and Peel (right) sit at opposite sides of a round library table, pen in hand, gloomily regarding blank sheets of paper. Peel: 'Oh! this Confounded Currency Question.' Wellington: 'Are you stuck fast too P—l I can't get farther than "My Lords & Gentlemen".' Between them, on the farther side of the table, Lyndhurst writes busily. A gibe at the King's Speech, not delivered till 4 Feb. In this there was an answer to the demands by Attwood, Cobbett, and others for depreciation of the currency. A violent attack on the Government followed. The cause of distress, it was maintained, was the 'surreptitious enhancement of the currency'.

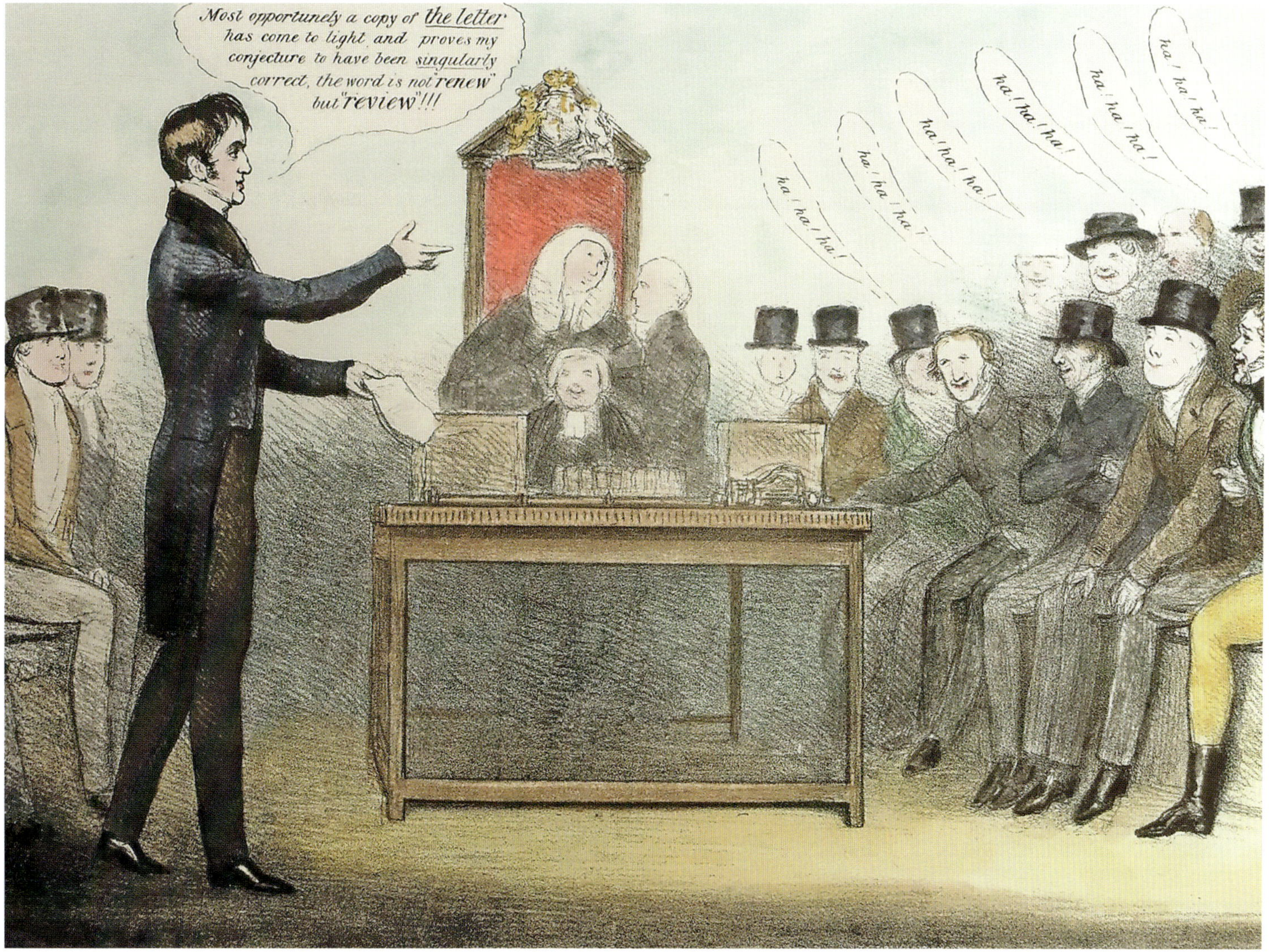

[3] ***No. 48, 'A Political Ruse' (published Feb. 1830)*** Below the title: "Ye Bankes & Braes"— A debate in the Commons, the Chair rather to the left of the design. Bankes stands primly in profile to the right, arm extended, addressing the Opposition benches. Behind him sits Peel watching with amused approval. Laughter, represented by six labels inscribed 'ha! ha! ha!', comes from the Opposition. Bankes: 'Most opportunely a copy of the letter has come to light and proves my conjecture to have been singularly correct, the word is not "renew" but review"!!!' On the front Opposition bench sit (left to right) Spring-Rice, Brougham, Mackintosh, and Lord Nugent. Among those behind are O'Connell and Burdett. The man on the extreme right is identified as Hume. A dispute over a letter from Lord Ellenborough relating to the East India Company. Bankes told the Commons (9 February) that 'he had since seen the only copy of that letter … [sent by Sir J. Grant to his son, and given by him to Ellenborough]. And in this copy, which, having been taken in India, must undoubtedly be considered the best authority, it appeared that his Lordship had said, not that we RENEW the Charter but that we will REVIEW the Charter.' See 'Parliamentary Debates', New Series, xxii, 283.

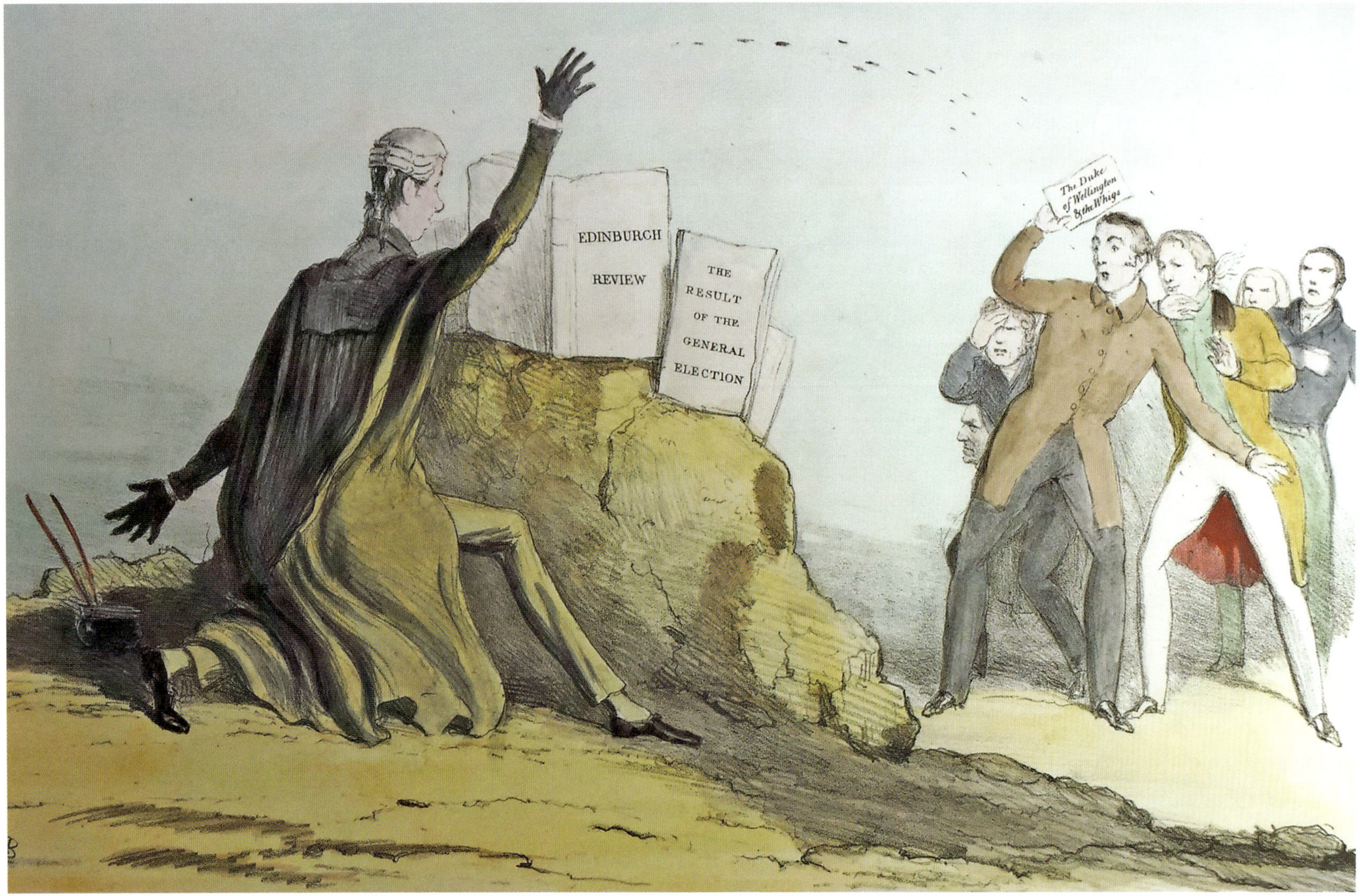

[4] ***No. 85, 'A Masked Battery' (published 4 Oct. 1830)*** Brougham (left), wearing wig, gown, and gloves, kneels behind a rock which is further fortified by large volumes: 'Edinburgh Review' and 'The Result of the General Election'. Beside him are ink-stand and pens. He hurls ink against his enemies, Wellington and his Ministers (right), who are in the open, and cannot protect themselves. The Duke holds up a small book, 'The Duke of Wellington & the Whigs', as if about to throw it. The Ministers, who try to take cover behind Wellington, are (left to right) Bathurst, Ellenborough, Peel, Lyndhurst, and Aberdeen. Brougham used the 'Edinburgh Review' for his (anonymous) propaganda. To his July article, 'The Ministry and the State of Parties', he added a note after his return for Yorkshire: 'Of all the most portentous signs for the present Ministry, the most appalling is the nearly unanimous choice of Mr. Brougham to be member for Yorkshire. This is assuredly the most extraordinary event in the history of party politics'. In the October number appeared Brougham's 'The General Election and the Ministry'. The book 'The Duke of Wellington & the Whigs' was published in 1830.

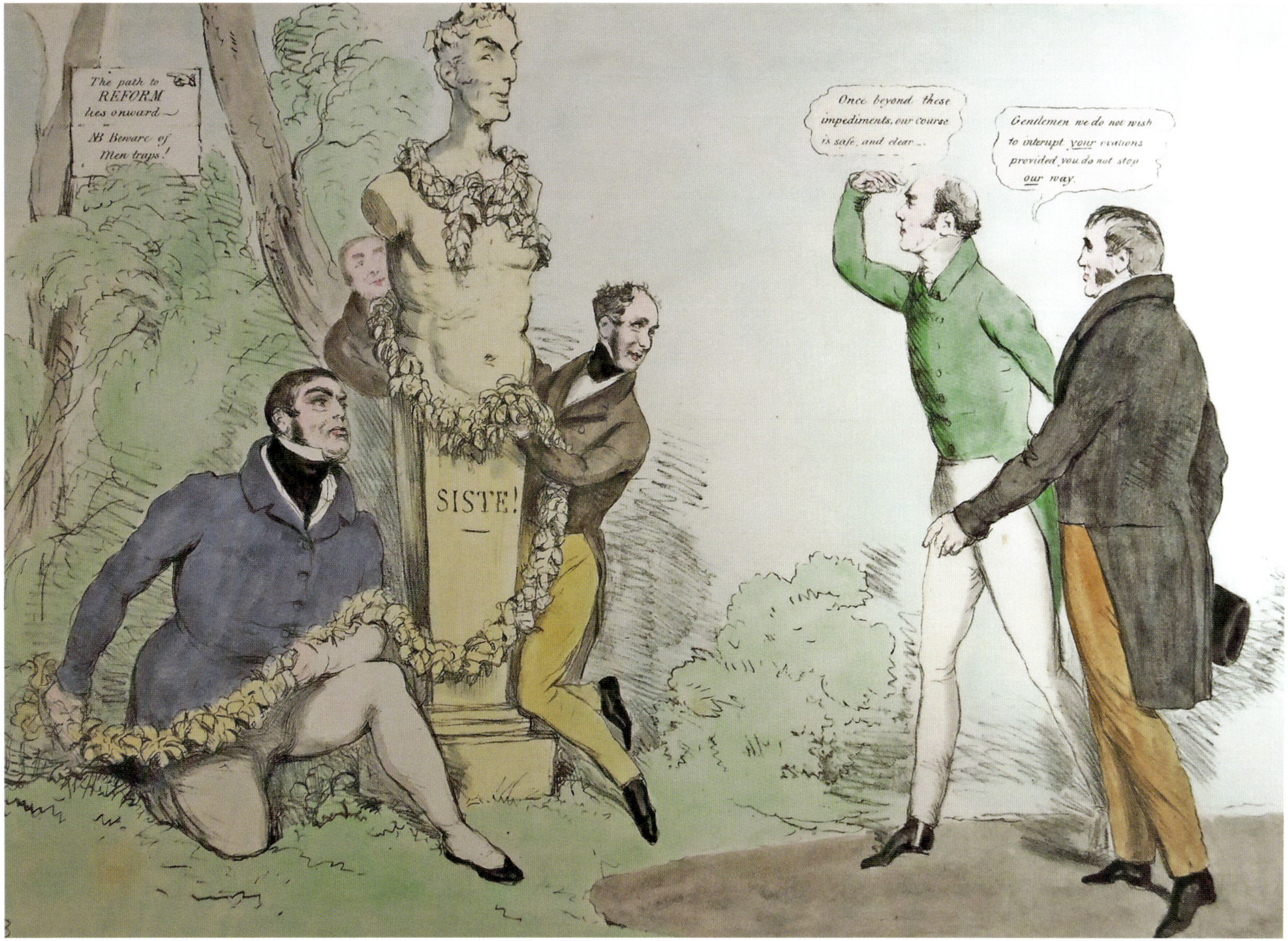

[5] ***No. 108, 'The Terminus of Reform' (published 12 Feb. 1831)*** Horace Twiss and Goulburn decorate with a long garland a terminal statue of Wellington (left) which has a satyr-like head and a nude torso. On the pedestal is the word 'Siste!' [stop!]. Twiss (left) kneels on one knee, Goulburn kneels on the plinth of the statue, both look in amused triumph at Grey and Althorp who have approached from the right. Peel, a dim figure, peers out from behind the term, which is backed by trees, among which is a placard: 'The path to REFORM lies onward—NB Beware of Men traps!'. Grey shields his eyes, saying, 'Once beyond these impediments our course is safe, and clear—'. Althorp says more sternly, 'Gentlemen we do not wish to interrupt your ovations provided you do not stop our way'. Their path seems to end in a thicket in front of which is the statue. Twiss's inveterate hatred of Reform was shown by his speech of 1 March which cost him his seat.

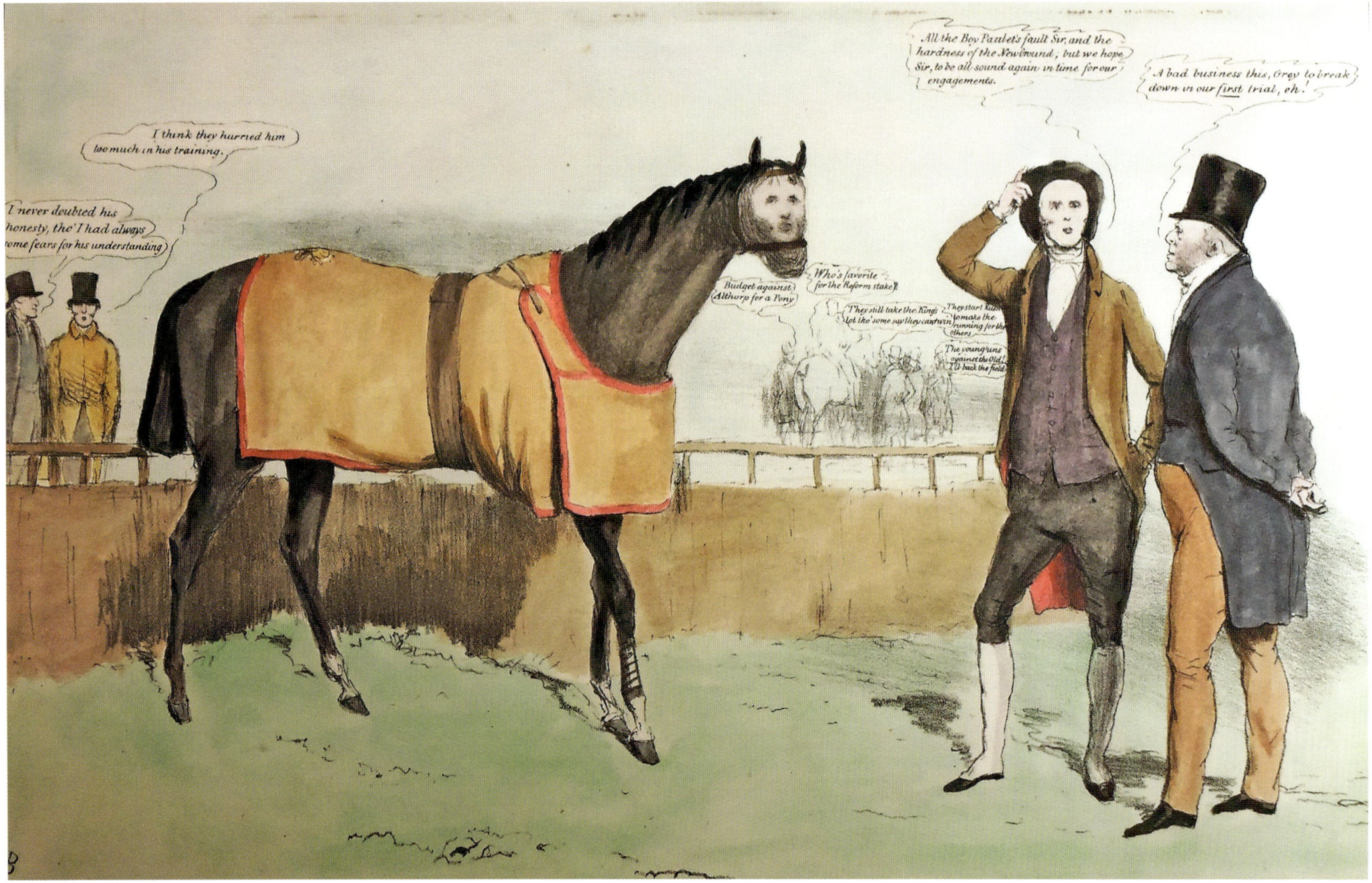

[6] ***No. 111, 'A Screw Loose' (published 1 Mar. 1831)*** A race-horse, with Althorp's head, with a scarred foreleg, is in a paddock and is covered with horse-clothes. William IV (right) inspects the horse and speaks to Grey: 'A bad business this, Grey to break down in our first trial, eh!'. Grey, touching his hat, 'All the Boy Paulet's fault Sir, and the hardness of the New Ground; but we hope Sir, to be all sound again in time for our engagements'. On the extreme left Peel and Wellington watch from outside the paling. Peel: 'I never doubted his honesty, tho' I had always some fears for his understanding'. Wellington: 'I think they hurried him too much in his training'. In the background (right) are betting men on a small scale; their words are: 'Who's favorite for the Reform stake?'; 'Budget against Althorp for a Pony'; 'They still take the King's lot tho' some say they cant win'; 'They start Russell to make the running for the others'; 'The young uns against the Old!'; 'I'll back the field'. Althorp's budget is condemned; Grey blames Poulett Thomson, Vice-President of the Board of Trade, Althorp's mentor in City matters. The opposition had high hopes from this Budget fiasco. According to Place the Budget was expected to do credit to the Ministry and confound their opponents, but was 'an exhibition of folly and weakness' which in other times 'would have destroyed the administration'.

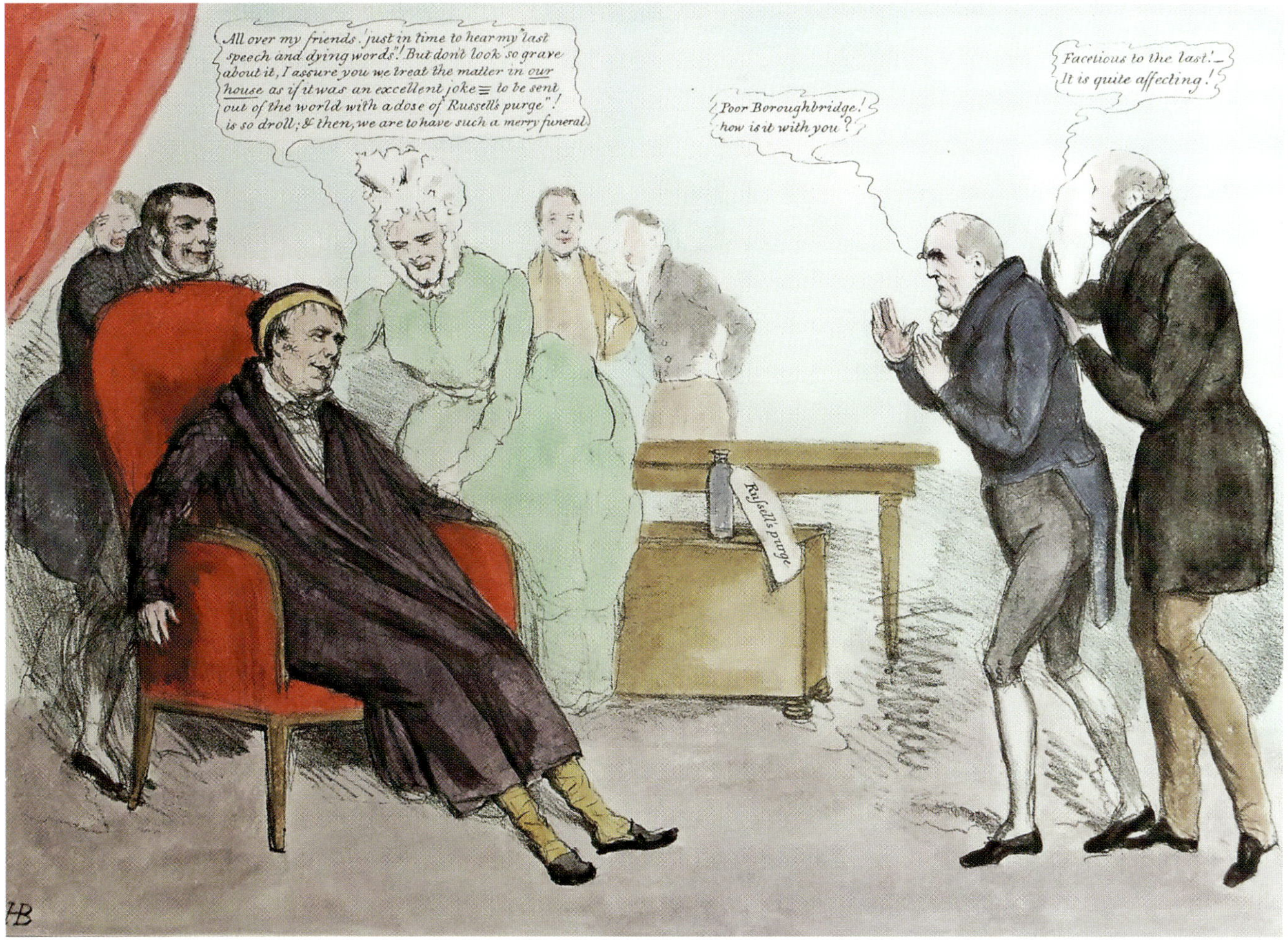

[7] ***No. 112, 'The Last of the Boroughbridges' (published 7 Mar. 1831)*** Wetherell (left), an invalid in dressing-gown and night-cap, reclines in an arm-chair, exhausted but laughing. Facing him stands Eldon in deep dejection, saying, with both hands raised, 'Poor Boroughbridge! how is it with you?' Cumberland, on the extreme right, stands behind Eldon, covering his face with his handkerchief; he says: 'Facetious to the last!—It is quite affecting!'. Horace Twiss leans on the back of Wetherell's chair; Chandos, dressed as a woman, stoops over the patient; both are smiling. Wetherell: 'All over my friends! just in time to hear my "last speech and dying words"! But don't look so grave about it, I assure you we treat the matter in our house as if it was an excellent joke—to be sent out of the world with a dose of "Russell's purge"! is so droll; & then, we are to have such a merry funeral'. On a commode is a bottle labelled 'Russell's purge'. Peel, smiling, and Goulburn, holding a handkerchief to his face and leaning on Peel, watch from the background. The print captures the reactions of ultra-Tories and Tories to Russell's exposition of the Ministerial Plan of Reform on 1 March, the sensation of which was the list of sixty boroughs to be disfranchised. These included Boroughbridge, Wetherell's constituency, and one of Newcastle's boroughs. Twiss (on 2 Mar.) and Wetherell spoke at length; the latter said he was 'rising to make his last dying speech … the last address of the dying member for Boroughbridge' ('Parliamentary Debates', 3rd series ii. 1220). 'He would call this Bill, Russell's Purge of Parliament … the nauseous experiment of a repetition of Pride's Purge' (ibid. 1240). Peel interposed only by 'Hear Hear' to Althorp's statement that the Bill promised 'to the people of England an overpowering influence in the choice of Representations' (ibid. 1143). He made a great speech on 3 March. Boroughbridge was to be par-excellence the abhorred and symbolic nomination borough and 'Russell's Purge' became a catch-phrase, used till after the Bill was passed.

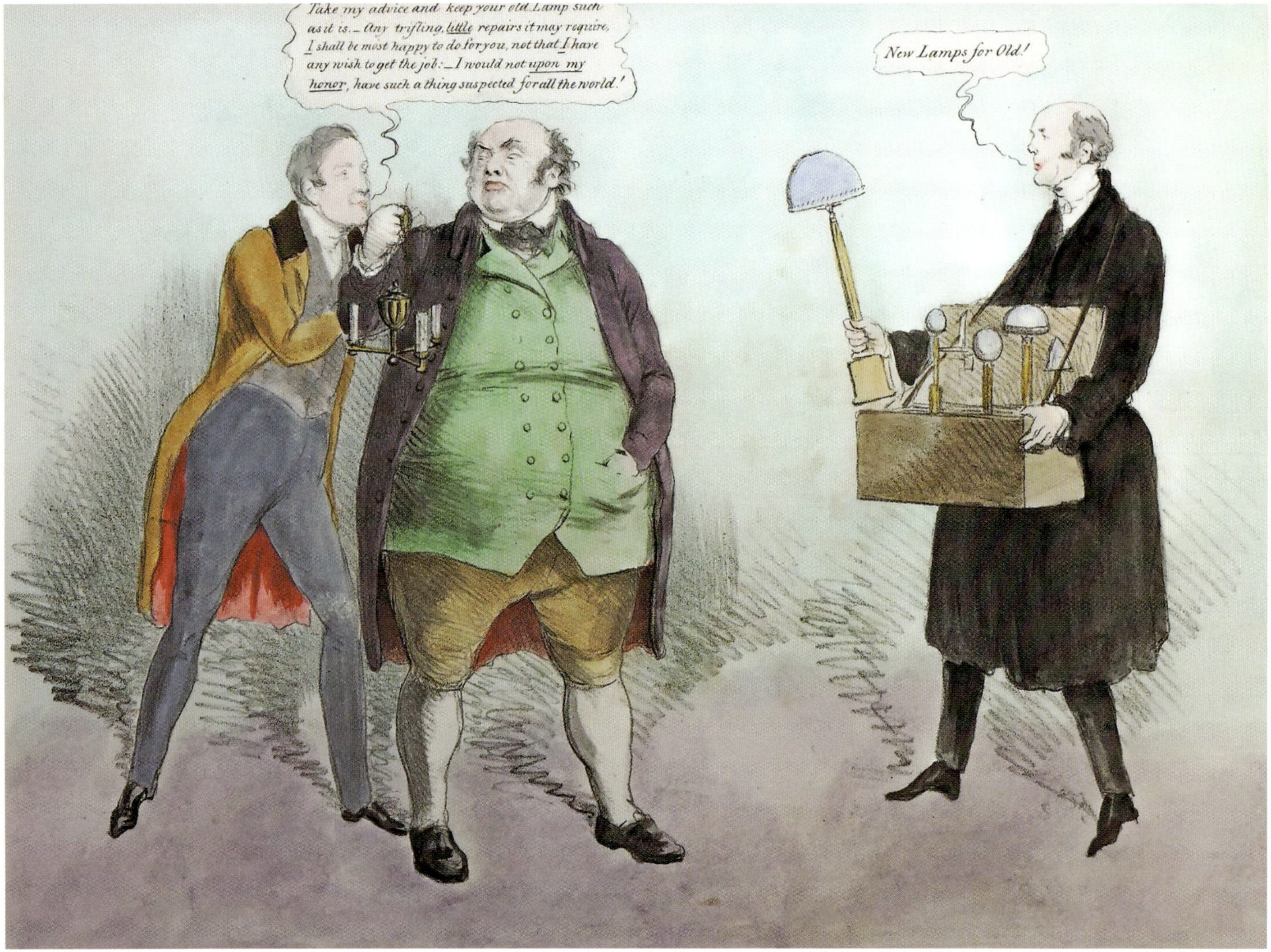

[8] ***No. 113, 'New Lamps for Old' (published 8 Mar. 1831)*** Grey (right), a box of lamps slung from his neck, offers one to John Bull, who holds up his old lamp, looking over his right shoulder at Peel who leans insinuatingly towards him. Grey's lamps, the light covered by a dome-shaped or a spherical shade, resemble the modern electric table-lamp; the old lamp is a hanging one with three lights in cylindrical shades round a centre-piece (a parable on the Constitution seems intended). Grey cries: 'New Lamps for Old!' Peel whispers to John Bull: 'Take my advice and keep your old Lamp such as it is—Any trifling, little repairs it may require, I shall be most happy to do for you, not that I have any wish to get the job:—I would not upon my honor, have such a thing suspected for all the world!'. John Bull looks distrustfully at Peel; his hand is in his waistcoat pocket. A satire on the Reform Bill. The allusion is probably to Lord John Russell's speech of 14 Dec. 1819, in moving the disfranchisement of Grampound; to go further than the disfranchisement of boroughs convicted of corruption would be 'to commit the folly of the servant in the story of Aladdin, who is deceived by the cry of new lamps for old …'. Grey had expressed the moderating of his own views on Reform in his speech of 13 June 1810. Peel, so often traduced as a rat-catcher and careerist, is also satirized. On 3 March he made 'a most effective address ... in favour of the present system' (J. C. Hobhouse, *Recollections of a Long Life*, (1910), iv. 90).

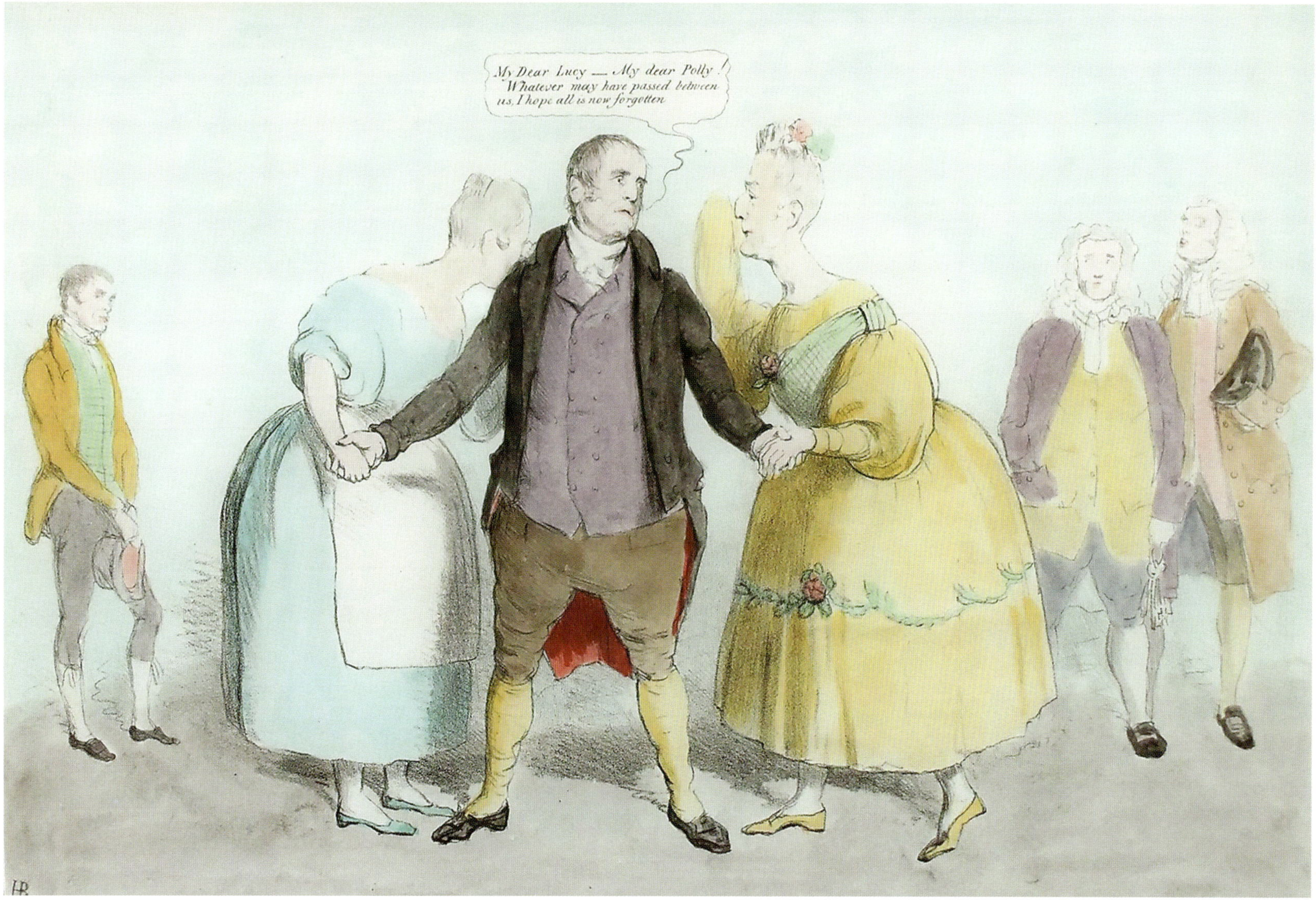

[9] ***No. 114, 'A Scene from the Beggar's Opera' (published 9 Mar. 1831)*** Wetherell as Macheath (but in his ordinary dress) stands between Peel (Polly) and Wellington (an elderly Lucy), both dressed for their parts. Peel rests his cheek on Wetherell's right shoulder; Wellington holds a handkerchief towards his face, which is puckered with weeping. Wetherell, taking a hand of each and turning to the Duke, says: 'My dear Lucy—My dear Polly! Whatever may have passed between us I hope all is now forgotten'. In the background Lord John Russell (in the dress of 1832) watches, hat in hand. Althorp and Grey (right), as jailors in period costume, wearing wigs and flapped waistcoats, watch from the right. There was much speculation on the relations of Wellington and Peel with the ultra-Tories. On 27 Feb. Burghersh wrote to the Duke expressing the desire of Eldon, Wetherell, and others for 'a general junction' (Wellington's *Despatches*, New Series, vii. 408). The cleavage between Wetherell and Peel was not to be bridged. One of many pictorial political applications of John Gay's *Beggars Opera*, charting the adventures of the celebrated highwayman Macheath.

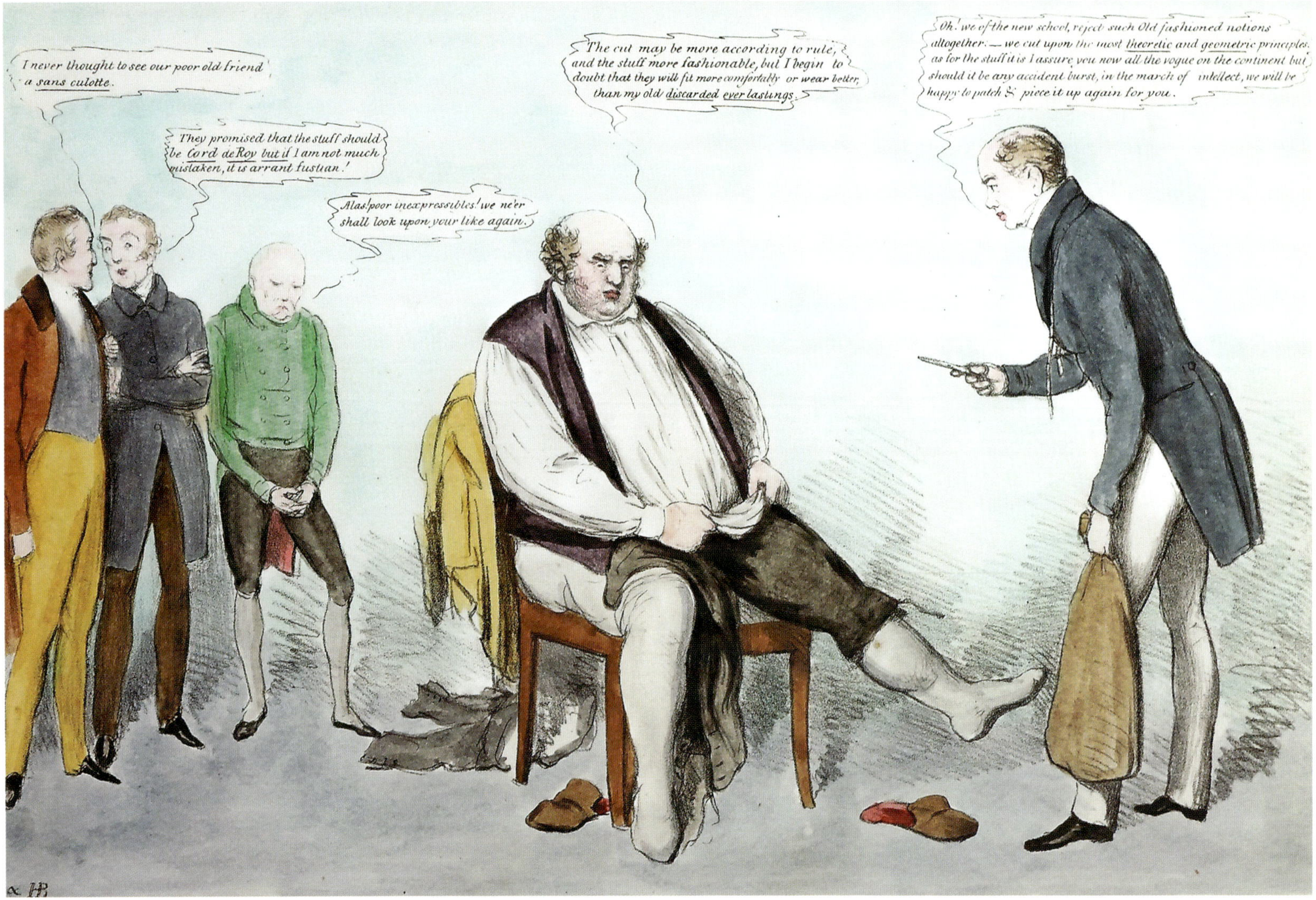

[10] ***No. 116, 'John Bull trying on his "bra" new Grey Breeks' (published 16 Mar. 1831)*** John Bull (larger in scale than the others) sits in an upright chair in his shirt and open waistcoat, tugging on a pair of breeches, his old ones on the floor behind him, his coat on the back of his chair. Lord Grey (right) as a tailor, holding a bag and a pair of shears, a tape-measure over his shoulders, bends deferentially towards him. John Bull, frowning slightly, says: 'The cut may be more according to rule, and the stuff more fashionable, but I begin to doubt that they will fit more comfortably or wear better than my old discarded everlastings'. Lord Grey: 'Oh! we of the new school, reject such Old fashioned notions altogether:— we cut upon the most theoretic and geometric principles, as for the stuff it is I assure you now all the vogue on the continent but should it be [sic] any accident burst, in the march of intellect, we will be happy to patch & piece it up again for you'. Tories behind John Bull (left) watch. Peel turns to Wellington: 'I never thought to see our poor old friend a sans culotte'. Wellington: 'They promised that the stuff should be Cord de Roy but if I am not much mistaken, it is arrant fustian!'. Eldon, a little apart, and more dejected: 'Alas! poor inexpressibles! We ne'er shall look upon your like again'.

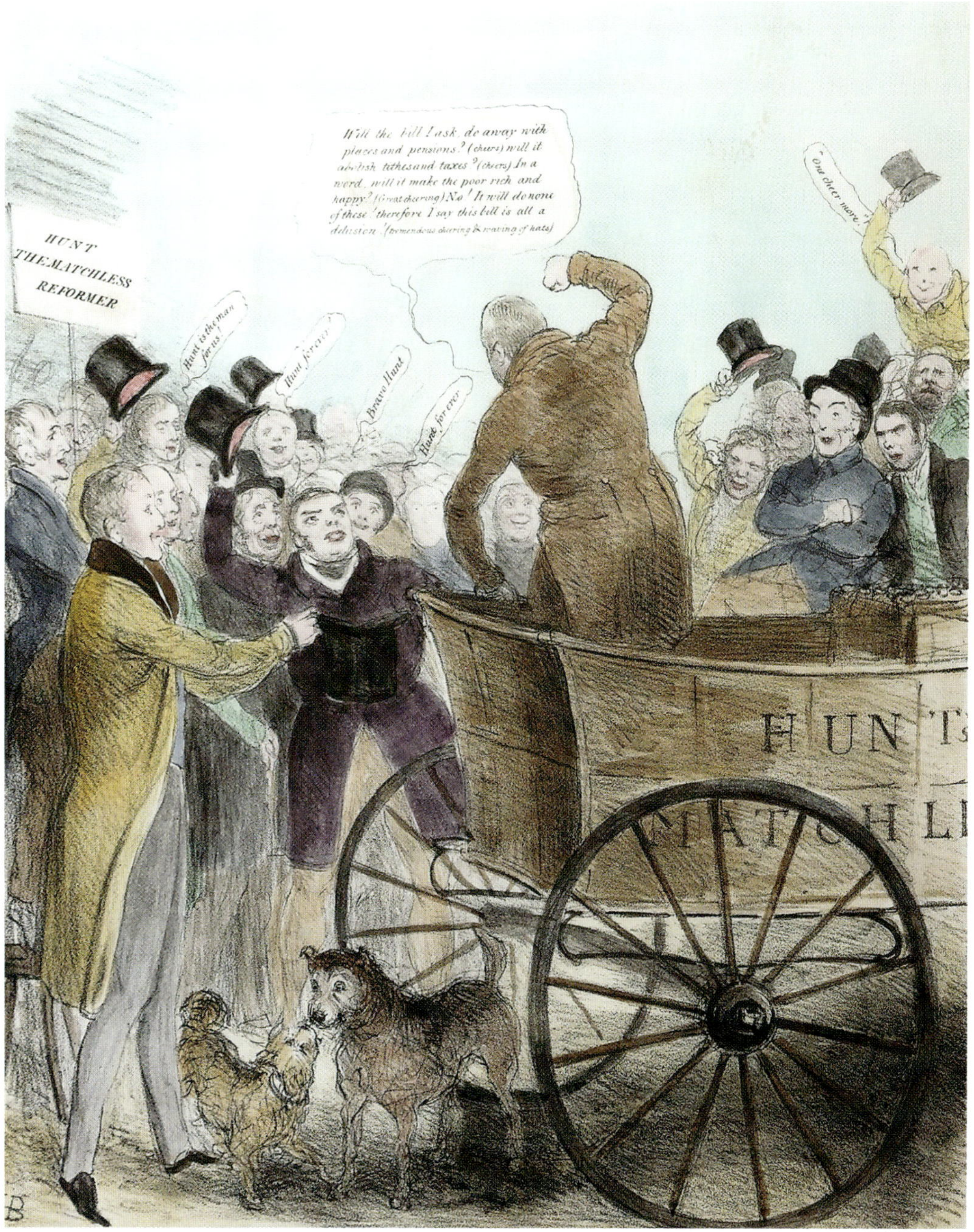

[11] ***No. 121, 'Anticipated Radical Meeting' (published 20 Apr. 1831)*** Henry Hunt speaks to an enthusiastic audience of Tories from a wagon (as at his Smithfield and other meetings). This is marked 'Hunt's Matchl'[ess Blacking], and contains a box of blacking jars. He is in back view stooping with his right fist raised: 'Will the bill I ask, do away with places and pensions? (cheers) will it abolish tithes and taxes? (cheers) In a word will it make the poor rich and happy? (Great cheering) No! It will do none of these! therefore I say this bill is all a delusion! (tremendous cheering & waving of hats)'. A standing crowd faces him, with Sugden on the extreme left, holding up a placard: 'Hunt The Matchless Reformer'. Peel in the foreground holds out his hat, next to him stands Goulburn. Twiss is prominent, waving his hat, while Wetherell grins over his shoulder. The shouts are 'Hunt for ever' [twice] 'Bravo Hunt', and 'Hunt is the man for us!'. On the right, on a stand hidden by the cart, is a seated group of peers. Wellington in front listens intently with folded arms; Ellenborough sits on his right, waving his hat, Aberdeen looks over Wellington's left shoulder. Behind is Cumberland, behind whom stands Eldon waving his hat and shouting 'One cheer more!'. Two (ill-matched) dogs sniff at each other in amity. Hunt opposed the Reform Bill on ultra-Radical grounds on 14 Apr.; O'Connell said he (Hunt) had shown the Tories 'he was a lumping pennyworth if they were disposed to purchase' ('Parliamentary Debates', 3rd series, iii. 1351).

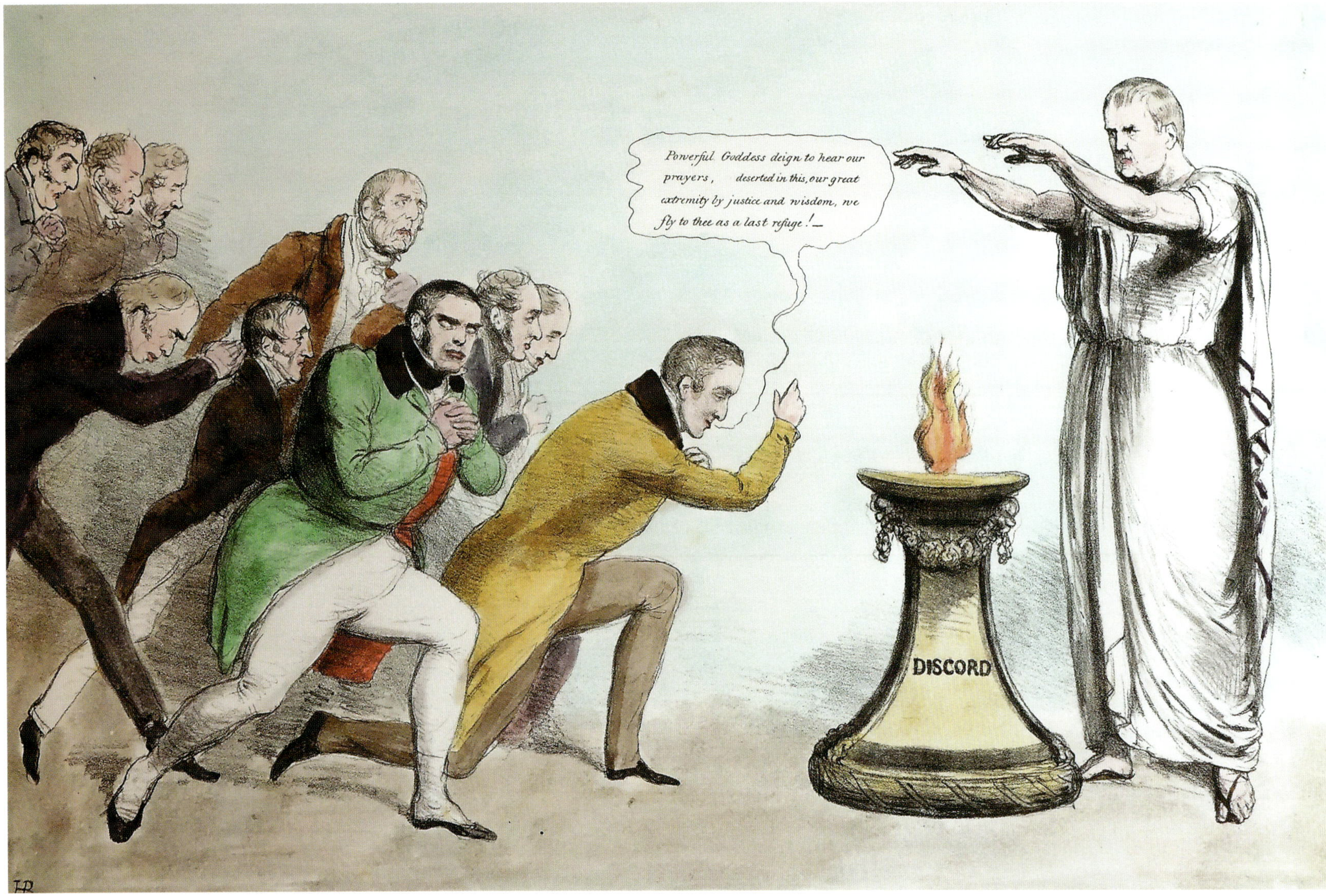

[12] ***No. 122, 'Votaries at the Altar of Discord' (published 20 Apr. 1831)*** Hunt (right), in classical draperies, presides over the Altar of 'Discord', extending both arms over the altar flame. Tories (left) kneel or bow in obeisance. In front of the others is Peel, the spokesman, with right arm raised, left hand on his breast; he kneels, declaiming: 'Powerful Goddess deign to hear our prayers, deserted in this our great extremity by justice and wisdom, we fly to thee as a last refuge!—' The three behind him are Twiss, the most prominent of the "Votaries", with clasped hands and sinister stare, Goulburn, and George Dawson, Peel's brother-in-law. The next three, striding forward (left to right), are Sadler, Sugden, and Wetherell. More aloof, but bending with clasped hands, are the peers: Wellington, Carnarvon, and Newcastle. On 19 Apr. the Government was defeated in Committee by eight votes, but Hunt voted for the Bill (as he had done for the Second Reading on 22 Mar.). See 'Parliamentary Debates', 3rd series, iii. 807, 1691.

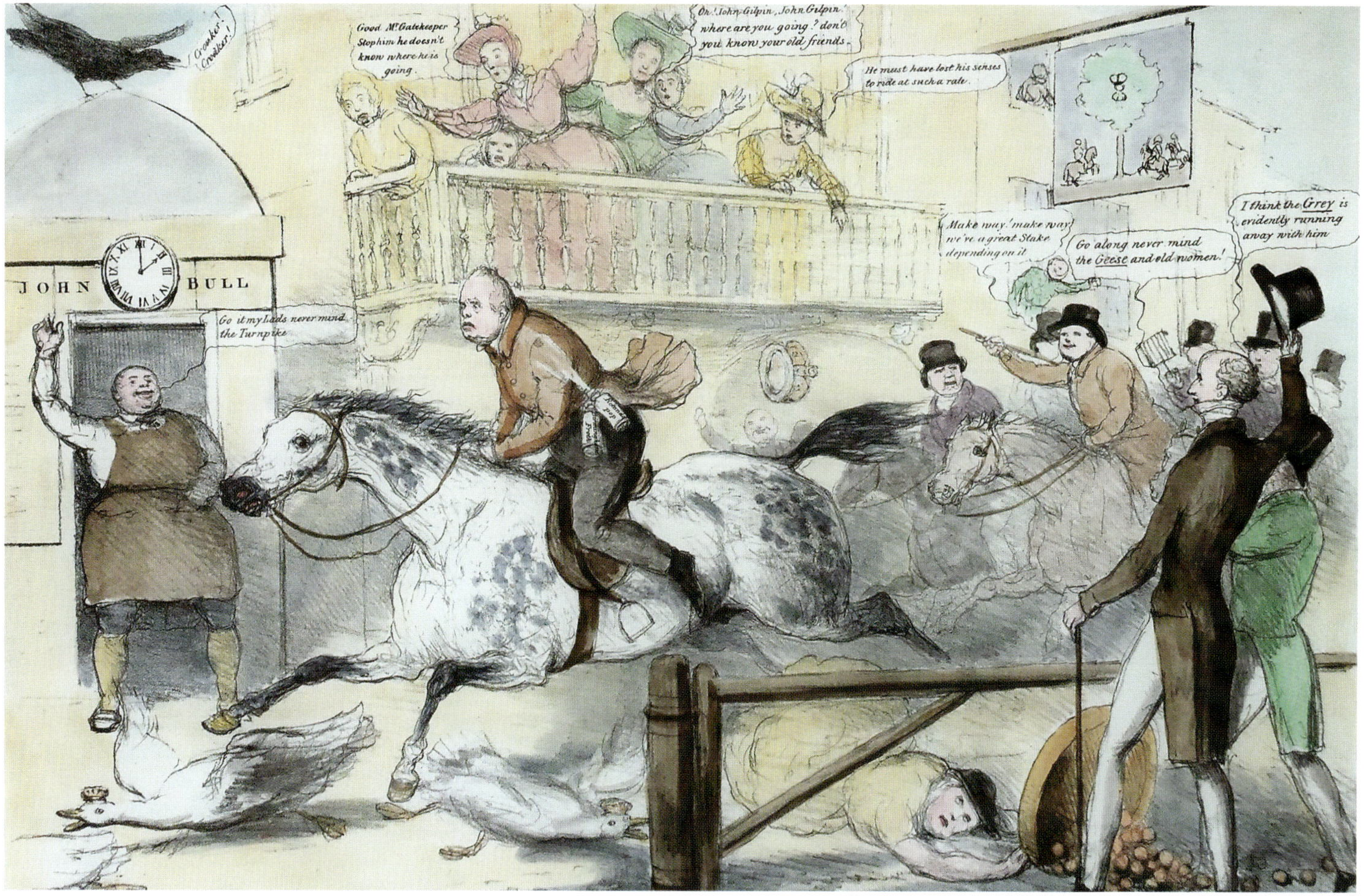

[13] ***No. 128, 'John Gilpin!' (published 13 May 1831)*** Below the title: 'Away went Gilpin, neck or nought; Away went hat and wig: / He little dream'd when he set out / Of running such a rig'. Based on William Cowper's poem 'The Diverting History of John Gilpin' (1782) - the sub-title quotes lines 97-100. William IV as Gilpin rides (right to left) a galloping grey horse (Grey) past the inn at Edmonton. He has lost his stirrups, his crown flies off, the beer-bottles at his belt explode; they are inscribed 'Rotunda Pop' and 'Birmingham Froth'. He rides over geese wearing coronets, and has overthrown an old apple-woman (Eldon). Two men follow on galloping horses, Hume and O'Connell, who shouts 'Make way! make way we've a great Stake depending on it'. Cobbett, holding his gridiron (by which he was always represented in caricatures) is indicated behind. In the foreground, behind a barrier, stand the Radical members for Westminster: Burdett lifts his hat, saying, 'Go along never mind the Geese [peers] and old women!'; Hobhouse: 'I think the Grey is evidently running away with him'. In a doorway (left) stands a fat John Bull as turnpike-keeper, grinning broadly and raising his arm; he shouts: 'Go it my Lads never mind the Turnpike'. In the overhanging balcony are six women (Gilpin's wife and her party), the most conspicuous being Wellington, who leans forward to shout 'Good Mr Gatekeeper Stop him he doesn't know where he is going'. Others (unrecognizable) are identified as Twiss, Peel, and Goulburn. The two latter say: 'Oh! John Gilpin, John Gilpin! where are you going? don't you know your old friends' and 'He must have lost his senses to ride at such a rate'. Perched above the turnpike door croaks a raven (Croker): 'Croaker! Croaker'. On the projecting sign is a tree on which a crowned head is suggested; below it are three tiny mounted men with drawn swords. A sequel to William IV's dramatic dissolution of Parliament, after which he pressed Grey to modify the Bill and conciliate its opponents. 'Birmingham Froth' represented the enthusiastic support for the Bill of Attwood's 'Birmingham Political Union', 'Rotunda pop' stands for sedition and profanity: the revolutionary ultra-Radicals at the Rotunda (Rotundanists) in Blackfriars Road were anti-Whig.

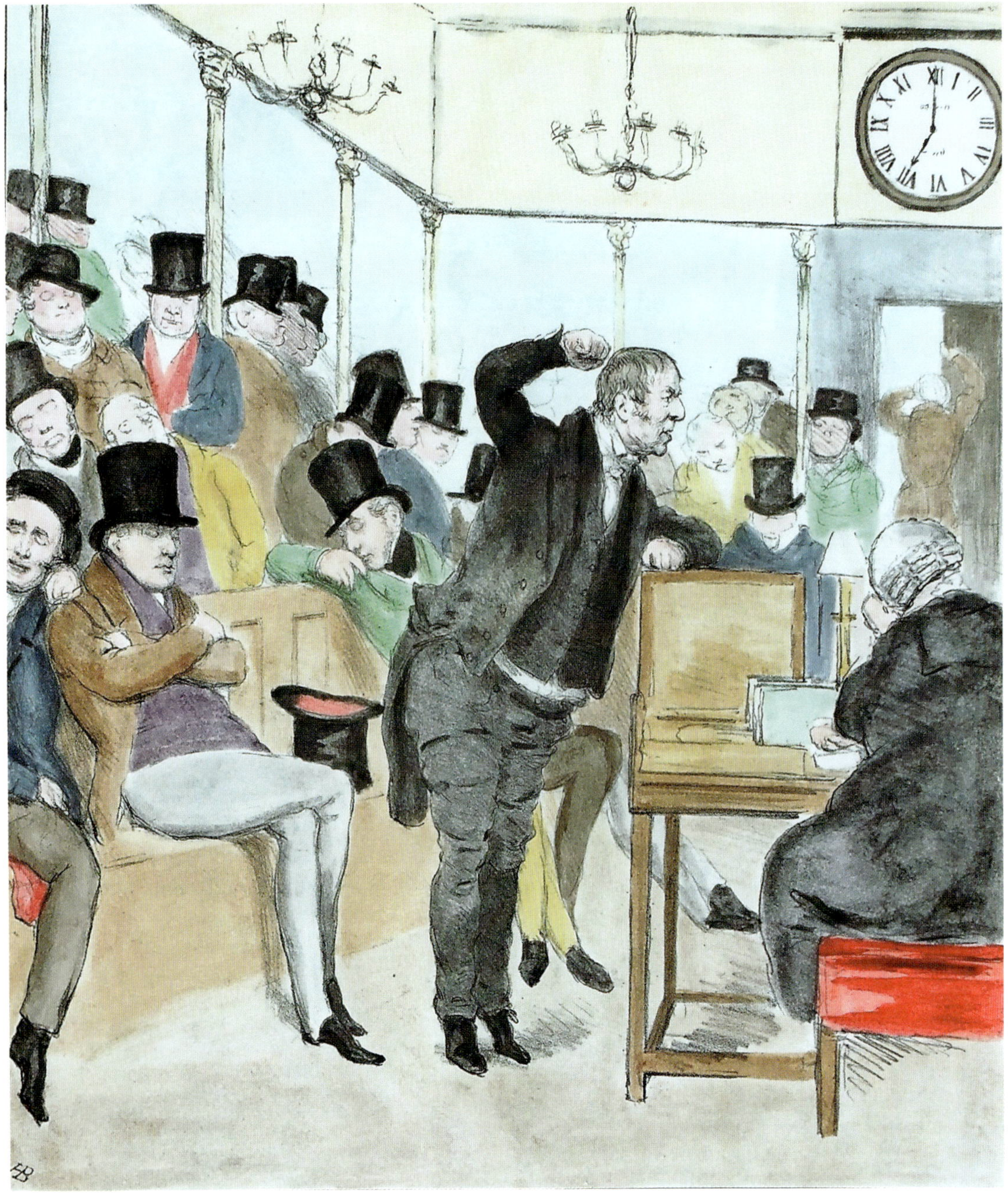

[14] ***No. 142, 'The House wot keeps Bad Hours' (published 18 July 1831)***
Below the title: 'Dedicated with all due respect to Sir Charles Weatherall. mem: Be it known for the benefit of posterity that the H. of Commons sat on Tuesday July 12th from 4 O'Clock in the Afternoon till 7 the following Morning:!!!'. Scene in the House of Commons with the Opposition benches on the left and the Table in the foreground, the Clerk, in back view, partly cut off by the right margin. The candles have burned to their sockets. A large clock on the gallery facing the Table points to seven. Wetherell, more than usually dishevelled, thumps a dispatch-box. All the members in view are asleep, except one who leaves the House, stretching his arms. On the front bench, Croker on the extreme left leans against Peel, who sleeps with folded arms. Goulburn leans against the back of the seat. In the third row are O'Connell and Hume, each leaning against a pillar. Wetherell and a few other Tories made repeated motions for adjournment on 12 July in order to obstruct the second Reform Bill in Committee, and the House sat till 7 a.m. Peel had left some hours earlier, having said that he 'would be no party to any thing like a vexatious delay' ('Parliamentary Debates', 3rd series, iv. 1144).

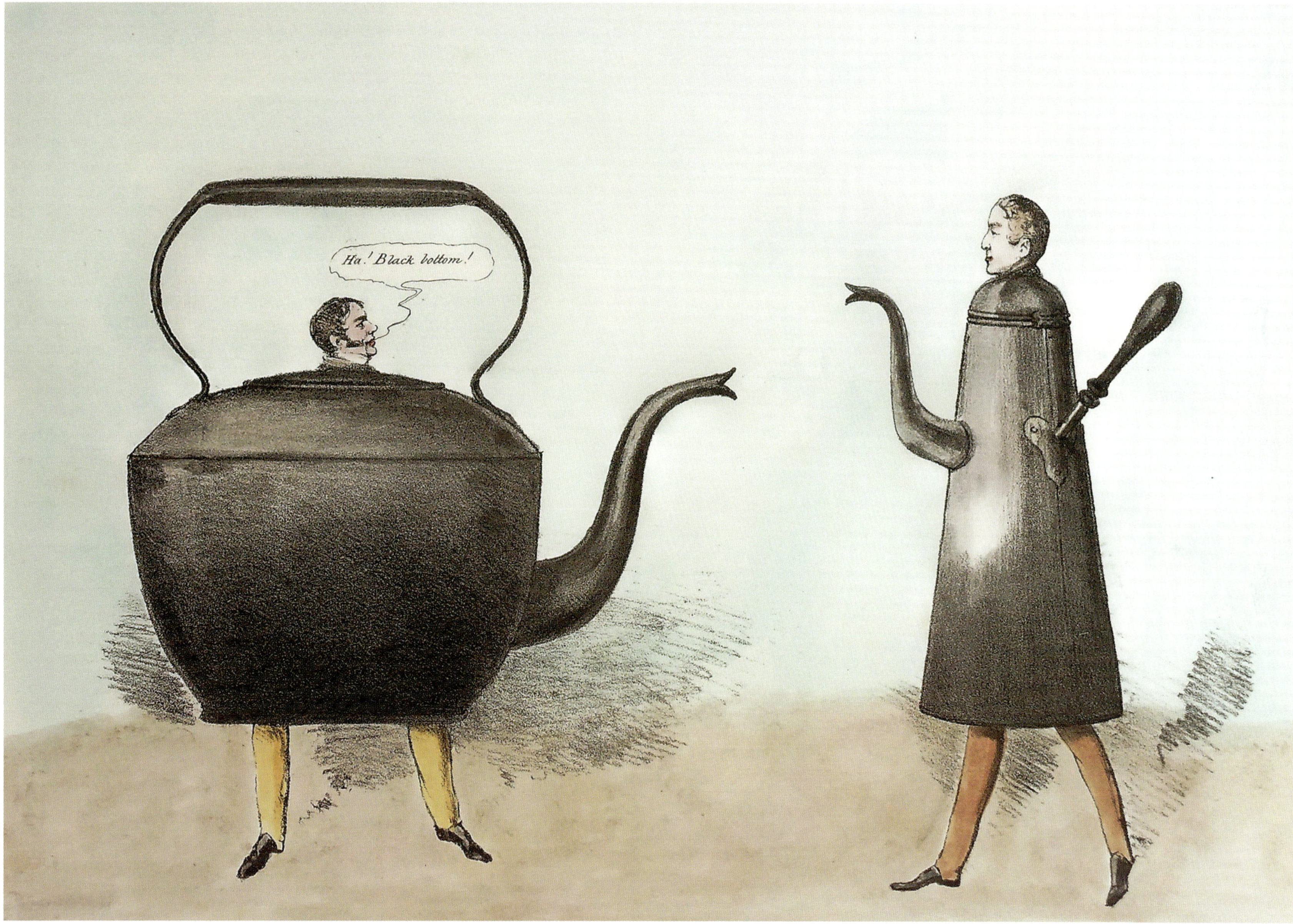

[15] ***No. 146, 'A New Illustration of an Old Joke' (published 5 Aug. 1831)*** Kettle (left) and coffee-pot stand with their spouts facing each other. The head of Lord John Russell tops the kettle-lid, that of Peel the lid of the coffee-pot. The latter is relatively tall and dignified. The kettle stands on Russell's legs, the coffee-pot walks forward on Peel's. Russell shouts to the silent Peel: 'Ha! Black bottom!'. Both men had been charged with change of front: Peel over Catholic Emancipation, Russell over the merits of nomination boroughs.

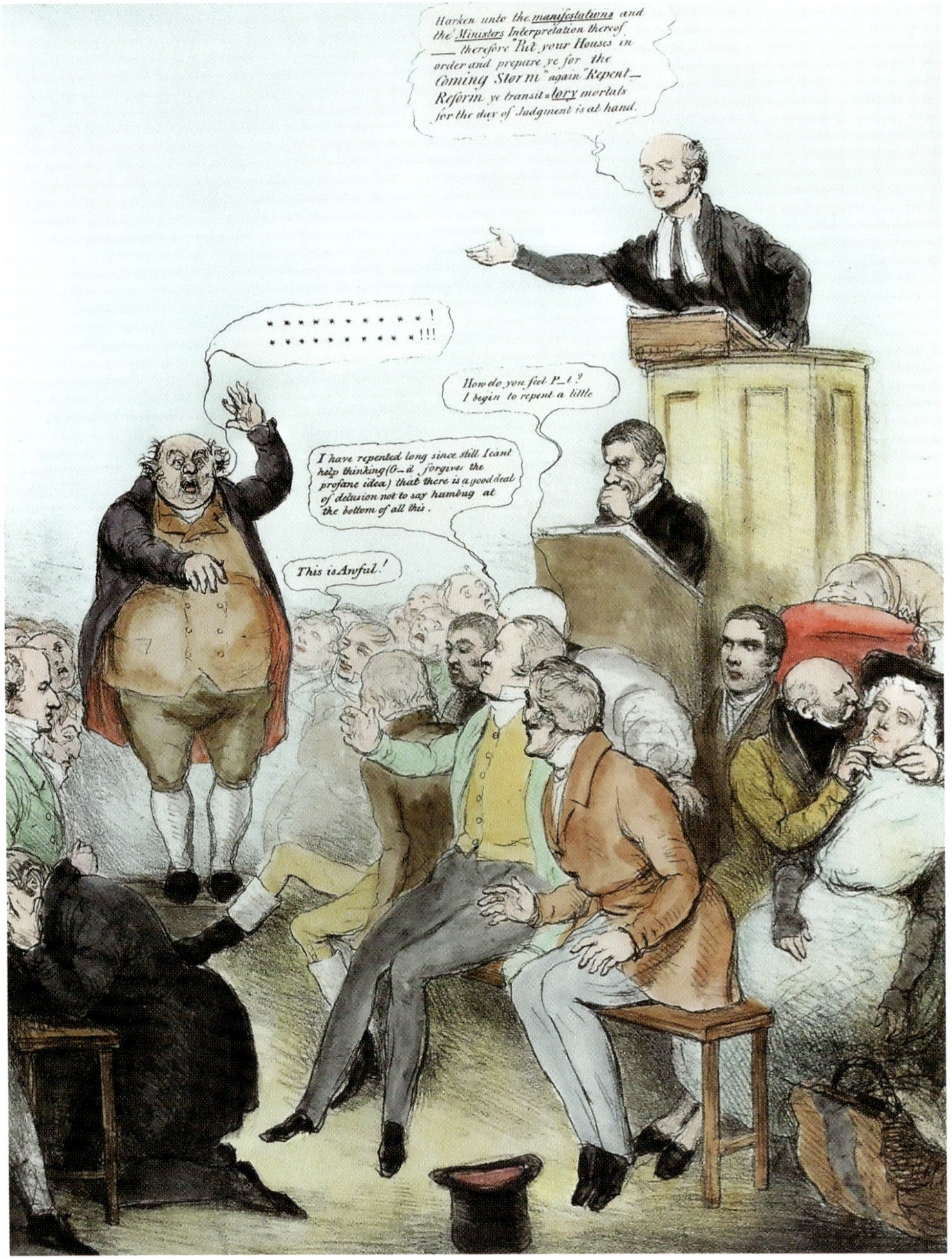

[16] ***No. 168, 'The Gift of Tongues' (published 26 Nov. 1831)*** A preacher in a high pulpit (right) addresses his congregation; he is Grey, taking the place of Edward Irving (the Evangelical preacher) at the Regent Square Chapel during a manifestation of 'unknown tongues'. The inspired or possessed speaker is John Bull who stands full-face on a form (left), pointing before him with the right hand, and raising the left. He utters: '**********! **********!!!' Grey, wearing a gown and bands, declaims: 'Hearken unto the manifestations and the Ministers Interpretation thereof—therefore "Put your Houses in order and prepare ye for the Coming Storm" again "Repent—Reform ye transit=tory mortals for the day of Judgment is at hand"'. Brougham, in the clerk's seat under the pulpit, grins slyly behind folded hands. On the extreme left, facing the pulpit, are Burdett and Hobhouse, with austerely lowered eyelids. Beside Burdett, kneeling at the form with his back to the pulpit, is (possibly) O'Connell (not identified) or perhaps Hume, peeping through his fingers. On the form facing them are Lord John Russell (among unidentified heads) listening, Lord Westmorland, in back view, much perturbed and restlessly raising a leg; he exclaims 'This is Awful'. Next to him sit Peel and Wellington (in the centre foreground), both disturbed. Wellington leans forward, saying, 'How do you feel P—l? I begin to repent a little'. Peel: 'I have repented long since still I can't help thinking (G—d forgive the profane idea) that there is a good deal of delusion not to say humbug at the bottom of this'. Behind Peel is Althorp's swarthy head. Next him an agitated bishop (the head concealed) leans forward. On a back bench (right) are Aberdeen, inscrutable or stupid, and Cumberland. The latter supports the fainting Eldon (an old woman), and with anxious concern holds a smelling-bottle to her nose. Behind these three and at a raised seat under the pulpit William IV, caricatured to the verge of sedition, rests his chin on a cushion, his eyes closed; he seems to wear a fool's cap. On 16 Oct. the first manifestation of 'unknown tongues', by a woman uttering incomprehensible sounds, occurred at Irving's chapel. She was followed by many others (see *The Times*, 19 Oct.). Irving maintained that this was a renewal of Pentecost. Here the application is to the acceptance by the Ministry of popular demonstrations and delusions as a stimulus to Reform (acting, Croker said, 11 Nov., in obedience to, and in encouragement of, the mob; see *The Croker Papers* [1884], ii. 136).

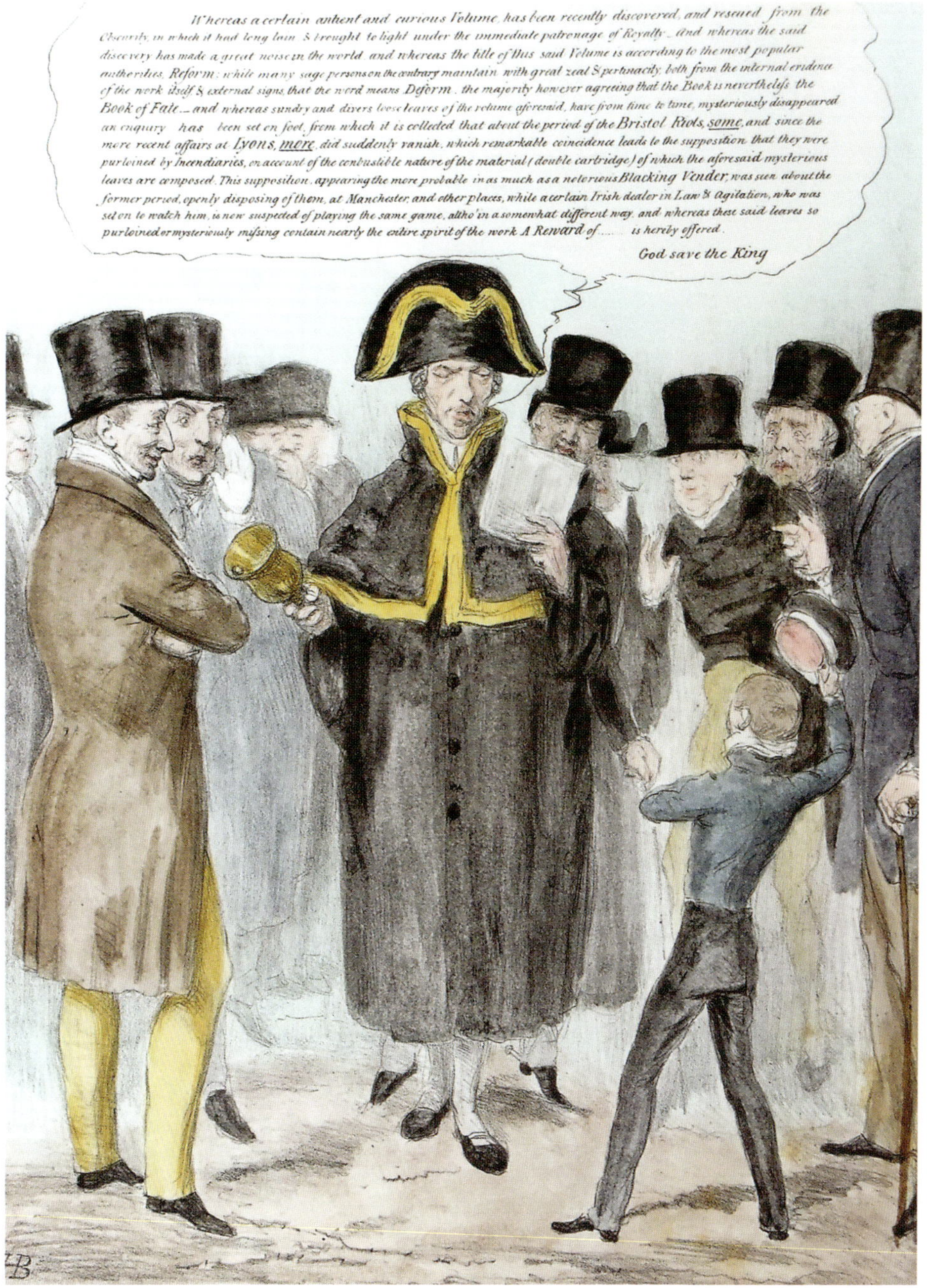

[17] ***No. 169, 'O yes! O yes! O yes!' (published 6 Dec. 1831)*** Brougham, as bellman or town-crier, stands erect, ringing his bell and reading from a paper. He wears cocked hat and long caped greatcoat. Tories press round him, listening with expressions ranging from amusement or satisfaction to astonishment or displeasure. He reads: 'Whereas a certain antient [*sic*] and curious Volume, has been recently discovered, and rescued from the Obscurity in which it had long lain, & brought to light under the immediate patronage of Royalty—And whereas the said discovery has made a great noise in the world, and whereas the title of this said Volume is according to the most popular authorities, Reform; while many sage persons on the contrary maintain with great zeal & pertinacity, both from the internal evidence of the work itself, & external signs, that the word means Deform, the majority however agreeing that the Book is nevertheless the Book of Fate.—and whereas sundry and divers loose leaves of the volume aforesaid, have from time to time, mysteriously disappeared an enquiry has been set on foot, from which it is collected that about the period of the Bristol Riots, some, and since the more recent affairs at Lyons, more, did suddenly vanish, which remarkable coincidence leads to the supposition that they were purloined by Incendiaries, on account of the combustible nature of the material (double cartridge) of which the aforesaid mysterious leaves are composed. This supposition, appearing the more probable in as much as a notorious Blacking Vender [Hunt], was seen about the former period, openly disposing of them, at Manchester, and other places, while a certain Irish dealer in Law & Agitation [O'Connell], who was set on to watch him, is now suspected of playing the same game, altho' in a somewhat different way, and whereas these said leaves so purloined or mysteriously missing contain nearly the entire spirit of the work A Reward of … … is hereby offered. God save the King'. On the extreme left and in shadow stands Peel, with a dry, appraising smile; next, Lord Wharncliffe, in the foreground smiling, Wellington astonished; next him are two scarcely characterized listeners: Hume (or Londonderry) tiptoes to read over Brougham's left shoulder; behind him is a bishop. Next stands Eldon, surprised and amused; Wetherell listens with melancholy apprehension; Cumberland on the extreme right is in profil perdu; beside him and in the foreground Prince George, in back view, holds up his cap as if cheering. A satire on the political trend between the prorogation of Parliament on 20 Oct. and its reassembling on 6 Dec. This was towards some modification of the Reform Bill, negotiations (abortive) taking place with Wharncliffe. A prorogation to January was also considered. Place and others feared great alterations in the Bill. There was also a proclamation against Political Unions on 22 Nov. In the interim, riots in major towns including Nottingham, Derby and Bristol; these were followed by an insurrection of French artisans at Lyons (the military were driven from the town, which was re-entered by Soult with reinforcements) and Grenoble.

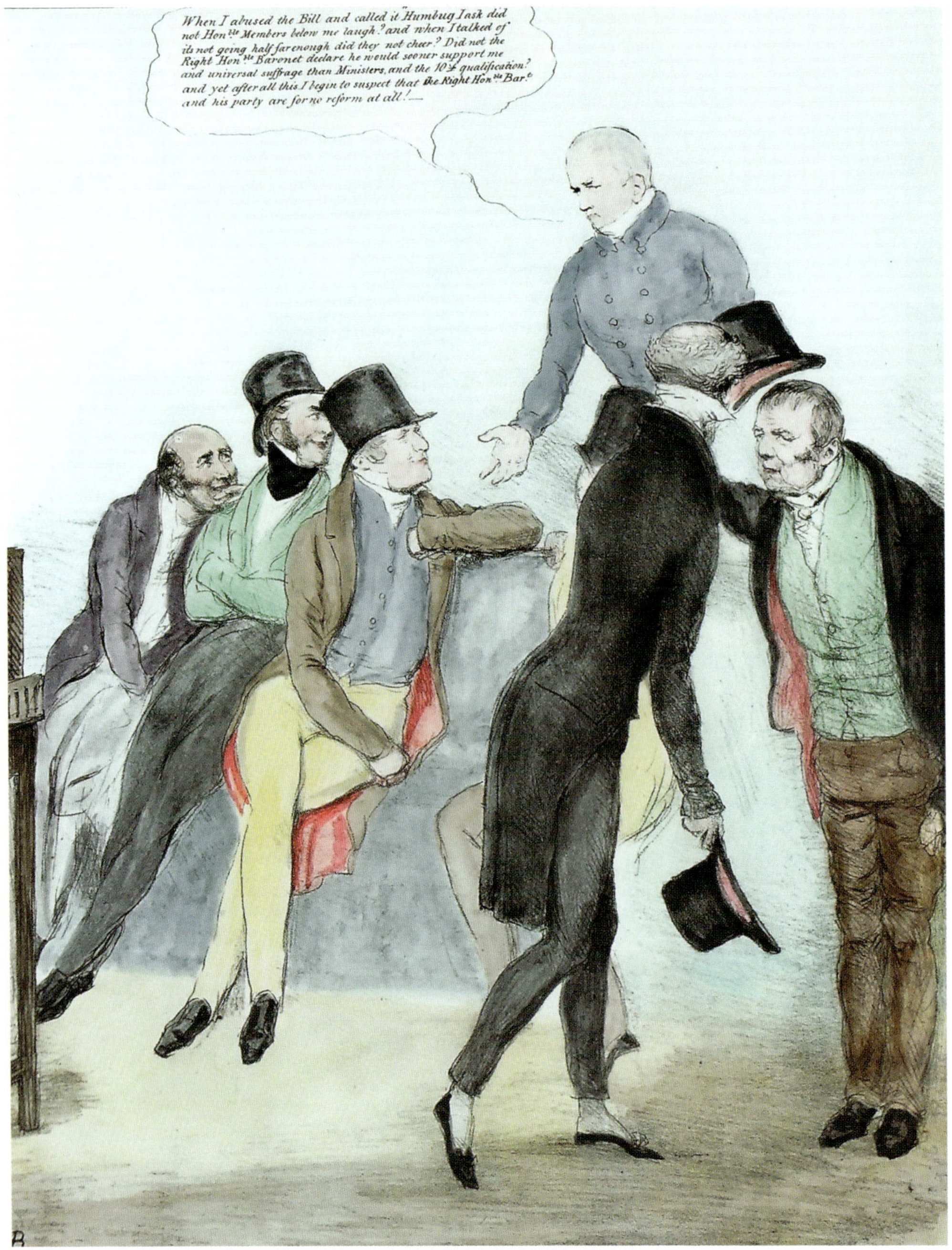

[18] ***No. 170, 'Political Symptoms on a small Scale' (published 12 Dec. 1831)*** Below the title: 'On a small scale. In which remarkable instances of interesting naiveté and Edifying courtesy appear'. A small section of the front Opposition bench in the Commons, with a corner of the Table on the extreme left. Close together sit (left to right) Croker, Goulburn, and Peel, all smiling over the left shoulder at Hunt who stands behind them, right arm extended. Hunt: 'When I abused the Bill and called it "Humbug" I ask did not Honble Members below me laugh? and when I talked of its not going half far enough did they not cheer? Did not the Right Honble Baronet declare he would sooner support me and universal suffrage than Ministers, and the 10£ qualification? and yet after all this I begin to suspect that the Right Honble Bart and his party are for no reform at all!—'. Standing in front (right) are Burdett in back view bowing elegantly, hat in hand, to Wetherell, who responds with stiff politeness, raising his hat. A satire on speeches on 7 Dec. Hunt said 'He did not mean to join those hon. Members on that (the Opposition) side of the House, many of whom, he was sorry to say, he now found to be no Reformers at all. From the tone of some of them he had expected that a more extensive measure would have met their approval than the late Bill'. He asserted that Peel had declared his preference for the household franchise of Preston to the £10 franchise (a perversion of Peel's statement). See 'Parliamentary Debates', 3rd series, ix. 101. Burdett explained his action in withdrawing from the Metropolitan Political Union, saying that Wetherell, 'whose talents and integrity he justly admired, had last night praised him for having withdrawn his name …' (ibid. 117).

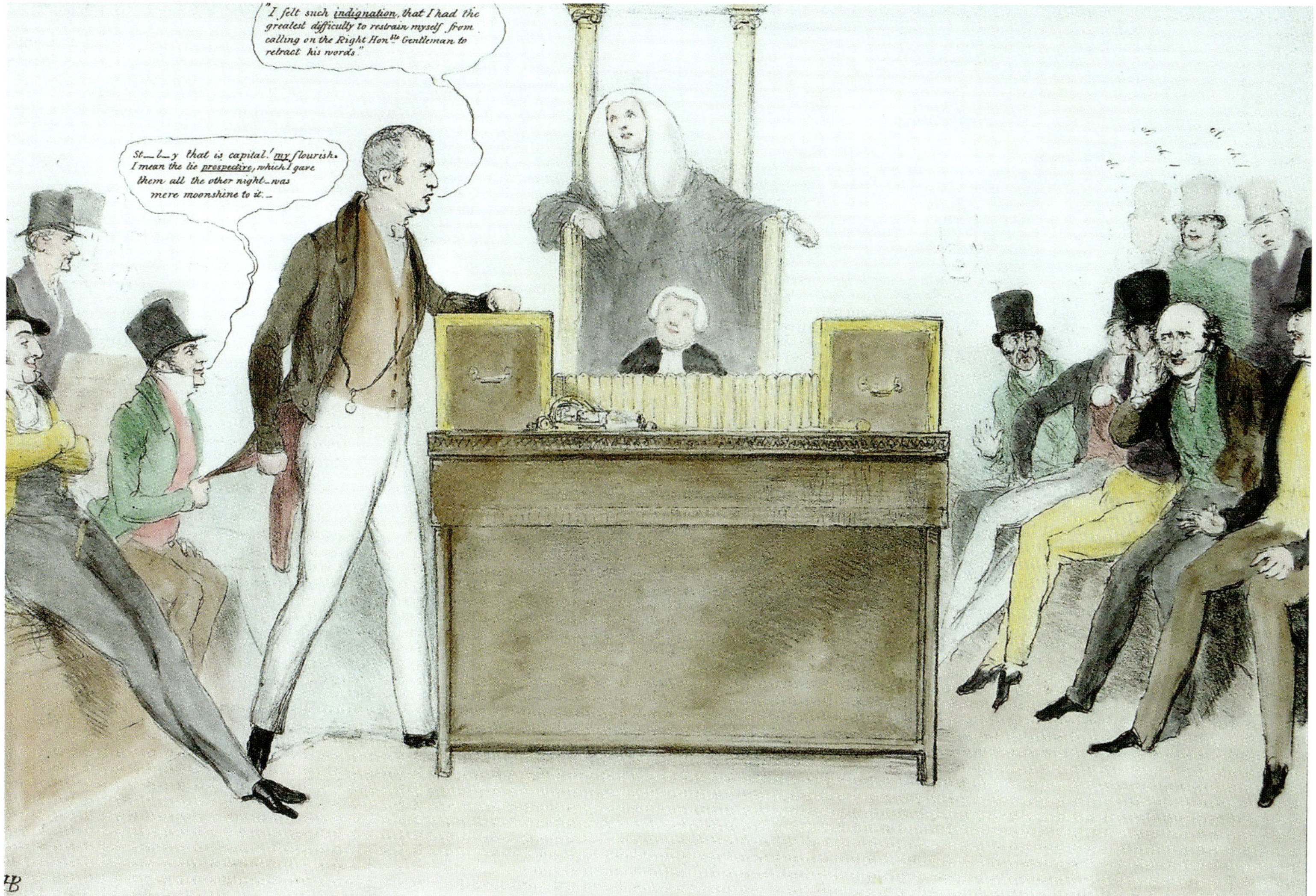

[19] ***No. 172, 'Parliamentary Eloquence' (published 24 Dec. 1831)*** Scene in the Commons centred by the Table and the Speaker's Chair. Stanley (left), standing in profile to the right, thumps the dispatch-box and glares at Croker (right), who leans forward, hand to his ear, trying to hear. He says: 'I felt such indignation, that I had the greatest difficulty to restrain myself from calling on the Right Honble Gentleman to retract his words.' Lord J. Russell, seated just behind him, tugs at his coat-tails, saying with a smile, 'St—I—y that is capital! my flourish. I mean the lie prospective, which I gave them all the other night—was mere moonshine to it—'. Sir James Graham, next Russell and on the extreme left, with arms folded and legs outstretched, smiles sardonically. Behind is the profile of Burdett. The Clerk smiles up at Stanley; the (Tory) Speaker (Manners-Sutton) watches him gravely. On the opposite bench Peel, next Croker and on the extreme right, registers surprise; at the left end of the bench Sugden manifests dismay. From three Members freely sketched behind the front bench come exclamations: 'oh oh!'. A satire on the debate, 17 Dec, on the Reform Bill, 'conspicuous … for a great speech from Edward Stanley, who lashed Mr. Croker so soundly as he had never been lashed before'; Hobhouse, *Recollections of a Long Life* (1910), iv. 156. Stanley said 'he never felt a deeper indignation … he never had a greater inclination … [&c.]'; 'Parliamentary Debates', 3rd series, ix. 516. For Croker's speech (16 Dec.) see *The Croker Papers* (1884), ii. 133–5.

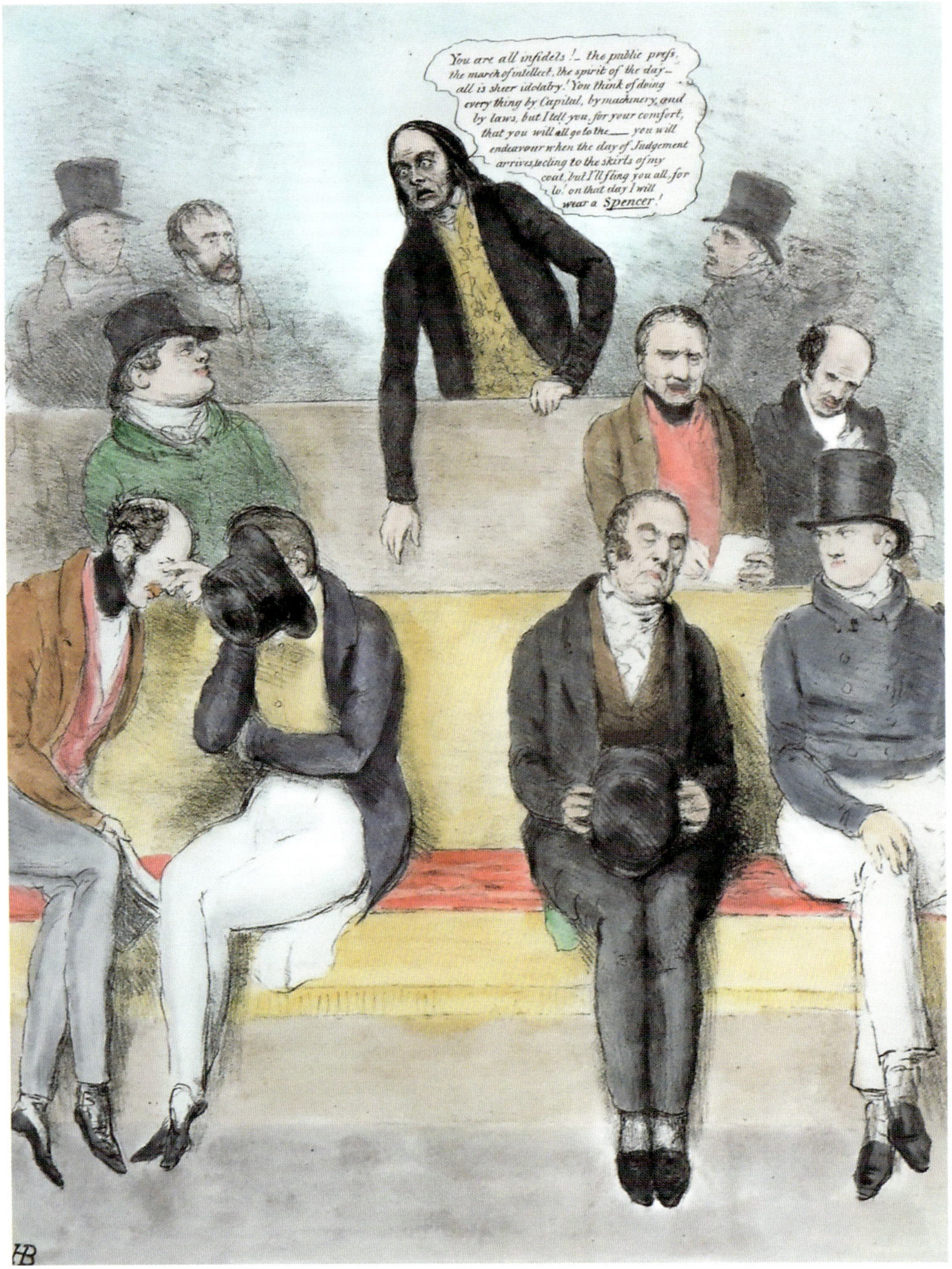

[20] ***No. 178, 'This is not Mr. Liston in the character of Mawworn' (published 6 Feb. 1832)*** A small section of Opposition benches (three tiers) in the Commons. Spencer Perceval, travestied as Maw-worm in Bickerstaffe's play 'The Hypocrite' (1769) leans forward from the third bench, addressing the House. The other members close their eyes or look away, embarrassed, bored, or contemptuous, except for shadowy black figures, one identified as Col. Sibthorp (on Perceval's right), and for O'Connell (left) who turns round from the second bench to stare appraisingly at the fanatic. On the front bench (left to right) Goulburn covers his eyes with his hand, Peel hides his face with his hat, Wetherell shuts his eyes, Hunt stares meaningly at Wetherell. Behind the last two sit the Radicals Hume and Warburton. Perceval has the lank hair, the glittering eyes, the tight black coat with light embroidered waistcoat of Liston in the part (a canting hypocrite, a vulgar copy of Cantwell in the play) as depicted in a coloured lithograph by J. W. Gear at this time. He says: 'You are all infidels!—the public press, the march of intellect, the spirit of the day—all is sheer idolatry! You think of doing every thing by Capital, by machinery and by laws, but I tell you for your comfort, that you will all go to the— —you will endeavour— when the day of Judgement arrives, to cling to the skirts of my coat, but I'll fling you all, for lo! on that day I will wear a Spencer!' [Maw-worm says in the last scene: "... I have one great and glorious consolation you'll all go to the D—l: I shall go up, but you'll go down... . You'll want my aid! you'll want me to take you with me! ... you'll attempt to lay hold of the skirts of my coat! but I'll fling ye all, for I'll wear a spencer!"].

On 26 Jan. Spencer Perceval, after calling for the withdrawal of strangers, made a fanatical speech (printed despite the absence of reporters), moving, as in Dec. 1830, for a General Fast on account of cholera, with many Old Testament quotations on Tyre and Sidon, Sodom, and Nineveh, saying, "You are all infidels. Look at the public press, the march of intellect —the spirit of the day is sheer idolatry"; 'Parliamentary Debates', 3rd series, ix. 895–903. The Fast evoked a violent anti-clerical demonstration: a parody of the Proclamation headed 'Farce Day', a mass meeting and procession of the National Union of the Working Classes.

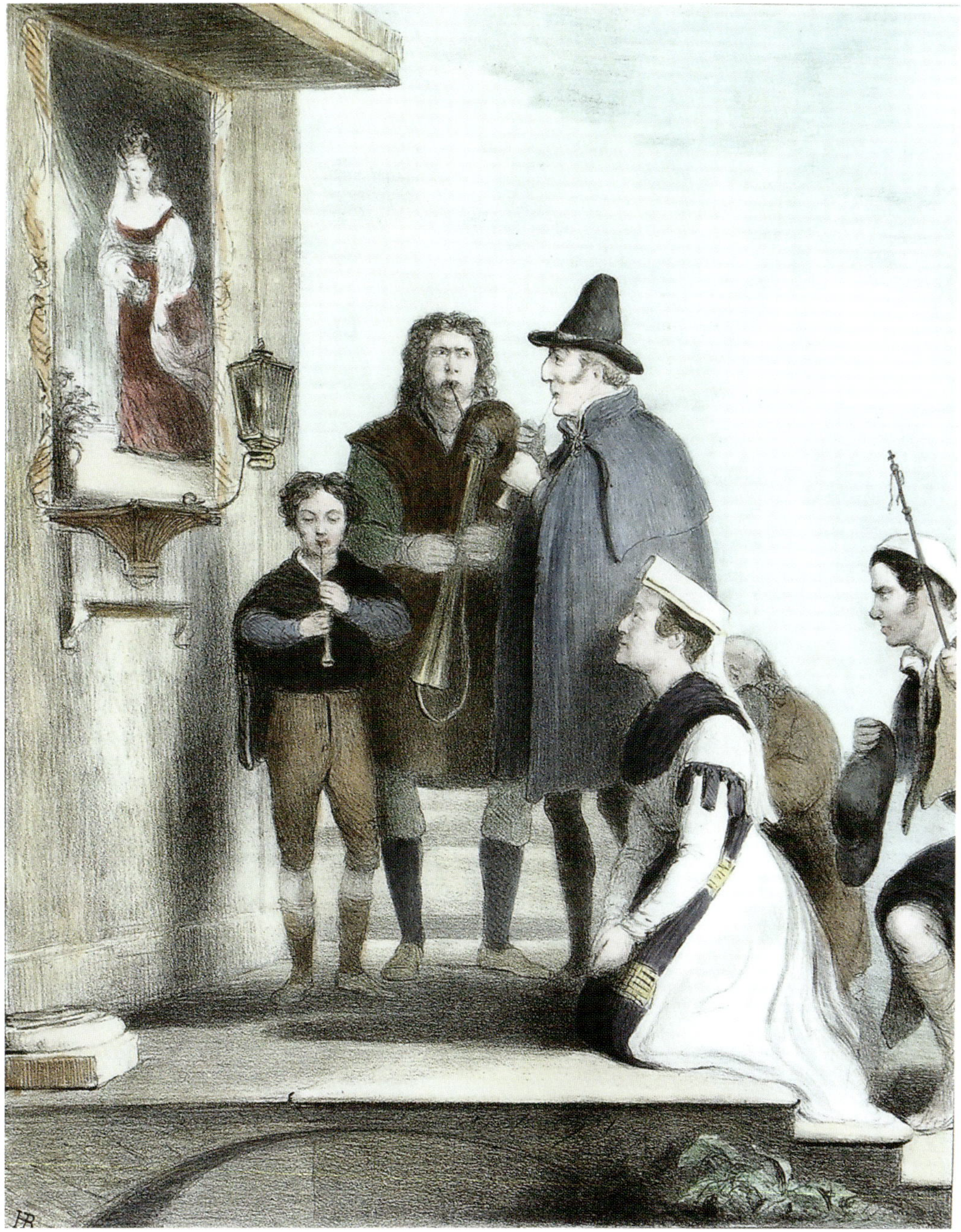

[21] ***No. 182, ''Le Tableau Vivant' (published 1 Mar. 1832)*** Below the title: 'Subject—Mr Wilkie's interesting Picture entitled "Calabrian Minstrels playing to the Madonna."' A travesty of Wilkie's picture, heavily shaded to suggest a painting. The Madonna is a W.L. portrait of Queen Adelaide on an exterior wall, and protected by a projection. Before it is a stone platform, reached by steps (right) on which three minstrels, shepherds in peasant costume, stand together: a boy (Lord Monson) full-face plays a pipe, next, Lord Ellenborough, tall, burly, shaggy-haired, plays the bagpipes (zampogna), looking sideways at Wellington, an elderly peasant in profile to the left, cloaked and wearing a conical hat. Beside him Peel, a woman, kneels devoutly; he wears a white cap with hanging drapery, white dress, and striped apron. Mounting the steps behind him is Aberdeen, holding his hat and a rod tipped with a small cross. The bowed and bulky back and bald head of Croker are more dimly seen behind Peel. The Queen is the patroness of the Opposition. Monson (b. 1809) was one of the 22 die-hard peers who voted against the third reading of the Reform Bill; he was small and childish in appearance.

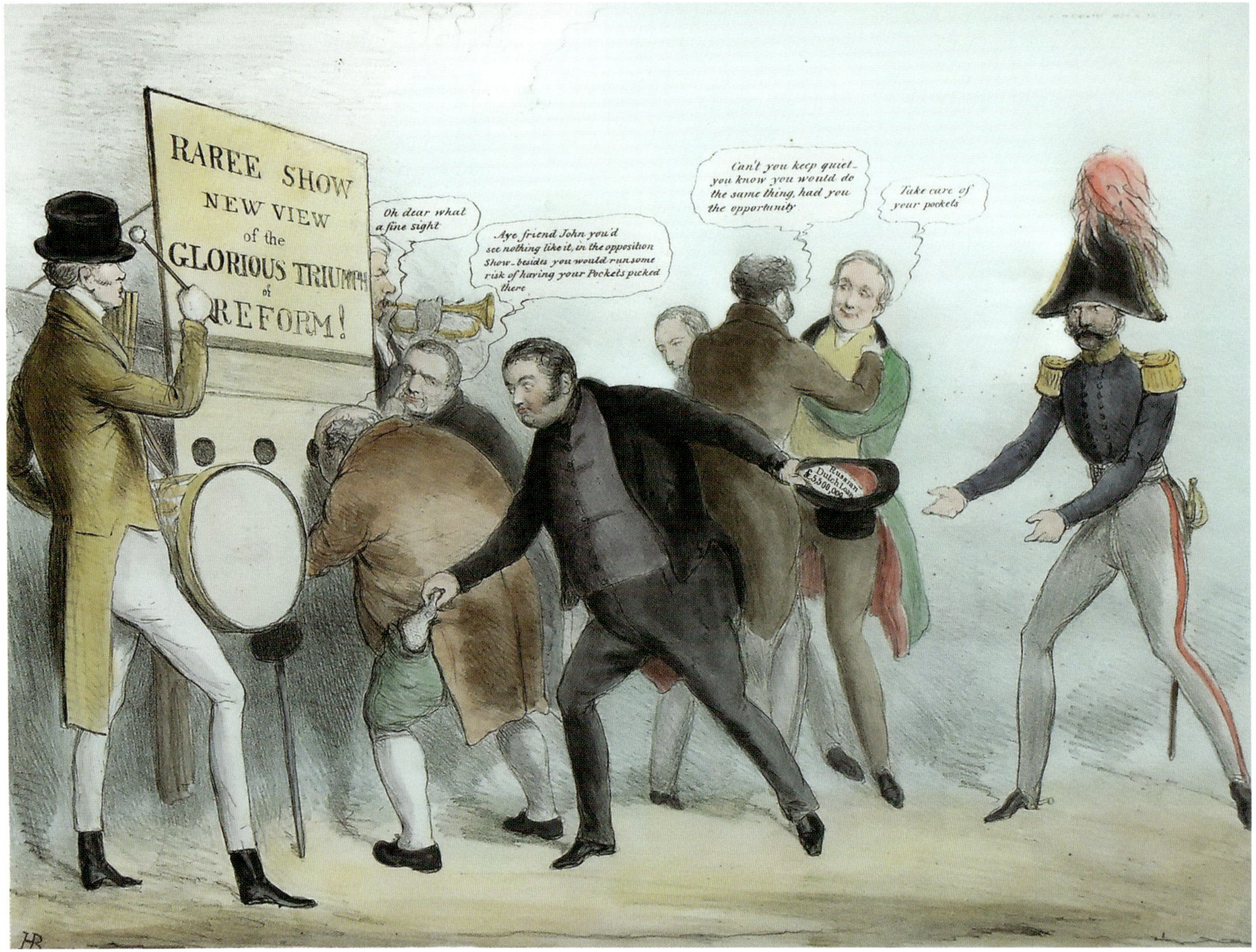

[22] ***No. 216, 'A Show-up' (published 1 Aug. 1832)*** Grey and Brougham display a peep-show to John Bull, who stoops to look through one of the round holes: Grey (left) blows pan-pipes and beats a drum, Brougham blows a trumpet. The show-box is placarded in big letters: 'Raree Show | New View | of the | Glorious Triumph | of | Reform!' John: 'Oh dear what a fine sight'. Hume, who stands beside him, slyly putting a finger to his nose, says: 'Aye friend John you'd see nothing like it, in the opposition Show—besides you would run some danger of having your Pockets picked there'. Meantime, Althorp, the centre figure, leans forward to take a purse from John's pocket, while he holds out in his hat to the Tsar a paper: 'Russian Dutch Loan £5,500,000'. Nicholas, on the extreme right, in uniform with cocked hat and sword, holds out both hands to grasp it, with a fixed and sinister stare. Back to back with Althorp is Palmerston who faces Peel, buttonholing him; the latter (as a policeman) says: 'Take care of your pockets'. Palmerston: 'Can't you keep quiet you know you would do the same thing had you the opportunity'. A satire on the debate on the Russian Loan on 16 July, when Hume said: 'It was no longer a question as to whether Ministers deserved censure … in this matter, but whether, on account of their foreign policy, he should consent to turn out Ministers, before the great measure [*sic*] of Reform are carried'. Peel made a statesmanlike and moderate speech on the principles of foreign policy involved, after an able speech by Palmerston.

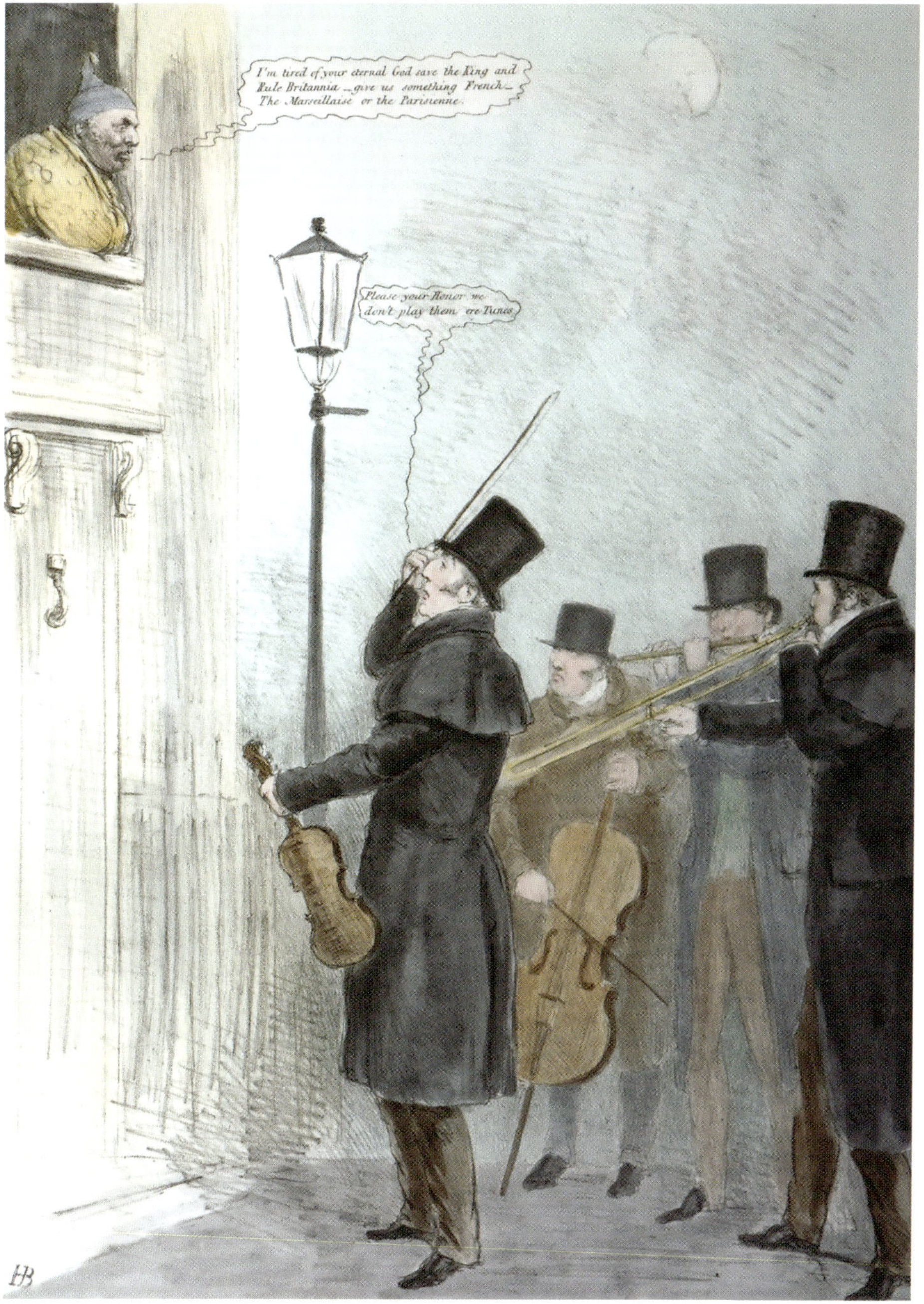

[23] ***No. 237, 'The <u>Waits</u>' (published 14 Jan. 1833)*** John Bull standing in the open window on the first floor of a house, requesting French music from a quartet of musicians standing in the street; the violinist (Duke of Wellington), standing in profile to left, holding a violin in his left hand and a bow in his right hand, refuses; the cellist (Lord Aberdeen), flutist (Sir Robert Peel) and trombonist (Lord Ellenborough) standing behind him to right, playing their instruments. This little band is composed of the Duke of Wellington, the Earl of Aberdeen, Sir Robert Peel, and Lord Ellenborough. The Duke is, of course, the leader: Lord Aberdeen handles the violoncello, the flute is breathed by Sir Robert Peel, and Lord Ellenborough sounds the trombone. They have wearied John Bull with their old-fashioned strains. John has taken up the humour of liking novelties, and, in perfect contempt for the melodies of native composers, calls for the Marseillaise and the Parisienne. But the leader 'does not play them 'ere tunes'. Not he – he would rather burn his fiddle; and so these waits are likely to wait a little longer before they receive John Bull's patronage.

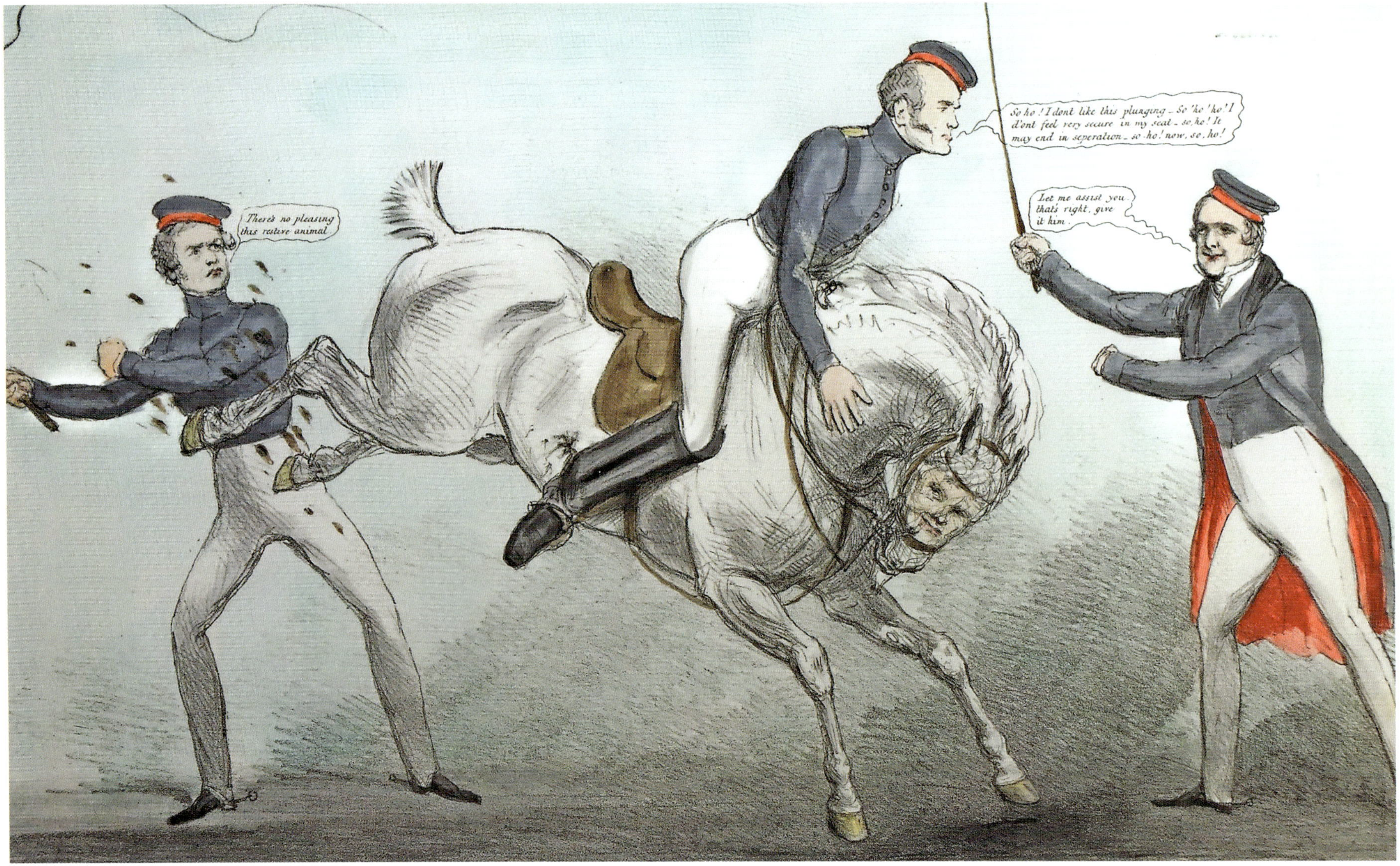

[24] ***No. 246, 'Military Rough-Riders breaking an Unruly Animal' (published 7 Mar. 1833)*** A man (Lord Grey), trying to ride a wild horse bearing a man's face (Daniel O'Connell), assisted by two men holding whips in their right hands, one standing to right (Sir Robert Peel), the other standing to left, spattered with soil by the horse (Edward Stanley). This sketch considers the agitation kept up in Ireland by Mr. O'Connell (leader of the Irish contingent in the House of Commons), and the attempts made by Lord Grey (as Prime Minister) and Mr. Stanley (as Chief Secretary to the Lord Lieutenant of Ireland) to suppress it. Mr. O'Connell is, of course, the unruly animal, and Lord Grey the rider in danger of losing his seat. The daring helper, who plies the whip behind, unmindful of the infuriated beast, that has already bespattered him with dirt, and threatens to deal him a mortal blow with his heels, is Mr. Stanley. The assistance proffered by Sir Robert Peel, and which seems to consist of adding fresh matter for irritation to the "animal," is of a rather doubtful character.

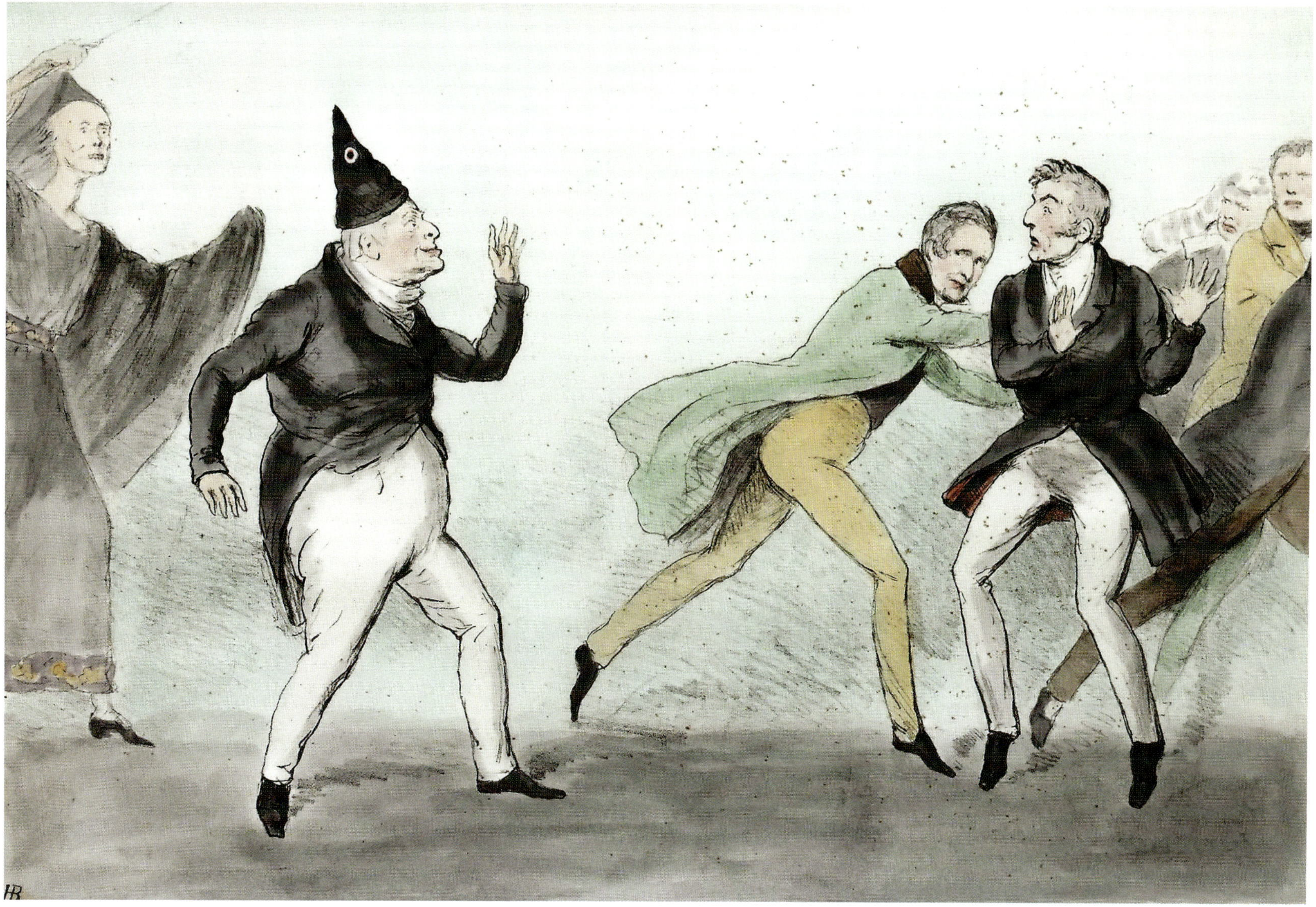

[25] ***No. 256, 'The Grim Grey Woman, No. 2' (published 25 Apr. 1833)*** A group of five frightened men, to right (Sir Robert Peel, the Duke of Wellington, Lord Lyndhurst and others) escaping from a man approaching from left, wearing a cap of liberty (William IV), directed from behind by a man dressed as a woman in grey clothes (Lord Grey). The transformation of William IV, a prince of the sober-minded House of Brunswick, into a harum-scarum revolutionist, running about with a cap of liberty on his head, and a tri-coloured cockade stuck upon it, was certainly sufficient to disguise him, so that his old servants, Sir Robert Peel and the Duke of Wellington, could not recognize him. Their terror, and the unconscious simplicity of the transformed, are well portrayed. Among the retreating party are Lords Lyndhurst and Ellenborough, while the Grim Grey Woman, otherwise Lord Grey, appears behind Sir Joddrill, enjoying the effects of her powerful spell.

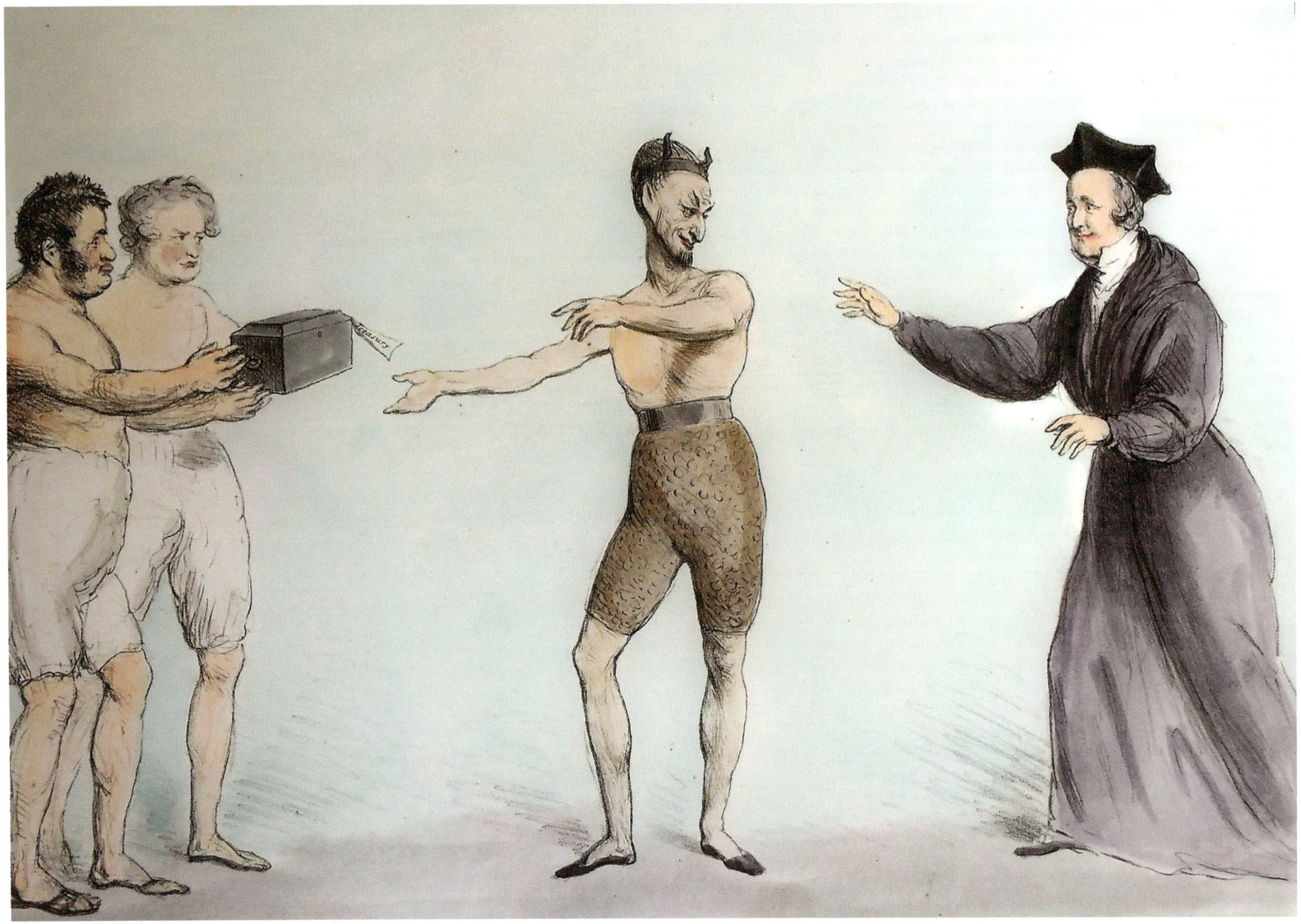

[26] ***No. 257, 'La Tentation, not from Faust' (published 29 Apr. 1833)*** Mephistopheles, in centre, trying to persuade Faust, to right (Sir Robert Peel), to sell his soul to two men standing to left (Lord Althorp and Edward Stanley), holding a box, from which hangs a piece of paper lettered 'Treasury'. Sir Robert Peel, in the character of Faust, is tempted by Mephistopheles to sell his soul to the Whigs, for the price of the office of First Lord of the Treasury. The Mephistopheles in this negotiation must be the demon of Ambition, not of Lucre; not Mammon, but Satan himself, in propriâ personâ, for Sir Robert is too wealthy to covet office for its emoluments; and if he desires it at all, must do so for the love of power and distinction. The bearers of the temptation are Lord Althorp and Mr. Stanley; and the keen and searching glance of the latter imply an inward conviction, arising from a congeniality of spirit, that over a mind like that of Sir Robert Peel the arts of the tempter will not prevail. The second part of Goethe's *Faust* was published in 1832.

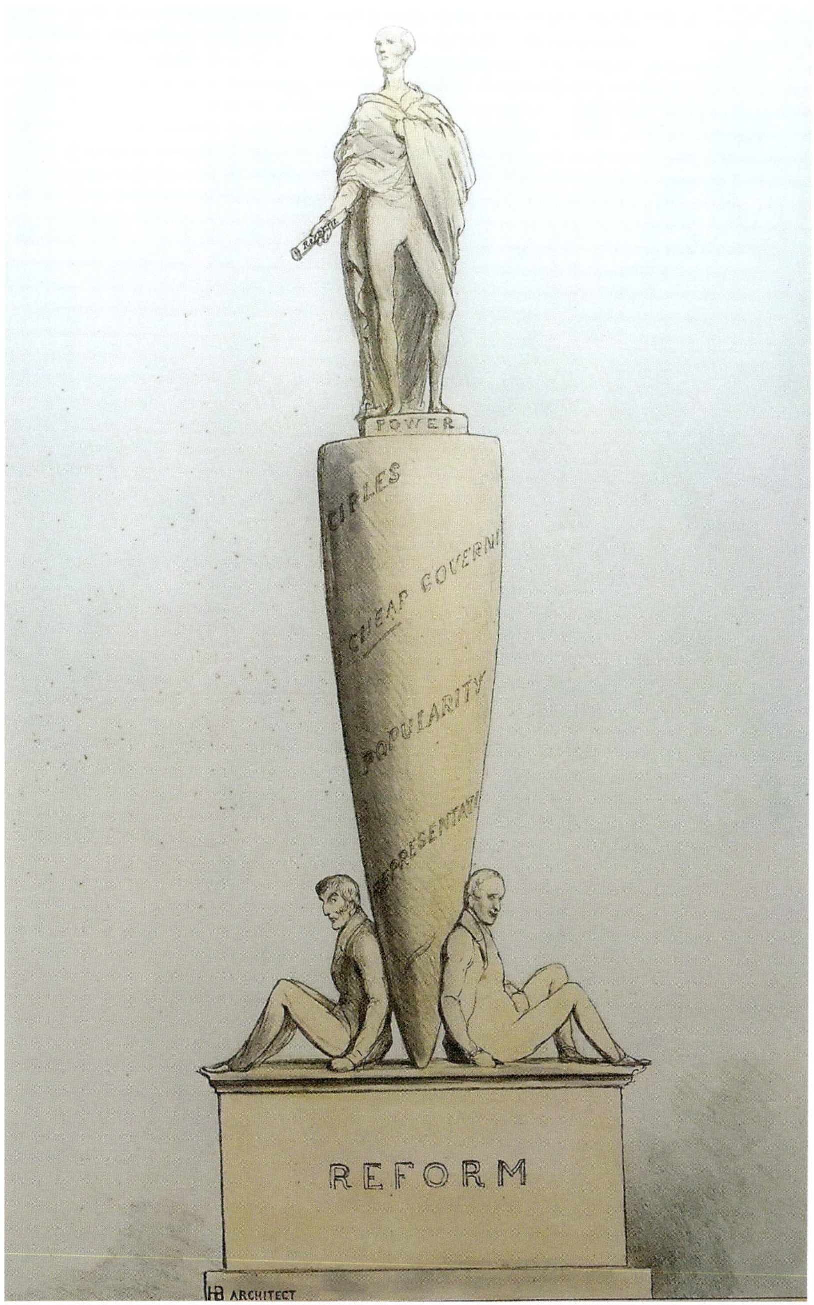

[27] ***No. 258, 'A Design' (published 4 May 1833)*** A cone-shaped monument, lettered with fragments of words 'ciples', 'cheap govern', 'popularity', representati'; a sculpture of a man on top (Lord Grey), standing on a slab lettered 'Power', holding a scroll lettered 'Reform'; two men (the Duke of Wellington and Sir Robert Peel) seated in profile at the base of the cone, with their backs turned towards each other, on a pedestal lettered 'Reform'. When it has been stated that the figure on the top of the monument is that of Earl Grey, and that the two involuntary supporters, sitting below, represent the Duke of Wellington (on the left) and Sir Robert Peel (on the right), and when the note explanatory has been read, very little more, in the way of explanation, will be wanted to render this sketch intelligible. That little may be thus told – Earl Grey remarks 'Hitherto society, in this happy island, has been constructed upon the model of a cone; the common people forming the base, the monarch the apex, and the various other classes ranging in order in the intermediate space. For my own aggrandizement I have reversed the figure. I well know that, if left to itself, this state of society could not endure, any more than a cone could stand unsupported upon its apex. But here is my master-stroke of policy. The broad base of the populace makes a firm footing for me; and my opponents are as much interested as I am in supporting me; because, if they desert me, the cone will fall, and anarchy, as fatal to them as to myself, will ensue'.

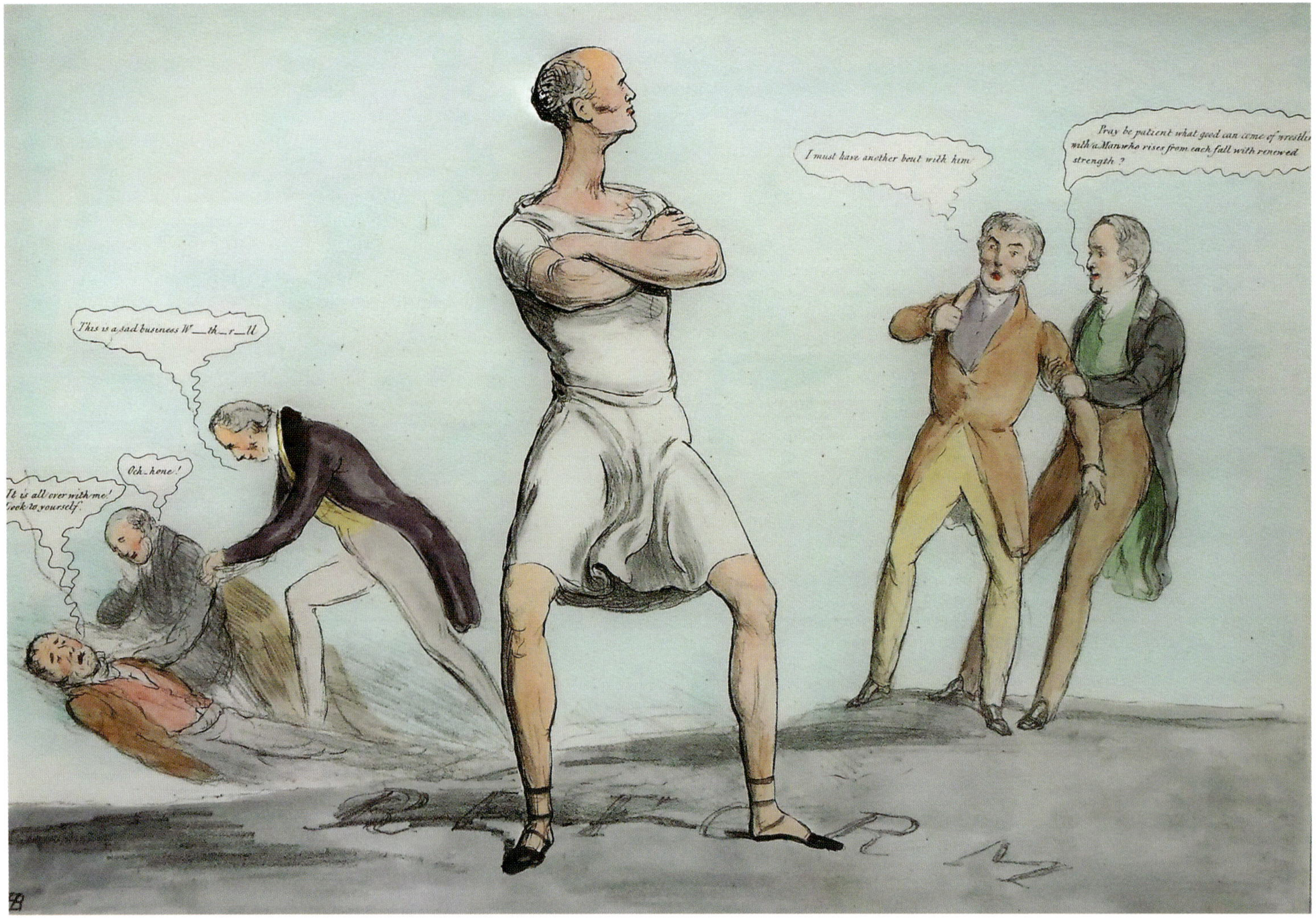

[28] ***No. 278, 'The Modern Antaeus' (published 31 July 1833)*** An athletic man standing outdoors in centre, with his arms folded and legs spread, on ground lettered with 'Reform' (Lord Grey); to left, a man lying on the ground in pain (Sir Charles Wetherell), attended by two men (John Wilson Croker and the Duke of Newcastle); a man standing to right on top of a small mount, ready to fight (Duke of Wellington), but being restrained by the man standing to far right (Sir Robert Peel). Antæus, the 'old original', was a giant of Libya, and the son of Terra (the Earth) by Neptune. He was also, as well he might be, the prince of wrestlers; for every fall was but to him an embrace of his mother, who took that opportunity of endowing him with fresh vigour. The Modern Antæus, (Earl Grey) a child of the spirit of Reform, gains, in like manner, renewed strength from his parent every time that he is baffled and thrown down by his political opponents. His last triumph is over Sir Charles Wetherell, who lies prostrate and irrecoverable. His bottle-holders, Mr. Croker and the Duke of Newcastle, endeavour in vain to raise him; he confesses that it is all over with him. The Duke of Wellington, however, is resolved to try a bout with the giant in spite of the remonstrance of Sir Robert Peel. The end of the real Antæus was, that Hercules, finding it of no use to throw him down, adopted the expedient of holding him up in the air, where his mother could not come to his assistance, and thus squeezed him to death: but 'H.B.' did not venture to represent the Duke of Wellington in the likeness of Hercules.

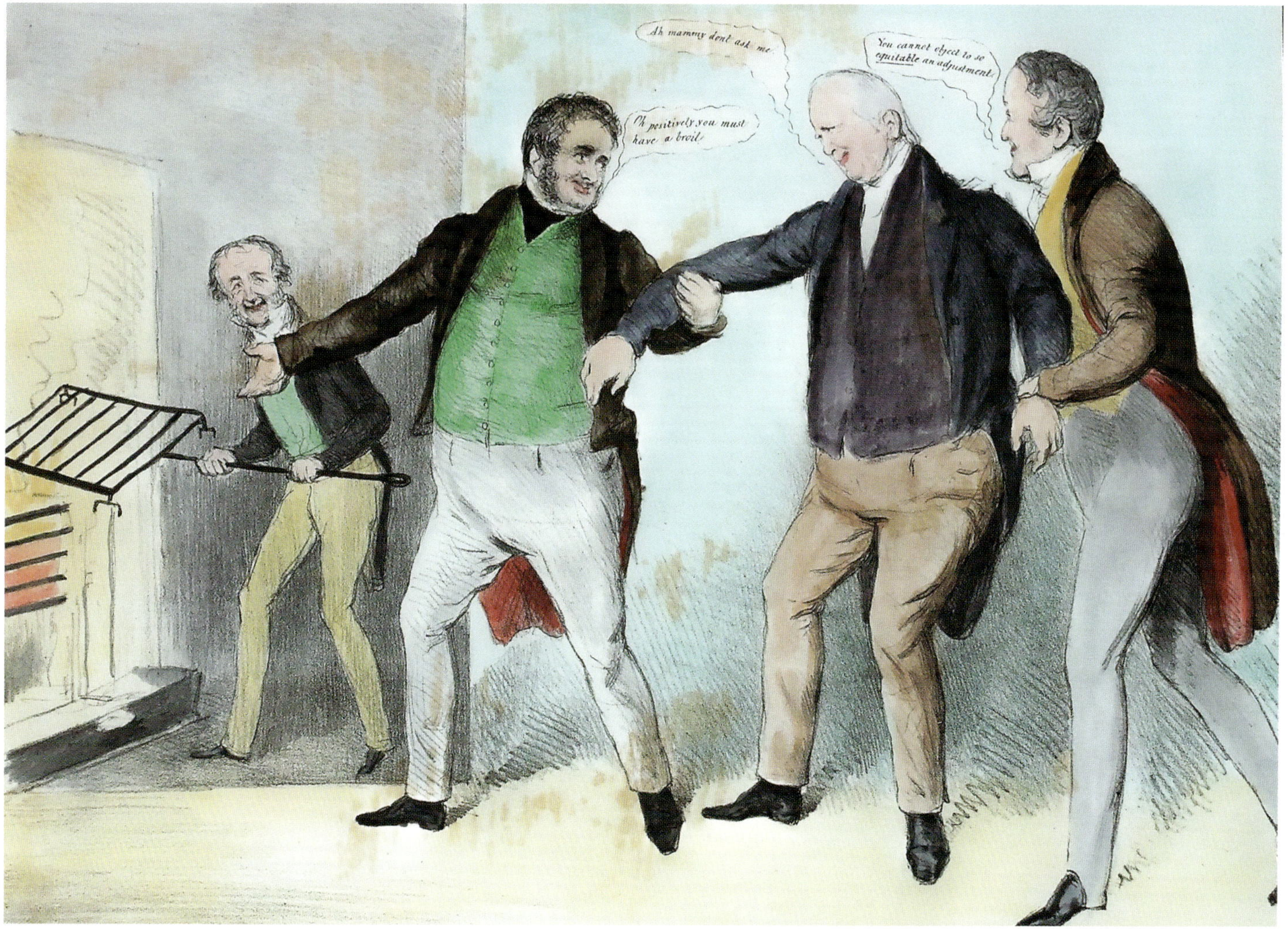

[29] ***No. 284, 'The Gridiron' (published 28 Aug. 1833)*** Two men (Lord Althorp to left, Sir Robert Peel to right) leading a third man (William Cobbett) by the arm towards a fireplace to left; a man standing next to the fireplace, holding a gridiron (Thomas Spring Rice). Mr. Cobbett, in his *Register*, emphatically declared, and often repeated the declaration, that so convinced was he of the impossibility of returning to cash payments, that he would pledge himself to suffer the punishment of being broiled on a gridiron if it should ever be effected; and, in commemoration of this pledge, he adopted the sign of a gridiron as a distinction for his *Register*; on every number of which it was to be seen for several years. His opponents contended that what he had deemed impossible was actually accomplished, and, therefore, he ought to go and be broiled: but Cobbett always maintained that there were qualifications in his prediction which exempted him, and many were convinced that he was right. Here, Lord Althorp is offering to hand Mr. Cobbett 'not where he is to eat, but where he is to be eaten', in the style of a gentleman handing a lady to her seat at dinner, and his soft persuasive eloquence seems well seconded by Sir Robert Peel behind, while Mr. Spring Rice, with a mouth that seems to water with a relish of the joke, is placing on the fire the primitive piece of culinary furniture on which the author of the *Weekly Register* had voluntarily offered to sacrifice himself. But it is clear that Mr. Cobbett is not willing to be brought to the bar. He delicately begs that he may not be pressed, and repeats the endearing term 'mammy' which he used in a previous sketch.

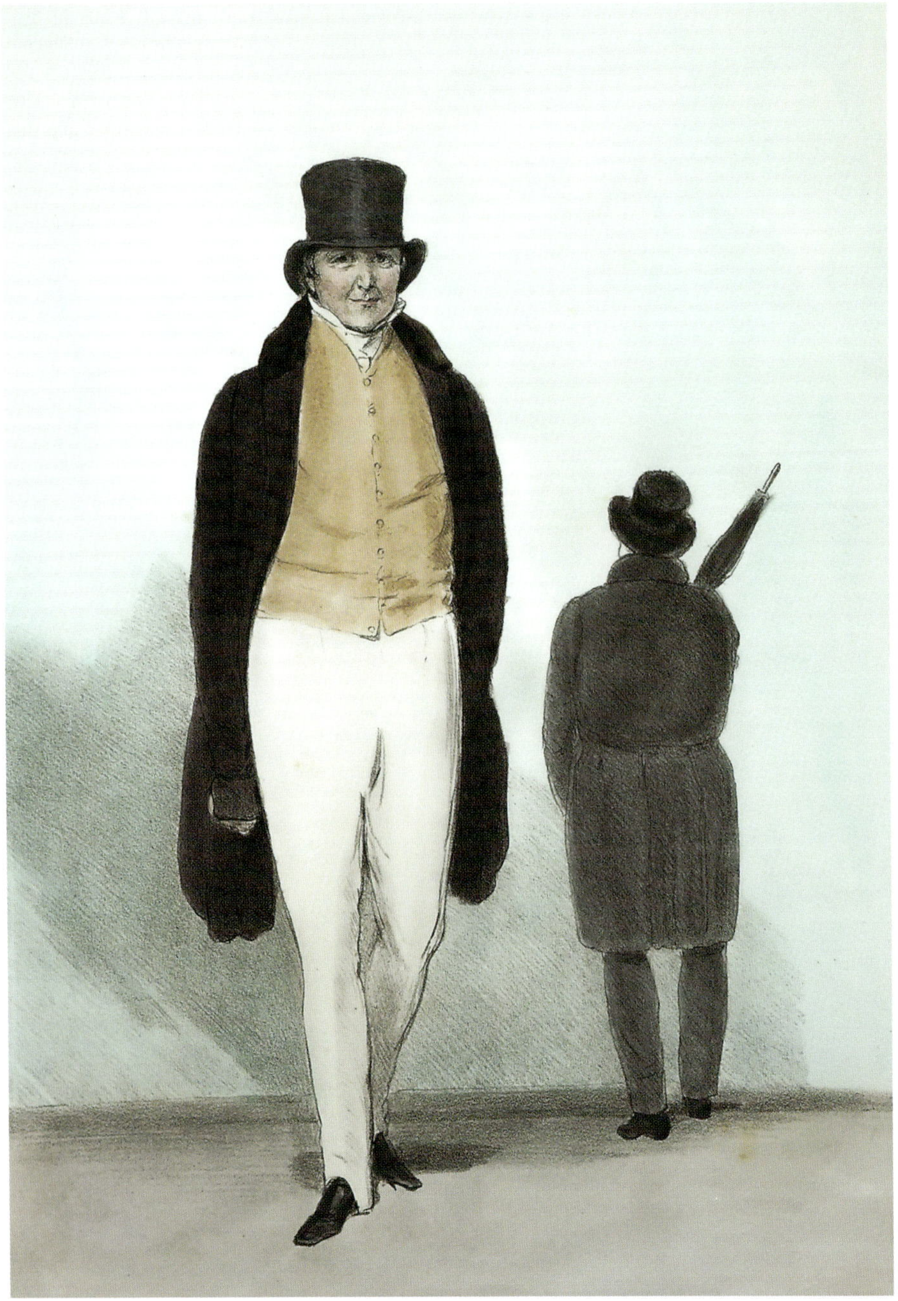

[30] ***No. 290, 'A Peel-er and a Re-pealer' (published 8 Dec. 1833)*** A man (Sir Robert Peel), standing to front with a smile on his face, wearing a top hat, dark open coat, white waistcoat and trousers; another man (Daniel O'Connell) standing in the background on right with his back turned, holding up an umbrella in front of his right shoulder. Sir Robert Peel (obverse) and Mr. O'Connell (reverse). Independently of the play on Sir Robert's name, he being the originator of the Police force, the individuals of which are, in Ireland, commonly called by the name of Peelers, gives authority for applying the same term to himself. Mr. O'Connell owes his title of Repealer to his advocacy of the project of a repeal of the Union between Great Britain and Ireland.

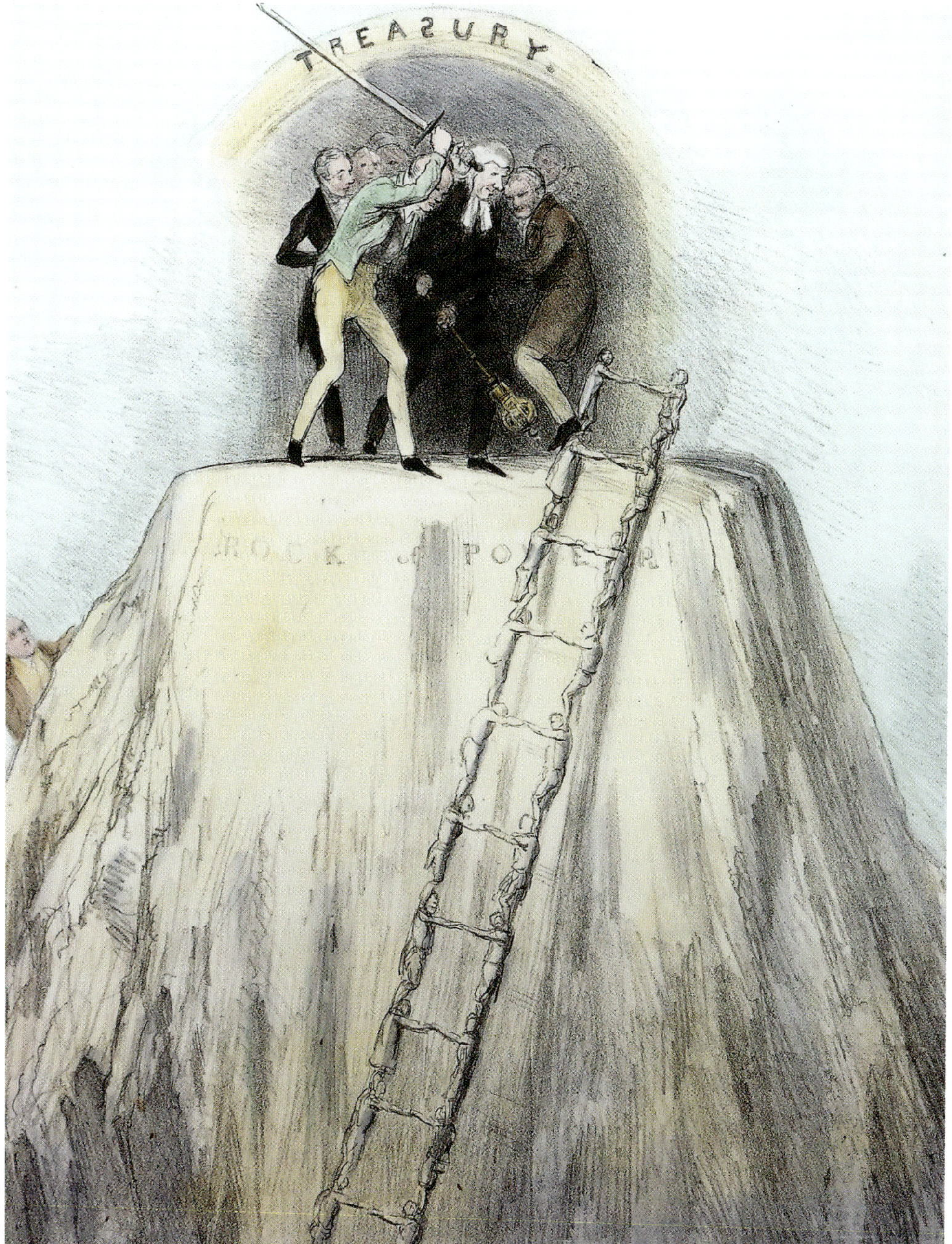

[31] ***No. 315, 'A Vision but no Dream' (published 28 Apr. 1834)*** A group of men standing on top of a rock lettered 'Rock of Power', under an arched entrance lettered 'Treasury'; the man in centre (Sir Robert Peel) attacking with his ceremonial mace a ladder formed by people which has reached the top of the rock, assisted by a man to left, swinging a sword. Based on a text from Henry Fielding, 'One of the maxims which the Devil, in a late visit to earth, left to his disciples, is, when once you are up, to kick the ladder from under you'. The ladder here represented is not Jacob's, for that was beheld in a dream only, but it is a ladder of real flesh and blood, being very ingeniously composed of reformers in pairs, joining hands to form the steps; and up this ladder the ministers, whom we see above, have climbed to the summit of political power. Safely landed there, they are acting upon the advice before mentioned, namely, kicking down the ladder. Lord Grey is using the sword of the Lord-High-Treasurer, and Lord Brougham handles his mace. The figure which peeps round from the left-hand side of the rock is that of Sir Robert Peel.

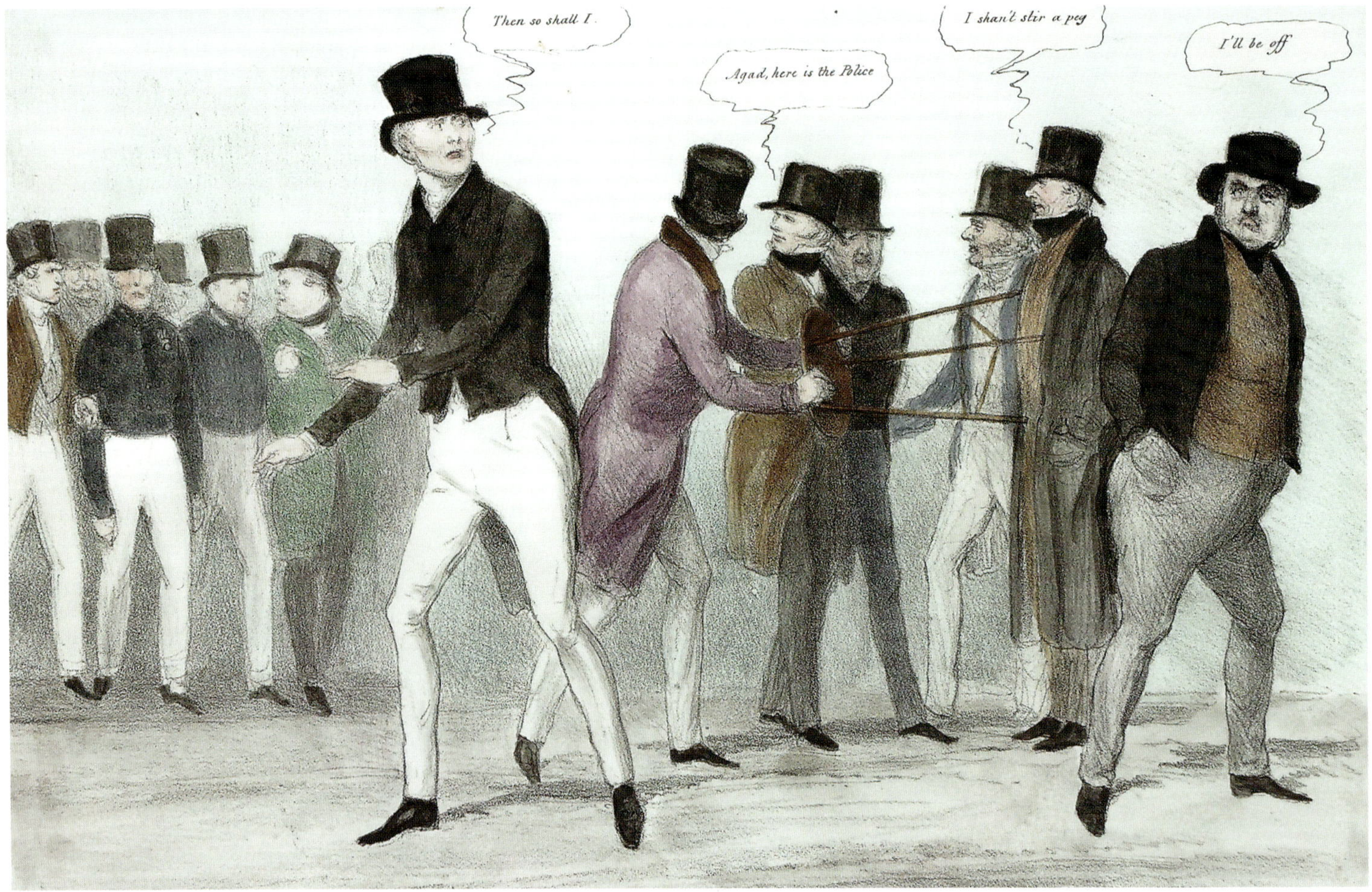

[32] ***No. 330, 'Dispersion of the Thimble Rig' (published 14 July 1834)*** A man in the centre, with his back turned (Edward John Littleton), carrying away a small table with three legs which was used to play the gambling game Thimble Rig (based on similar principles to the card-game 'find the lady'). The thimble-rigger (or confidence trickster, who can always ensure that he wins the game) makes away, after realizing the arrival of the police; next to him stand four fellow gamblers (Lord John Russell, Thomas Spring Rice, Lord Melbourne, Lord Brougham); one man is fleeing the scene to right (Lord Althorp), another to left (Lord Grey); the man in background to far left (Edward Stanley) has brought along the police (Duke of Cumberland, Duke of Wellington, Sir Robert Peel), joined by a man from the mob (Daniel O'Connell). The administration of Lord Grey was broken up within a very short period, a few days only, after the debate in which Mr. Stanley made his Thimble-rig speech. Lord Grey, in communicating to the House of Lords the fact of his having resigned office, stated that in consequence of what had passed in the House of Commons between Mr. Littleton (the Chief Secretary to the Lord Lieutenant of Ireland) and Mr. O'Connell; and also in consequence of other circumstances growing out of those proceedings, Lord Althorp had thought proper to tender his resignation, accompanied by a statement, that his resolution was final and unalterable; and that his own resignation was the unavoidable result of his losing Lord Althorp, whom he described as the right-arm of his Ministry. 'H.B.' has represented Lord Althorp as the first to say 'I'll be off', and Lord Grey as taking his departure for that reason, and exclaiming, 'Then so shall I'. Mr. Littleton is snatching up his table; Lord John Russell is giving the alarm of the approach of the Police; and Mr. Spring Rice is standing close to Lord John Russell. Lord Brougham is made to say, 'I shan't stir a peg' (a comment on his speech in reply to the Duke of Wellington, upon the evening referred to). The gentleman on the left-hand, who is bringing down the police, is Mr. Stanley. The serjeant of the Police, wearing a Waterloo medal, is the Duke of Wellington, and close to him is Sir Robert Peel. Mr. O'Connell comes with them, as one of the mob.

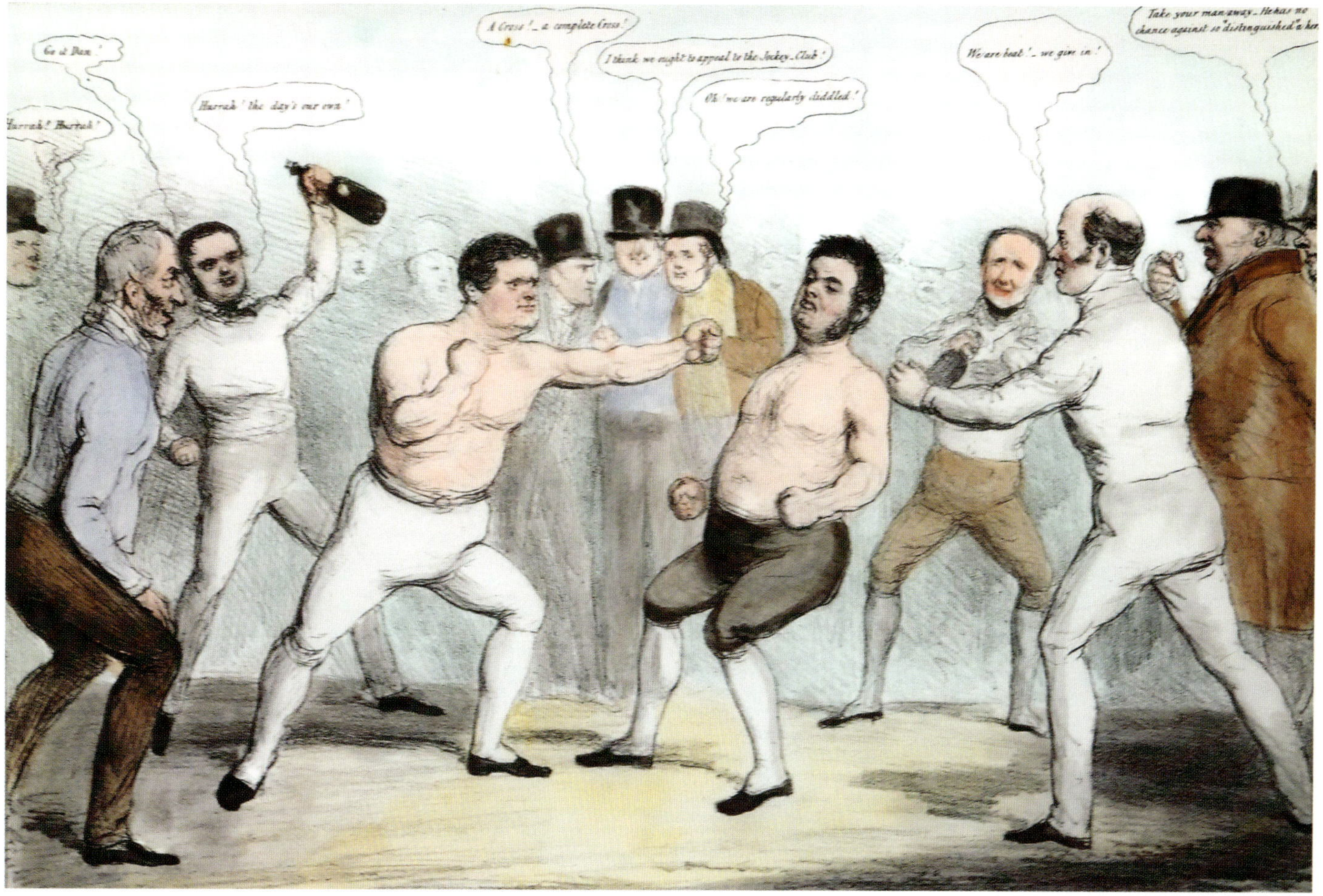

[33] ***No. 338, 'A Fancy Sketch' (published 11 Aug. 1834)*** Two men engaged in a fist-fight in the centre: the one to the left (Daniel O'Connell) punching the other (Lord Althorp); to the left, a man holding up a bottle in his left hand (Richard Lalor Shiel); a man standing to the far left watching in excitement (Edward Southwell Ruthven); behind the loser, two of his supporters (Thomas Spring Rice, Edward John Littleton); to the far right, John Bull holding a watch; behind him the partial profile of a man calling for the loser to be taken away (Lord Brougham); three men standing in centre background, engaged in conversation (Thomas Langlois Lefroy, Sir Robert Peel, Sir Robert Harry Inglis); more spectators watching from the background. Among the professors and admirers of pugilism, the science is frequently mentioned by the delicate term 'The Fancy' and 'a cross' is a term which signifies a fight, in which, though the combatants and their seconds appear to be animated by no other desire than that the best man should win, it is, nevertheless, previously settled which of the two shall win, and how the loser shall appear to yield to superior strength and science, when, in fact, he gives up by collusion and not by collision. The stake for which the Government appeared to be contending was a certain portion of the Irish Tithe Bill, which Mr. Shaw, Mr. Irton, and other opposition-members, alleged that Government did not sincerely support, but voted one way, while they wished and allowed the question to be carried the other. Mr. O'Connell and Lord Althorp, two heavy weights, are the principals; the former, pushing on for victory with a determined look, while the latter drops his arms and pretends to be beaten, though evidently without a scratch. Mr. O'Connell's second is his colleague, Mr. Ruthven; and his bottle-holder, Mr. Shiel. Lord Althorp is waited on by Mr. Littleton and Mr. Spring Rice, the former of whom, in the secret of 'the cross', is crying out 'we are beat; we give in'. The three Conservatives in the middle, Mr. Lefroy, Sir Robert Peel, and Sir Robert Inglis, have discovered the trick, and confess themselves taken in. John Bull holds his watch, as umpire of the fight, and Lord Brougham, coming in from behind, as if he were a disinterested spectator, assists the deception, by begging that the beaten man may be taken away.

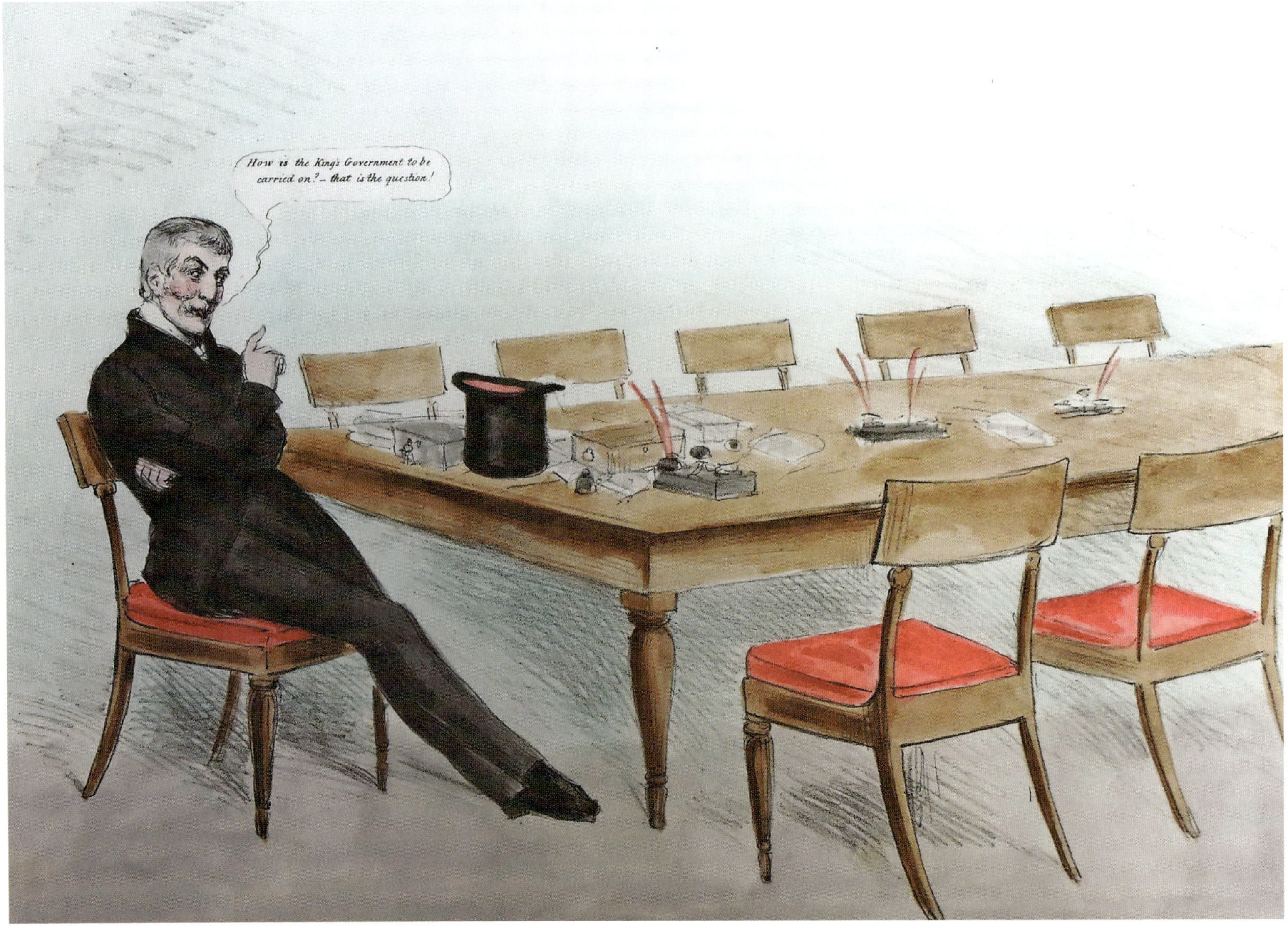

[34] ***No. 355, 'A Cabinet Council' (published 28 Nov. 1834)*** A man seated on a chair on left, at the end of a long table with seven empty chairs, speaking, as if he was addressing a meeting (Duke of Wellington). During the discussions on the Reform Bill, the Duke of Wellington descanted, with great force, on the inconveniences which must arise in the practical working of the business of government, when the minister should have lost his influence over the House of Commons, which his Grace contended would be the consequence of destroying the nomination boroughs; and in the course of one of his speeches on this subject, he very emphatically put the question, 'How is the King's government to be carried on?'. Being now, himself, the Ministry (for between the dissolution of the Melbourne Cabinet, and the return of Sir Robert Peel to England, the Duke was said to represent, in his own person, all the principal offices of state), he is placed by 'H.B.' alone at the council board, asking himself the same very pertinent and difficult question, 'How is the King's government to be carried on?'. The empty chairs, placed in order round the table, have a very ludicrous effect.

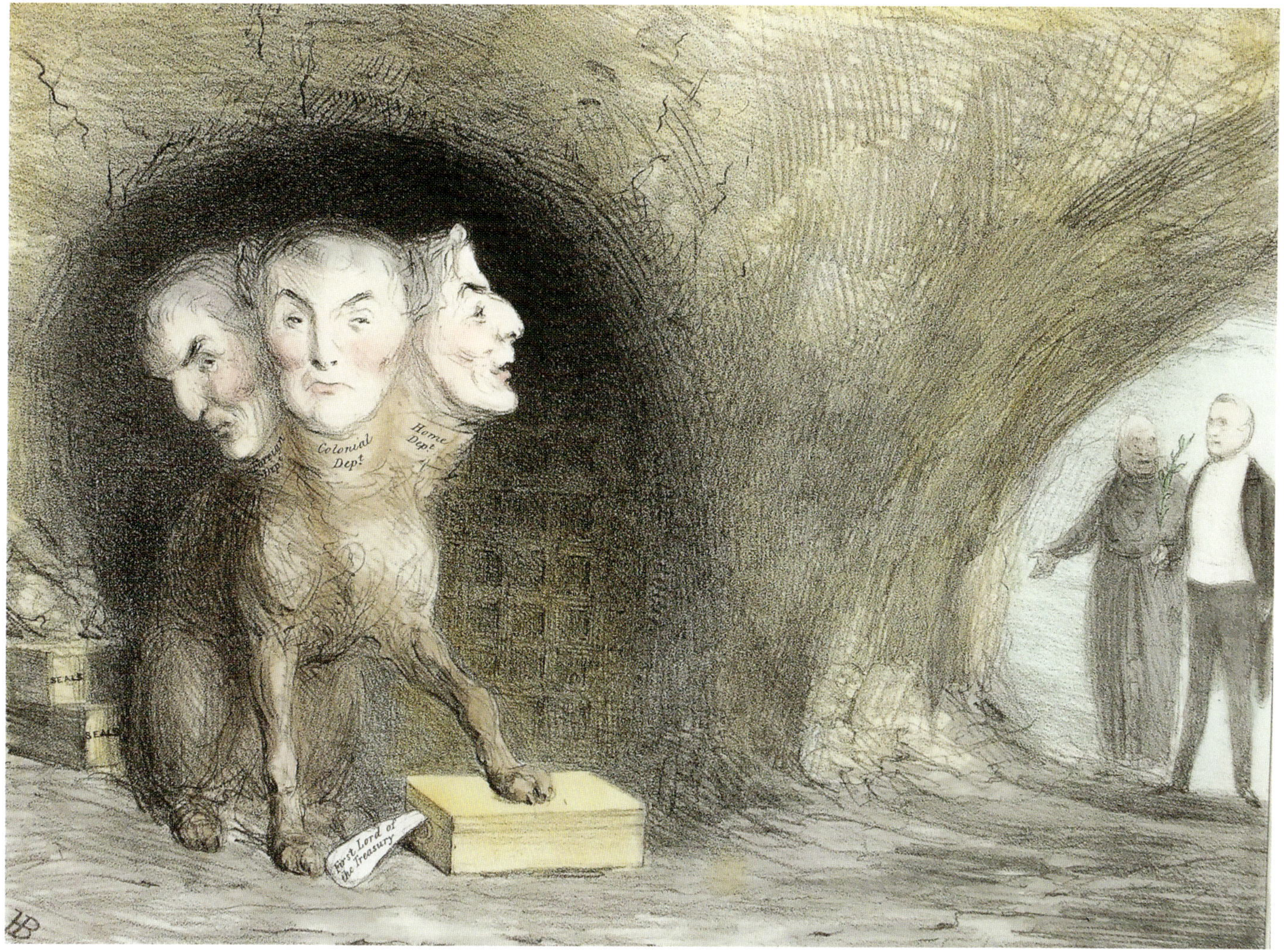

[35] ***No. 360, 'The state Cerberus' (published 11 Dec. 1834)*** In a cave, Cerberus (the mythological three-headed dog which guarded the gates of the underworld), with heads of a man (Duke of Wellington), wearing collars lettered with 'Foreign Dept.', Colonial Dept.' and 'Home Dept.', seated on the ground in front of two boxes lettered with 'Seals', with his left foreleg on a wooden box lettered with 'First Lord of the Treasury'; one of his heads, in profile to right, looking towards the entrance of the cave, from where approach a man in the character of Æneas (Sir Robert Peel) and a man dressed as a woman, in the character of Sibyl (King William IV). After the dissolution of the Melbourne cabinet, Sir Robert Peel, to whom the King intended to assign the task of forming a Ministry, being abroad, the Duke of Wellington undertook to carry on the public business until Sir Robert's return to England; and, for that purpose, held (as it was said) the seals of the three great offices of the Secretaries of State. In this sketch, therefore, 'H.B.' has drawn him as a political Cerberus guarding the seals of office. The reader will not fail to observe, that he lays his paw on a box, which is labelled 'First Lord of the Treasury'; from which it might be inferred that he intended to hold this appointment himself; but this was not the case, Sir Robert Peel having received the appointment immediately on his return. Sir Robert is enacting pious Æneas (a heroic figure in Greek and Roman mythology), and entering the infernal regions under the guidance of William IV in the character of the Sybil (or prophetess).

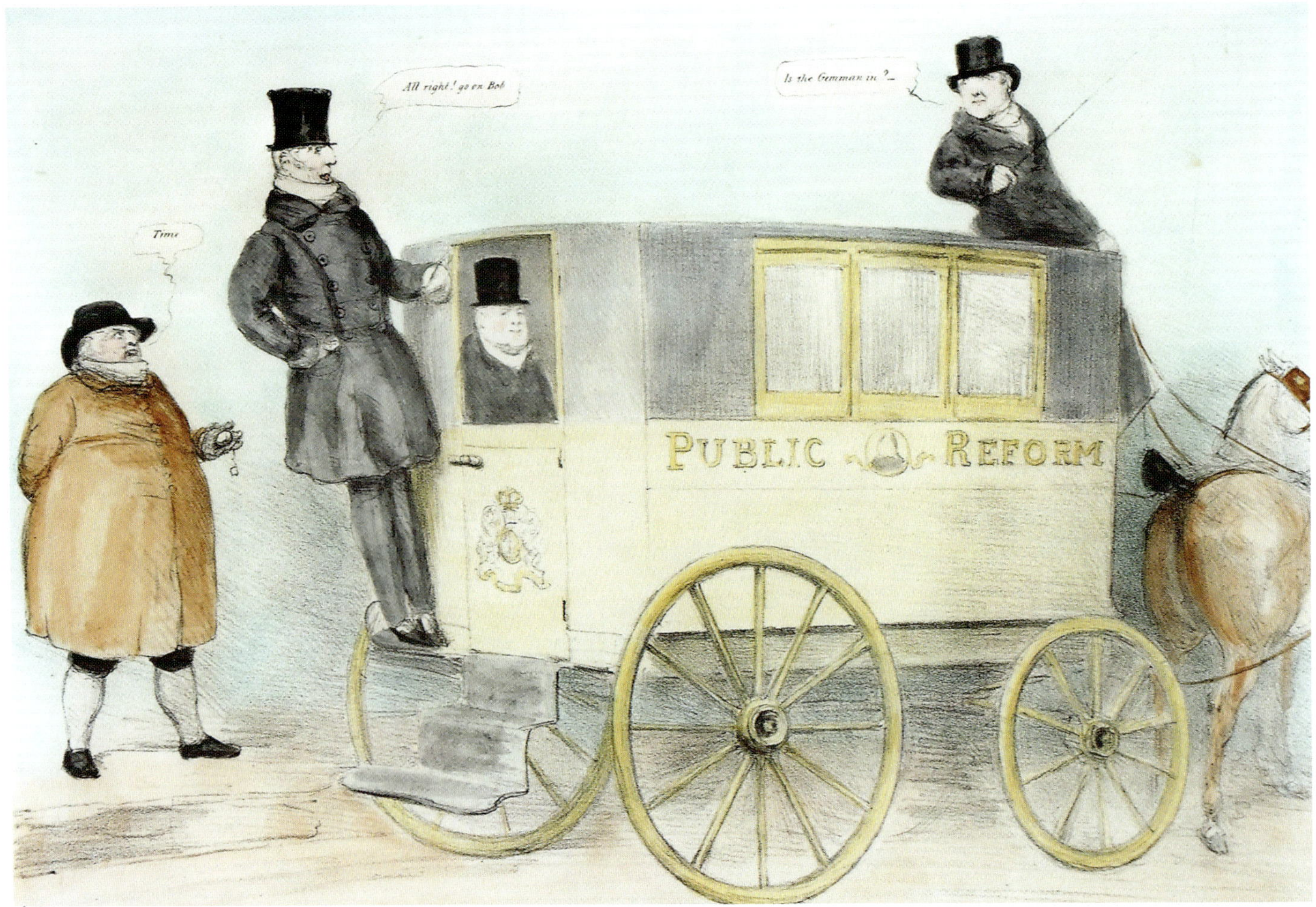

[36] ***No. 363, 'The State Omnibus' (published 24 Dec. 1834)*** An omnibus, lettered on its side with 'Public Reform', drawn by two horses from left to right, with one man seated inside (King William IV), and another travelling on the step outside to left, holding on to a handle (Duke of Wellington); driven by a coachman, holding the reins in his left hand and a whip in his right hand, with his head turned slightly to left, looking back (Sir Robert Peel); to far left, a man standing with his right arm behind his back, holding a watch in his left hand (John Bull). Sir Robert Peel is now mounted in his seat, and has the reins in his hands, but his start seems not to be a very promising one; for, except for his gracious master, the proprietor of the concern, he has not a single passenger. John Bull, in the character of a time-keeper, with watch in hand, admonishes him to set off; and when it is considered how long the public had waited, first, for Sir Robert's return from abroad, and afterwards for his completing his ministerial arrangements, it can hardly be said that John Bull is too quick upon him. His chief dependence, for the success of the undertaking, seems to be upon the Duke of Wellington, who is serving in the very arduous and useful office of his conductor or cad. 'H.B.' thus revives an image pioneered in William Heath's representation of the Wellington government in 1828–1829; 1st. The Man wot drives the Sovereign, viz., the Duke of Wellington, then Prime-Minister to George IV, as a coachman. 2nd. The Guard wot looks after the Sovereign; viz. the Marchioness of Conyngham, in the dress of a mail-coach guard. 3rd. The Cad to the Man wot drives the Sovereign; viz., Sir Robert Peel, then Leader of the House of Commons, in the character of a cad; and 4th. The great Swell wot drives whenever he likes; viz., George IV., in the dress of a coachman of a superior order. It is with reference to these prints, that the Duke, in the present sketch, is called 'The Man wot is Cad to the Man wot was Cad to the Man wot drove the Sovereign'.

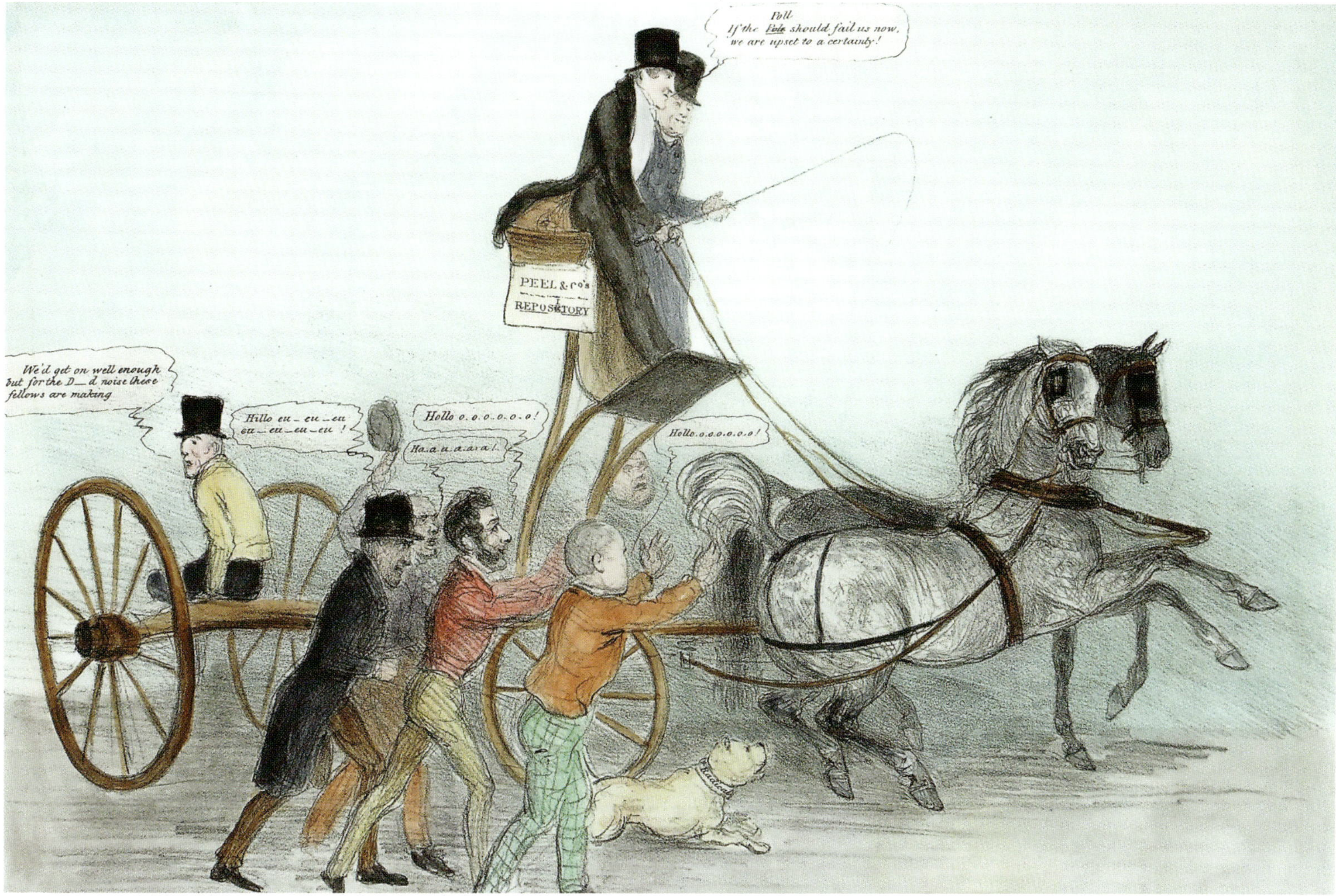

[37] ***No. 365, 'Breaking in the Reform Colt, Or Symptoms of Restiveness' (published 7 Jan. 1835)*** A coach lettered with 'Peel & Co's Reposetory [the second 'e' crossed out, replaced with 'i']', drawn by two horses along a road from left towards right; the coachman standing on a high platform, holding the reins and whip (Sir Robert Peel); a man standing next to him (King William IV); a man seated on the axle-tree to far left (Duke of Wellington); a dog wearing a collar lettered with 'Radical' running along the side of the coach, followed by four shouting men (Joseph Hume, Thomas Slingsby Duncombe, Daniel Whittle Harvey, Stephen Lushington). The King, as the proprietor of the concern, of which Sir Robert Peel is the driver, sits at his side, and the Duke of Wellington, like the old hostler and chief manager of the stable, sits on the axle-tree behind, ready to put to rights whatever may happen to get out of its place. The horses (His Majesty's liege subjects, over-fed with promises of reform, and hopes of improvement) are evidently unmanageable, and their natural skittishness is mightily aggravated by the shouting of a group of the stable-men and drivers, whom the proprietor has recently discarded to make way for his new coachman. Referring to the approaching general election, the driver observes, that everything depends on the poll; and that, should it fail, they must be upset to a certainty. The ragamuffins, following and shouting, are Mr. Hume, then M.P. for Middlesex (in the plaid brogues), Mr. Thomas S. Duncombe, M.P. for Finsbury; Mr. D. W. Harvey, late M.P. for Southwark; and Dr. Lushington, M.P. for the Tower Hamlets.

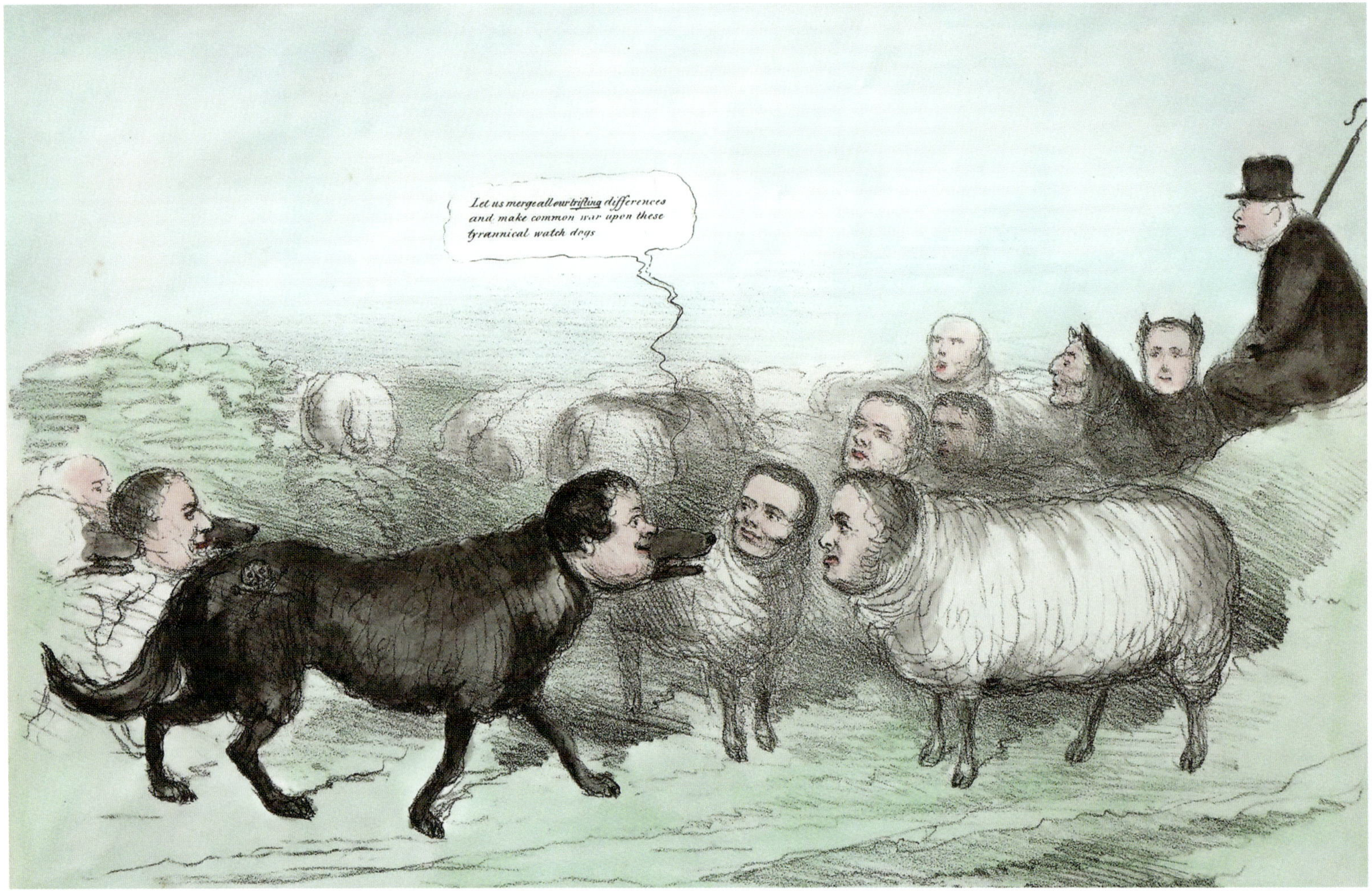

[38] ***No. 367, 'Coalition' (published 18 Jan. 1835)*** A scene with animals with men's faces; a shepherd seated on a rock to right (William IV); in front of him, two sheepdogs (Sir Robert Peel to right, the Duke of Wellington to left); in foreground to right, a large sheep (Lord Spencer, formerly Viscount Althorp) engaged in conversation with a wolf approaching from left (Daniel O'Connell); between them, a small sheep looking at the wolf (Lord John Russell); behind to the right, three sheep watching the scene (Lords Melbourne, Durham and Grey); another wolf to far left (Joseph Hume). A satire based on the fable of the wolves who proposed to the sheep to merge their own trifling differences, for the purpose of making common war upon the watch-dogs. Here the fable satirises the coalition against Peel's government formulated between the Whigs and Radicals (formalised in Feb. 1835 in the so-called 'Lichfield House compact'). King William IV is the good old shepherd and the two faithful animals at his feet, ever watchful over his flock, are the Duke of Wellington and Sir Robert Peel. The fat sheep in the foreground, in conference with one of the wolves (whom, by the mark of Death's head and cross-bones, we know to be Mr. O'Connell), is Earl Spencer; and that smaller animal, who looks up in the face of the ruthless ravager, is Lord John Russell. Immediately behind them, and listening to the terms of the treaty, though taking no ostensible part in it, is Lord Melbourne; behind him, with a look that seems to show very little personal interest in the matter, is Lord Durham; and, quite in the background is Lord Grey. The conference is managed by the wolf already described; but he is backed by another, a Scotch variety of the species, whose countenance strongly resembles that of Mr. Joseph Hume, then member for Middlesex.

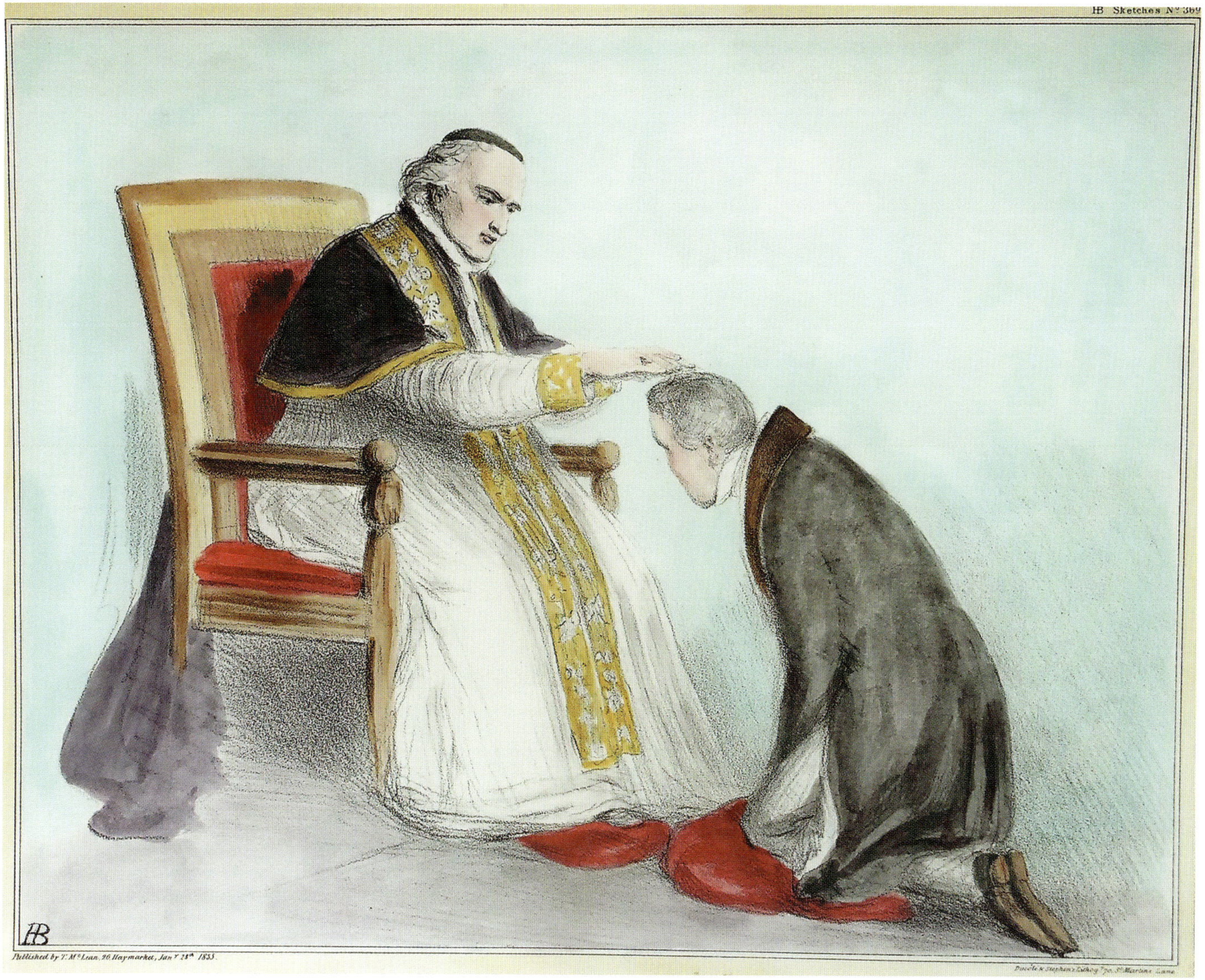

[39] ***No. 369, 'Absolution' (published 28 Jan. 1835)*** A pope seated in an armchair on left, touching with his right hand the head of a man, kneeling in front of him on right (Sir Robert Peel). It was at Rome that the messenger Hudson found Sir Robert Peel, bringing him the commission to become Prime Minister. Peel took a respectful leave of the Pope, and set off in obedience to his Sovereign's commands. This sketch represents Sir Robert Peel in the act of taking leave of the Pope, but 'H.B.' has taken a poet's license with the fact, and made his representation retrospective. Sir Robert Peel was, for a long series of years, the great champion of the Protestant cause; and, in that character, steadily, ardently, and resolutely opposed the bill for granting Catholic Emancipation. But having, at length, brought forward a bill for granting emancipation, and succeeded in carrying it into a law (1829), it may be imagined that Peel had merited absolution and, being at Rome, he is receiving it (by the favour of 'H.B.') at the hands of the Sovereign Pontiff, Gregory XVI.

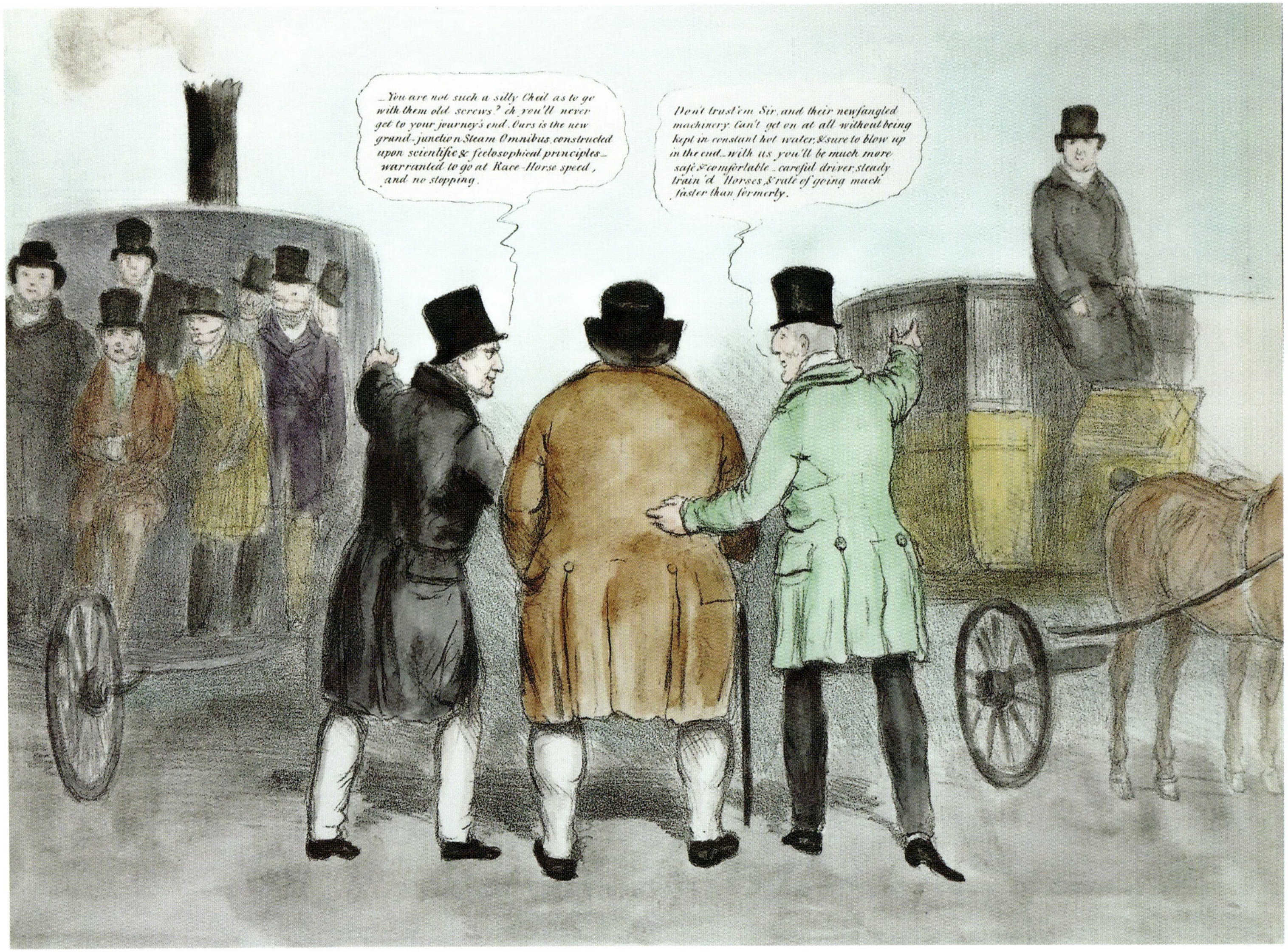

[40] ***No. 370, 'The Hopposition Buses' (published 28 Jan. 1835)*** Three men in centre; the one to the left (Joseph Hume) and the one to the right (Duke of Wellington) trying to persuade John Bull, in the middle, to embark on two different stage-coaches; the horse-drawn coach, to right, is driven by a man (Sir Robert Peel) and no passengers can be seen; there are six men standing and seated on the steam-driven coach, to left (Daniel O'Connell, Lord Melbourne, Lord John Russell, Thomas Spring Rice, Lord Palmerston). The Duke of Wellington on the right, and Mr. Joseph Hume on the left, are making their separate attempts to get John Bull as a passenger into their respective carriages; the Duke's is an old-fashioned stage-coach-looking concern, drawn by horses, of which Sir Robert Peel is the driver; the other is a nondescript vehicle, of which steam seems to be the moving power, and in the front may be recognized the figures of Mr. O'Connell, Lord Melbourne, Lord J. Russell, Mr. Spring Rice, and Lord Palmerston. Whether they are conductors, managers, or passengers, it is not easy to determine, or if managers, who is the chief.

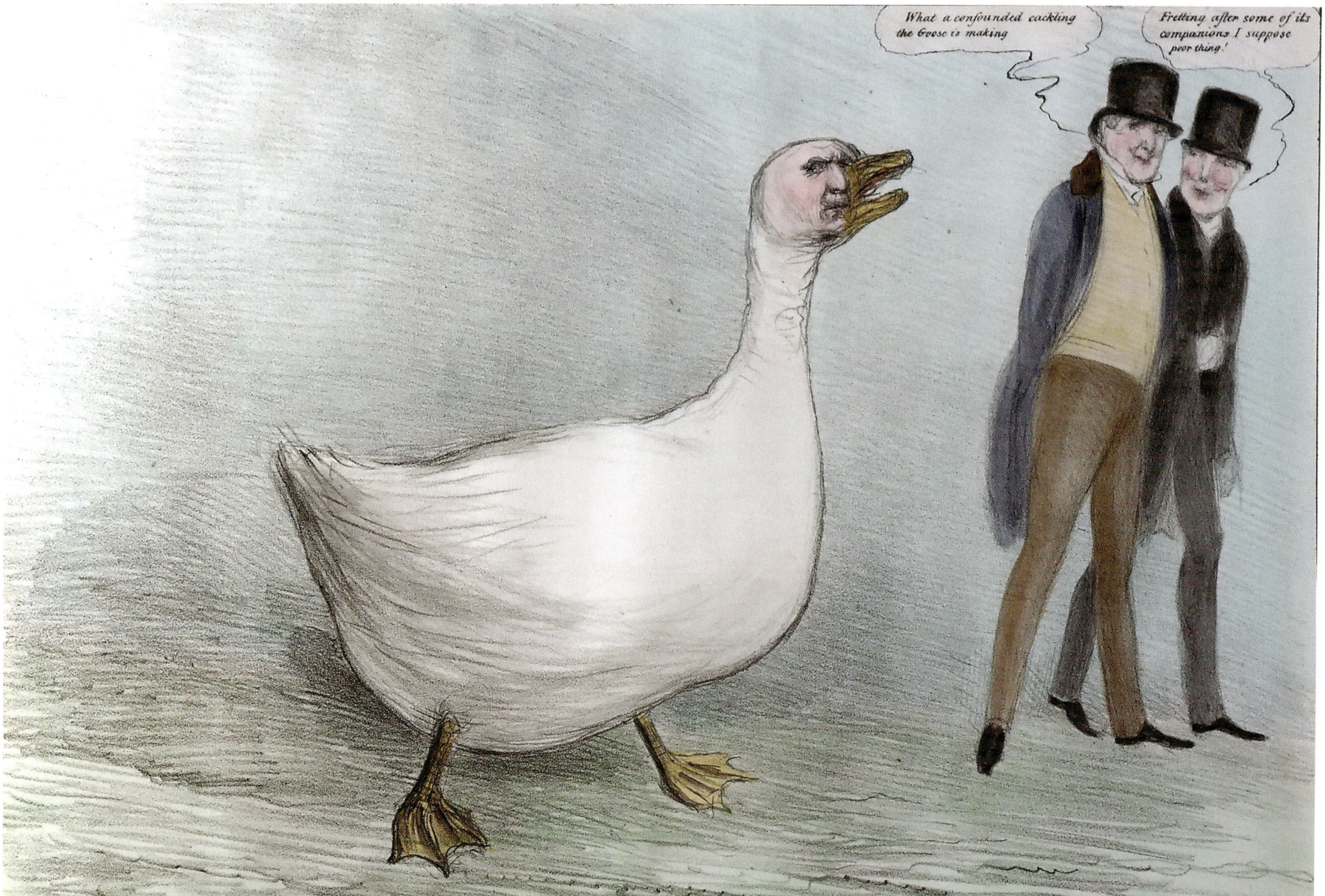

[41] ***No. 371, 'The Goose of the Capitol' (published 26 Jan. 1835)*** A large white goose, with the face of a man (Joseph Hume), standing at the centre, cackling; to right, two men wearing top hats (Sir Robert Peel to the left, the Duke of Wellington to the right), turning back towards the goose in surprise. Joseph Hume (whose countenance is worn by the goose), in one of his harangues to the electors of Middlesex, reminded them, with reference to some former speech which he had delivered, that the cackling of a goose had saved the capitol of Rome. Sir Robert Peel and the Duke of Wellington are the two persons who seem surprized at the cackling of the goose; perhaps they are intended for two of the Gauls, whom the goose is scaring away.

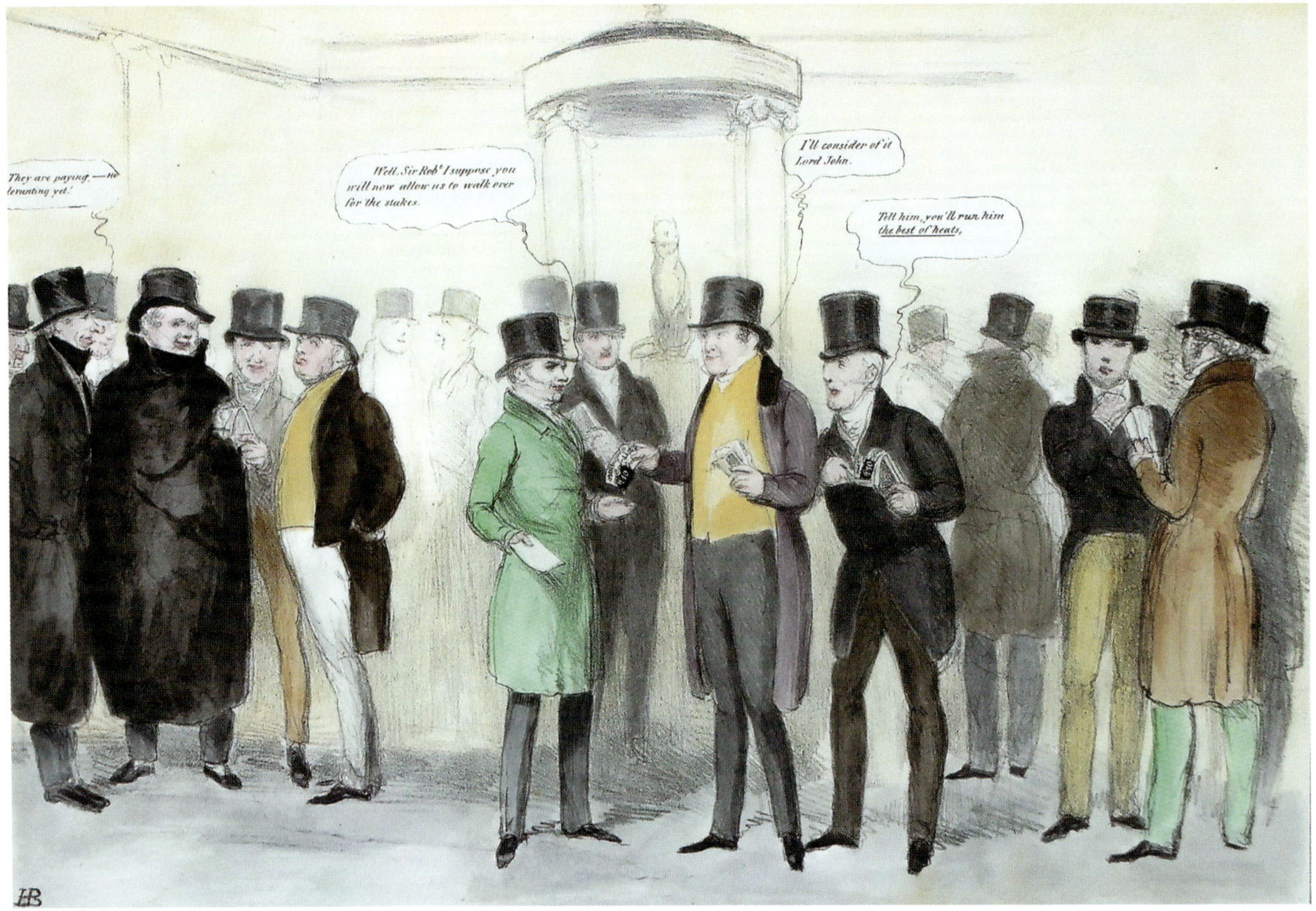

[42] ***No. 377, 'Settling Day at Tattersall's' (published 5 Mar. 1835)*** A scene at Tattersall's (the auctioneers of race-horses) at Hyde Park Corner; in front of the domed structure with the sculpture of a kangaroo in the centre, a man standing in foreground to right (Sir Robert Peel), handing over a £10 note to the man standing to left (Lord John Russell), observed by a man to the right, pointing to a £10 note held in his left hand (the Duke of Wellington), and a man in the background behind the group (Lord Stanley); to the far right, two men engaged in conversation (Lords Aberdeen and Ellenborough); to the left, a group of men engaged in conversation (Joseph Hume, Lord Brougham, Daniel O'Connell, Thomas Spring Rice, Lord Spencer); two men standing in the background behind them (William Cobbett and Francis Burdett). The Duke of Cumberland's back can be seen behind Lord Aberdeen. The division on the choice of a Speaker was the first assault on the Peel ministry. The race for the majority was run between the Conservatives and the united Whigs and Radicals, and the Conservatives were beaten. Sir Robert, as the loser, is handing over a £10 note (the number of the majority was ten) to Lord John Russell, who shrewdly suggests that, after this trial of strength, Sir Robert may as well let him walk over the course, and take quiet possession of the stakes; that is to say, of the government. Sir Robert promises to consider the proposal; and the Duke of Wellington endeavours to avert the loss that is sure to follow the placing of everything upon a single point, and proposes to run him the best of heats. Lord John is much too knowing for this. The parties most immediately interested in the race for political power are disposed in the fore-ground on either side of the room. Behind Sir Robert Peel and the Duke of Wellington are Lord Aberdeen and Lord Ellenborough, and behind Lord John Russell are Lord Spencer (with his hands in his coat-pockets), Mr. O'Connell (in his cloak), and Lord Brougham (great-coated and neck-clothed up to his chin). Mr. Joseph Hume is peeping over Lord Brougham's shoulder; and between Mr. O'Connell and Lord Spencer appears the ever-smiling countenance of Mr. Spring Rice. In the back-ground are Mr. Cobbett and Sir F. Burdett, but it is no settling-day with them. Near to Lord John, but at some distance behind, as if the affair did not immediately concern him, is Lord Stanley, to whom Sir Robert Peel had made overtures to join his Ministry, without success.

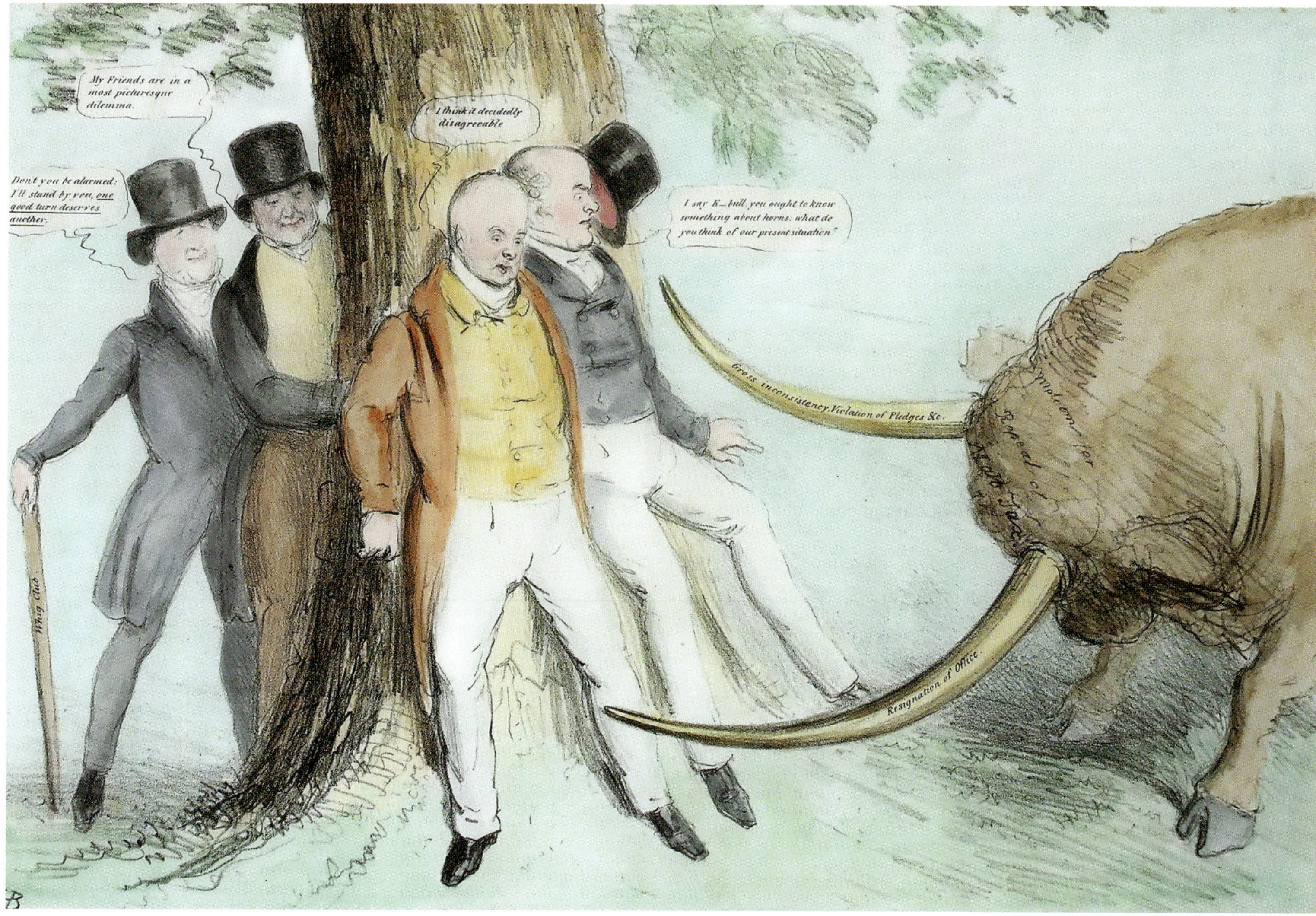

[43] ***No. 380, 'A Rural Subject' (published 16 Mar. 1835)*** Two men standing with their backs against a tree (Sir Edward Knatchbull and Alexander Baring), retreating from a bull charging from the right (representing Lord Chandos), its right horn lettered with 'Gross inconsistency, Violation of Pledges &c.', left horn with 'Resignation of Office.', and head with 'Repeal of Malt Tax'; two bemused men watching the scene from behind the tree (Thomas Spring Rice and Sir Robert Peel), the one to left holding a club lettered with 'Whig Club.'. Sir Edward Knatchbull and Mr. Baring (afterwards Lord Ashburton), being considered as representatives of the landed interest, were expected, by their constituents, to vote for the repeal of the malt-tax; but, as members of Sir Robert Peel's administration, they stood in a new position, and felt the necessity of opposing the repeal of any and every tax whatever; notwithstanding which, the Marquess of Chandos, charging the Ministry like a wild bull, with his motion for the repeal, placed the two gentlemen in the disagreeable situation of having to choose between forfeiting their places, or disappointing the expectation, and incurring the disapprobation of their constituents. Sir Robert Peel, without such a pledge, or a rural constituency, evinces much more complacency than might be expected on the occasion, were he not certain of the votes of the late Ministry. As Spring Rice intimates, the ex-government intends to support him by opposing the motion.

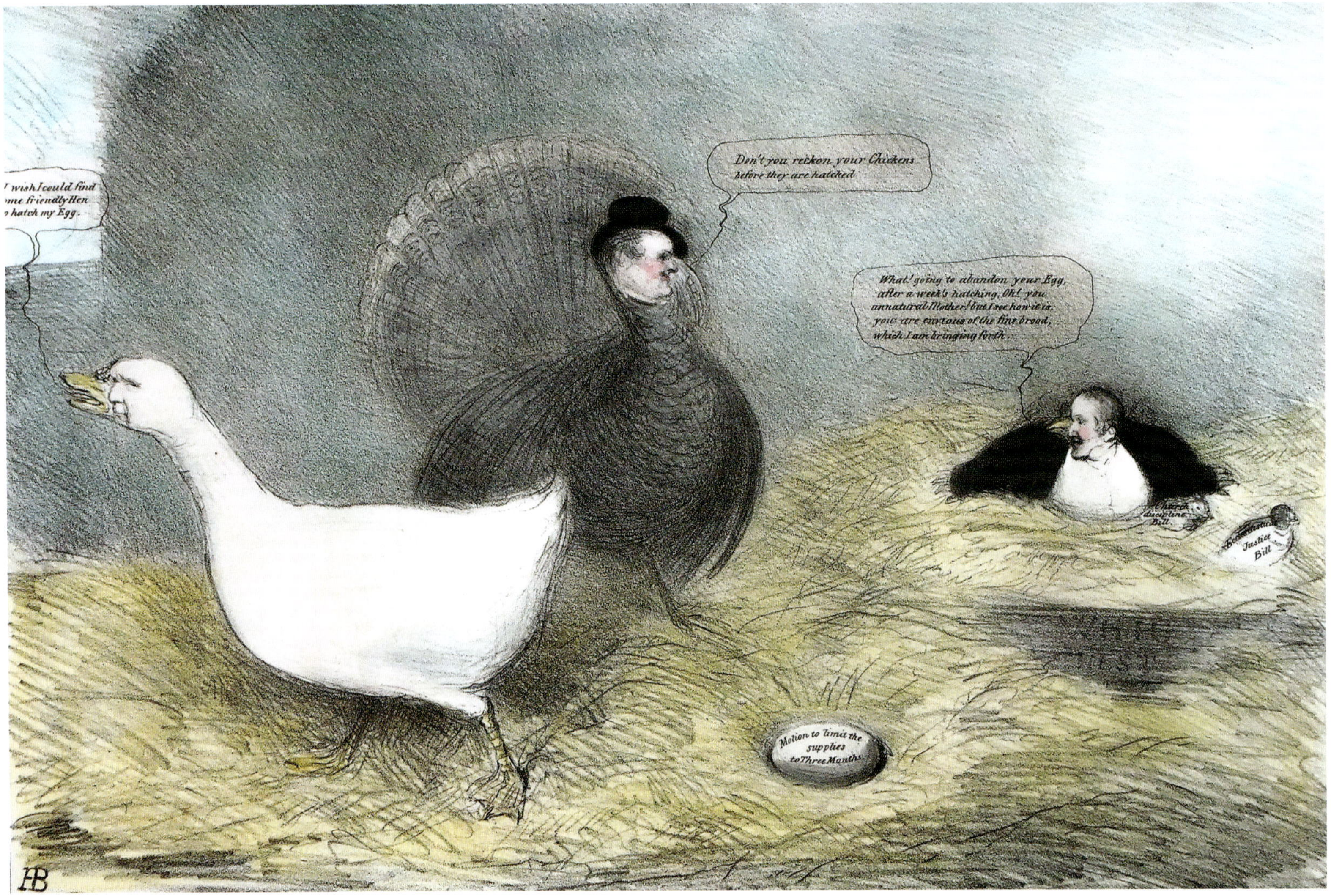

[44] ***No. 381, 'Incubation Extraordinary' (published 17 Mar. 1835)*** Scene involving farm animals with men's heads; on straw, a turkey standing in the centre (Daniel O'Connell), interfering with a hen hatching her eggs, to the right (Sir Robert Peel); two chicks, lettered with 'Church discipline Bill.' and Ecclesiastical Justice Bill', lying on straw to the right; a large egg, lettered with 'Motion to limit the supplies to Three Months.', lying in the foreground, abandoned by a goose, running away to the left (Joseph Hume). Sir Robert Peel is sitting in the 'Whig nest', and upon the Whig eggs, that is to say, measures that were in embryo when the Whigs were turned out of office. His hopes of hatching them seem likely to be blighted, by the mischievous interposition of the great turkey-cock, Mr. O'Connell. Mr. Hume, as the Middlesex goose, has laid a solitary egg, in the shape of a notice of a motion to limit the supplies to three months, a modification of the threatened motion of the Attorney-General, who talked of stopping the supplies altogether. But the goose has abandoned her egg, finding no probability of her being able to raise warmth enough to hatch it. When it is recollected how suddenly the former occupiers of the nest were driven away, and how long a time the eggs had to cool before Sir Robert returned to supply their place, it will not seem surprizing that they were all addled. On 12 Mar., Mr. Hume, then member for Middlesex, in a debate on the Ecclesiastical Courts Bill, said, 'The Right Honourable Baronet has asked me whether the introduction of this bill was

[44] ***No. 381*** (continued)

one of the reasons which have induced me to alter the course I originally intended to pursue with regard to the supplies. My answer is, that in changing that intention, the measure under consideration never, for a moment, entered into my contemplation. It would seem that the Right Honourable Baronet assumes great merit for the introduction of this bill. The fact is, however, that the Right Honourable Baronet has merely crept into the nest of the old administration – that he is now hatching one of their eggs'. To this Sir Robert Peel replied, – 'The Honourable Gentleman has talked of hatching eggs – Why, the Honourable Gentleman himself has laid an egg in this House which it seems that neither he himself, nor any of his friends, can hatch. What has become of the egg which the Honourable Gentleman laid last week? Last night the Honourable Gentleman stated it to be a matter of doubt, whether he or some other friendly hen would sit upon it; but to-night, it appears, that, notwithstanding the incubation, all attempt to bring forth the chicken is to be abandoned'. Mr. O'Connell remarked 'The Right Honourable Baronet should not count his own chickens before they are hatched, for he will probably find the chicken of my Honourable Friend, the member for Middlesex, a good fighting-cock yet'. Four days later, in the course of a discussion on the intention of Government to send the Marquess of Londonderry upon an embassy to St. Petersburgh, said, 'The Right Honourable Baronet, with his cuckoo-note of "a fair trial," is the reverse of the cuckoo in his habits; for instead of laying his eggs in other birds' nests for them to hatch, he hops into other birds' nests himself, and hatching their eggs, takes credit for a most goodly brood of reform chickens'.

[45] ***No. 382, 'A Study for a Damocles' (published 24 Mar. 1835)*** A man seated on a bench in three-quarter profile to right, next to an open box filled with papers (Sir Robert Peel), looking up at a sword hanging above him, lettered with 'Adverse Majority', held on a thread by three men among clouds in the sky (from left to right, Lord Stanley, Lord John Russell, Joseph Hume). Damocles was prevailed on by Dionysius to undertake, for a while, the charge of royalty, and be convinced of the happiness which a Sovereign enjoyed. He ascended the throne, and while he gazed upon the wealth and splendour that surrounded him, perceived a sword hanging over his head by a single hair. The sword (bearing the inscription of 'adverse majority') suspended over the head of Sir Robert Peel, is held by Lord Stanley, Lord John Russell, and Mr. Hume, as the leaders of the three parties, two of which, namely, the ex-Ministers and the Radicals, were decidedly and actively hostile, and the third, or Stanley party, not, at that time, friendly. It is evident that the three persons above-mentioned had it in their power, by uniting their forces, at any time to put an end to the Government of Sir Robert Peel.

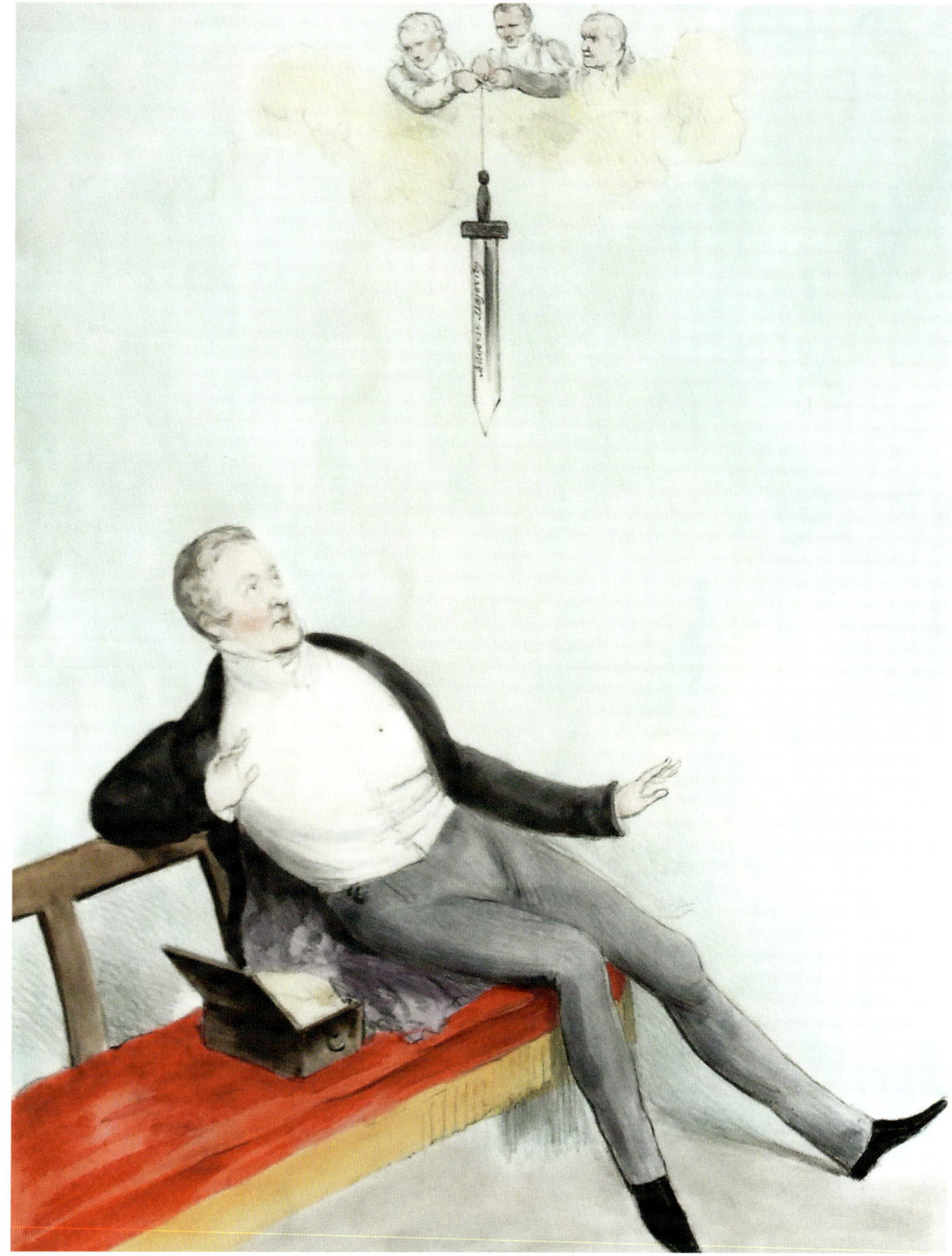

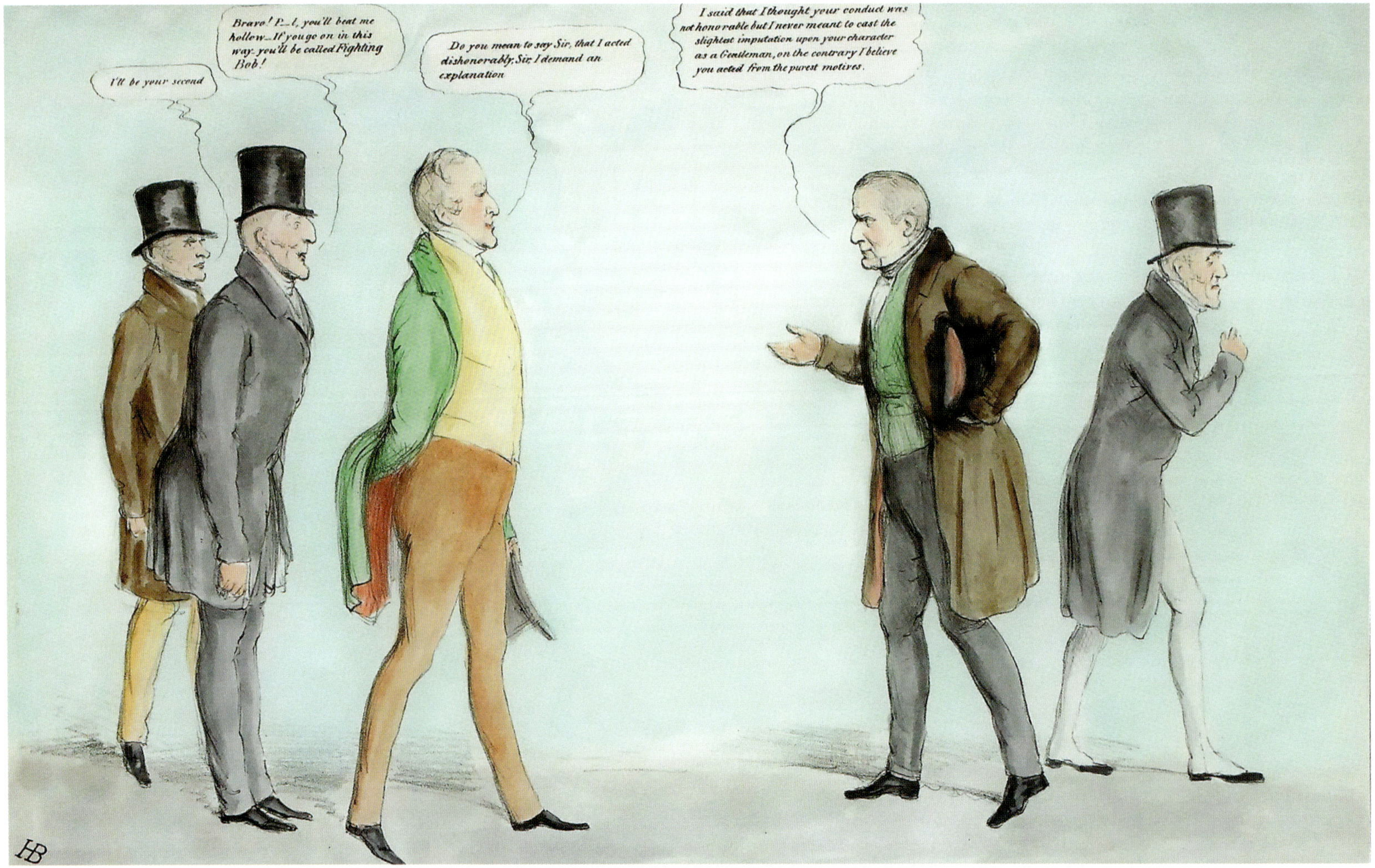

[46] ***No. 384, 'A nice distinction, or a Hume-iliating Rejoinder to a Warlike Ap-Peal' (published 26 Mar. 1835)*** Two men confronting each other (Sir Robert Peel at centre left, Joseph Hume at centre right); two men, standing at left, making remarks (Sir Henry Hardinge and Duke of Wellington); a man to right turning his back to them, silently walking away (Stephen Lushington). In a debate on Sir Henry Hardinge's Irish Tithe Bill, Mr. Hume, alluding to the conduct of Sir Robert Peel with reference to the matter under discussion, said, 'I myself positively could not, consistently with the feelings of a man of honour, have recourse to the bringing in of a measure which had been "Condemned and thrown out of the other House by my friends"'. This expression called up Sir Robert Peel to ask Mr. Hume if he really meant to say that he (Sir Robert) was acting in a manner inconsistent with a man of honour? In the House Mr. Hume did not explain his meaning to Sir Robert Peel's satisfaction, and, therefore, Sir Robert sent him a letter calling on him to disavow the imputation apparently conveyed by the objectionable passage in his speech; to which letter Mr. Hume made the following reply, 'What I intended to say was, that I could not say what your feelings of honour were, but that I, as a political man, should not have considered it honourable conduct if I had so acted. It is, therefore, quite clear in my recollection, that whilst I made my observations in allusion to what I would have done, I did not impugn your honour as a gentleman in the course you had taken'. Sir Robert Peel, followed by the Duke of Wellington and Sir Henry Hardinge, advances with a bold front to demand satisfaction; which Mr. Hume, with his hat under his arm, as he usually disposes of it while addressing the House, is offering with Hume-ility. The gentleman retreating is Dr. Lushington, between whom and Sir Robert Peel a misunderstanding had arisen on a previous night; but, happily, had been explained without bloodshed.

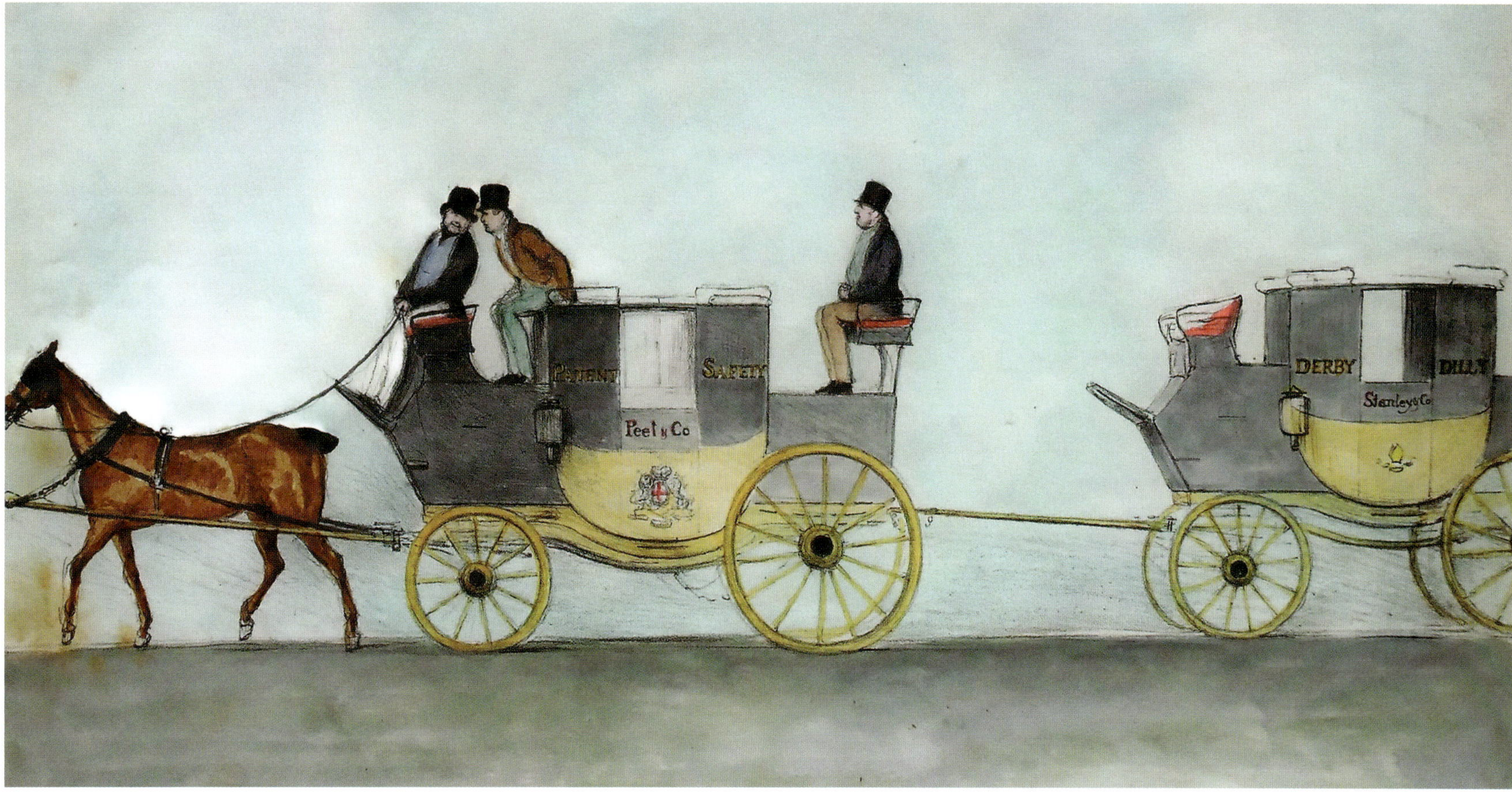

[47] ***No. 406, 'The Derby Dilly taken in tow by the Patent Safety' (published 10 Aug. 1835)*** A coach lettered with 'Patent Safety Peel & Co' on its side, drawn by a horse from right towards left, towing an empty coach lettered with 'Derby Dilly Stanley & Co' on its side; the coachman holding the reins (Sir Robert Peel), listening to the man seated behind (Lord Stanley); another man seated on the back seat (Sir Robert Inglis). The Derby Dilly had not been on the road six months before it was given up. Lord Stanley, after declining the proposals of Sir Robert Peel to join his administration, had continued to sit, in the House of Commons, on the same benches with his former friends, the Whigs; but he soon found that his neutral position was untenable in every respect; that, in politics, whoever was not for Mr. O'Connell must be against him; and that the very benches and cushions were so identified with the politics of those who sat upon them, that the seats on the ministerial side of the House were stuffed with thorns for those who did not go the full length of the ministerial policy. Lord Stanley, therefore, went over to the other side, and thus explained his motives in so doing: – 'When he found that one night, after discussing the details of a measure, upon the principles of which they were agreed, having left his seat, for the purpose of voting according to the best of his judgment, he was received, on his return, with ironical cheers, which, in any other place and under other circumstances, would have amounted to personal insult – cheers, which, coming from the quarter from which they did, intimated the opinion that he was not fit for their society, (an opinion in which he humbly acquiesced), he could not be mistaken in the conclusion at which he had arrived. There was no choice left him on which he could for a moment pause. Determined, on the one side, not to permit insult which he could find the means of preventing; and, on the other, to give no offence, no alternative remained for him but to withdraw from a society which did not like his presence, and for which he confessed he was unfit'. Thus, then, we see the Derby Dilly given up, and hooked, on to the 'Patent Safety', the owner of the latter having taken the concern to add to his own. Sir Robert Peel, the proprietor of the Patent Safety, is driving home his new acquisition, and chatting with Lord Stanley on the precarious state of the coach trade, and the success of their rivals on the road. The person who occupies the back seat, and is a terror to those mischievous rogues who delight in throwing stones and dirt at the king's-arms, is Sir Robert Inglis.

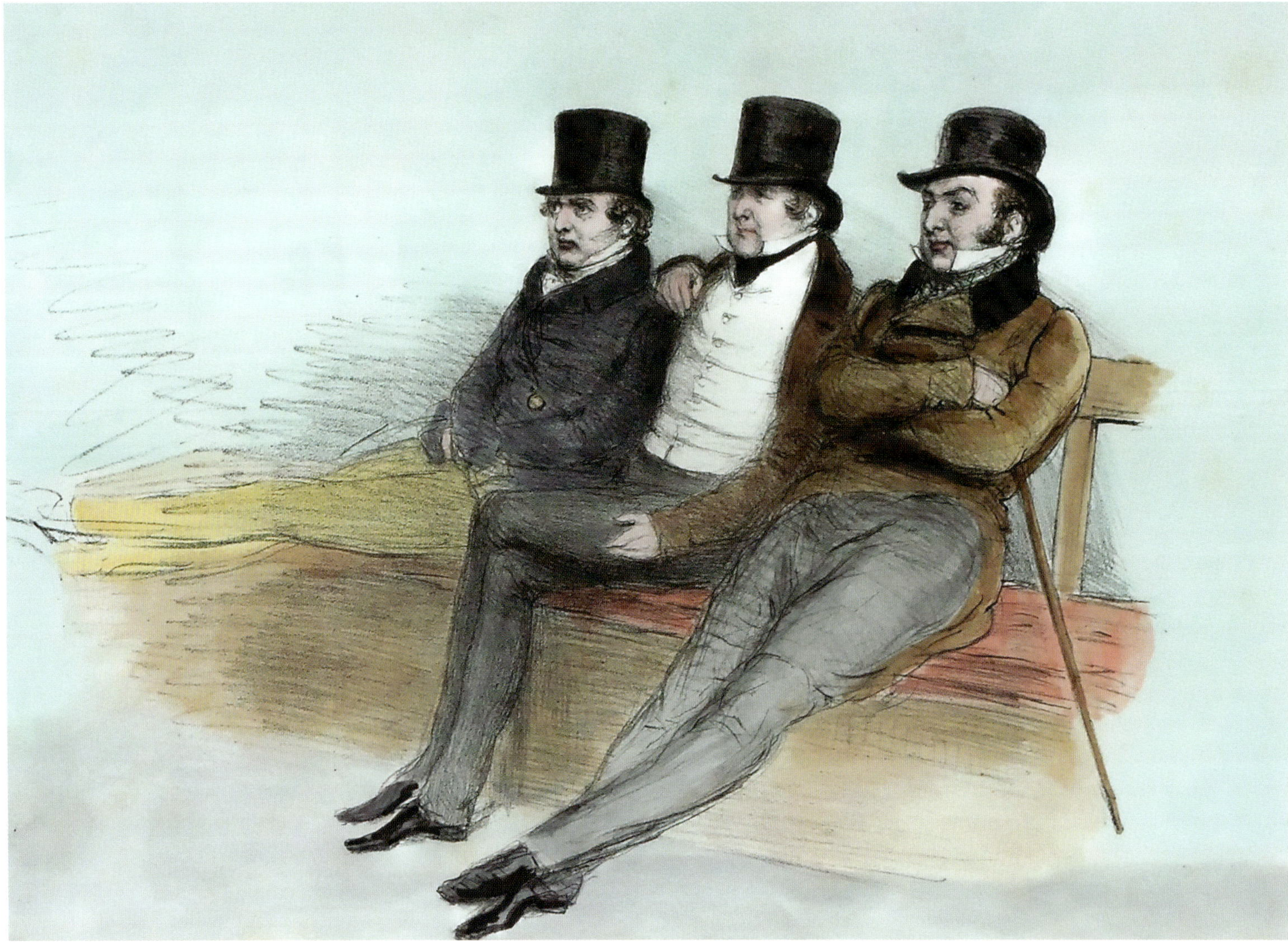

[48] ***No. 426, 'Old Attitudes in New Positions, or a corps of observation from the combined forces of the HOLY Alliance' (published 7 Mar. 1836)*** Three men seated on a bench next to each other, facing left; the one at left with his legs outstretched (Lord Stanley), the one in the centre with his right hand on his shoulder (Sir Robert Peel), the one at the right with his arms crossed, holding a walking stick under his left arm (Sir James Graham). This satire represents the three very eminent and highly-talented men who were now, by the force of circumstances, brought together, and united in one course of policy, within so short a time after that in which one of them (Sir Robert Peel), was diametrically opposed to the other two. The scene hints that their new position was inevitable. They themselves appear to think so; and, finding the change of position natural, are enjoying the freedom of their accustomed attitudes. The reference to the Holy Alliance reminds the audience not only of the post-1815 agreement between Russia, Austria and Prussia (mocked as the 'Holy Alliance') to work together in the interests of conserving the status quo but also the fact that religious questions (notably, defence of the Church of Ireland) have been crucial in the formation of the new political alliance between Peel, Graham and Stanley.

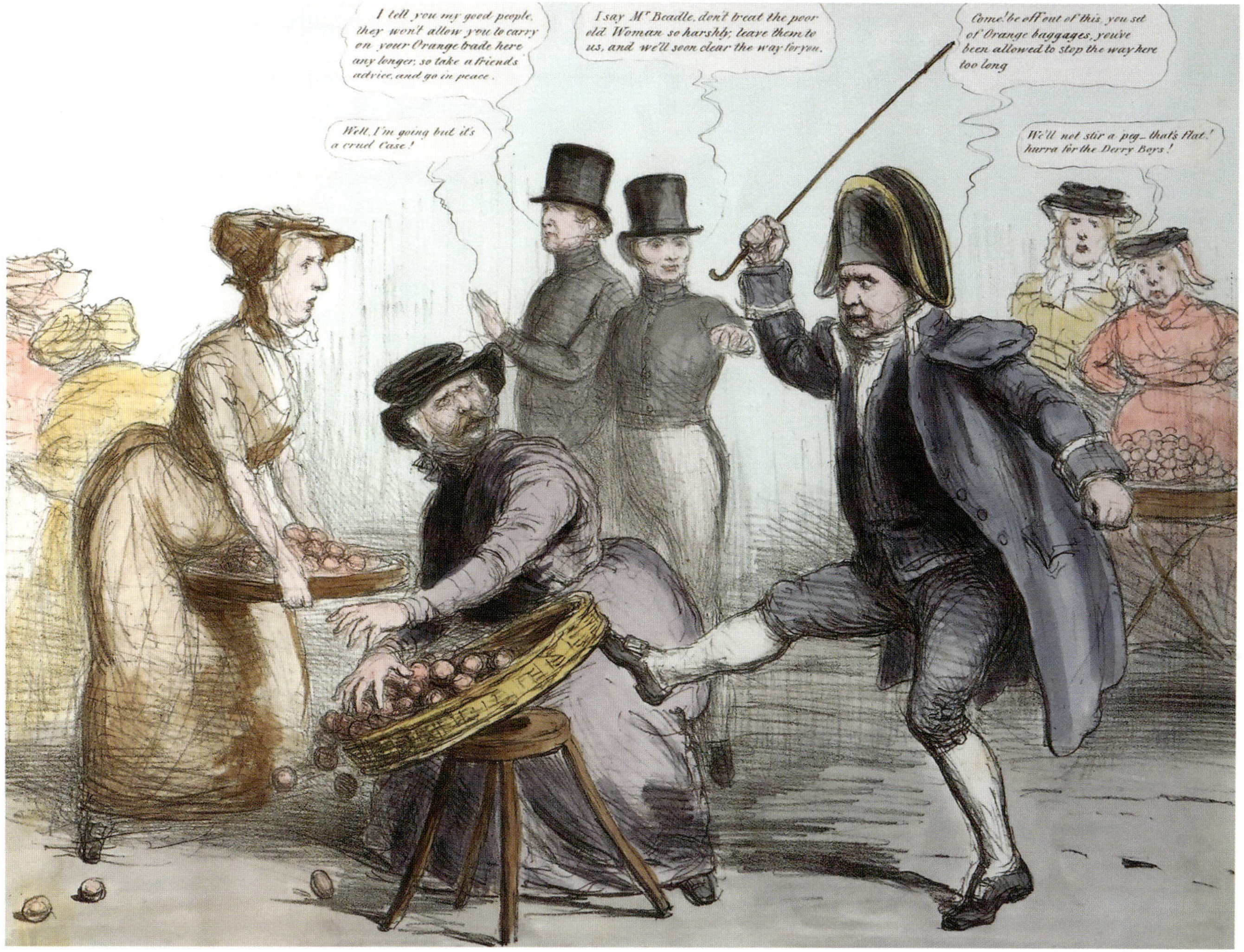

[49] ***No. 427, 'A Regular Kick-Up!' (published 7 Mar. 1836)*** A street market, with men dressed as female orange sellers; a parish beadle, at the right (Joseph Hume), holding up a stick in his right hand, kicking a basket of oranges off the stool of the orange seller at the centre (the Duke of Cumberland); another orange seller standing at the left, watching in fear (Lord Kenyon); in the centre background, two policemen walking past, appearing to defend the women (Sir Robert Peel, Lord John Russell); two orange sellers watching from the background, at the right (Lord Roden, Sir Harcourt Lees). Mr. Hume moved, in the House of Commons, an address to His Majesty, for the purpose of suppressing the Orange Societies, which were accordingly put down by royal proclamation. The parish beadle, exerting himself with so much vigour against the unlucky orange women, is Mr. Hume; the orange woman whom he attacks is the Duke of Cumberland, at that time the Grand Master of the Orange Association; and the other is Lord Kenyon, a distinguished member of that body. Sir Robert Peel and Lord John Russell, as policemen, are endeavouring to mitigate the wrath of the parochial functionary, and to accomplish the suppression by milder methods; the interpretation of which is, that, in lieu of Mr. Hume's resolution, Lord John Russell proposed an address to the King upon the subject, which amendment was agreed to by Sir Robert Peel, and voted by the House. The two orange women in the distance are Lord Roden and Sir Harcourt Lees, influential leaders of the Orange party in Ireland.

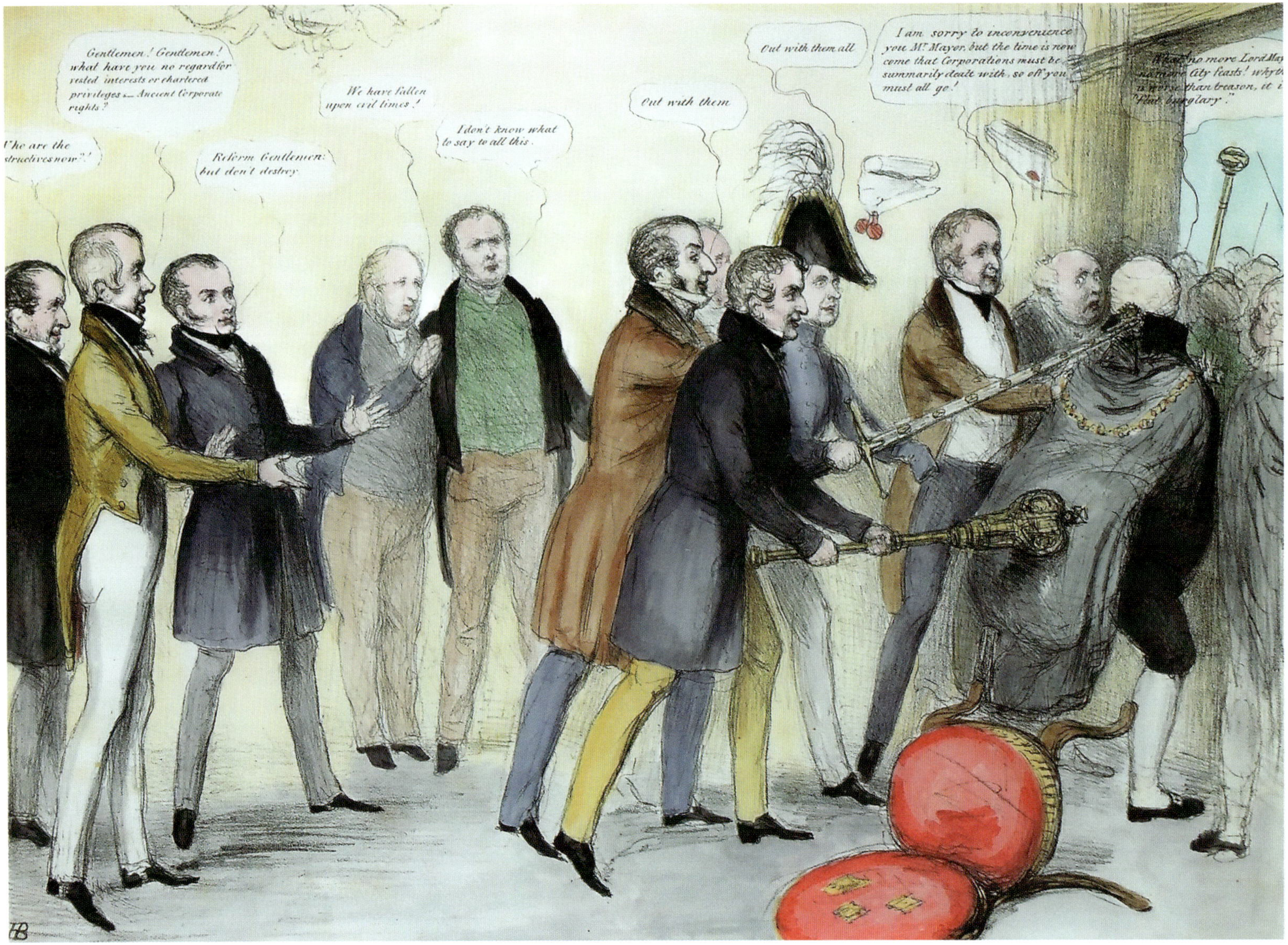

[50] ***No. 430, 'Turning the Tables' (published 25 Mar. 1836)*** Four men in the centre (three recognisable, Sir James Graham, Lord Stanley, holding a mace, Sir Henry Hardinge, holding a sword), and a man next to them at the right (Sir Robert Peel), pushing a high official and a group of his companions out of a room (the Lord Mayor, Arthur Morrison, and Corporators of Dublin); five men watching from left (Thomas Spring Rice, Lord Morpeth, Lord John Russell, Sir Robert Inglis, Frederick Shaw); an upturned chair lying in foreground at right. The Conservative members are turning out the officers of the Irish Corporations. The characters are (beginning on the left-hand) Mr. Spring Rice, Lord Morpeth, Lord John Russell, Sir Robert Inglis, Mr. Shaw (the Recorder of Dublin), Sir James Graham, Lord Stanley (with the mace), Sir Henry Hardinge (in military costume), Sir Robert Peel, and the Lord Mayor and Corporators of Dublin.

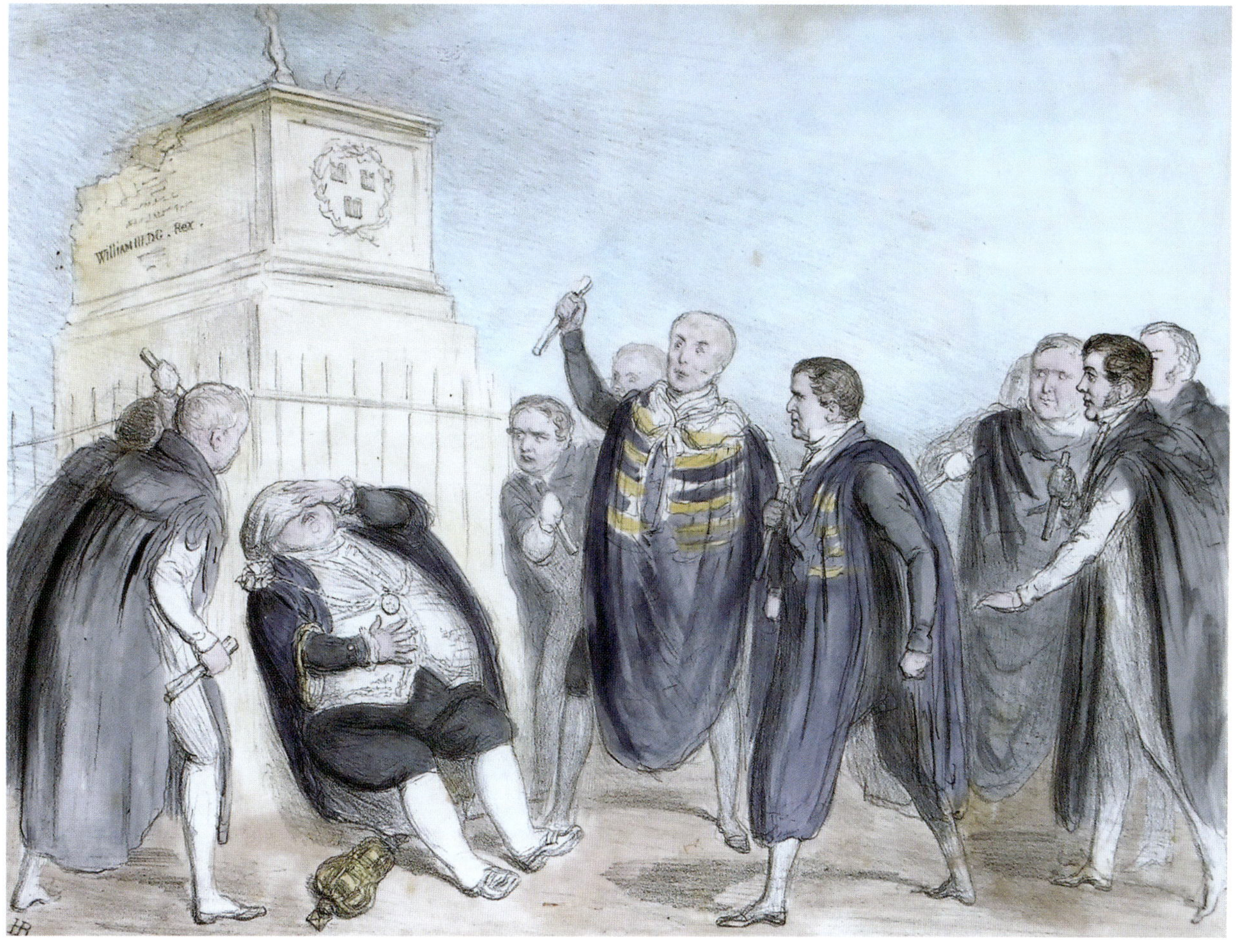

[51] ***No. 434, 'A Rude Design for a Grand Historical Picture, The Death of Caesar' (published 29 Apr. 1836)*** Below a ruined statue, lettered on the plinth with 'William III. DG. Rex.', a blindfolded man collapsing with his back against the fence (Arthur Morrison); a mace lying in front of him on the ground; two men approaching from the left, holding papers as if they were daggers (the one in front, Sir James Graham), four men approaching from the centre (three recognisable, Lord Stanley, Duke of Wellington, Lord Lyndhurst), and a group of four men approaching from the right (two recognisable, Sir Robert Peel and Francis Egerton). The subject of this sketch is the vexatious question of Irish Municipal Reform. The preamble to the Bill which the Government introduced, for the purpose of reforming the Irish Corporations, set forth that they were the cause of great discontent, and the source of much mischief; that having been established as bulwarks for the protection of the Protestant party, they were highly offensive to the Catholics; and thereupon it was proposed to introduce into them such reforms as would admit all parties to corporate rights and privileges, without distinction of religion. The opposition party met this Bill by admitting all the evils described in the preamble, but proposing a different remedy. 'At present, the corporations are a scourge inflicted by Protestants upon Catholics, but the proposed Bill will be a still greater scourge to be inflicted by Catholics upon Protestants. Our remedy is to do away with corporations altogether, and provide for their duties in some other way'. This stab at the existence of Municipal Corporations in Ireland, is here compared to the assassination of Cæsar, who is personated by the Lord Mayor of Dublin (Arthur Morrison). The conspirators are the leaders of the opposition. The Duke of Wellington, who is most conspicuous, and stands out boldly with his dagger (the Lords' amendments) in his hand, is most probably intended for Brutus. Under his right arm Lord Stanley creeps, and on the other side Lord Lyndhurst is rushing in. Behind are Sir Robert Peel, Lord Francis Egerton, and Sir James Graham. The civic Cæsar is ludicrously represented as falling at the feet, or foot (for one only remains) of the statue of King William III, which was mysteriously blown up with gunpowder and destroyed on the night of the 7th of April, 1836.

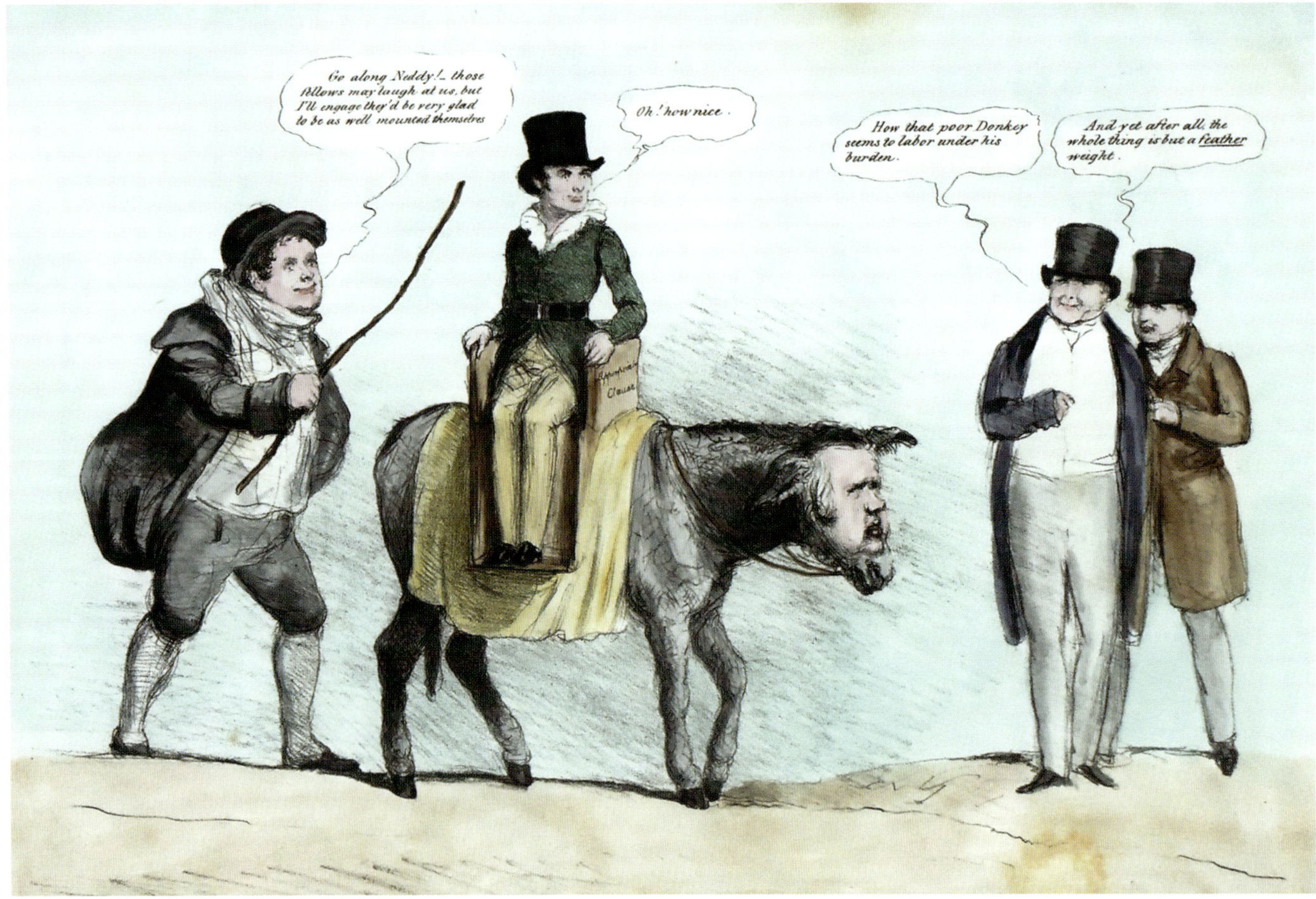

[52] ***No. 436, 'A Classical Subject' (published 10 May 1836)*** Beneath the title: 'Demitto auriculas ut iniquæ mentis asellus cum gravius dorso subiit onus'. From Horace's 'Satires' (1.9), 'I happened to be walking on the Sacred Way' concerning a last-minute delivery from an overpowering enemy. A man seated on a seat lettered with 'Appropriate [Appropriation] Clause' (Lord John Russell), on the back of a donkey with a man's face (Lord Morpeth, Chief Secretary of Ireland), walking along a road from left towards right, driven from the back by a man holding a stick in his right hand (Daniel O'Connell); two men watching from the roadside at right (Sir Robert Peel, Lord Stanley). It was the following extract from a speech of Sir Robert Peel, on 25 Apr. 1836, in a debate on the Irish Tithe Bill, which furnished the subject of this sketch. Speaking of the appropriation clause (which provided for the application of the surplus funds of the Protestant Church in Ireland to secular uses), he said, 'that the promise of the noble Lord (Morpeth) to submit a mere formal resolution, did not imply that His Majesty's government were prepared to abandon their former pledge, [hear, hear.] At the same time, he could not help feeling that there was something in the expressions used by the noble Lord that might, with reference to that part of the question, particularly where he mentioned his inability to shake it off, – [great laughter] there was something in the expression and significant action with which that expression was accompanied, and which was formed according to the models of the ablest orators, that convinced him that he would have fled if he could from the embarrassment of that question. The noble Lord's manner and appearance, during that part of the speech, reminded him strongly of the graphic picture drawn by Horace when he says Demitto auriculas ut iniquæ mentis asellus, cum gravius dorso subiit onus'. Lord Morpeth having the charge of bringing in and carrying through its several stages the measure alluded to, is aptly represented as the 'asellus iniquæ mentis', or vicious donkey; and although his rider, Lord John Russell, looks not much like a 'gravius onus', yet, on closer inspection, it will be seen that his unsparing driver, Mr. O'Connell, has fixed him into the appropriation clause by way of a chair, which all the kingdom knows was too great a load for any minister to carry, and which has been ultimately kicked off. Sir Robert Peel, with Lord Stanley looking over his shoulder, is enjoying the agonies of the poor creature, whose ears are painfully expressive.

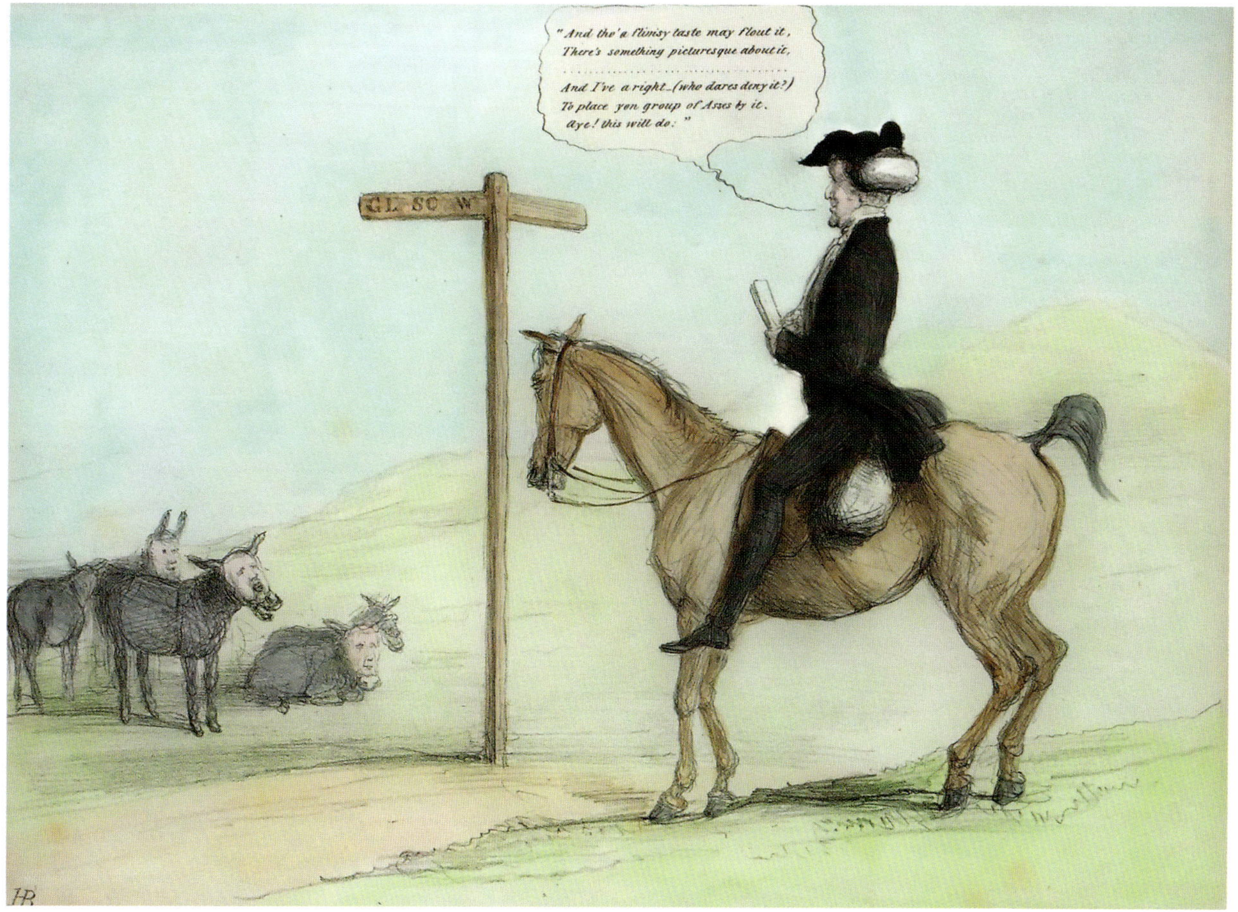

[53] ***No. 465, 'Doctor Syntax "on his humble but faithful Steed"' (published 31 Jan. 1837)*** A man on horseback at right, in the character of Dr Syntax (Sir Robert Peel), shown in profile to left, holding papers in his left hand, stopping at a road sign lettered with 'Glasgow', looking at a group of donkeys with men's faces, standing and lying behind the sign at left (Thomas Spring Rice, Lord Morpeth). The reference point is 'The adventures of Doctor Syntax in search of the Picturesque', a humorous poem published by Ackerman. The comparison, instituted in this sketch, of Sir Robert Peel to the learned hero of the poem, was suggested by the following extract from his speech at Glasgow University on the occasion of his being installed Lord Rector, in January 1837: – 'I am not a stranger to Glasgow. No, when my education was completed, I burnt with anxiety to see Scotland. I came to this city, I wished to see something of Scotland which I could not have seen from the windows of a luxurious carriage; I wished to see other habits and manners of life than those which the magnificent hospitable castles of the nobility presented. Yes, in Glasgow I hired an humble but faithful steed; I travelled partly on horseback and partly on foot through almost every county that lies southern of Inverness; I have read the map of Scotland upon the great scale of nature, from the summits of Ben Nevis and Ben Lomond; I have visited that island, whence savage and roaming bards derived the benefits of knowledge, and the blessings of religion. Yes, amid the ruins of Iona I have abjured the rigid philosophy which would conduct us indifferent and unmoved over any ground that has been dignified by wisdom, by bravery, and by virtue. I have stood on the shores of Staffa, – I have seen the temple not built with hands, – I have seen the mighty swell of the ocean, – the waves of the great Atlantic beating in its inmost recesses, and swelling notes of praise nobler than any that ever pealed from human organs. I have lived on the banks of the Spey, – two autumns have I spent on the margin of that river; I want no guide to the mountains and Glens of Badenoch; I could find my way tomorrow from Corriarick to Loch Logan; many a day have I climbed the mountain side with no other companion than a Highland shepherd; many an hour have I passed in converse with him, listening to his simple annals and artless views of human life'.

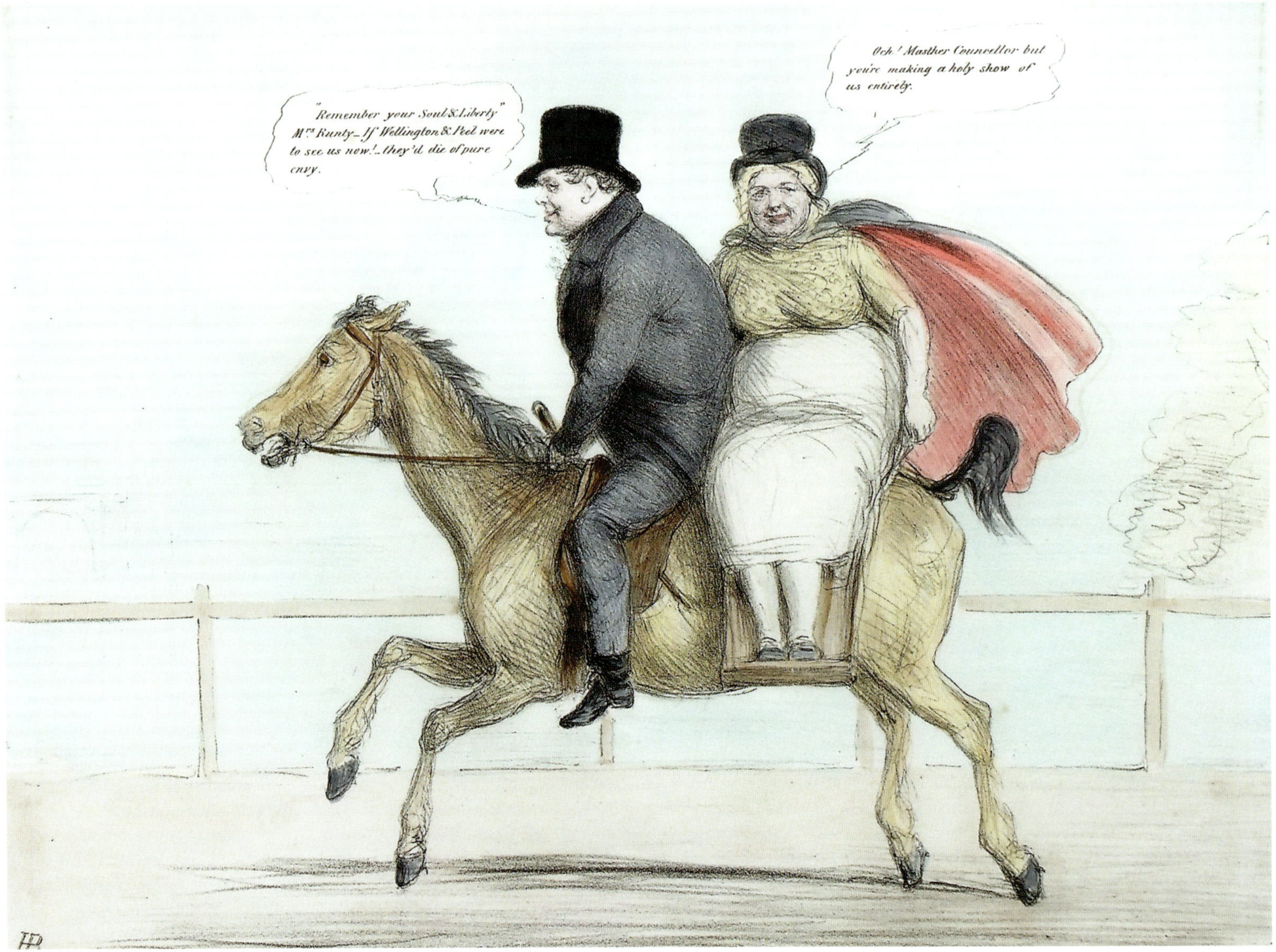

[54] ***No. 472, 'A Study for Rotten Row, Hyde Park' (published 16 Mar. 1837)*** A man riding a horse at high speed, from right towards left, in Rotten Row, Hyde Park (Daniel O'Connell), engaged in conversation with a woman seated behind him on a chair, facing front (Mrs Prunty). The lady mounted on a pillion behind Mr. O'Connell, upon the back of a beast which seems in all respects wild, rough and frisky, ill-fed, and over-burdened, is one Mrs. Prunty, a female politician of no little importance. For the zeal and energy which she displayed at a contested election, and her services in bringing electors to the poll, 'nolentes volentes', she received the public thanks of the liberal party, and was presented with a new pair of panniers, to enable her and her donkey to carry on, with greater credit and respectability, their daily avocations as itinerant merchants and dealers.

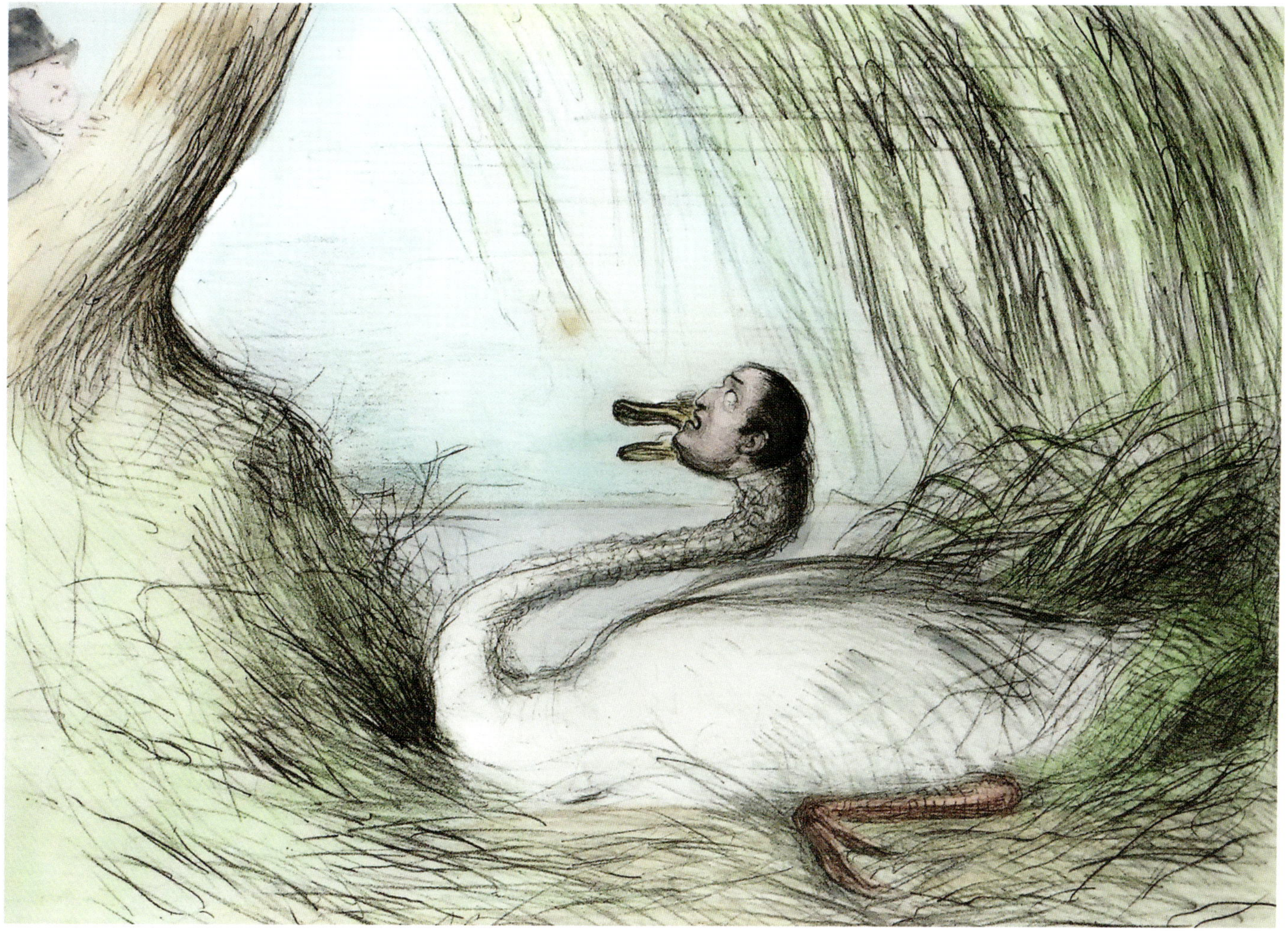

[55] ***No. 473, 'A Dying Swan' (published 13 Mar. 1837)*** A swan with a man's head (Sir John Cam Hobhouse), lying at centre among vegetation under a willow tree, with his eyes turned up; at top left, a man watching from behind the tree trunk (Sir Robert Peel). In the debate on the Irish Municipal Corporation Bill, in the House of Commons on 8 Feb. 1837, Sir John Cam Hobhouse, who is here represented as the dying Swan, having replied to a very powerful speech of Sir James Graham's, was followed, and somewhat roughly handled, by Sir Robert Peel. The comparison of Sir John Cam Hobhouse to the dying Swan is contained in the following passage:- 'The Right Honourable Baronet has asked me – I think, rather improperly – what course I mean to pursue, when I receive an appointment which, till the Right Honourable Baronet himself spoke, I had not the slightest expectation of obtaining. As I doubt the Right Honourable Gentleman's authority or competence to confer the appointment, I must say I do not recognize his right to catechise me as to the principles I mean to follow on the contingency, which, till this night, I thought was a remote one; and now, what between his funeral speech – between the notes of the "dying Swan" – and his declaration that it is in vain for me to hope to be able to conduct the Government, the Right Honourable Gentleman has left me in complete doubt as to the position in which I really stand'. 'H.B.' has admirably followed up Sir Robert Peel's image, and suited it with everything that is appropriate. The expiring bird has retreated to a sedgy and secluded nook, and at the foot of a willow-tree 'Which grows aslant the brook, And shews its hoar-leaves in the glassy stream', is turning up his eyes, and laying down his head, to die in music. Sir Robert Peel, from behind the tree, is witnessing the sorrowful scene.

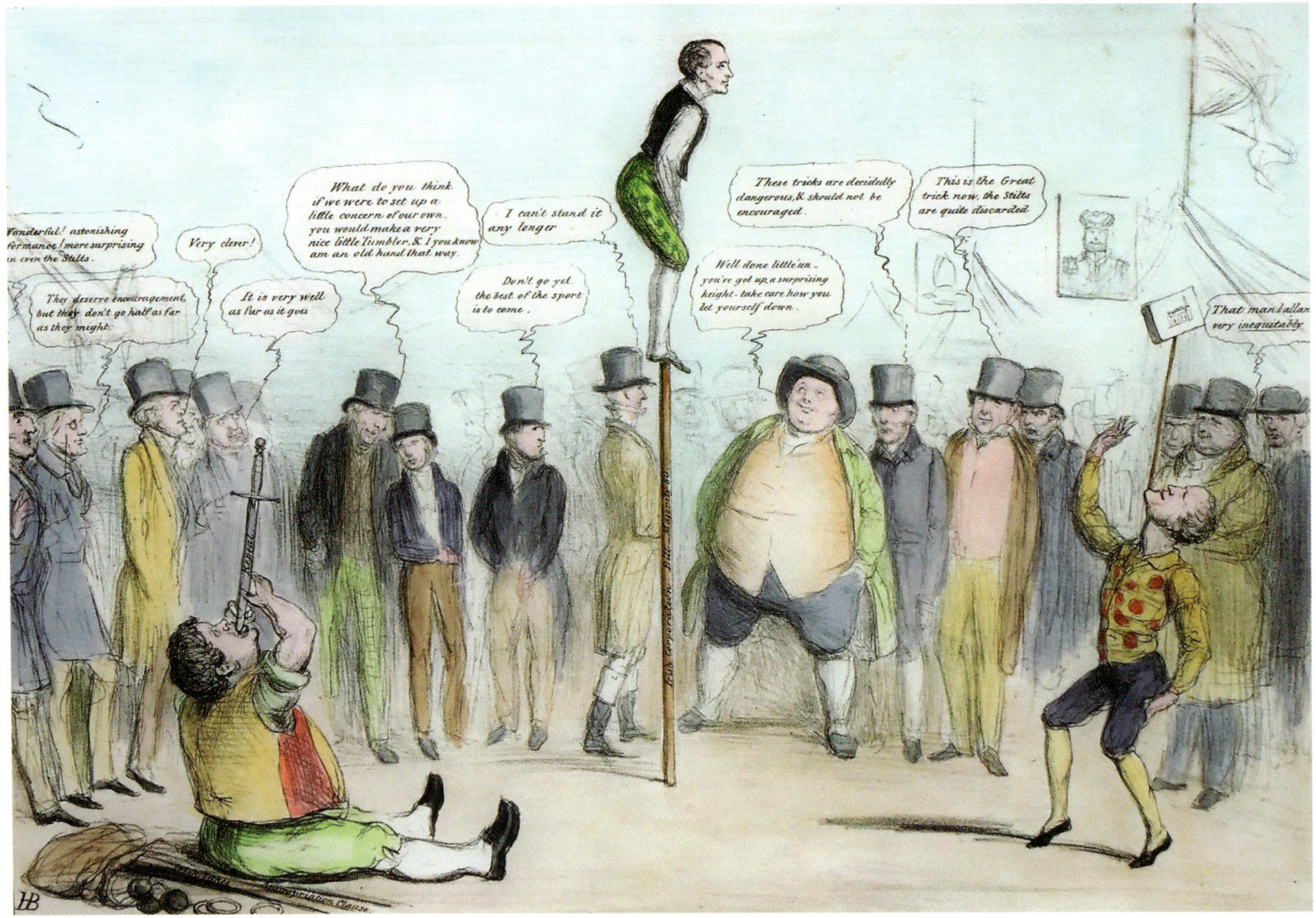

[56] ***No. 477, 'A cant phrase for doing anything in an extravagant way – known it is presumed to most persons – "Going to the Fair with it"' (published 30 Mar. 1837)*** A group of men watching street performers; at left, a man seated on the ground in front of poles lettered with 'Irish Tithes' and 'Appropriation Clause.', swallowing a sword lettered with 'Repeal' (Daniel O'Connell); in the centre, a man standing on top of a pole lettered with 'Irish Corporation Bill – Majority 80' (Lord John Russell); at the right, a man balancing an object with the image of a church on a long pole on his chin (Thomas Spring Rice); their audience standing in the background (from left to right, Lord Ebrington, Sir William Molesworth, Charles Buller, Joseph Hume, Lord Brougham, John Arthur Roebuck, Sir John Cam Hobhouse, Sir Francis Burdett, John Bull, the Duke of Wellington, Sir Robert Peel and Lord Stanley). This sketch exhibits Ministers in the act of performing, before a numerous assemblage, the extravagancies necessary to keep up excitement. The most conspicuous figure is Lord John Russell, balancing himself on a pole which bears the inscription of 'Irish Corporation Bill – majority 80'. His Lordship is manifestly so placed to represent that the whole administration depended for support on the measure referred to, and the majority in its favour. The ticklish trick of balancing the church is performed by Mr. Spring Rice, in allusion to the measures which he proposed with regard to reforming the church-rates. The other performer, (Mr. O'Connell) though not strictly one of the administration, may be said to be one of their party, and his grand trick is the swallowing of the sword on which 'Repeal' is inscribed. It is understood, however, that though he swallows the sword, he does not swallow the handle, but makes use of it to draw the sword out again, and flourish it over the heads of his foes as terrifically as ever. The bye-standers are all men of political importance. Beginning at the left-hand they are as follows – Lord Ebrington, Sir William Molesworth, Mr. C. Buller, Mr. Joseph Hume, Lord Brougham, Mr. Roebuck, Sir John Hobhouse, Sir F. Burdett, John Bull, the Duke of Wellington, Sir Robert Peel, Lord Stanley, Lord Lyndhurst, Sir Robert Inglis, and the Archbishop of Canterbury (William Howley), and each of them is making some appropriate remark.

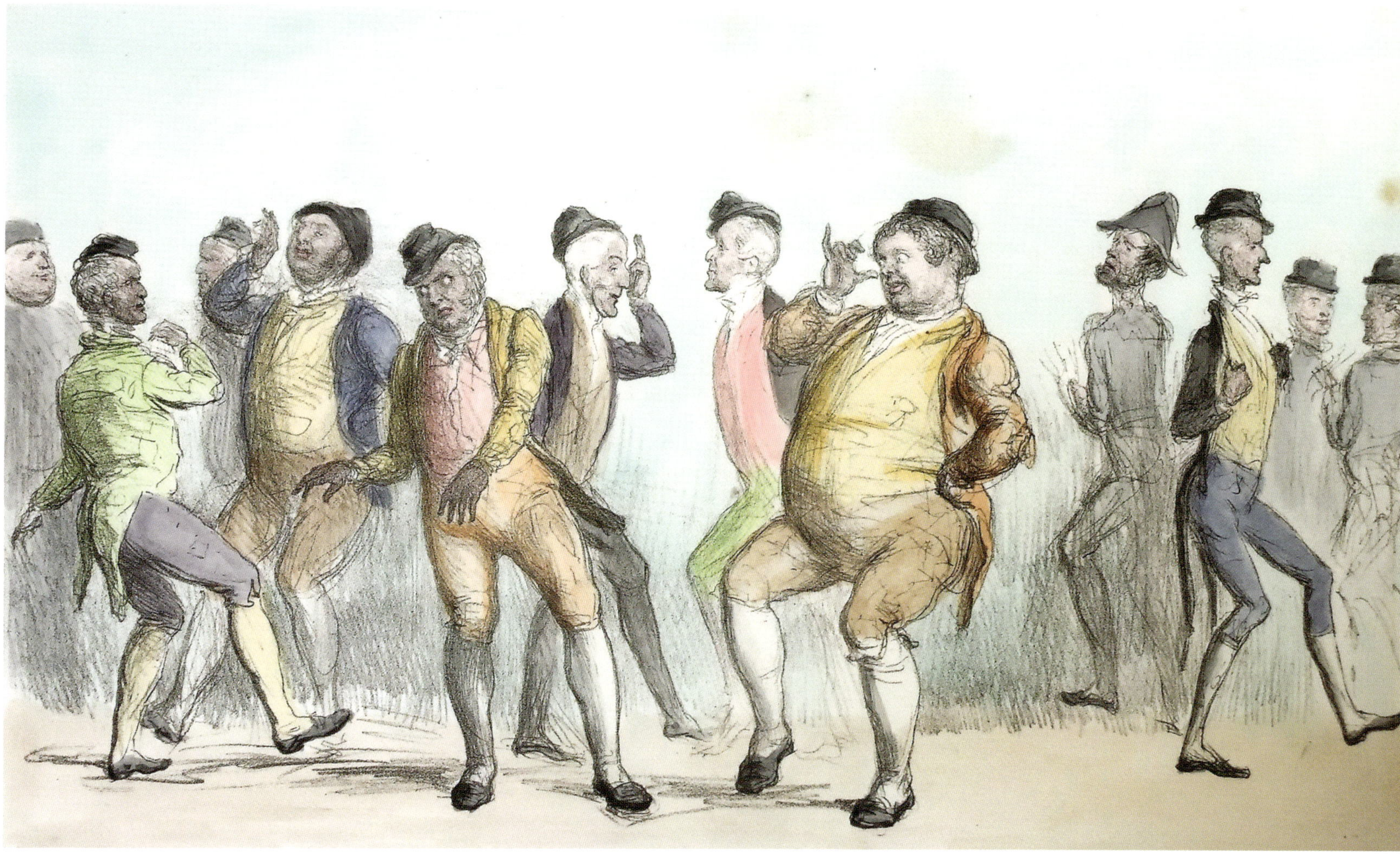

[57] ***No. 478, 'Fancy – Jim Crow Dance and Chorus' (published 17 April 1837)*** A group of black men dancing (from left to right, Lords Abinger, Stanley, Lyndhurst, Sir James Graham, Lord Melbourne, the Duke of Wellington, Sir Robert Peel, Daniel O'Connell, General Evans, Sir Francis Burdett, Lord John Russell, Thomas Spring Rice). In 1837 Jim Crow was the fashion, and to 'jump Jim Crow' was the favourite expression to signify any kind of inconsistency. It originated in a dramatic piece, played at the Adelphi Theatre, in which an American actor, Mr. Rice, performed the part of a negro, and sang a song describing all sorts of persons and things, and the facility with which he had accommodated himself to every change. The burthen of the song, which was accompanied by a peculiar dance, was very nearly as set forth in the sketch: – 'Turn about, and wheel about, And do just so; And every time I turn about I jump Jim Crow'. Here are eleven of the leading men of modern days, and all brought to the same acknowledgment of Jim Crow-ism, each variety strikingly appropriate to the character of the performer. In the left-hand corner is Lord Abinger, formerly Sir James Scarlett, and a Whig, till, tired of waiting for Whig-ascendancy, he 'jumped Jim Crow' and was made Attorney-General, by the Duke of Wellington, in the reign of George IV. Next to him is Lord Stanley, a scion of an old Whig stock. His grandfather may be seen among the most conspicuous of the Whig politicians, in the caricatures of Gillray, and his Lordship was a member of Lord Grey's reform government, and a Whig, 'until the pressure from without' (Lord Grey's well-known expression) drove the Whigs into lengths which Lord Stanley was not prepared for, and then he 'jumped Jim Crow' and took his seat on the opposition benches. The jolly figure with an upturned face, to whom Lord Stanley is setting, is Sir James Graham. In former days, when Toryism was predominant,

[57] ***No. 478*** (continued)

Sir James went great lengths the other way, and his notions on the subject of the national debt were considered very heterodox. As a member of Lord Grey's cabinet he prudently suppressed all extravagant notions, and confined himself within proper Whig limits. The circumstances which produced the change in Lord Stanley operated in like manner upon Sir James Graham, and he took precisely the same opportunity to 'jump Jim Crow'. Between these two, in the back-ground, is Lord Lyndhurst. It is said, that when a young man, and before he had entered on political life, he was ultra-latitudinarian in his political creed; and that, notwithstanding the strict truth of his assertion, that his political life has been consistently conservative, he did originally 'jump Jim Crow'. The two figures occupying the centre of the fore-ground it is not possible to mistake. Lord Melbourne, who, when in office under Mr. Canning, made several speeches against reform in Parliament, was next a member of Lord Grey's cabinet, by which reform was carried, and subsequently, as Prime-Minister, went much greater lengths towards democracy than either Lord Grey or Lord Althorp would venture to go; if he did not actually make, yet consented to enjoy the advantage of, an alliance with Mr. O'Connell, the sworn enemy of the Protestant Church in Ireland, and the advocate of a repeal of the union. Lord Melbourne has 'jumped Jim Crow' as high as any of them, but his aristocratic and courtly sensibilities are evidently shocked at finding that his jumping Jim Crow has at length brought him into close contact with the 'Irish Agitator', and he turns in disgust from the 'individual' who, with his thumb to his nose, and his left-arm stuck in his side, lets him see that it is too late to be squeamish when he has become dependent. The attitude of Mr. O'Connell is that of 'toeing it and heeling it'. In the centre of the back-ground are the Duke of Wellington and Sir Robert Peel. Wellington voted against Catholic emancipation for years, whilst Sir Robert Peel was the chosen champion of the opposition to this great measure, yet it was carried at last by this very pair of Ministers. On the right is Sir Francis Burdett. Formerly drawn through the City of Westminster in a triumphal car, decorated with everything symbolical of liberty and popularity, and preceded by a banner, on which was inscribed 'Westminster's Pride and England's Glory', he turned to Conservatism in 1837 and sat as a Conservative M.P. until 1844. The figure in the cocked hat is Sir De Lacy Evans, M.P. for Westminster. His attitude, like that of a person receiving corporal chastisement, very readily suggests the reason for including him among the group of jumpers. In obtaining the seat for Westminster, he triumphed over Sir John C. Hobhouse. Among other topics then touched upon, was that of flogging in the army, and Sir John C. Hobhouse being then Secretary-at-War, and unable, in that character, to carry out the professions of which he had once been so lavish with respect to the abolition of military punishment, General Evans shone by contrast a brilliant abolitionist. Nevertheless, when commanding the British legion at St. Sebastian, the General flogged his soldiers without any scruple, and 'H.B.' has accordingly put him into his sketch as one of those who, when it suited their purpose, could 'jump Jim Crow'. The next person is Lord John Russell, who used to compare himself to Aladdin, who was too sensible of the value of his old lamp to exchange it for a new one. Grave and sometimes querulous, he is here presented as having 'jumped Jim Crow'. The last person in the company is Mr. Spring Rice, on whom it is unnecessary to fix any specific charge of Jim Crowism, since the mere fact of his jumping into the office of Chancellor of the Exchequer, where it was his bounden duty to defend every item of the expenditure, and to resist every assault upon the revenue, which, while in opposition, he had been accustomed to join in, was quite sufficient to give him admittance into the company.

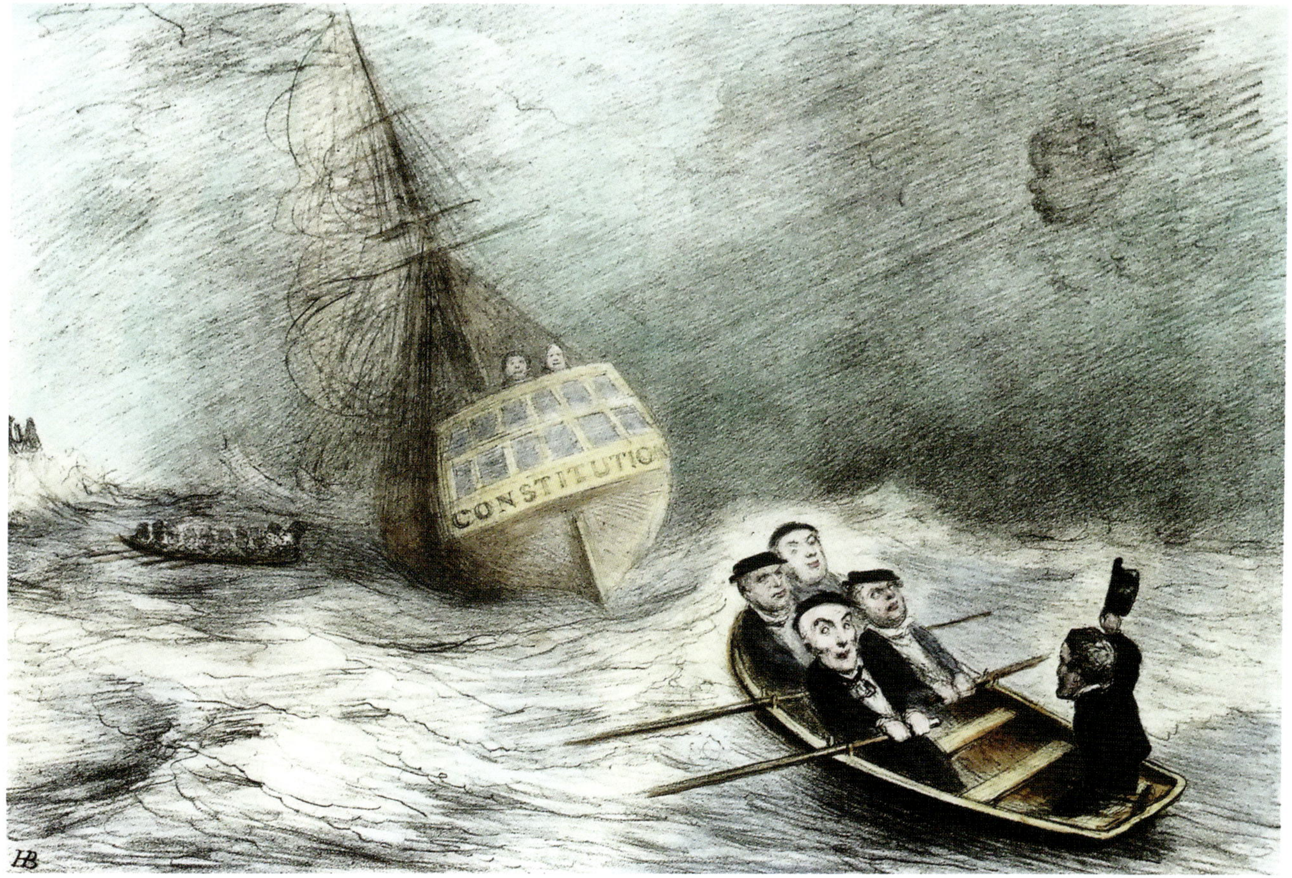

[58] ***No. 479, 'A Conservative vision – a little premature – Something between the Sublime & the Ridiculous' (published 27 Apr. 1837)*** A ship at the centre, lettered with 'Constitution' on its front, with two men on board (John Bull and King William IV), blown by wind from top right, impersonated by the two men (Daniel O'Connell at left, Lord Brougham at right); a rowing boat with ten men escaping towards left (two recognisable, Lords Melbourne and John Russell); five men in another boat in foreground at right, rowing towards the ship (steered by Sir Robert Peel, opposite the Duke of Wellington, Lord Stanley, Lord Lyndhurst and Sir James Graham). It was Sir Robert Peel, who, in reply to some observations made in the House of Commons, on the difficulty of forming a Conservative Ministry, made use of the metaphor which has given occasion to this sketch, and stated his belief, that if the vessel of the state should be deserted by its crew, there would be found a sufficient number of hands willing and able to take the helm, and steer the ship through the dangers by which she might be surrounded. 'H.B.' has given an excellent representation of the idea. The vessel is evidently on a lee-shore, thither driven by the furious blasts of Mr. O'Connell and Lord Brougham, who are blowing great guns upon her weather-quarter. The crew are making their escape in the jolly-boat, leaving the owner (John Bull) and the captain (William IV) to take their chance with the ill-fated bark. Assistance, however, is at hand; a boat steered by Sir Robert Peel, and rowed by the Duke of Wellington, Lord Stanley, Lord Lyndhurst, and Sir James Graham, is making for the vessel. But what of the sublime and the ridiculous? This is the point in the sketch. To describe, in fervent language, a patriotic statesman rushing forward to take the helm of government, when the nation is sinking amidst the storms of contending factions; – this is sublime. To talk of such things when all the world sees that politicians, ready and eager for office, are waiting at every corner, and are thinking less of the dangers of the state than of the salary and patronage which placemen enjoy. There are the raging sea, the stranded ship, the forsaken owner and his captain, the runaway crew, and the gallant preservers in the life-boat. These ingredients would compose a sublime subject; but a single glance at the two heads peeping over the stern of the vessel, the Boreas [North wind] with trumpeters' cheeks blowing from the clouds, and the dwarfish figures in the two boats, show that there is a just proportion of the ridiculous in the composition. Edmund Burke had written *A Philosophical Enquiry into the Origins of Our ideas of the Sublime and Beautiful* (1757).

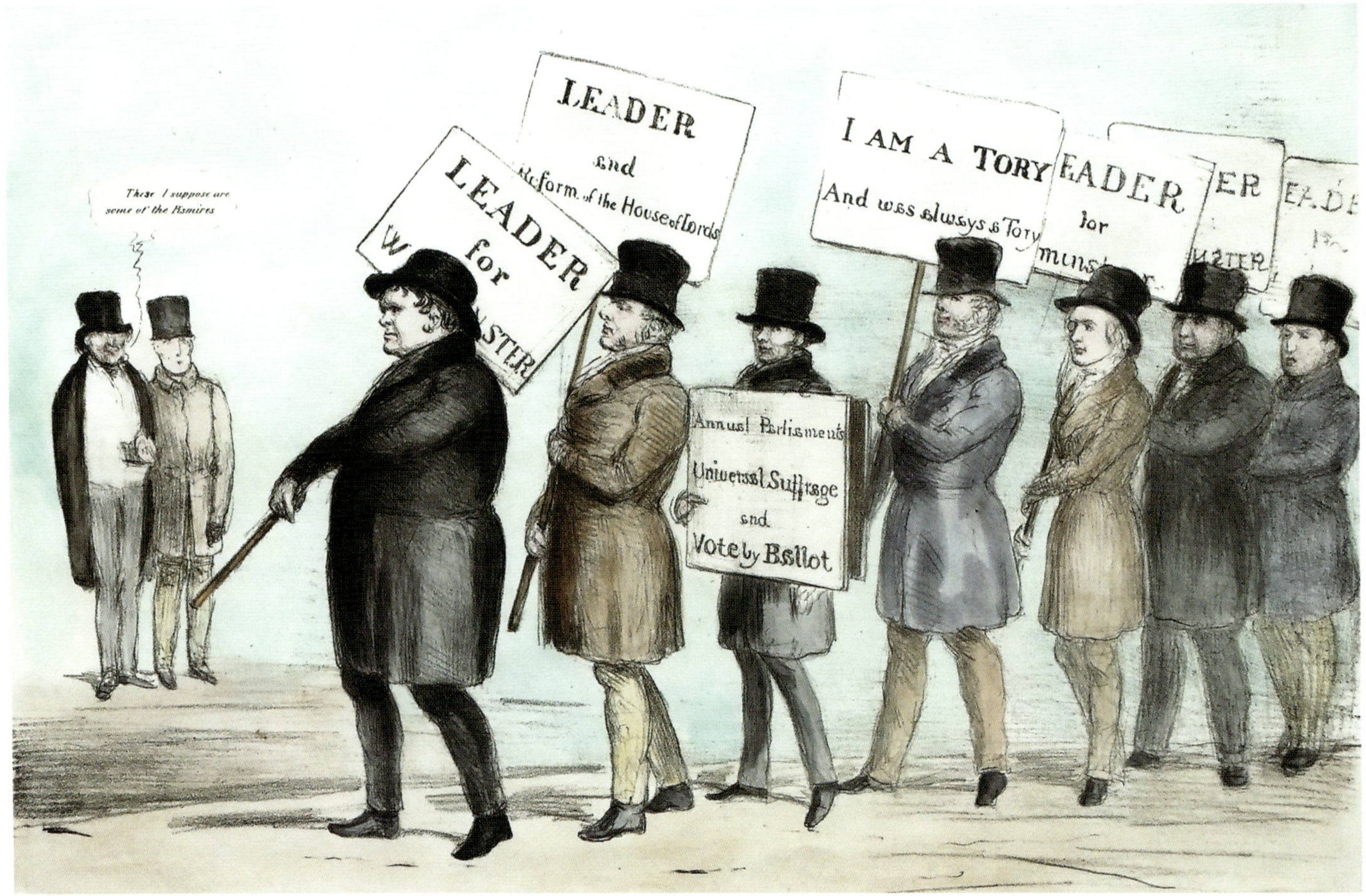

[59] ***No. 482, 'Following the Leader' (published 12 May 1837)*** A group of men walking in a row along a street, from right towards left, carrying banners (Daniel O'Connell, Lords Melbourne, John Russell, Palmerston, Sir William Molesworth, Joseph Hume, Sir John Cam Hobhouse), observed by two men standing on the roadside in the background at left (Sir Robert Peel and the Duke of Wellington). For some time previously to the date of this sketch, Sir Francis Burdett had absented himself from the House of Commons, and it had become pretty evident that he had conceived a distaste either for the persons or principles, or both, of the leading men among the party to which he had formerly belonged. The persons who put themselves forward as the organs of the City of Westminster, pressed him for an explicit avowal of his sentiments, and after some correspondence, equally unsatisfactory to both parties, they called on him to resign his seat, which he did in a letter containing the following remarkable passage:- 'It affords me an opportunity, and I trust a justification of complying, to use the fashionable patriotic slang, with the wants and wishes of this portion of the people. The gauntlet is thrown down thus publicly, and I take it up and accept the challenge thus publicly given. I will apply for the Chiltern Hundreds, and then call upon the electors of Westminster to declare themselves for or against a zealous supporter and firm adherent, as I have ever been, and still am, of the laws, institutions, and constitution of England. I should not, however, venture upon this decision, provoked to it as I am, "nettled and stung by pismires", were I not satisfied by recent appearances that no unfair advantage will thereby be given, or can be taken by either party; all will start fair and upon equal terms'. The person brought forward to oppose Sir Francis, was John Temple Leader, Esq., then the sitting member for Bridgewater. This sketch, exhibiting four Cabinet Ministers, Lord Melbourne, Lord John Russell, and Lord Palmerston, immediately following Mr. O'Connell and Sir J. Hobhouse, bringing up the rear behind Mr. Hume and Sir William Molesworth, indicates very plainly the extraordinary exertions made by Ministers and their friends to procure the election of Mr. Leader, who nevertheless was, on this occasion., beaten by a considerable majority.

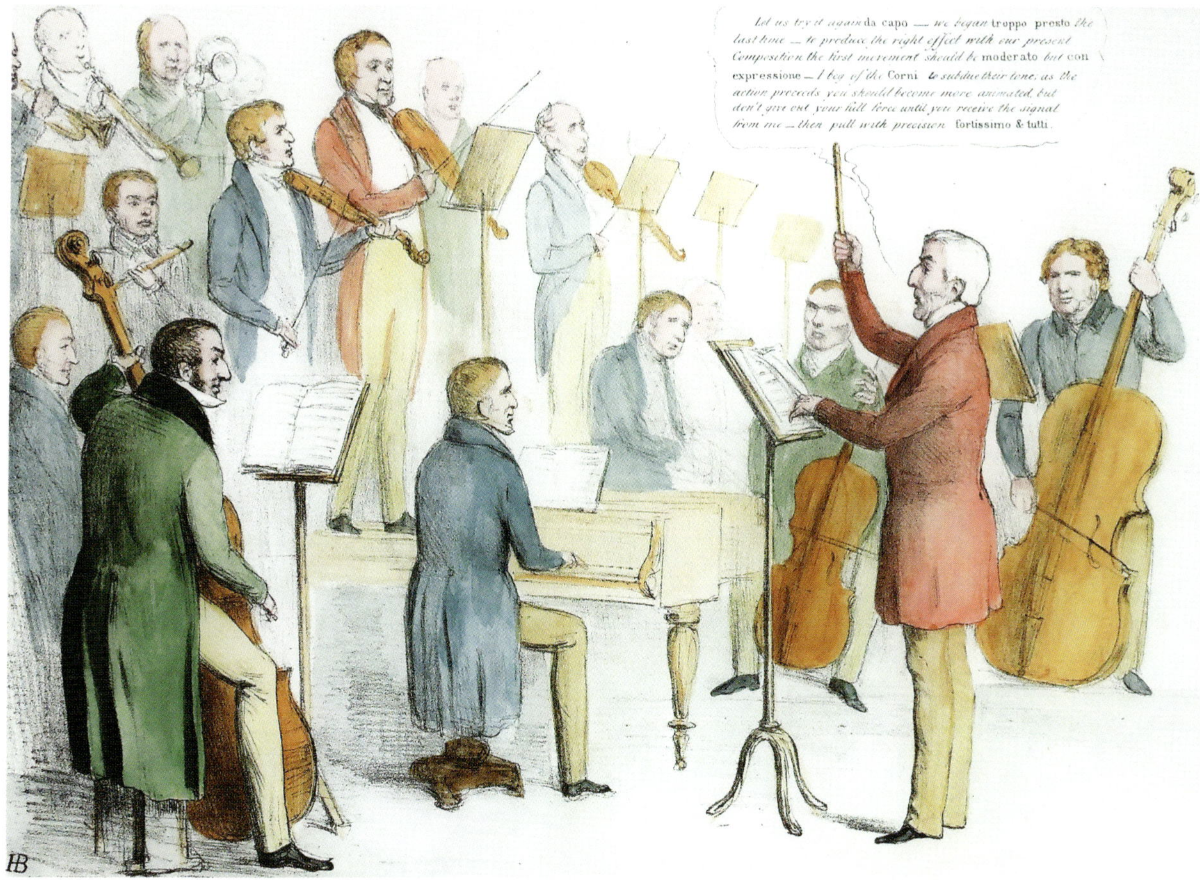

[60] ***No. 538, 'Ancient Concerts' (published 14 May 1838)*** A conductor standing in the foreground at the right behind a music stand (the Duke of Wellington), holding up a baton in his right hand, addressing the members of the orchestra: violinists (Sir Robert Peel, Lord Stanley), a flautist (Sir William Follett), trumpeters (Sir Henry Hardinge, Lords Wicklow and Londonderry), a man playing the double bass in foreground at the left (Sir James Graham), with a man behind at far left (Sir Frederick Pollock), a pianist (Lord Lyndhurst), a man behind the piano (Lord Burghersh), a cellist (Lord Aberdeen), and another man playing the double bass at far right (Lord Ellenborough). In politics, as well as in music, it is impossible to produce the desired effect, unless the parts be individually well sustained, and, at the same time, well blended by the precision, taste, and skill of an able conductor. It was said that, on some occasions, the Conservatives failed to make that impression on the country which they had anticipated, and that their failure was owing to the want of a perfect understanding among themselves. In short, the speech which the conductor, the Duke of Wellington, is addressing to his band, is a close translation into musical terms of the language held by the Ministerial papers on the subject of Conservative tactics. The discrimination and humour of 'H.B.' are very conspicuous in the selection of instruments for the several performers. Sir Robert Peel is, of course, the leader, and plays first violin; but Lord Stanley, at his side, handles his bow with the air of a performer, who knows that the leader of the second violin is very little less important in his place than he who leads the first. Just below Lord Stanley, is Sir William Follett, more conspicuous as second flute than Sir Frederick Pollock, who sits lower still, and who, of course, is the flauto primo. Above these are the Corni, Sir Henry Hardinge, Lord Wicklow, and Lord Londonderry, who are requested by the conductor to subdue their tones till he shall give them the signal, being too apt to blow away fortissime without attending to the directions of the composer. The quiet and masterly air which distinguishes Lord Lyndhurst at the piano-forte is exceedingly good. Behind Lord Lyndhurst sits Sir James Graham, handling with graceful ease his double bass. Does the artist by this insinuate a pun on the baronet's tergiversation? Lord Aberdeen and Lord Ellenborough are the violoncellos, the latter, who sits on the right, has an easy independent air, but Lord Aberdeen keeps his eye entirely fixed upon the conductor, anxious only to follow his direction. The Duke of Wellington was, at this time, one of the Directors of the Ancient Concerts and of the Royal Academy of Music.

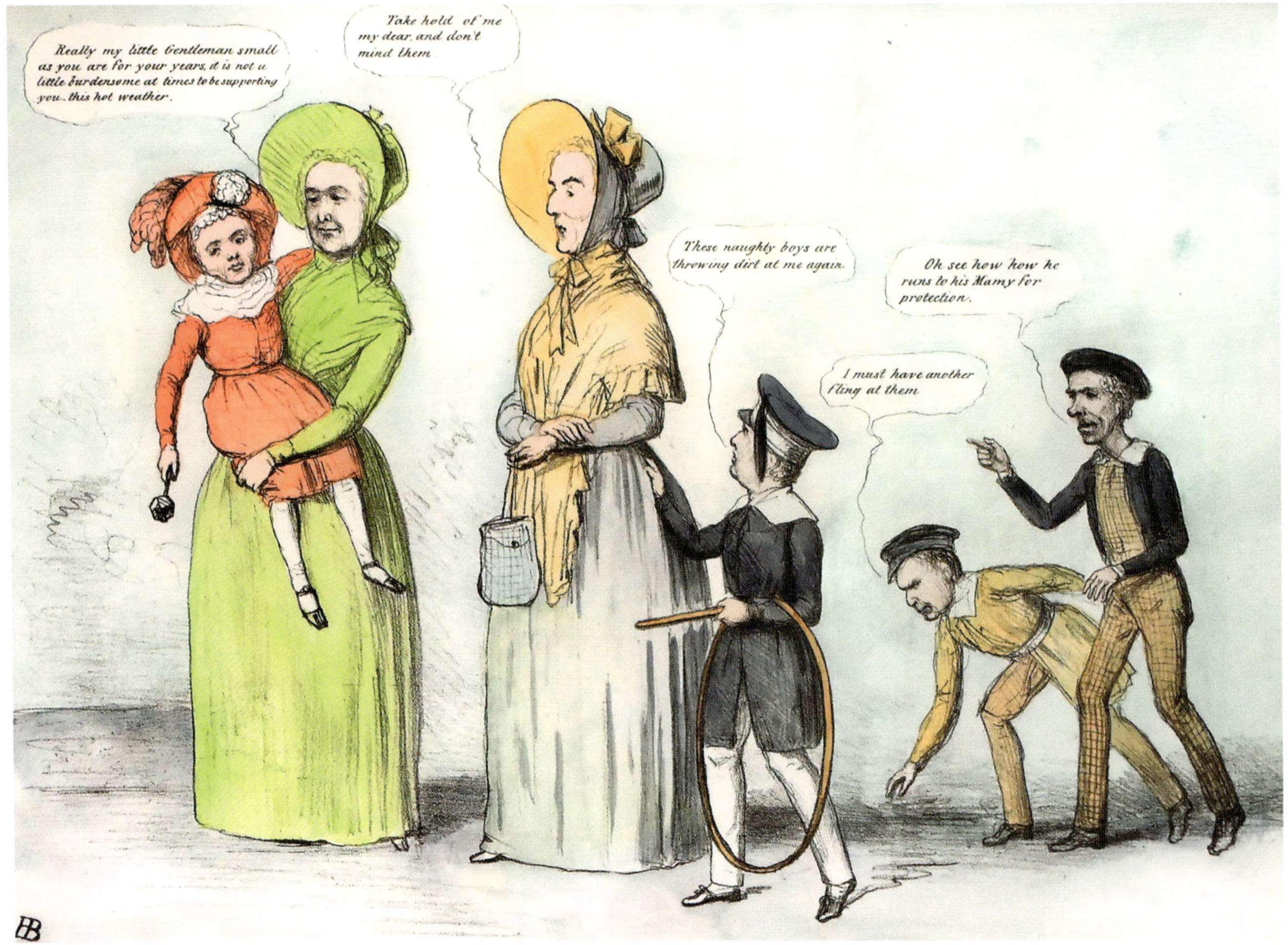

[61] ***No. 551, 'Dry Nurses' (published 21 July 1838)*** Two men dressed as women, walking along a street from right towards left with two children; the one at the left (Sir Robert Peel) holding a young boy, dressed as a girl (Lord John Russell), the one at the centre (the Duke of Wellington) next to a boy, holding a hoop (Lord Melbourne); they are attacked by two youths, with older men's faces, following them from the right (Lords Lyndhurst and Brougham). The position of parties, and their relative numbers and strength, produce some very curious results. The Radicals, regarding the Tories with that sort of feeling with which a rat regards a terrier, or a vagrant eyes the hat and staff of an authorized street-keeper, were ever ready to support Ministers when the Tories agitated a question in which the security of the Ministry was involved; but when the same Radicals, presuming on the value of their services in the hour of need, would push their demands for organic changes, and projects which Ministers were not disposed to encourage, the latter had only to cry out 'Constitution in danger', and the Tories would come instantly to the rescue, and the Radicals be driven back discomfited. This was all notoriously true of the parties, collectively considered. Nevertheless, there were individuals, and even small sections of the extreme parties, namely, the Tories and Radicals, who did not join heartily, and sometimes would not join at all, in supporting Ministers, but 'took a pride to gird at them' on every occasion, careless of any consequences. Lord John Russell, in the arms of Sir Robert Peel and Lord Melbourne, under the protection of the Duke of Wellington, is taking shelter from the attacks of Lord Lyndhurst and Lord Brougham, who, being extreme members of the extreme parties, prove the truth of the proverb that extremes meet. Lord John Russell is evidently ashamed of his weakness, and seems to remonstrate with destiny on the hardness of his lot, in being a Minister, and a wilful and wayward one, too, but yet unable to run alone. Lord Melbourne is evidently a spoiled child, and fully sensible of the advantages of being one.

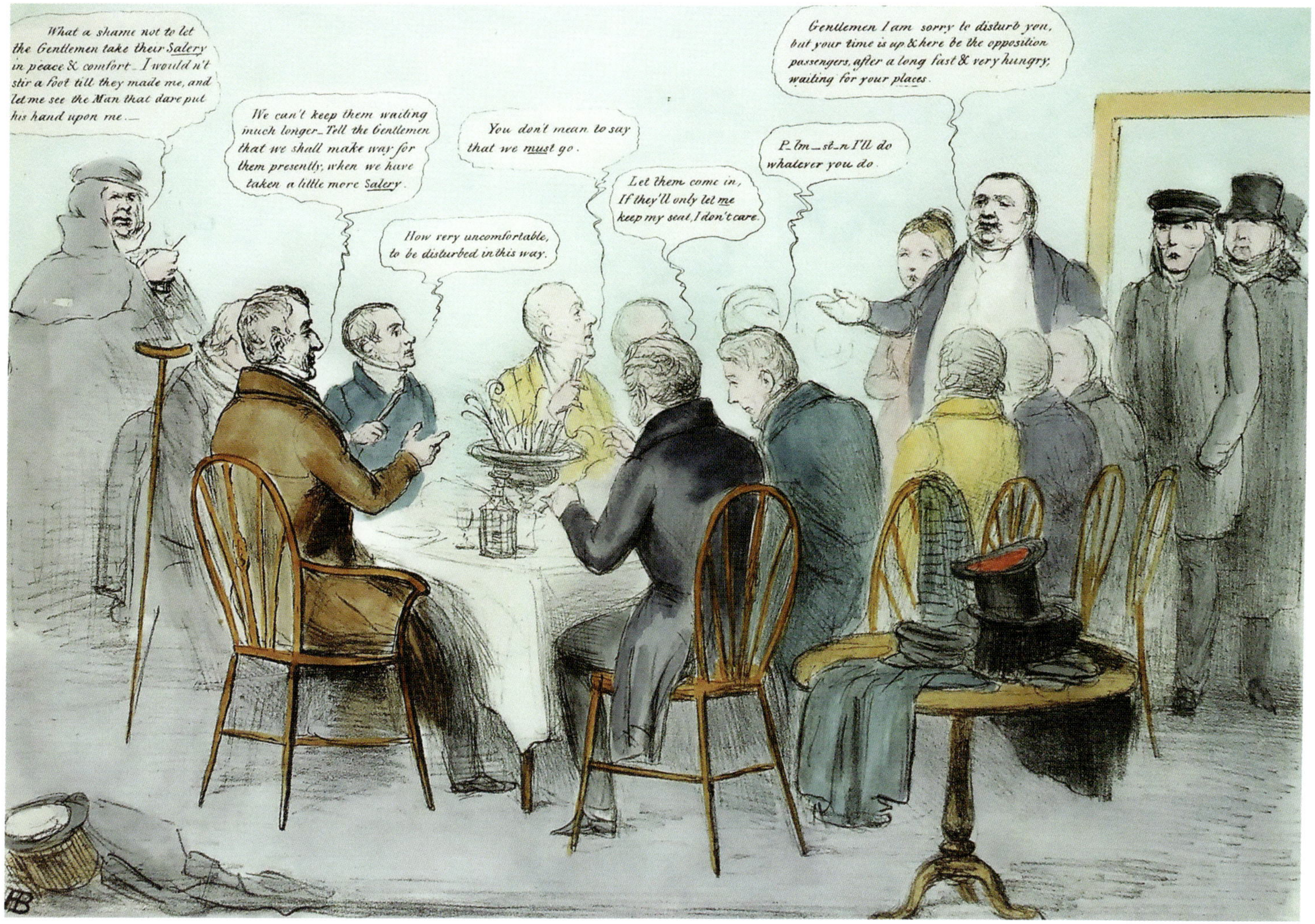

[62] ***No. 567, 'Coach Dinner – Castle Inn – Windsor' (published 31 Dec. 1838)*** A group of men seated at dinner (from left to right, Lord Holland with a crutch, Lords Melbourne, John Russell, Duncannon, Palmerston, Glenelg), responding to John Bull, standing at right, with a young woman behind him (Queen Victoria), announcing that they must make room for the opposition passengers, entering the door at far right (the Duke of Wellington and Sir Robert Peel); a man standing at far left, wearing a cloak (Daniel O'Connell). The ill-success of Ministers in some of their most important measures, and particularly those relating to colonial affairs (notably in Canada, following the rebellion there), encouraged the idea that they must resign, and 'H.B.' has seized, as usual, the ruling topic of the day to discuss it after his own peculiar style and manner. The Ministers, travellers by the first coach (we will call it the Sovereign), are seated at dinner at the 'Castle Inn, Windsor'. The opposition coach has overtaken them, and the travellers (the Duke of Wellington, Sir Robert Peel, and the rest) are being introduced by John Bull to the same table, somewhat pre-maturely as it appears, since the Ministers have not yet quitted their places. In fact, not one of them seems willing to move. The table is filled by Lord Holland (whose seat is pointed out by his crutch), Lord Melbourne, on his right hand, Lord Palmerston and Lord Glenelg (expressing their determination to remain if possible, let who will go), Lord Duncannon, and Lord John Russell. Behind them, as the guard of the coach, stands Mr. O'Connell. Over the shoulder of John Bull appears the head of Queen Victoria.

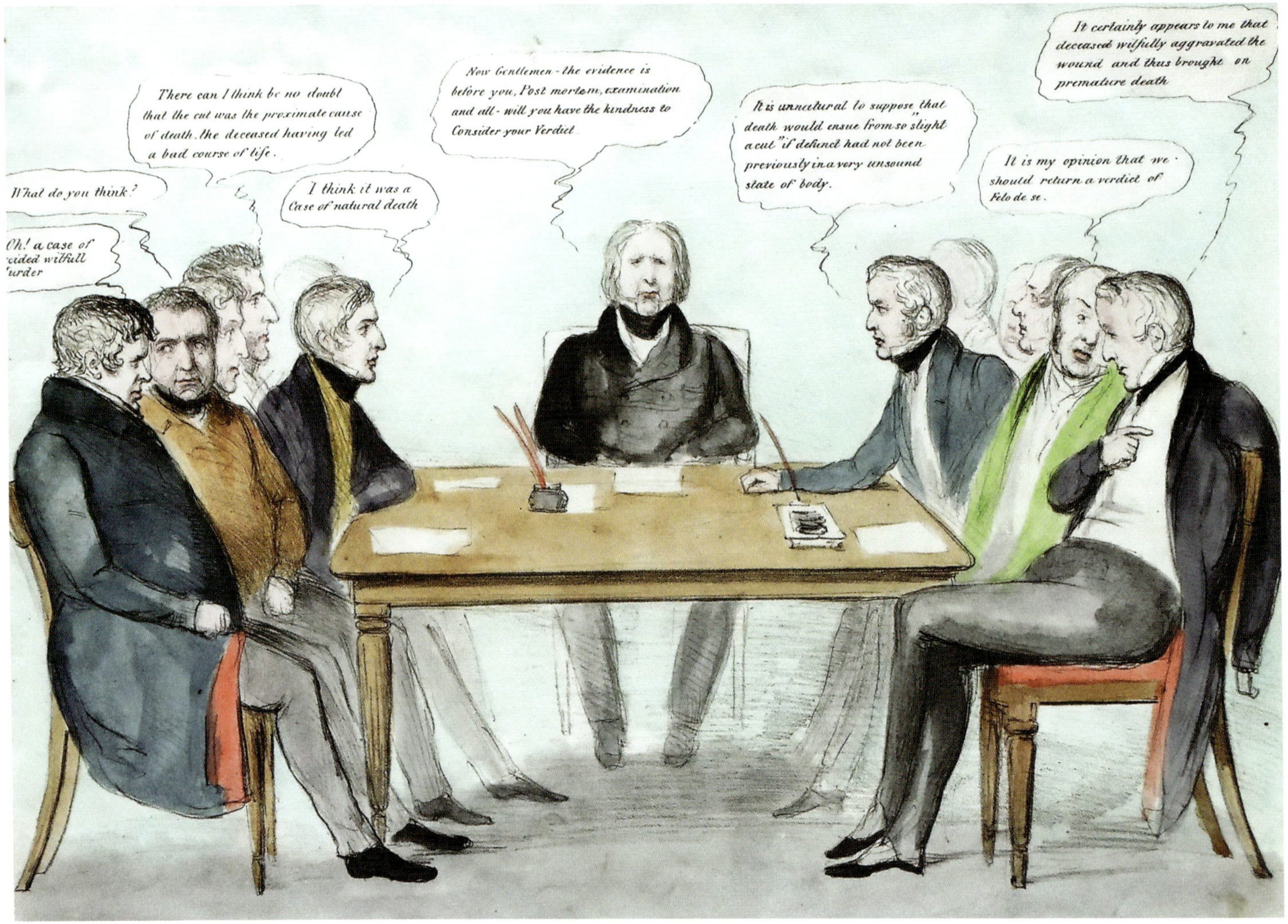

[63] ***No. 589, 'A Coroner's Inquest' (published 1 May 1839)*** In a meeting room, a group of men seated around a table, addressed by the coroner (Thomas Wakley), seated at centre (seated at left, Daniel O'Connell, Joseph Hume, Edward Bulwer, George Grote, John Temple Leader; seated at right, from right to left, Sir Robert Peel, Sir James Graham, Lord Stanley). The speeches of Sir George Sinclair, if not the most edifying, are certainly among the most amusing, that are delivered in the House of Commons. In a debate on the ministerial arrangements, after the temporary resignation of Lord Melbourne, he congratulated the Hon. Member for Finsbury (Mr. Wakley,) upon his being re-cently elected to the office of Coroner for Middlesex, and added that if, in that character, it should ever become his duty to hold an inquest on the body of the defunct Cabinet, he was sure that he would charge the jury to bring in a verdict of felo-de-se, and find that they had committed suicide by constant truckling to their enemies, and frequent treachery to their friends. 'H.B.' has caught up this idea, and embodied it in the present sketch. Mr. O'Connell, Mr. Hume, Sir E. L. Bulwer, Mr. Grote, and Mr. Leader, sit on the left hand. They are not unanimous, as appears by the expressions on their several labels, except that they all seem to agree that the deceased had violence offered; but the gentlemen on the right, who are Sir Robert Peel, Sir James Graham, and Lord Stanley, rather incline to the opinion that the case is one of suicide. Mr. Wakley, the coroner, who sits at the head of the table, does not lead the jury, as Sir George Sinclair supposed that he would, but, with the utmost impartiality, calls on them to give their verdict.

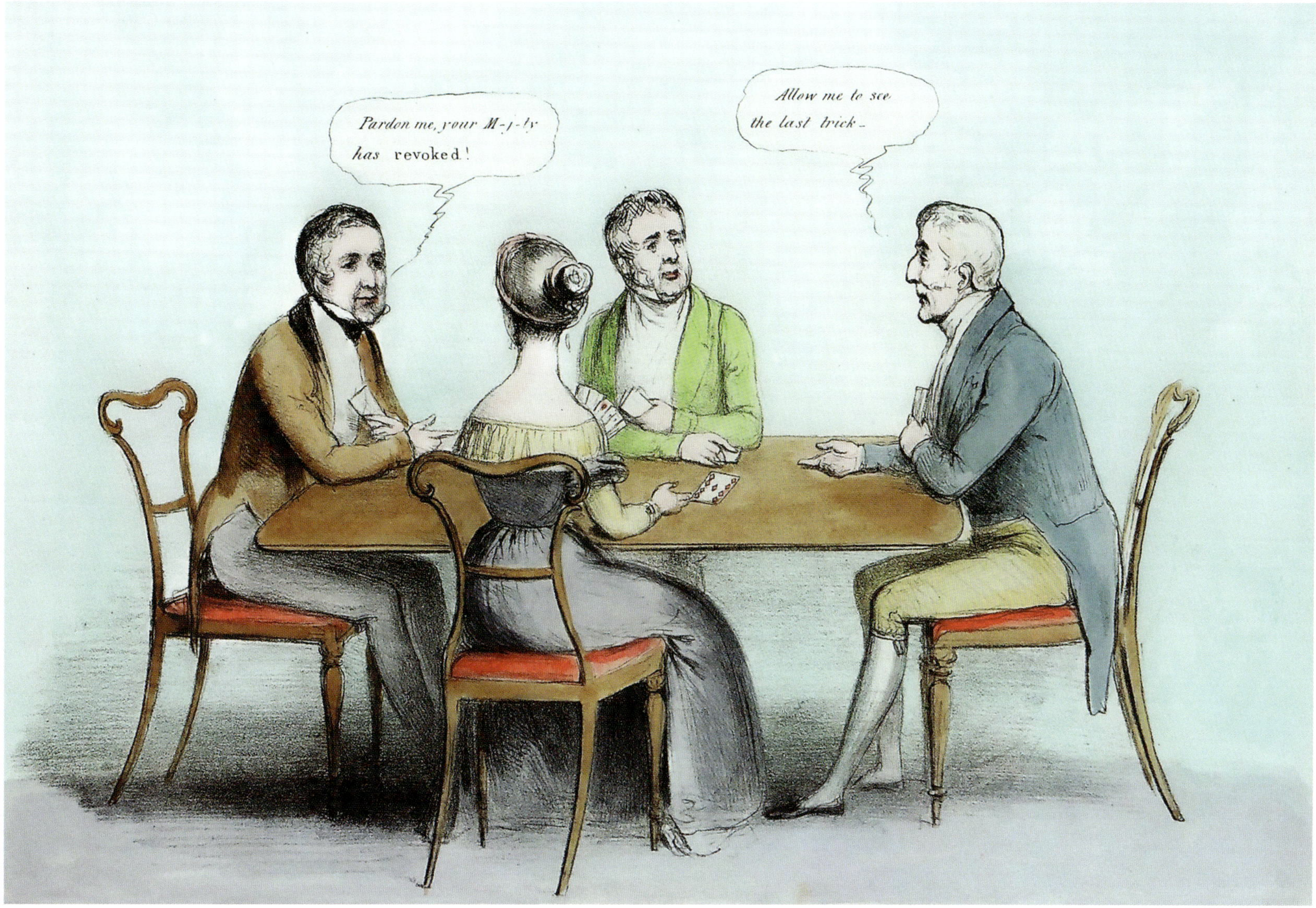

[64] ***No. 590, 'Whist!' (published 20 May 1839)*** Four card-players playing Whist, seated around a table; a man seated at the left (Sir Robert Peel) playing in partnership with the man seated at the right (the Duke of Wellington), the former reproaching the woman seated with his back turned (Queen Victoria), and the latter asking her partner, seated at the opposite side of the table (Lord Melbourne), to see the last trick. This sketch refers to the unexpected resignation, and still more unexpected return to power, of the Melbourne Cabinet, after the vote of the House of Commons on the Jamaica Bill. Queen Victoria having called upon the Duke of Wellington and Sir Robert Peel to form a new administration, and having suddenly broken off the negotiation, is here represented playing at Whist with Lord Melbourne for her partner, against the Duke of Wellington and Sir Robert Peel. Sir Robert, finding himself over trumped by Her Majesty, when he fancied that the game was in his hands, very innocently suggests to Her Majesty that she has revoked, while his partner, the Duke, always taking the shortest and surest method to prove his case, desires to see the last trick.

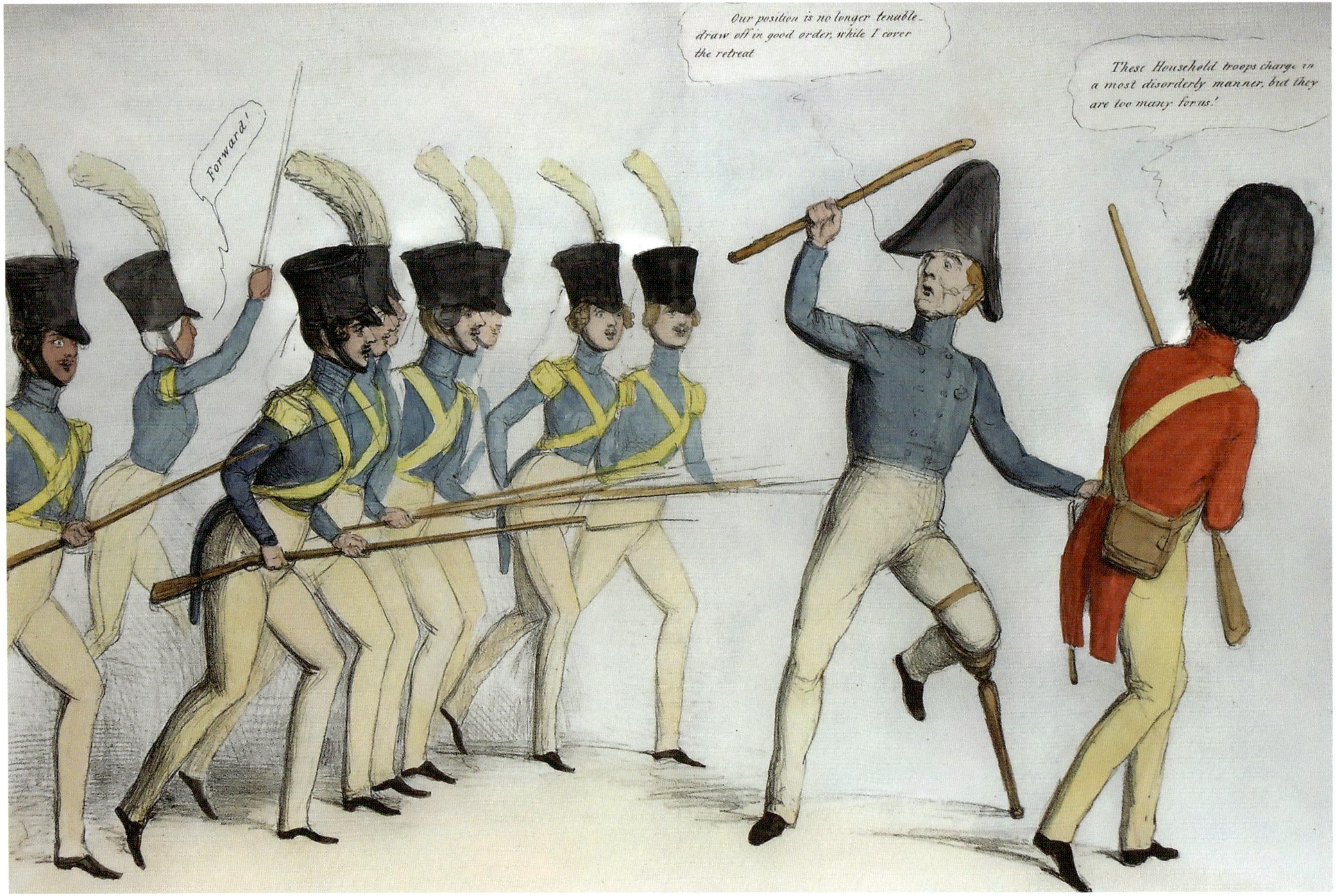

[65] ***No. 591, 'Scene from the Farce of "The Invincibles"' (published 23 May 1839)*** A parody of Thomas Morton's play 'The Invincibles' (1828); a group of female soldiers (Ladies of the Household), cheered on by one in the background at the left (Queen Victoria), putting two male soldiers, in the characters of Brusque and O'Slash, to rout at the point of a bayonet (the Duke of Wellington and Sir Robert Peel). In the second scene of the first Act of the farce, two old soldiers, Brusque and O'Slash, are charged and driven nearly off the stage by a company of ladies in the disguise of soldiers, and 'H.B.' has sported with the comparison between this incident in the farce, and the rumoured defeat of the Duke of Wellington and Sir Robert Peel through the manoeuvres of the ladies of the bed-chamber.

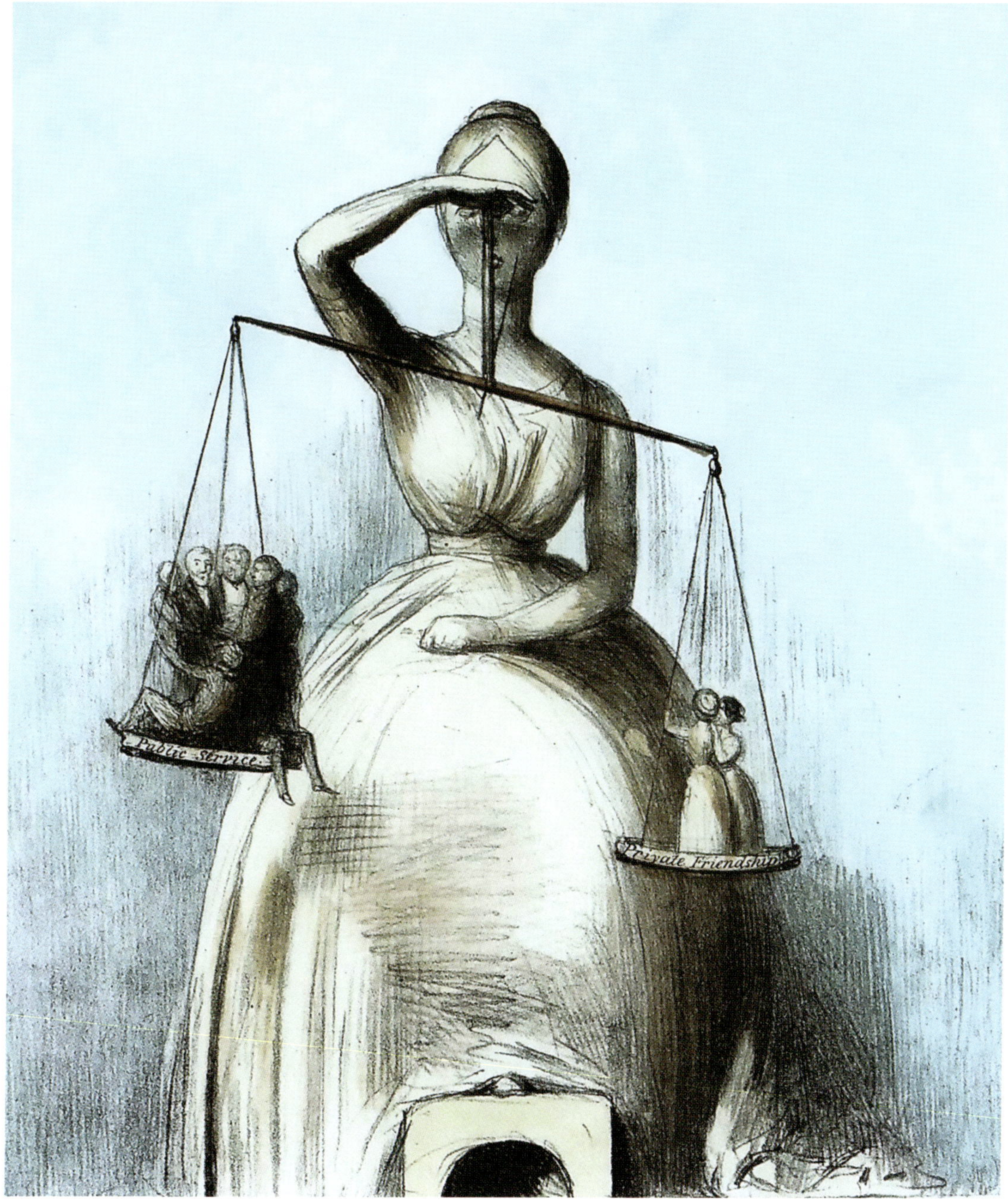

[66] ***No. 592, 'The Balance of Power' (published 5 June 1839)*** Below the title: Figure proposed to displace the old one of Justice at the top of Constitution Hill'. A woman in the character of Justice (Queen Victoria), holding scales; the left pan, lettered with 'Public Service', containing a group of men (among them the Duke of Wellington, Sir Robert Peel and Lord Stanley), weighed down by the right pan, lettered with 'Private Friendship', containing two women (Ladies of the Household). The point of the satire if that the Queen appears to have preferred consulting her private feelings to providing effectually for the public service by refusing to change any of her ladies of the bedchamber in order to accommodate the request of Sir Robert Peel. The scale marked 'Private Friendship' contains two female figures – two ladies, doubtless, belonging to the court, and of the highest worth and purest moral character. The other scale contains some half-dozen statesmen, who hesitate to undertake a government, while the two ladies are suffered to go about the court and talk without restriction. Is friendship so common, and are statesmen so rare, that two tried and devoted friends should not outweigh a whole council of administration-makers? 'H.B.' seems to think not; for he has given to the Queen a firm position, an earnest look, and a steady hand. He has made the fulcrum to look as if it were held with an even as well as with a powerful hand; and the state of the scales appears to be the natural result of gravitation.

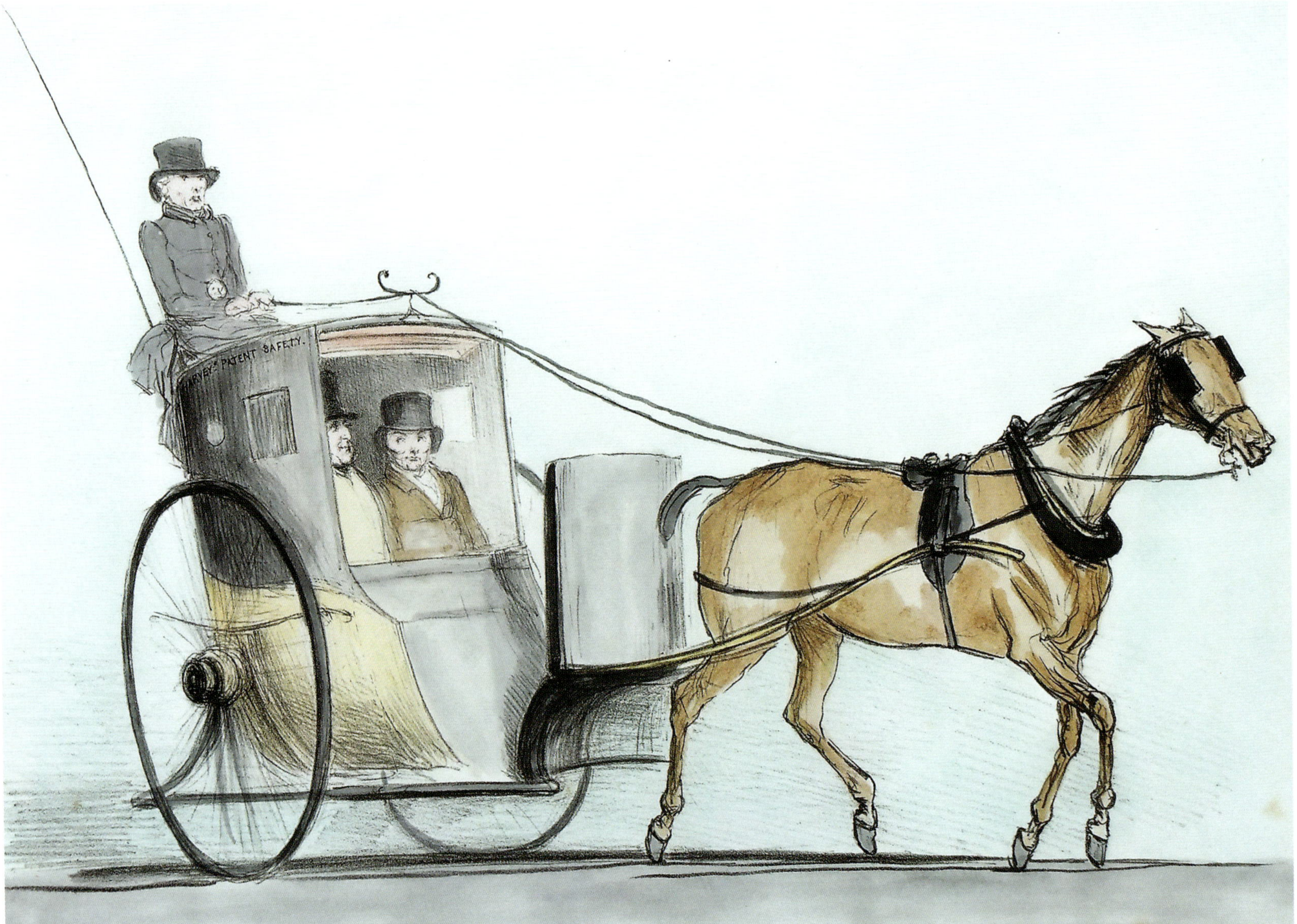

[67] ***No. 596, 'New Patent Safety Cab' (published 14 June 1839)*** A coach, lettered with 'Harvey's Patent Safety', drawn by one horse along a road from left towards right, driven by the coachman seated on top, holding the reins (Daniel Whittle Harvey), carrying two passengers (Sir Robert Peel and Lord John Russell). Mr. Daniel Whittle Harvey, in one of his caustic speeches, suggested the idea of a coalition between Lord John Russell and Sir Robert Peel. This idea is embodied by 'H.B.', by placing the rival leaders side by side in a cab, of which the ingenious inventor of the notion is owner and driver.

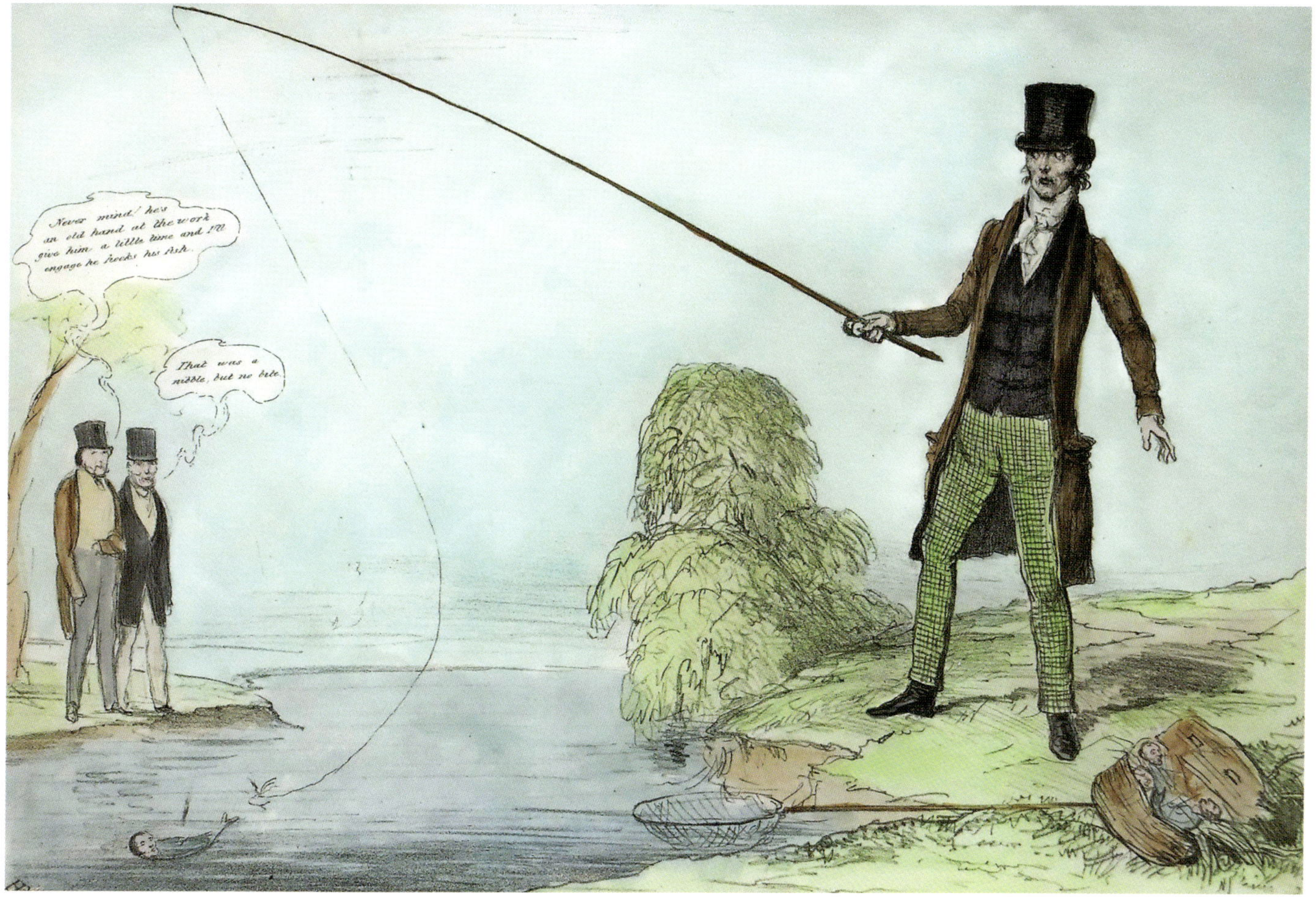

[68] ***No. 598, 'The Complete Angler' (published 24 June 1839)*** An angler standing on a riverbank at right (Henry Warburton), fishing; at left, in the water, a fish with a man's face, avoiding biting the bait (Lord John Russell); at left, two men standing arm-in-arm on the opposite bank, commenting on the situation (Sir Robert Peel, the Duke of Wellington). Soon after the return of the Melbourne Ministry to office, following their short resignation upon the Jamaica Bill, and while they were scarcely secure in their places, Mr. Warburton, the member for Bridport, made a very earnest and energetic appeal to the Ministers in general, and to Lord John Russell in particular, to say something in order to rouse the dormant spirits of the Radical electors; to make, at least, a show of a desire to concede some portion of what they were known to desire, such as the ballot, the abolition of the tax-paying clause in the Reform Act, shorter parliaments, or so forth. 'For here we go on, supporting you against your rivals, the Tories, though you yield us nothing in return; and what sort of an account can we give to our constituents, while we play such an unprofitable game?' Lord John Russell was not to be caught. He knew well enough that the Radicals had no choice – that they must support him, and could not help themselves; that, between them and the Tories, there was no more possibility of coalition than between the hounds and the foxes; and that, as a party, they had no existence, every one being himself a party, or, to speak more properly, an original. In the basket of the Honourable Member are three or four fishes (simple gudgeons) that he has succeeded in hooking, but the one for which he is now plying his rod with all the skill of which he is master, is no gudgeon, but a wary old Jack, who will not bite. The Duke of Wellington and Sir Robert Peel stand looking on. The circumstance which gives a sharper point to this sketch is, that Mr. Warburton is most devotedly fond of that branch of the piscatorial art which has been wittily described as 'a stick and a string', and he is known to spend all his leisure in the enjoyment of the Waltonian sport (i.e. Izaak Walton, author of *The Compleat Angler* [1653]).

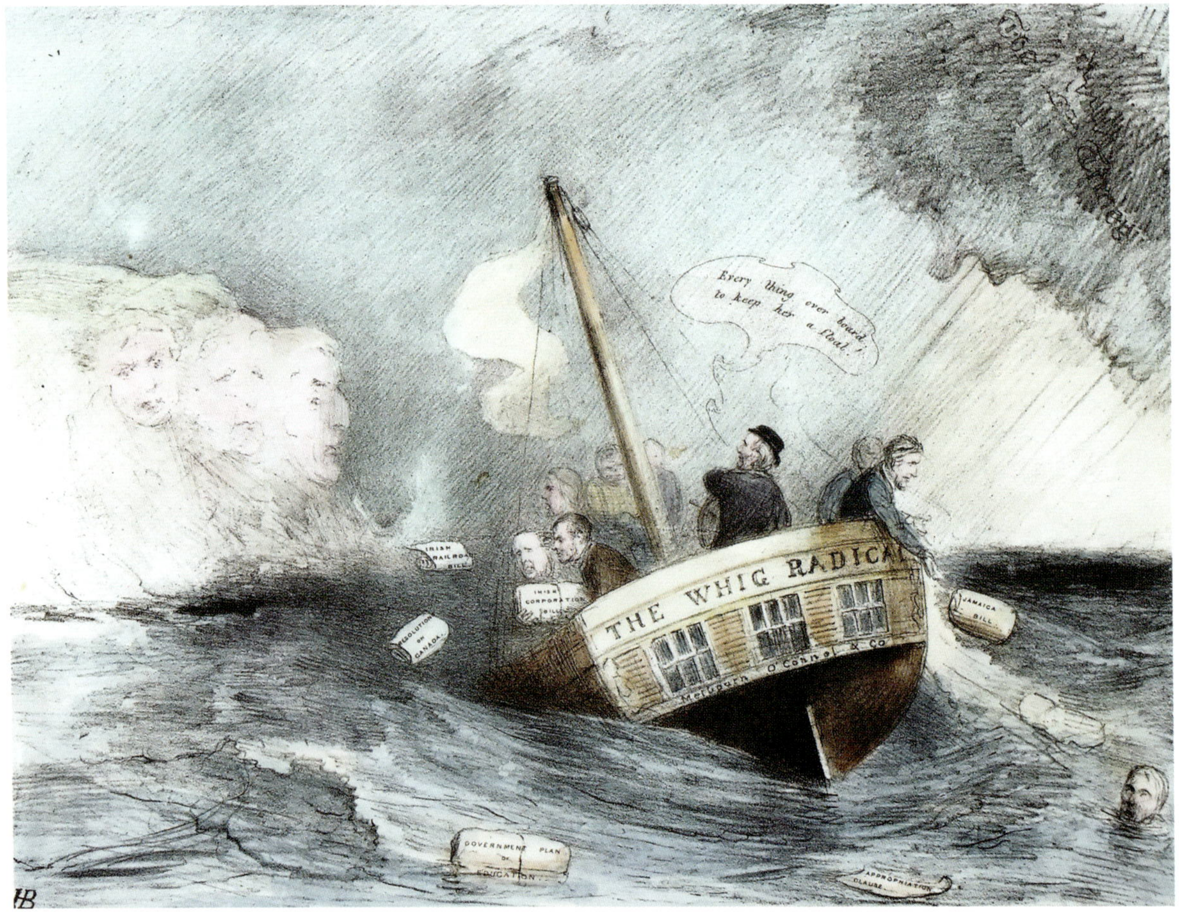

[69] ***No. 601, 'A Ship in Distress – Crew throwing the cargo over board' (published 5 July 1839)*** A ship lettered with 'The Whig Radical' and 'Melbourn O'Connel & Co', sinking at rough seas; its passengers (from left, Thomas Spring Rice, Lord John Russell, Lords Morpeth, Melbourne and Mulgrave), throwing overboard scrolls and packets of papers, lettered with names of parliamentary bills; in the foreground at the far right, a man in the water (Lord Glenelg); in the top right corner, clouds, lettered with 'The Times', with the outline of men's profiles (Lords Brougham and Lyndhurst); at the left, cliffs, with men's heads (Lord Stanley, Sir Robert Peel, the Duke of Wellington). Lord Melbourne's Cabinet, having been reinstated, after their resignation in May 1839, abandoned several measures, on which the numbers of those who held opposite opinions were known to be very nearly balanced. This policy of the government forms the subject of the present sketch. The vessel of the State, bearing the name of the 'Whig-Radical', is still in distress; and to lighten her and give her a chance of riding out the storm, several bulky measures have been flung overboard. The Jamaica Bill is being tossed out by the Marquess of Normanby, as Colonial Secretary; and Lord Monteagle and Lord John Russell are exerting their utmost strength to throw over the Irish Corporation Bill, another measure which the Government had very little chance of carrying. Under the vessel's lee the white cliffs of Albion, presenting the likenesses of Lord Stanley, Sir Robert Peel, and the Duke of Wellington, whose nose forms the bluff-head of the promontory, frown upon the 'Whig-Radical' and her crew; and the dark portentous clouds that hang over the tempest-tossed bark, and seem to threaten it with instant destruction, exhibit the heading of *The Times* newspaper and the countenances of Lords Brougham and Lyndhurst. The 'man overboard' is an allusion to a well-known 1823 picture of William Daniell's, representing a vessel in a gale of wind off the Cape of Good Hope, and a man overboard to whom a hen-coop has been tossed out as the only chance of assistance that can be given him under the distressful circumstances in which the vessel and her crew are placed. In the present sketch, the 'man overboard' is Lord Glenelg; however, here, there is evidently no chance of his receiving any assistance from the crew.

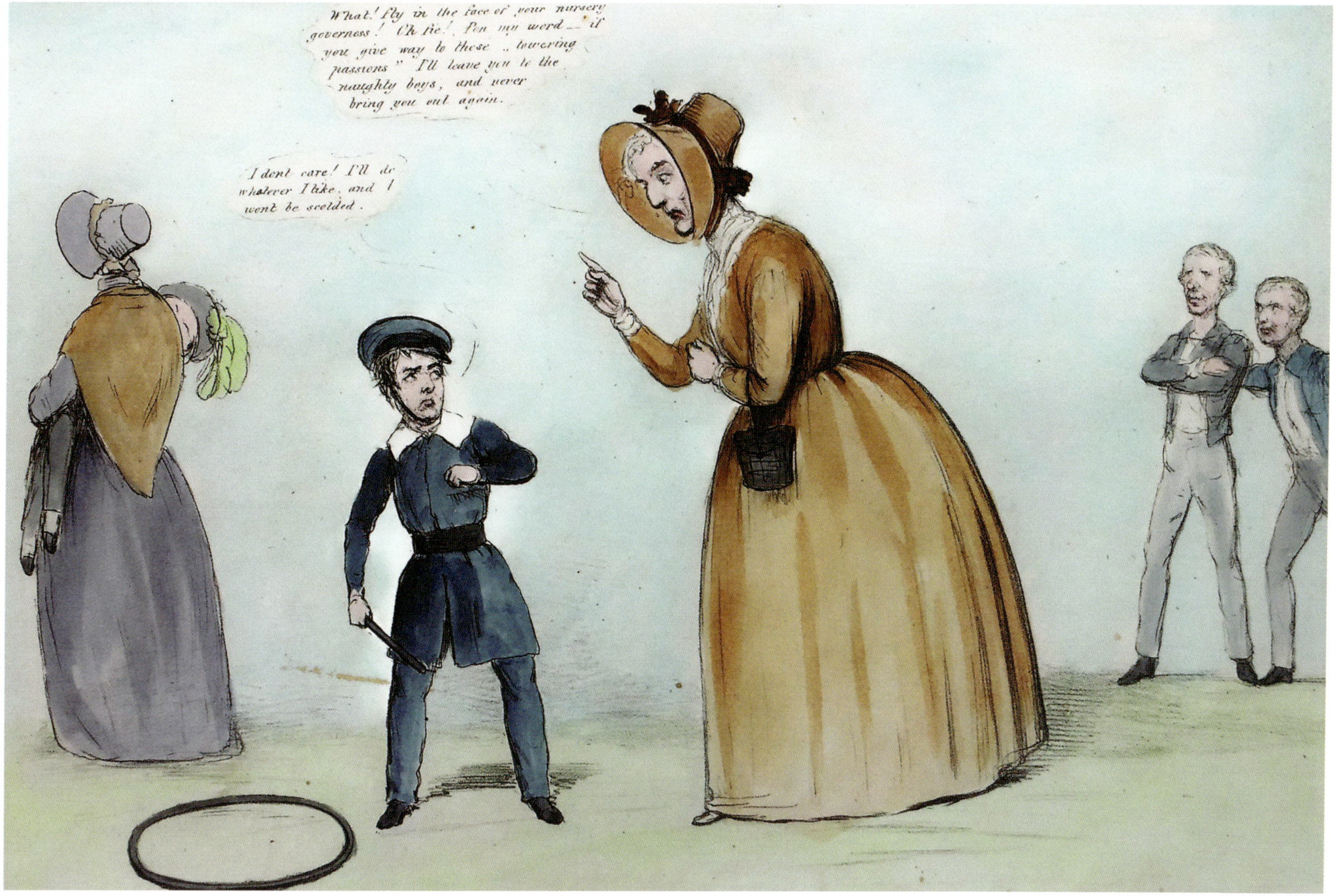

[70] ***No. 607, 'Symptoms of Insubordination' (published 1 Aug. 1839)*** A boy in temper, standing at centre left, with a hoop lying in front of him on the ground, holding a stick (Lord Melbourne), reproved by a man dressed as a woman, standing at the centre right (the Duke of Wellington); at the left, a man dressed as a woman (Sir Robert Peel) carrying a boy in his arms (Lord John Russell), walking away; at the right, two boys watching the scene (Lords Brougham and Lyndhurst). The protection afforded to the Whig Ministry by the Duke of Wellington and Sir Robert Peel, on occasions when the Ministry was assailed either by the most violent of the Radicals, or the most headstrong of the High Tories, however timely and needful, was still too humiliating to be pleasant, and the Whigs were glad of any opportunity to assert, if they could not maintain, their independence. It would also happen that the Duke, conscious of his power, would sometimes exercise a control over the ministry to which they were under the hard necessity (more humiliating still) of yielding submission. The present sketch refers to one of these occasions, and is a sequel to an earlier sketch. Here are the same dry nurses, the same spoiled children, and the same naughty boys, as represented in the former sketch. On this occasion the bigger of the pets (Lord Melbourne) has fallen out with his nurse (the Duke of Wellington), who threatens to withdraw his protection, and leave him to the naughty boys (Lords Brougham and Lyndhurst). There were several occasions about this date, when Lord Melbourne complained heavily, but ineffectually, of the opposition which was given by the Duke of Wellington to the measures of his Government.

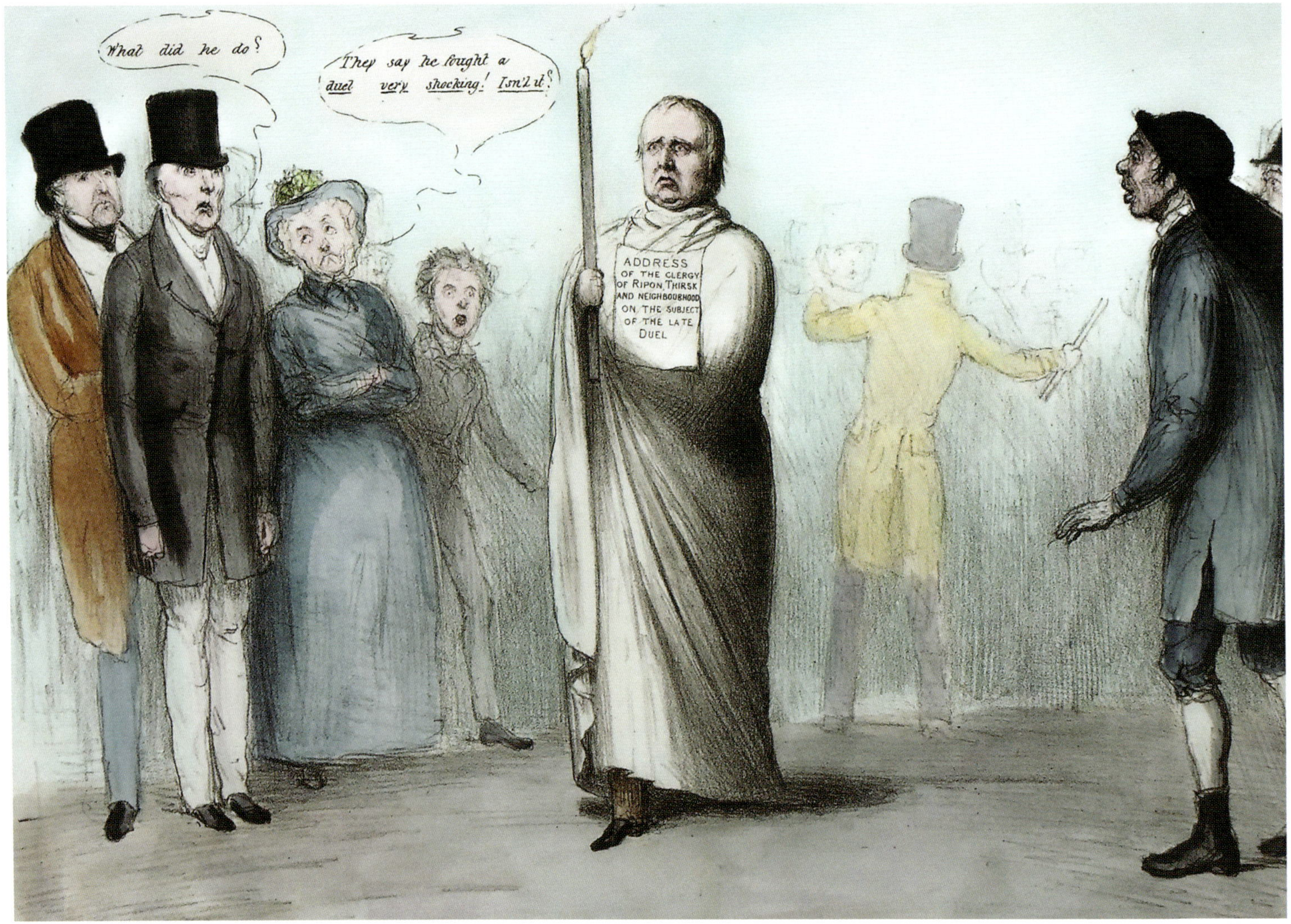

[71] ***No. 617, 'Doing Penance in a White Sheet A LA JANE SHORE' (published 17 Oct. 1839)*** Below the title: Being an awful warning to Duelists [*sic*] in general and certain high individuals in particular. A man holding a burning candle in his right hand, wearing a sheet (Lord Londonderry), walking along a street towards front with a note around his neck, lettered with 'Address of the clergy of Ripon, Thirsk and neighbourhood on the subject of the late duel', watched by an astonished crowd (at the far left, Sir Robert Peel and the Duke of Wellington). The Marquess of Londonderry having fought a duel with Mr. H. Grattan, the clergy of Ripon, Thirsk, and their neighbourhoods addressed to him a representation on the occasion, urging, in forcible terms, the sinfulness of duelling. To this the Noble Marquis wrote a very spirited and characteristic reply, claiming for himself, as a soldier, and for the rest of his profession, the unfettered right of being the best judge and arbiter of his own honor, and submitting that while he exposed his life in doing what he considered to be his duty, in upholding the altar and throne, when attacked, he should find mercy rather than wrath. The figure of the Marquess undergoing his sentence after the fashion of Jane Shore (one of Edward IV's mistresses, who underwent public penance), is very humorously portrayed, and Sir Robert Peel, and the Duke of Wellington, the former of whom sent a challenge to Mr. Hume, and the latter of whom fought a duel with the Earl of Winchilsea (1829), are very naturally interested spectators of the awful scene.

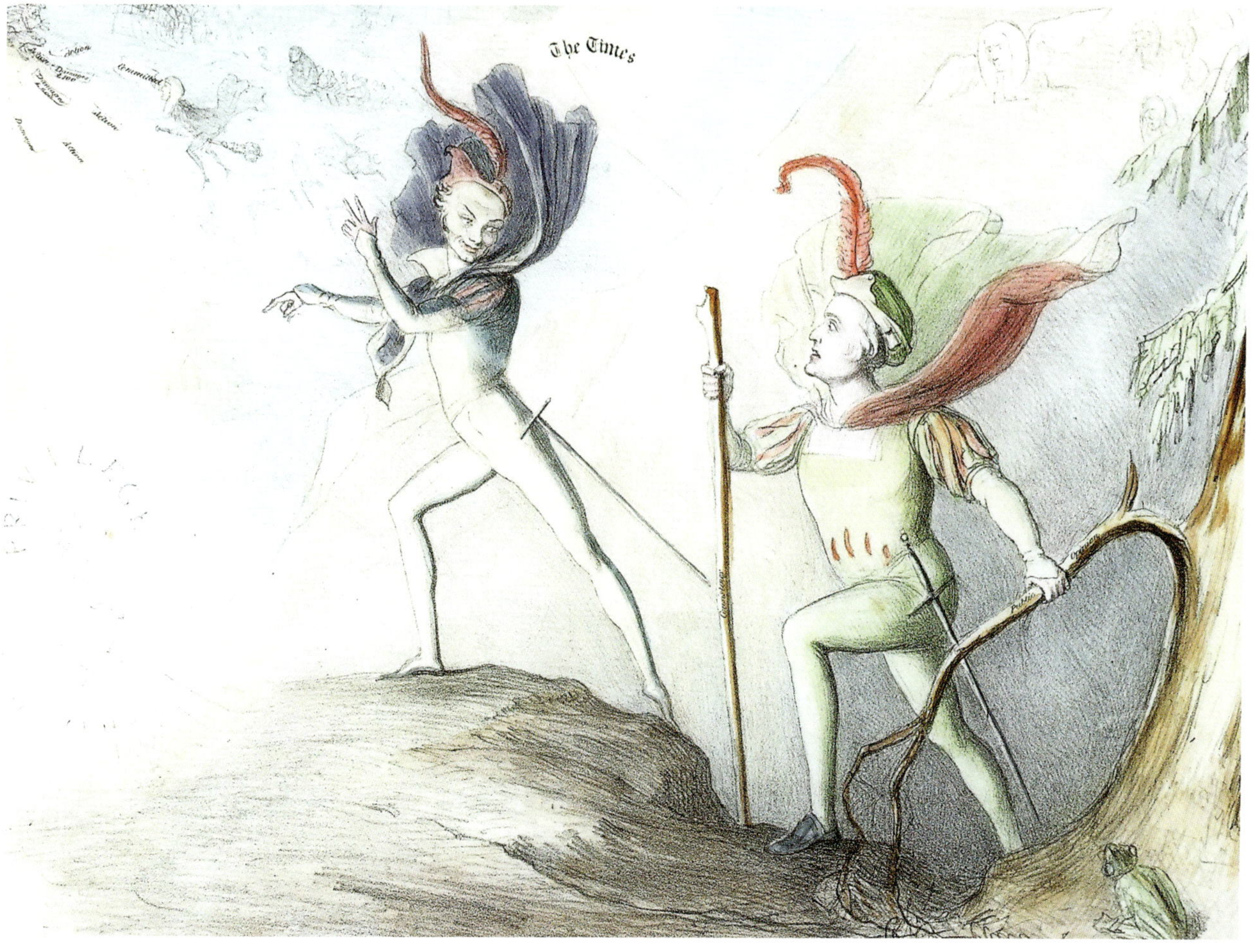

[72] ***No. 626, 'A Scene from Faust freely translated from Retzsch's outlines' (published 26 Feb. 1840)*** Friedrich August Moritz Retzsch (1779–1857) produced 26 plates based on Goethe's Faust, which 'H.B.' parodies here. A man in the character of Faust (Sir Robert Peel), holding a walking stick in his right hand, breaking a branch of a tree, lettered with 'Public Opinion', with his left hand, following a man in the character of Mephistopheles (Lord John Russell), walking ahead of him towards a spot of light at the left, with the outline of a small creature, with 'Privilege' lettered above, pointing towards figures in the sky; the sun shines from top centre, lettered with 'The Times'; men wearing long wigs are flying in the sky at the top right. Sir Robert Peel, as Faust, is led by Lord John Russell as Mephistopheles, in pursuit of the ignis fatuus Privilege which is seen dancing in the distance; and so intent is Sir Robert on the object before him, that he heeds not the bright beams which emanate from the great luminary above, (*The Times* newspaper) or hesitates for a moment to tempt the uncertain ground before him, though public opinion is breaking beneath him. The friendly spirits whom he leaves behind are the Judges, headed by the Lord Chief Justice Denman; and the supernatural beings flitting before the tempter Mephistopheles are the Speaker of the House of Commons (Charles Shaw-Lefevre), Serjeant at Arms (Sir William Gosset), &c. The sketch refers to the vexed question of parliamentary privilege. In 1839, John Joseph Stockdale sued the official parliamentary publisher, Hansard, for defamation. Hansard was ordered by the House of Commons to plead that he had acted under their order and was protected by parliamentary privilege. The Court of Queen's Bench, led by Denman, rejected this defence and awarded damages to Stockdale. However, the sheriffs empowered to carry out the orders were imprisoned by order of the Commons. The dispute was ended by the Parliamentary Papers Act of 1840 which legislated that all civil or criminal proceedings against anyone for the publication of papers which either House of Parliament had ordered to be printed could be prevented on production of a certificate of authority. 'H.B.'s print references Peel's keen defence of the privileges of the House.

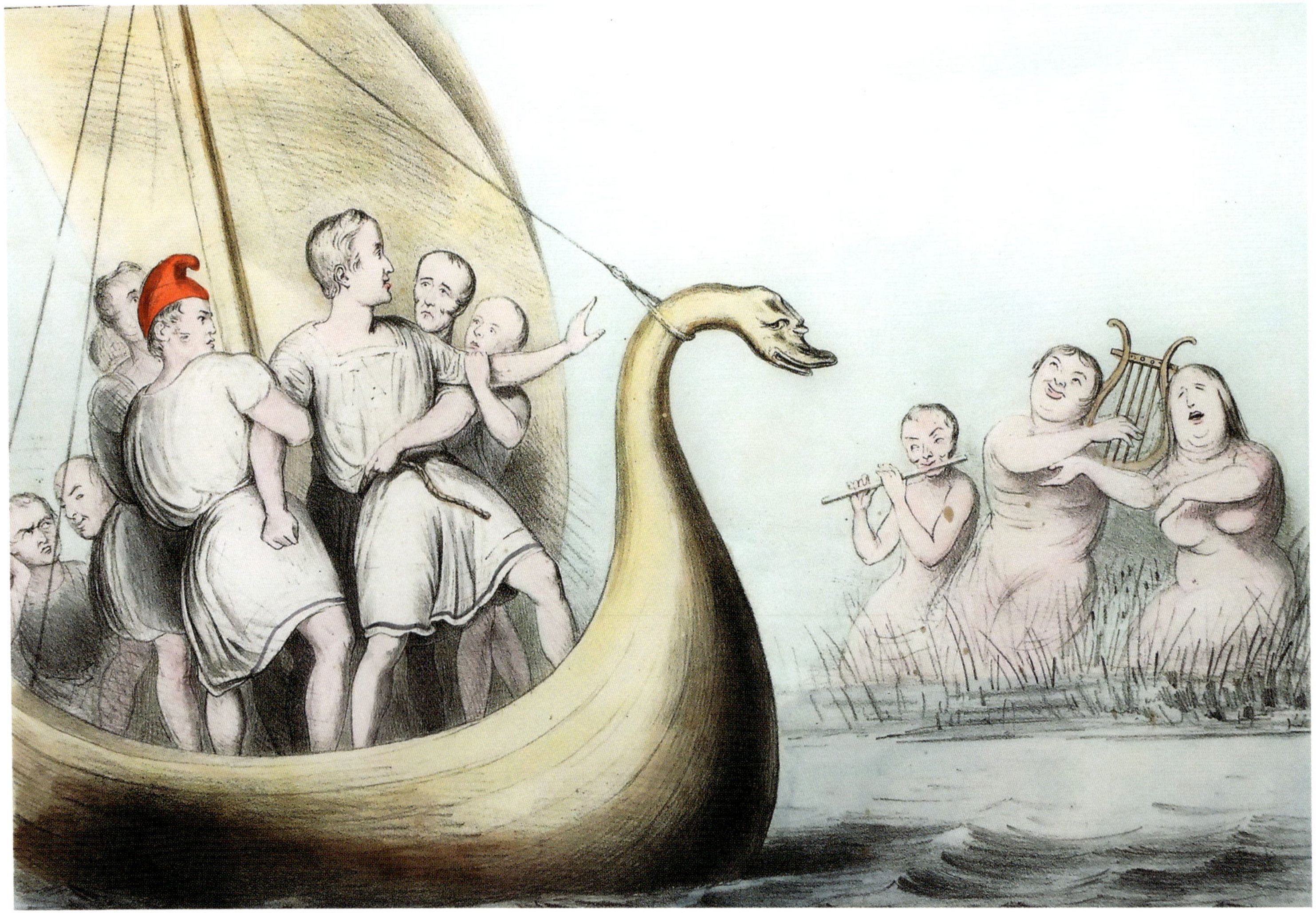

[73] ***No. 628, 'Ulysses and the Syrens' (published 3 Mar. 1840)*** A man in the character of Ulysses (Sir Robert Peel), tied to the mast by men standing around him on boat in the shape of a swan (on his right, Charles Law, on his left, Sir Edward Sugden); two men seated in the stern at the far left (Lord Stanley and Sir James Graham); at the right, three men kneeling among reeds, in the characters of syrens, the one at the left playing the flute (Lord John Russell), the one at the centre the lyre (Daniel O'Connell), and the one at the right singing (Thomas Wakley). Sir Robert Peel, the Ulysses of the Conservative party, is in the act of encountering one of the dangers, of which his prototype was warned by Circe, when he commenced his voyage home, namely the sweet and enchanting voices of the Syrens. These dangerous ladies appear in the likenesses of Mr. Wakley (somewhat redundant in his personal attractions), Mr. O'Connell luting, and Lord John Russell fluting. Not only is it impossible for the three performers to unite in harmony, but they are actually performing different pieces: Lord John Russell pipes, 'Come live with me and be my love', – Mr. O'Connell twangs, 'The Groves of Blarney', – and Mr. Wakley practices, 'Ah! How Sophia'. Ulysses is cleared touched by the force of the spell: and it is with difficulty that Sir Edward Sugden on his left, and the Hon. Charles Law on his right, are able to restrain him; 'heaping brand on brand', according to the injunctions of the goddess. In the stern of the boat is Lord Stanley looking stern; and Sir James Graham is putting up his ample shoulders to assist those, who, to master Sir Robert are tying him to the mast.

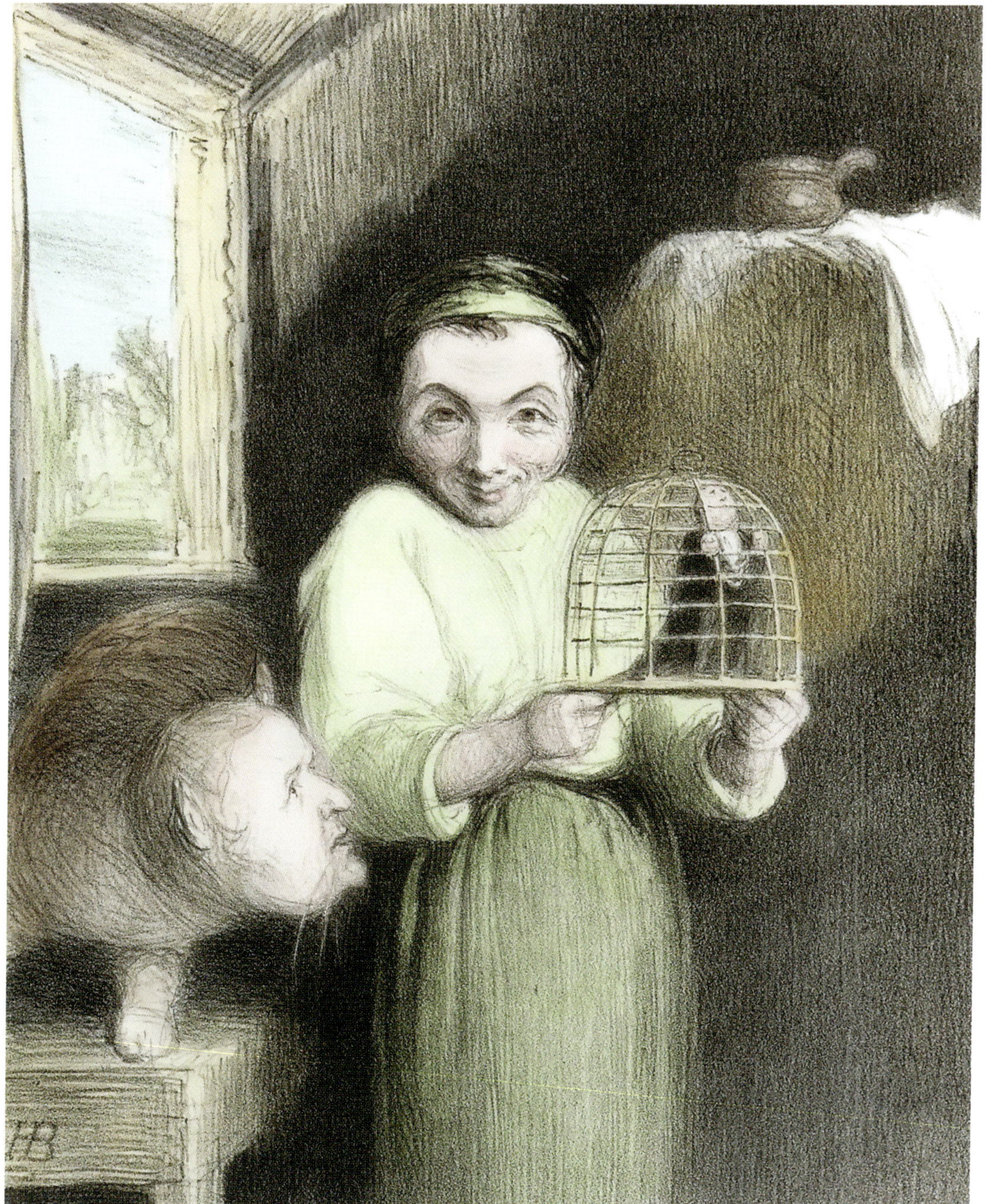

[74] ***No. 629, 'Muscipula' (published 14 Mar. 1840)*** A man dressed as a little girl (Lord John Russell), standing in a room at the centre, holding a cage with a small man inside it, holding onto the bars (Sheriff William Evans), watched by a cat with a man's face (Sir Robert Peel), standing on a table under the window at left. An allusion to Sir Joshua Reynolds's picture 'Muscipula' – the Mouse Trap, of which this is a parody. Sir Joshua's picture represents a sly little girl delighted beyond measure with the success of her wiles, in having entrapped a poor unfortunate mouse, who has infringed the privileges of the kitchen or larder. In her delicious enjoyment of the power obtained over her victim, the sly looking little puss is tempting and tantalizing a graver mouser, who looks eagerly at the prize, and is evidently her rival in the art of ingeniously tormenting. Here, the owner of the Mouse Trap is Lord John Russell, the mouse, the Sheriff of Middlesex (Evans) and the trap, the place where the Serjeant at Arms confines those who are committed to his custody; the whiskered tabby is Sir Robert Peel. The case of the Sheriff was particularly unfortunate, inasmuch as he was placed between two traps, and could only escape one by running into the other. As Sheriff he was bound by his office, to execute the writ against Hansard, and to obtain the damages awarded by the Court of Law; for disobeying the writ he was liable to be punished as a false Sheriff, for obeying it he was punished as a breaker of the privileges of the House of Commons.

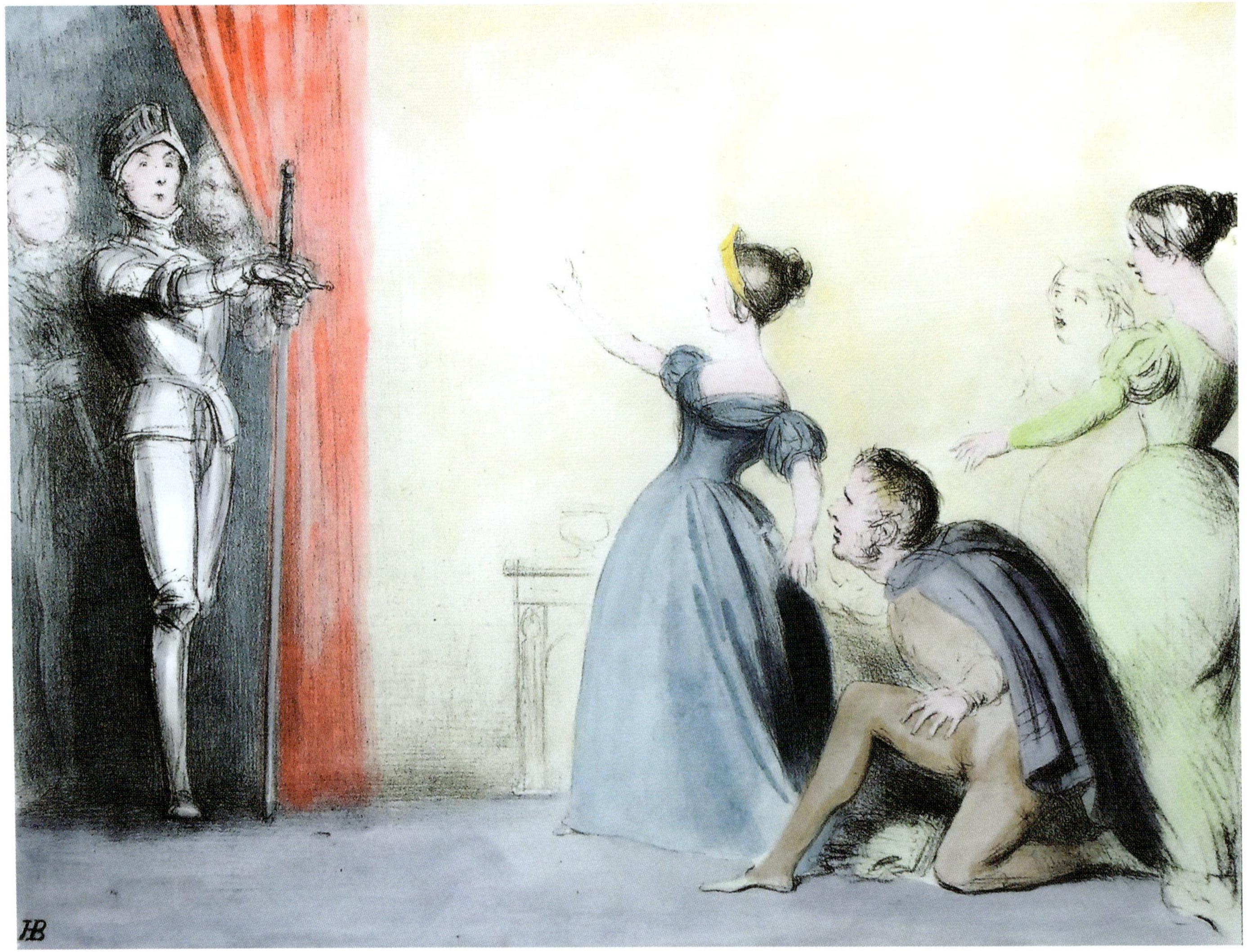

[75] ***No. 630, 'Tableau from the New Play of "Mary Stewart" – Sketched with great freedom' (published 16 Mar. 1840)*** A man standing at left in the character of Lord Ruthven from 'Mary Stuart' (Duke of Wellington), wearing armour, holding a large sword vertically on the floor; two men standing behind a curtain behind him (Sir Robert Peel, and Lord Lyndhust in the character of the Earl of Morton); at right, a man in the character of Rizzio (Lord Melbourne), kneeling on the floor on his left knee, next to three women, the one at the centre in the character of Mary Stuart (Queen Victoria). Mr. Haynes's 'Tragedy of Mary Stuart' had a great run at the period, at which this sketch is dated; and the scene in which Rizzio is murdered, presented a tableau of which this sketch is a faithful copy. Its adaptation to political circumstances and to the personages portrayed in the sketch, is a freedom greater than 'H.B.' is in the habit of taking with facts. In the spirit of these representations, Melbourne is here sketched as the well-known David Rizzio, the favourite of the unfortunate Mary Queen of Scots, and the object of the jealousy and hatred of certain of the nobility, who desired to obtain a control over the queen's actions. The Duke of Wellington stands for Lord Ruthven, 'in complete armour, looking pale and ghastly, as one scarcely recovered from long sickness', and behind him is Lord Lyndhurst in the character of the cruel and relentless 4th Earl of Morton (who was amongst those that burst into Mary's bedchamber and murdered her secretary, David Rizzio).

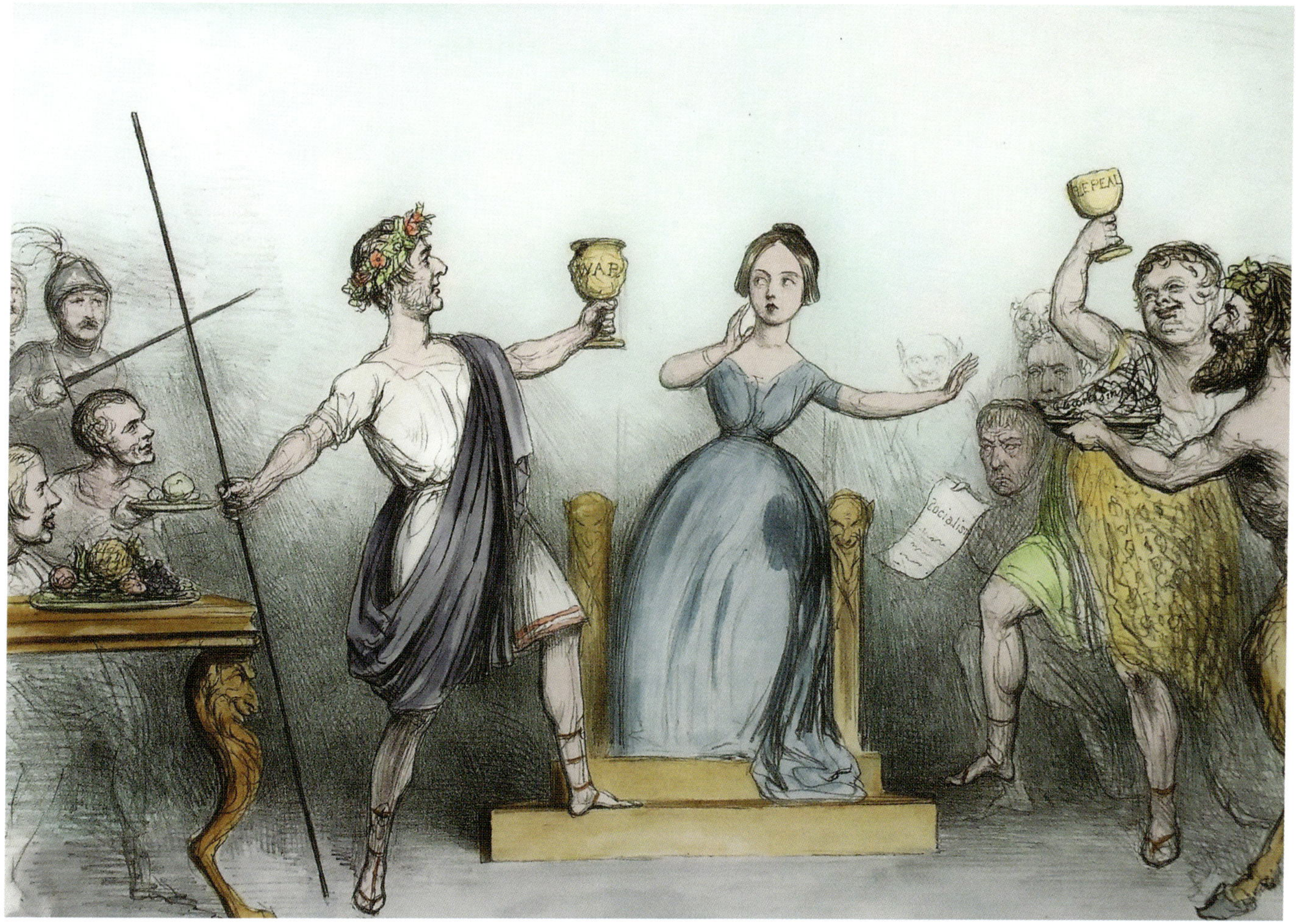

[76] ***No. 632, 'Comus and the Lady' (published 9 Apr. 1840)*** A young woman seated on a throne (Queen Victoria), surrounded by revellers, who offer wines and fruit; two seated at a table at the left (Lords Morpeth and John Russell), one standing at the centre left in the character of Comus (Lord Melbourne), with his left foot on the platform of the throne, holding a cup lettered with 'War'; at the right, a man kneeling, holding a piece of paper lettered with 'Socialism' (Robert Owen), a man seen behind him (Joseph Hume), another man holding a cup lettered with 'Repeal' (Daniel O'Connell), and a satyr at the far right holding a bowl with a boar's head, lettered with 'Chartism' (Mr Muntz); in the background at the left, two soldiers arriving to rescue the woman (Sir Robert Peel and the Duke of Wellington). Lord Melbourne as Comus (the Greek god of festivities and revelry), having succeeded in charming the Queen into the seat, is offering her his cup inscribed with 'War' by which it is intended to be understood that the policy which the queen had been persuaded to adopt respecting Egypt was very likely to lead to this result. On the left hand of Lord Melbourne is Lord John Russell offering fruit, and farther still to the left is the head of Lord Morpeth. The monsters forming 'the midnight crew', are composed of Mr. Muntz (one of the Members for Birmingham), in the likeness of a hairy satyr, holding a dish in which lies a boar's head inscribed 'Chartism'. Mr. O'Connell flourishing a cup on which is written 'Repeal', Mr. Hume, and a cadaverous wretch holding up a paper wherein is inscribed the word 'Socialism'. Lord Melbourne had introduced Owen at Court, leading to a severe denunciation by the Bishop of Exeter (Henry Phillpotts) in the House of Lords, and by the journals of the Conservative party. In the background, behind Lord Morpeth and Lord John Russell, the Duke of Wellington and Sir Robert Peel, as the two brothers, are seen rushing in with drawn swords to rescue the lady, even as, in the character of Conservatives, they have rescued the Queen from the influence of the Whigs.

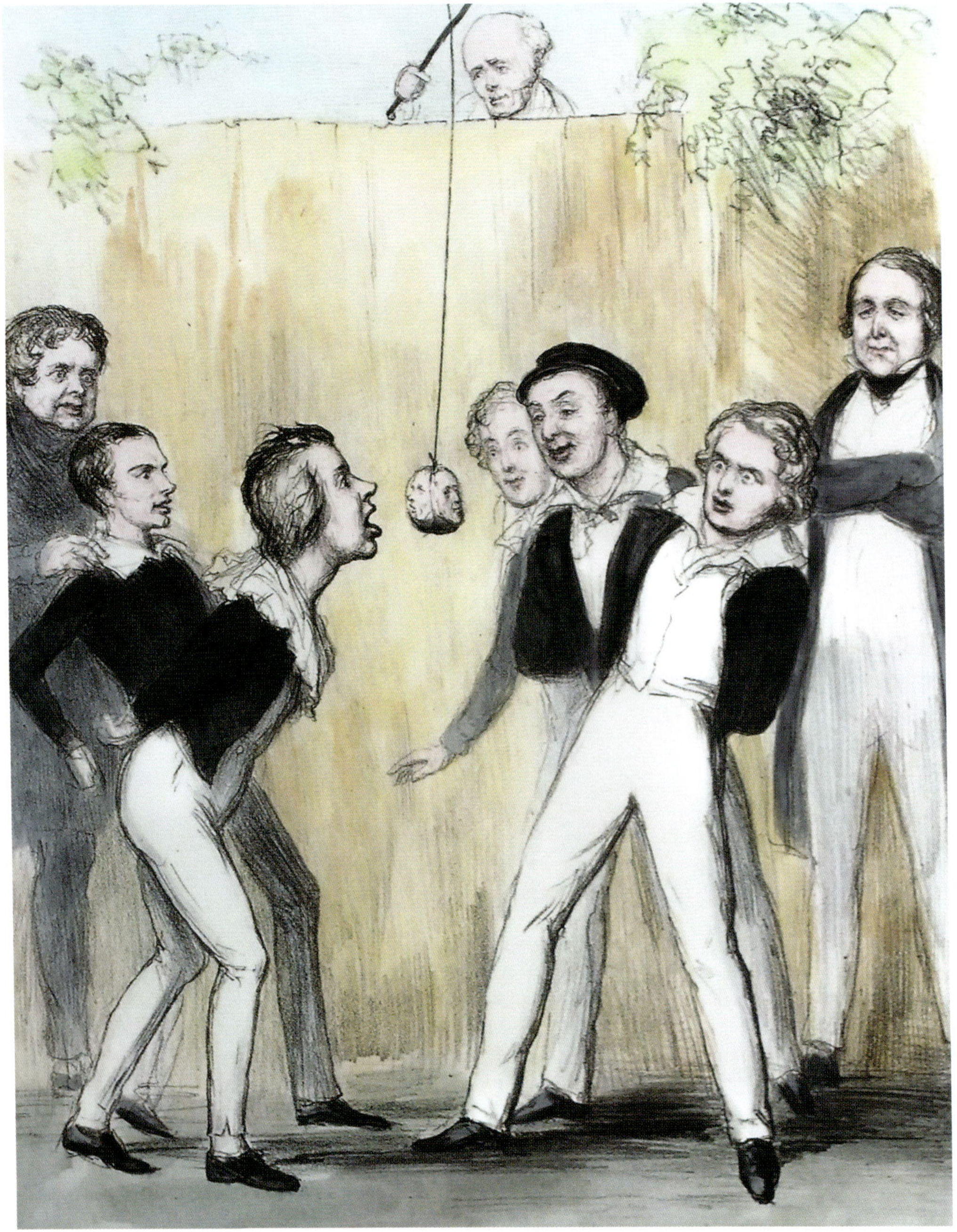

[77] ***No. 646, 'New Game of Snap Apple' (published 1 July 1840)*** A man looking over a wall in the background at the centre (Lord Grey), holding a string with an apple with two men's faces (Lord Howick and Charles Wood), which five boys are biting at alternately (at left, Lords John Russell and Morpeth; at right, Emerson Tennent, Sir James Graham, Lord Stanley); two adults looking on at the far left (Daniel O'Connell) and the far right (Sir Robert Peel). The two seceding Members, Lord Howick and Mr. Charles Wood, are represented in this sketch as a prize, for which the rivals, Lord Stanley and Lord Morpeth, are contending, after the fashion of the well-known school-game of Snap Apple. The resemblance of the scene to the play-ground of a school is rendered perfect by the friends of the two antagonists respectively taking sides. Lord Stanley, on the right, is assisted by Sir James Graham and Mr. Emerson Tennent; and Lord Morpeth, on the left, by Lord John Russell. Behind his Lordship stands Mr. O'Connell, as an umpire on one side, and behind Lord Stanley Sir Robert Peel stands as the umpire on the other. The game, however, is not left to chance, or to the skill of the players; for, over the wall, unobserved, as it seems by any one, the venerable Earl Grey is using a little paternal influence to direct the suspended fruit into the mouth of Lord Morpeth.

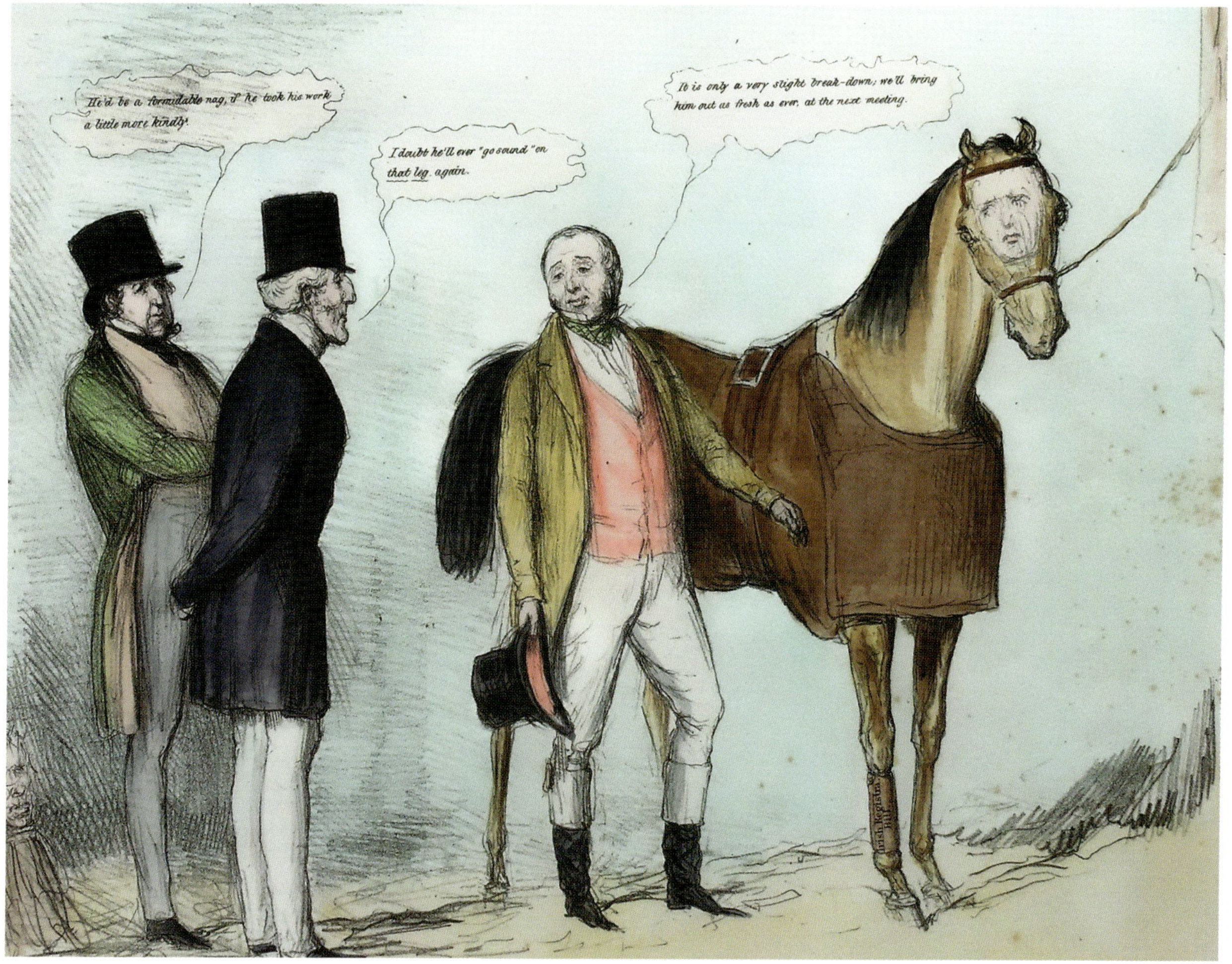

[78] ***No. 648, 'The Derby Favourite a little amiss' (published 6 Aug. 1840)*** Two men standing at the left (Sir Robert Peel and the Duke of Wellington), talking to a horse groom, standing at the centre (Sir James Graham), about the chances of recovery of a horse, with a man's face, standing at the right (Lord Stanley); at the far left, a broom with a man's face (Lord Brougham). The Derby favourite, or in sporting phrase, the favourite for the Derby, is, of course, Lord Stanley, the eldest son of the Earl of Derby. His Bill to amend the system of registering votes in Ireland, threatened at its commencement to prove the destruction of the Ministry, and the successive majorities obtained by his Lordship in divisions upon the Bill in its early stages, led to a belief that it would certainly pass the House of Commons; but the opposition given to it by Mr. O'Connell, created so much delay, that Lord Stanley, unwilling to press too hard on his party, by keeping Members in constant attendance to the end of the session, gave up the Bill in something like disgust, announcing at the same time his intention to resume it next session. The Derby favourite is here exhibited as having broken down; his off fore leg, on which is a bandage inscribed 'Irish Registration Bill', has given way, and consequently he is, in the language of the turf, 'a little amiss'. His groom, Sir James Graham, speaks with confidence of his speedy and perfect recovery, but the Duke of Wellington, having much more experience in such cases, predicts with certainty the irreparable nature of the injury. Sir Robert Peel hints that the accident is in some measure owing to the impetuosity of the 'favourite's temper'. Having completed the composition of the picture, 'H.B.' appears to have indulged a whim, which perhaps was an after-thought, and presented itself in a manner so tempting that he could not resist it. That invariable inmate of a stable, a birch-broom, stands in the corner, and 'H.B.' has been pleased to give it the exact likeness of a certain ex-Lord Chancellor (Henry Brougham) in his robe and band.

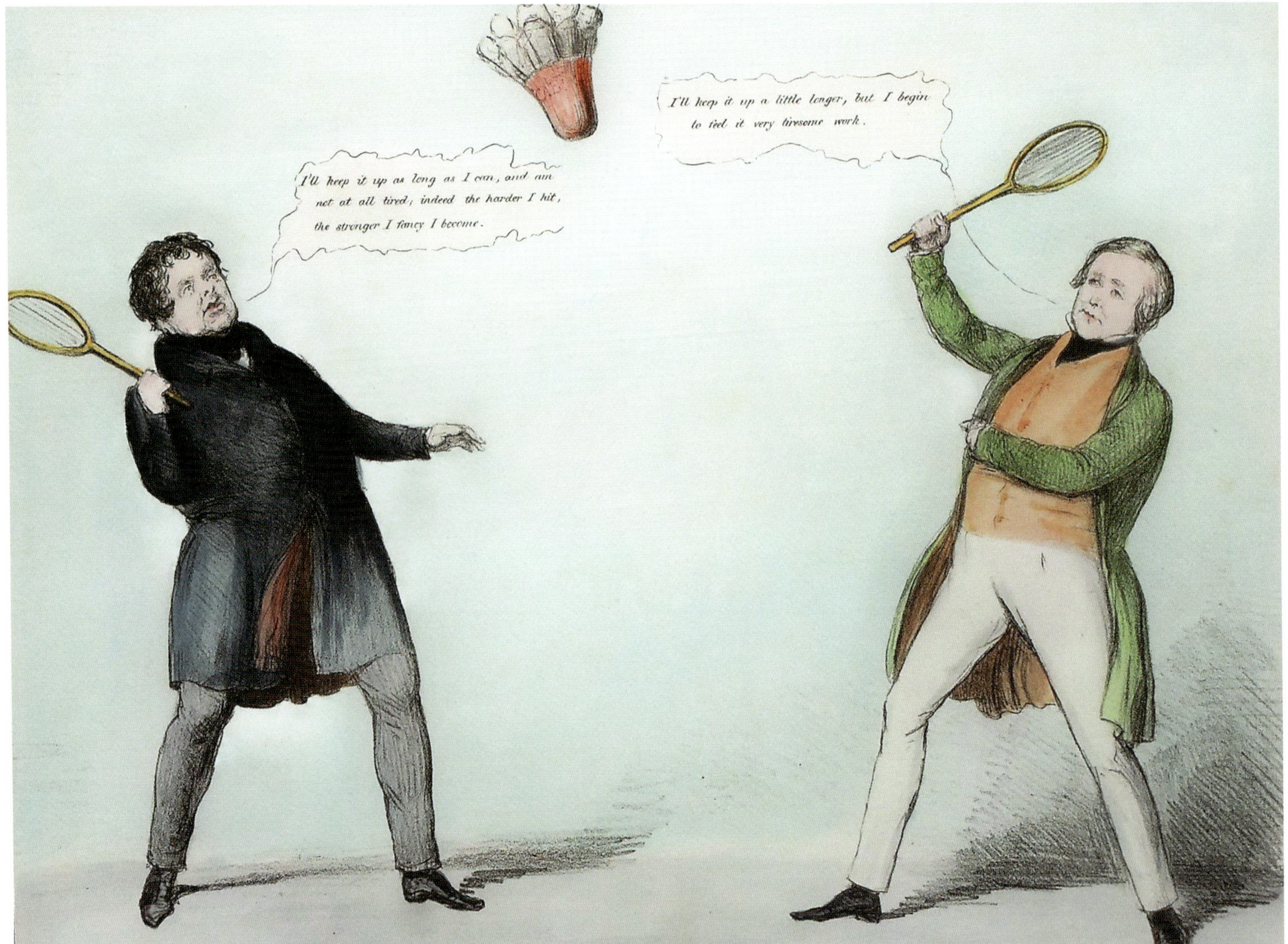

[79] ***No. 649, 'The Shuttlecock Ministry' (published 7 Aug. 1840)*** Two men playing badminton, holding rackets in their right hands, one standing at the left (Daniel O'Connell), the other at the right (Sir Robert Peel); a shuttlecock flying in the air at the centre, with feathers in the shape of men's heads and torsos, representing the Whig Ministry. It was said more than an hundred times by every Conservative journal, and repeated a thousand times by every Conservative both in and out of Parliament, that the Whig Ministry was maintained in its position by the opposite efforts of the other two parties; that the Conservatives supported the Ministers against the efforts of the Radicals, to push them into measures dangerous to the Monarchy and the Church; and that the Radicals supported them, when the Conservatives made any attempt to drive them from their places. This state of things is aptly represented by a game of shuttlecock, between Sir Robert Peel, the Conservative leader, and Mr. O'Connell, the leader of the Irish party, or if not the leader, the most important and influential Member of the Radical body. The same conceit had been used by caricaturists in the 1780s and 1790s to represent the political dispute between Charles James Fox and Pitt the Younger.

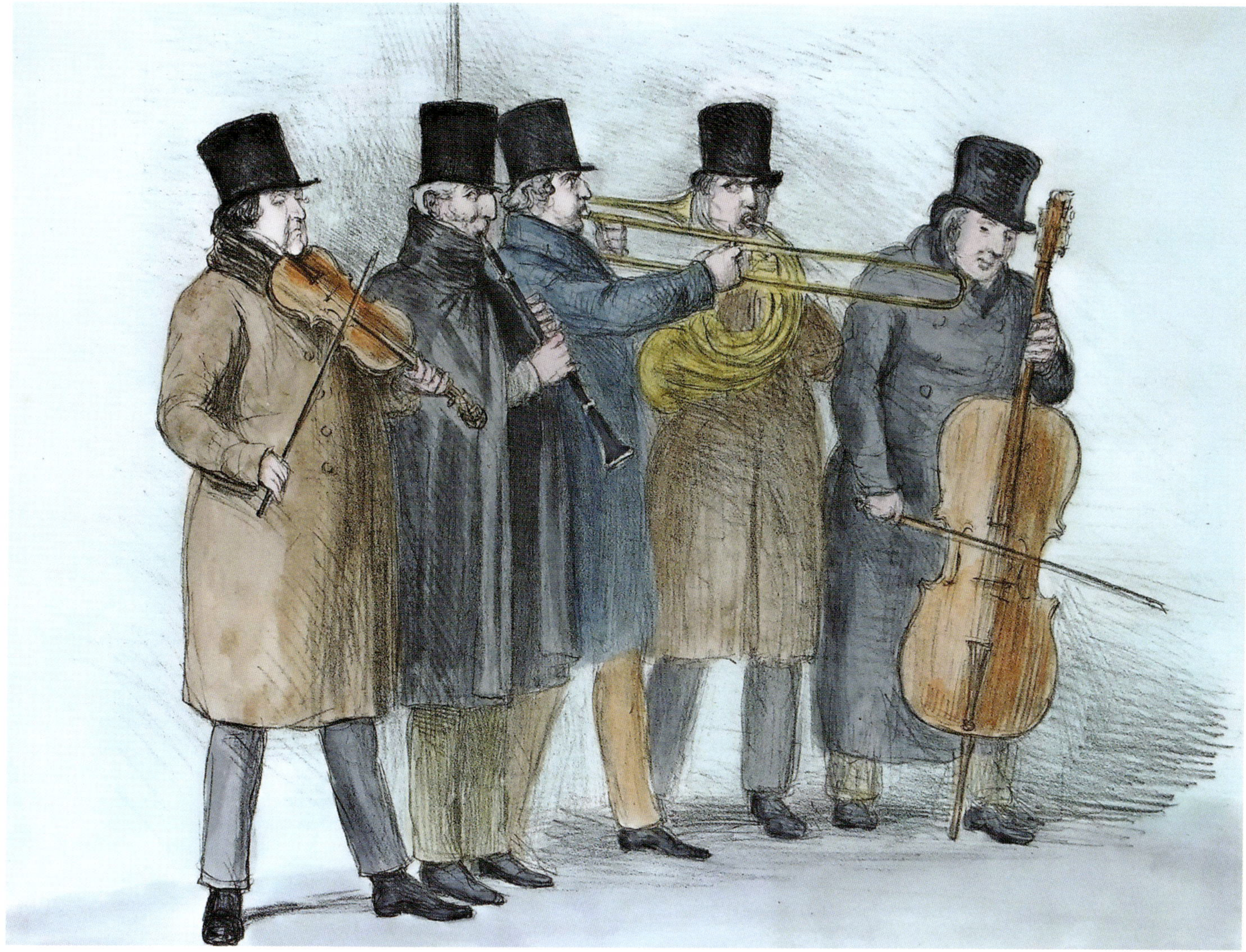

[80] ***No. 668, 'The Waits – Caution "These are the old genuine <u>Waits</u>; all others are pretenders!"' (published 31 Dec. 1840)*** A group of five musicians muffled up in the cold, playing the violin (Sir Robert Peel), clarinet (Duke of Wellington), trombone (Lord Stanley), French horn (Lord Lyndhurst) and cello (Sir James Graham). 'H.B.'s last sketch of 'The Waits' appeared in January 1833. These, the inscription below the sketch informs us, are old Genuine Waits, and so, it is to be presumed, they have a right to call themselves, notwithstanding the changes which have been made by the wear and tear of eight long years. The band of the old original and genuine Waits, is not entirely composed of different individuals from those who were in existence in 1833. The leader is still the same, namely the Duke of Wellington who was 'waiting' in 1833, and still waiting at the date of this sketch. He has changed his instrument from the violin (which he has handed over to his second Sir Robert Peel) to the clarionet. The other three are comparatively new performers in this old genuine band. The trombone player is Lord Stanley, the French-horn is Lord Lyndhurst, and the Violoncello Sir James Graham.

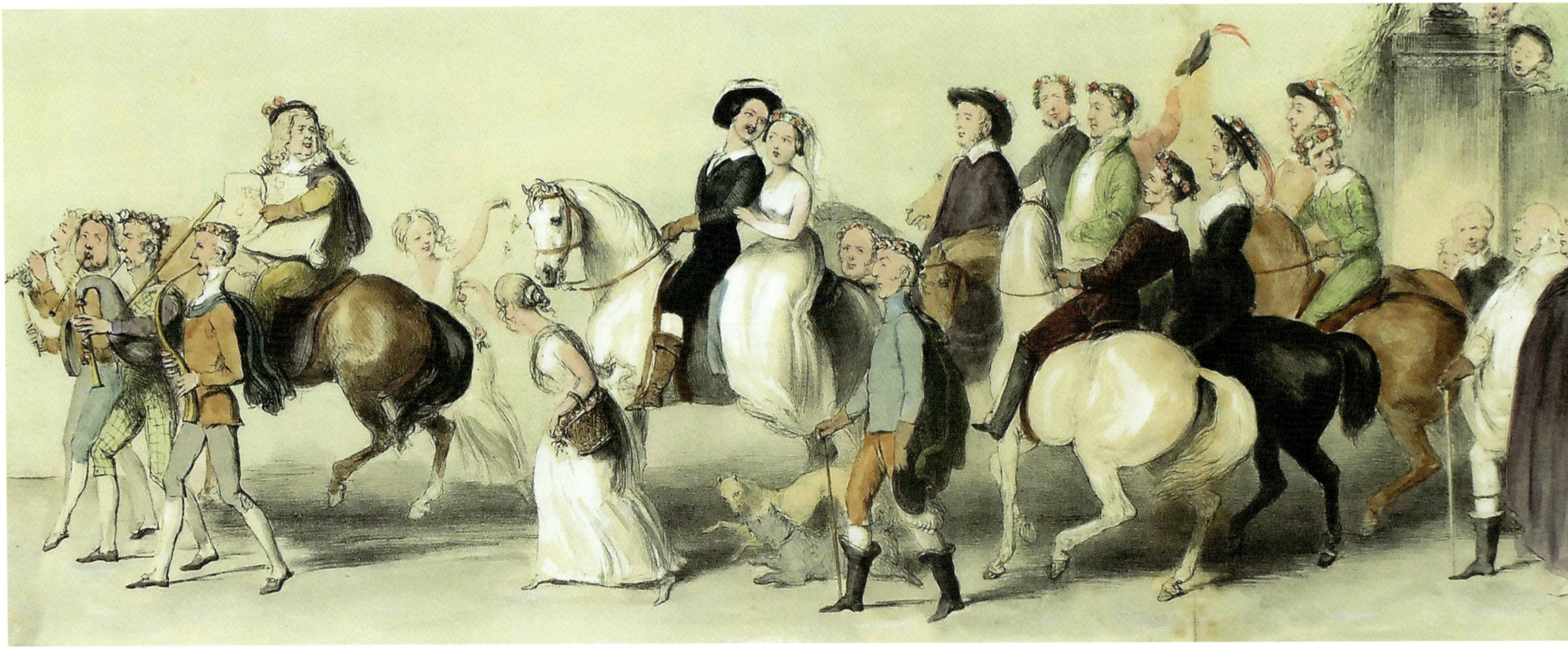

[81] ***No. 669 & 670, 'The Procession of the Flitch of Bacon'*** A procession moving along a street from right towards left, led by four musicians, men playing the oboe (Lord Duncannon), pipe and tabor (Lord Morpeth), bagpipes (Lord Brougham), serpent (Sir Francis Burdett), a man on horseback, carrying the flitch (Lord Cottenham), young girls scattering flowers before a couple on horseback (Prince Albert and Queen Victoria), attended by two men (Duke of Wellington and Lord Palmerston), and followed by three men (Lords Melbourne and Normanby and Sir Robert Peel), three riders (Lord John Russell, the Duchess of Kent, Lord Stanley), a man on foot in background (Sir James Graham), and three men on foot in foreground (the Archbishop of Canterbury (William Howley) and the Dukes of Cambridge and Sussex); two men looking down from a garden wall in background at the right (Lord Howick and Charles Wood). The satire relates to the ancient custom, variously dated from the time of Henry III onwards, to the presentation of a flitch of bacon to every married couple, a year and a day after marriage, who could declare on oath that they had never repented of their marriage nor sought another partner. The custom had been illustrated in a painting by Thomas Stothard, R.A., afterwards engraved by Mr Watt (1832). In 'H.B.'s composition, the first, and by far the greatest, share of attention is claimed by the Bride; the cavalcade is not very numerous. It is preceded by four musicians, who, if they contribute nothing to the harmony of the occasion, are accounted, separately, good performers on their peculiar instruments. The farthest is Lord Duncannon, the first Commissioner of the Woods and Forests. The second (Lord Morpeth), who is reported to be a pupil of a well-known Irish performer on the Union Pipes, plays the pipe and tabor with so much glee, that he cannot refrain from dancing to his own music. The third (Lord Brougham), is a composer of great celebrity, and is chiefly known for his variations of the air of 'Buy a Broom:' and the fourth (Sir Francis Burdett), playing a serpent, was in former times, as sure of an engagement at Covent Garden, as the season was sure to come round, but since the decline of the regular drama, he has been obliged to take to the provinces, and has at present, a good engagement in North Wiltshire (where he was returned as a Conservative M.P. in the 1837 General Election). Close behind the musicians follows the Lord Chancellor, Lord Cottenham, who, next to the bride and bridegroom, is the most important person in the procession. He rides, not like one whom fortune alone raised to eminence, which he is all unqualified to hold, but evidently keeps his 'seat' with 'judgment.' In his arms he bears the Flitch, which may be termed the ensign or great seal of his office; and surely he is great as a Lord Chancellor, for Bacon is his predecessor. To him succeed two young ladies, whose pleasant occupation is that of 'herb-women' in this coronation of domestic felicity. They are throwing flowers on the route with a degree of grace and native elegance which betoken them of gentle blood. They are but a few steps in advance of the Bride and Bridegroom, who, mounted on the same horse, the 'observed of all observers' are pacing on in that 'sober certainty of waking bliss', so likely to have arisen in their minds from the contemplation of their favoured condition and recent triumph. Those following the bride are led by Wellington, the oldest, truest, and most tried friend of her family. The wreath around his

[81] ***No. 669 & 670*** (continued)

brow gives him the look of the great Caesar; and truly he is a soldier of no little renown – 'The Hero of a Hundred Fights'. Veteran as he is, his step seems firm and his carriage bold and upright. He appears to attract the special admiration of the pedestrian on his right, Lord Palmerston, whose attention is not so much fixed on the subject of the procession as on 'foreign affairs'. Behind them, is an interesting group on horse-back. The most conspicuous among whom is the wearer of the hat and cloak, Lord Melbourne. He also is one of the guardians of the Bride; and, though not present at her birth, appears to take as much interest in her welfare as if his own were blended with it. He regards the happy couple as if he had been in some degree instrumental in effecting their union, and had the best reason to be satisfied with the result. Most probably he is intended for the 'Lord of the Bride's Treasury'. The Marquess of Normanby, turning round with a self-complacent smile, is now the major domo, or manager of the 'Home Department' in the Bride's establishment; and the nearer one, Sir Robert Peel, who looks straight forward and smiles not, formerly held the same post in the establishment, when the Bride's uncle (George IV) was the head of the family. The youthful-looking rider of the high horse, Lord John Russell, has the bold and confident appearance of one who is accustomed to lead those whom it requires great address to manage. At the same time that he takes care of such of the Bride's possessions and estates as lie at a distance from home, he takes an active part in regulating the proceedings of the under-tenants of the 'Commons'. The bride's mother (the Duchess of Kent) observes with heartfelt pride and gratification the married happiness of her daughter, tracing it to the affectionate care which they have bestowed on their education. The two persons who close the cavalcade appear to have joined it rather for their own amusement than having any direct connexion with it. The bigger one Sir James Graham, looks as bold and as powerful as a 'Cumberland Yeoman' and the other, Lord Stanley, wearing a garland, gives no attention to the scene before him, but is making observations on the by-standers. It is not difficult to discern in his countenance, the appearance of the driver of the 'Derby Dilly'. The procession appears to be closed by three personages on foot; – one of them, the Archbishop of Canterbury, is the good priest who officiated at the marriage of the happy pair; the others are, no doubt, two of the Bride's uncles, and seem lost in admiration of the scene. The two figures who are looking over the garden wall are members of the family, who might have claimed each a place in the procession but for some insubordination of conduct.

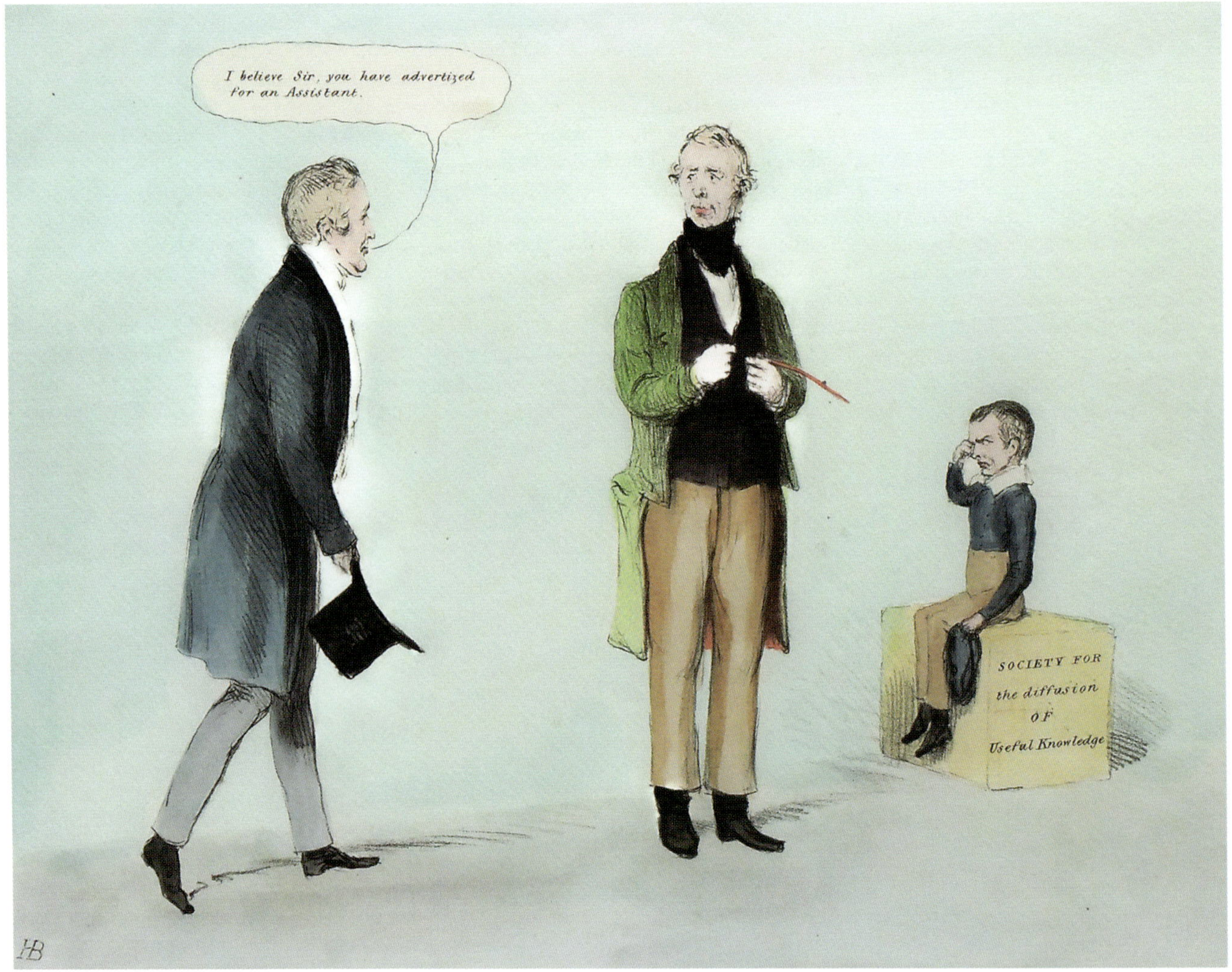

[82] ***No. 672, 'Nicholas Nickleby's Introduction to Squeers' (published 25 Feb. 1841)*** A man in the character of Nicholas Nickleby, at the left (Sir Robert Peel) asking a man in the character of Squeers, standing at the centre (Lord Brougham), if he had not advertised for an assistant; at the right, a disconsolate small boy seated on a box lettered with 'Society for the Diffusion of Useful Knowledge' (Lord John Russell). The scene relates to the introduction of the hero of Charles Dickens' novel (1838–1839), at his first entrance upon the world, to Mr. Squeers, the Yorkshire Schoolmaster, at the Saracen's-Head, Snow-Hill. The application of this incident in the novel is for the purpose of illustrating the relative positions of Lord Brougham and Sir Robert Peel, with regard to the subject of national education, and the extension of knowledge among the humbler classes of Society. Lord Brougham was closely connected with the foundation of both the University of London and the Society for the Diffusion of Useful Knowledge. On 19 Jan. 1841, at a Meeting held at Tamworth, relative to the Establishment of a Library and Reading-room in that town, Sir Robert Peel, in his character of President, delivered an address setting forth the objects and regulations of the institution, and likewise the pleasures and advantages resulting from the extension of useful knowledge, and the pursuit of intellectual improvement. In this undertaking he is represented by 'H.B.' as an humble assistant to the Veteran Pedagogue, Lord Brougham, and the humour of the piece is heightened by seating Lord John Russell on the box, in the character of the little boy whom Squeers was about to take down to the Establishment at Dotheboy's Hall.

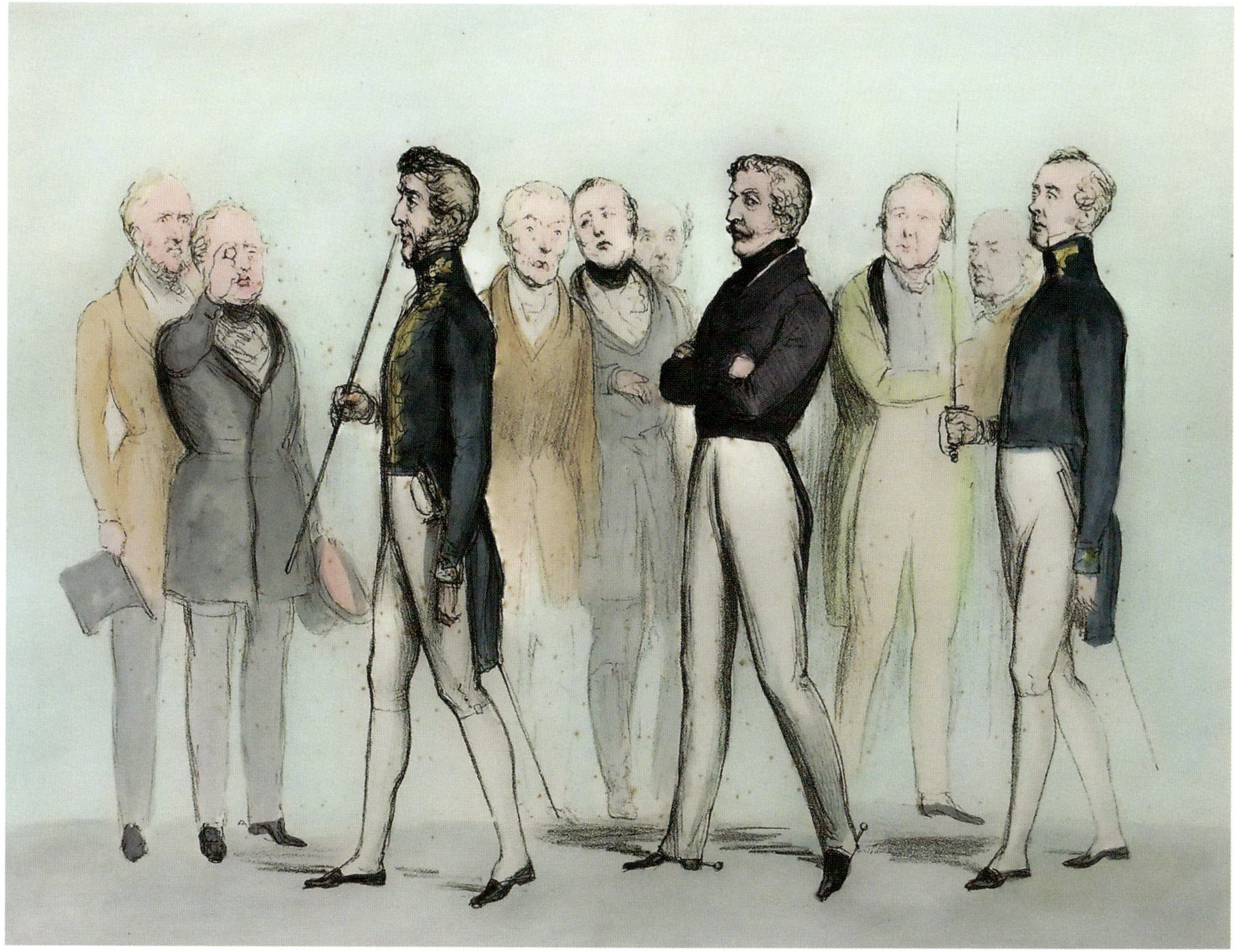

[83] ***No. 673, 'A Criminal in Custody – Query – "Which is the Malefactor?"' (published 25 Feb. 1841)*** Three men walking in a procession in foreground from right to left, the one leading at the left holding a staff in his right hand (Sir Augustus Clifford), the one at the centre with his arms folded (Lord Cardigan), the one at the right holding up a sword in his right hand (Mr Pulman); a group of spectators watching from the background (from left, Lords Anglesey and Londonderry, the Duke of Wellington, Lord Winchilsea, an unidentified man, Sir Robert Peel and Sir Henry Hardinge). The subject of the duel between the Earl of Cardigan and Captain Tuckett engaged a large share of public attention from the 12 Sept. 1840, when the duel was fought, till the trial and acquittal of his Lordship by the House of Lords in February, 1841. This sketch represents Lord Cardigan in the custody of Sir Augustus Clifford, the usher of the Black Rod, who walks before the Earl, and Mr. Pulman, the Deputy Usher, who brings up the rear. The spectators of this procession are all persons who, at some period of their lives have either fought duels, or sent challenges. Beginning on the left-hand, there is the Marquess of Anglesey, holding his hat in his hand, and the Marquess of Londonderry, with his glass at his eye; the Duke of Wellington and the Earl of Winchilsea in conversation, standing between the Serjeant-at-arms, and Sir Robert Peel and Sir Henry Hardinge, between Lord Cardigan and the Deputy Usher. In such an assembly, 'H.B.' very naturally inquires, in the language of the Sexton in 'Much Ado about Nothing' (1598–1599), 'Which be the Malefactor?'

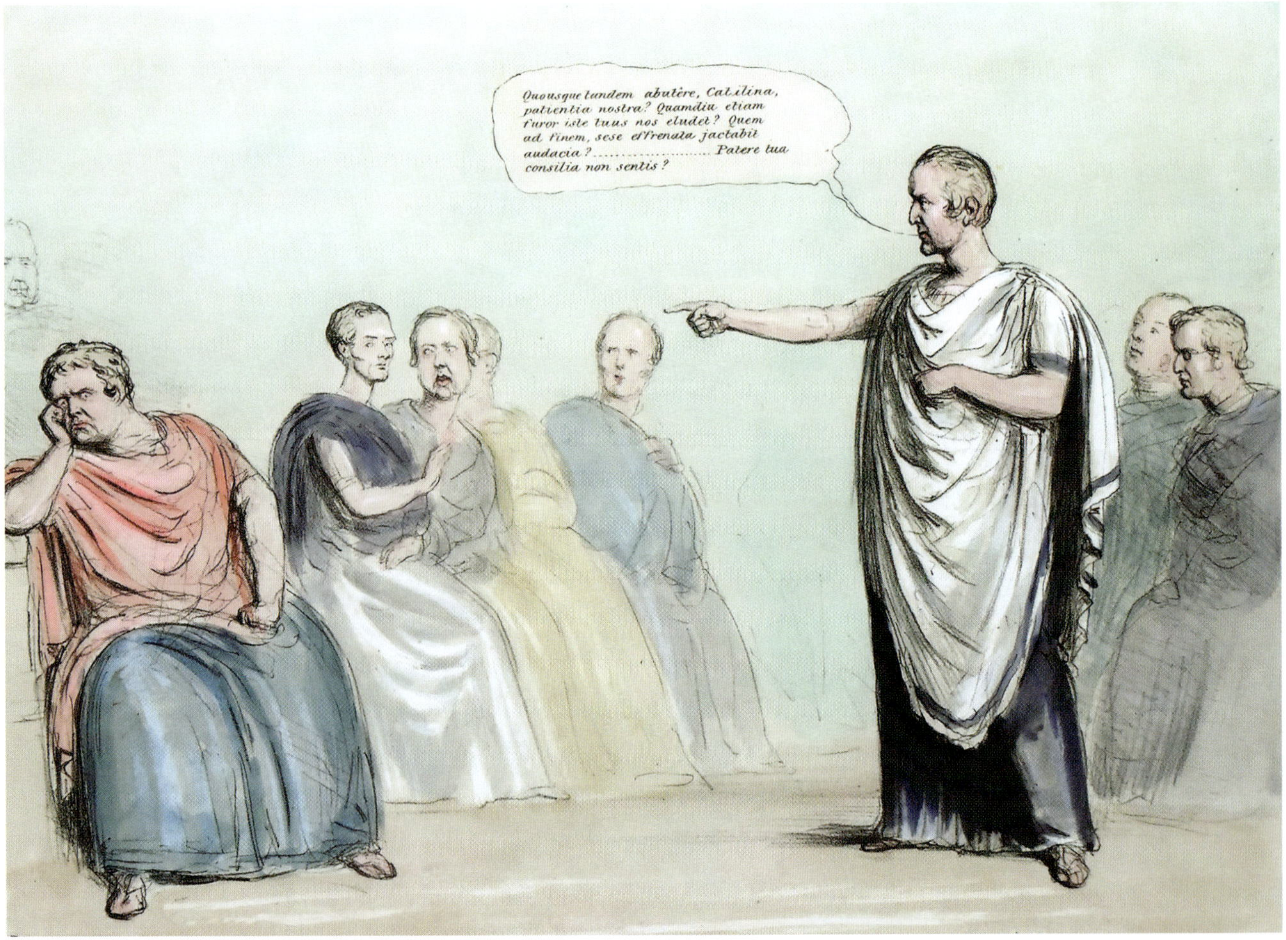

[84] ***No. 675, 'Cicero in Catilinam – A Classical Fragment' (published 22 Mar. 1841)*** A scene at the Roman Senate, representing the House of Commons; a man standing at the right in the character of Cicero (Sir Robert Peel), denouncing a man seated at the far left in the character of Cataline (Daniel O'Connell); a man's head in the background behind him at the far left (Joseph Hume); a group of men seated at the centre (Lords John Russell, Morpeth and Palmerston); two men seated at the far right (Sir James Graham and Lord Stanley). This sketch converts the House of Commons into the Senate of Rome, and Sir Robert Peel into Cicero, addressing Mr. O'Connell in the very words which the Roman orator addressed to Cataline. 'How long, O Cataline, will you abuse our patience? and how long shall that madness of thine mock us? at what object does your unbridled insolence aim? Do you not perceive that your designs are seen through?' The nearest approach to the reality of this scene, and that which perhaps suggested the idea of the present sketch, occurred on the last night's debate of Lord Morpeth's Irish Registration Bill, when Mr. O'Connell held out a threat that, unless the House should pass the Bill, and thereby conciliate the Irish, there would be danger that in the event of a war between Great Britain and France, or Great Britain and America, the alienated people of Ireland might yield to the temptation of an opportunity of severing for ever their connection with the British Empire. To this Sir Robert Peel replied that Mr. O'Connell, in alleging the probability of such conduct was a slanderer of the Irish people, whose loyalty could not be doubted. The classical toga ascribed to O'Connell is in contrast to the vulgarity of his attitude and figure. His countenance shows that he feels the force of the castigation which he is made to undergo. Lord John Russell, equally cool and classical, sits next to him, but at some little distance; and appears to behold the infliction with tolerable fortitude. However, the look of Lord Morpeth is one of mingled horror, fear, and pity. Beyond Lord Morpeth sits Lord Palmerston, and behind Sir Robert Peel are Sir James Graham and Lord Stanley. The head of Mr. Hume, just above the figure of Mr. O'Connell, is witnessing the scene with the most stoical indifference and appears to wonder why all parties seem so much affected.

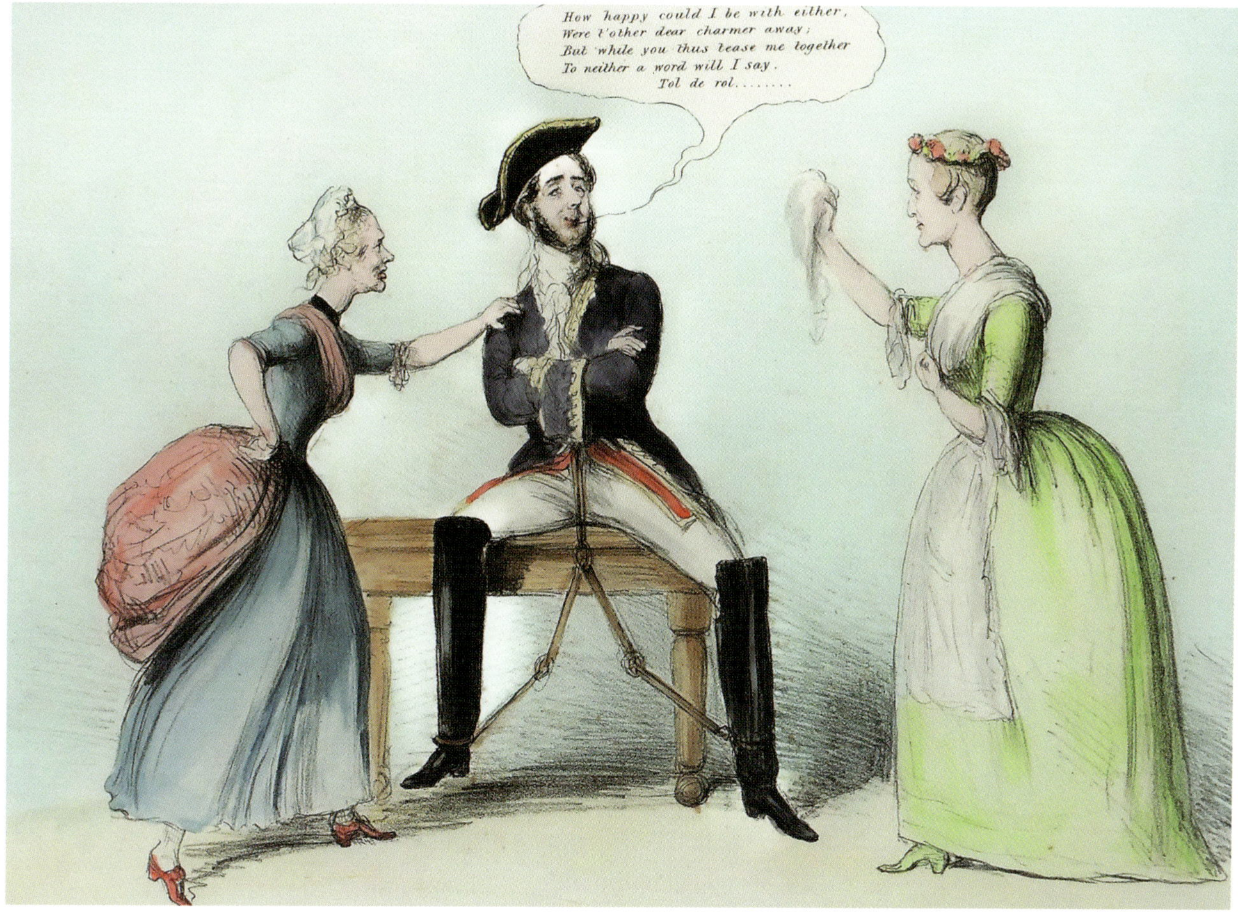

[85] ***No. 677, 'Scene from the 'Beggar's Opera'' (published 14 April 1841)*** A scene from John Gay's runaway eighteenth century hit 'The Beggar's Opera'; a man seated on a bench at the centre, in the character of Macheath, the highwayman in chains (Thomas Duncombe), singing when approached by two men, dressed as women, rivals for his attention, one from the left in the character of Lucy (Lord John Russell), the other from right, in the character of Polly (Sir Robert Peel). This sketch contains a reference to the particular debate which supplied 'H.B.' with his subject. The seat for the Borough of St. Albans having become vacant, was strongly contested between Mr. Benjamin Bond Cabbell and Lord Listowel, one of the Lords of the Queen's bedchamber. It was reported that when the Queen heard of Mr. Cabbell's having offered himself for the Borough upon the strength of the Earl of Verulam's interest, she issued her command to Lord Listhowell to 'go down to St. Albans and beat the Grimstones'. Enormous bribery was proved before a Committee of the House of Commons appointed to inquire into the merits of the election. At the same time an election had taken place at Canterbury, where, as it was alleged, bribery had been practised as extensively by the Tories as at St. Albans by the Whigs. A petition had been presented, and the merits of the election were under investigation before a Committee. In both cases, it was said the bribery was proved beyond any doubt, but the evidence to connect the sitting member with the acts of bribery was wanting, and both Committees reported the sitting member duly elected. It was openly said, however, that this conclusion was the result of a compromise between the opposite parties. Thomas Duncombe, Esq., M.P. for Finsbury, who in an indignant speech full of virtuous indignation (2 Apr. 1841), exclaimed, 'Is it to be borne. Sir, that a Beggar's Opera scene is to be enacted at Election Committees? Are Committees to meet in a room and say, like Peachum and Lockit, "Brother, brother, we are both in the wrong; we could both hang one another; and so let us shake hands?"' The two rival parties of Whig and Tory, the one represented by the likeness of Lord John Russell, and the other by that of Sir Robert Peel, are the Lucy and Polly of the scene, and the independence of the Honourable Member for Finsbury is proclaimed by his singing the well-known song of Macheath, 'How happy could I be with either!'.

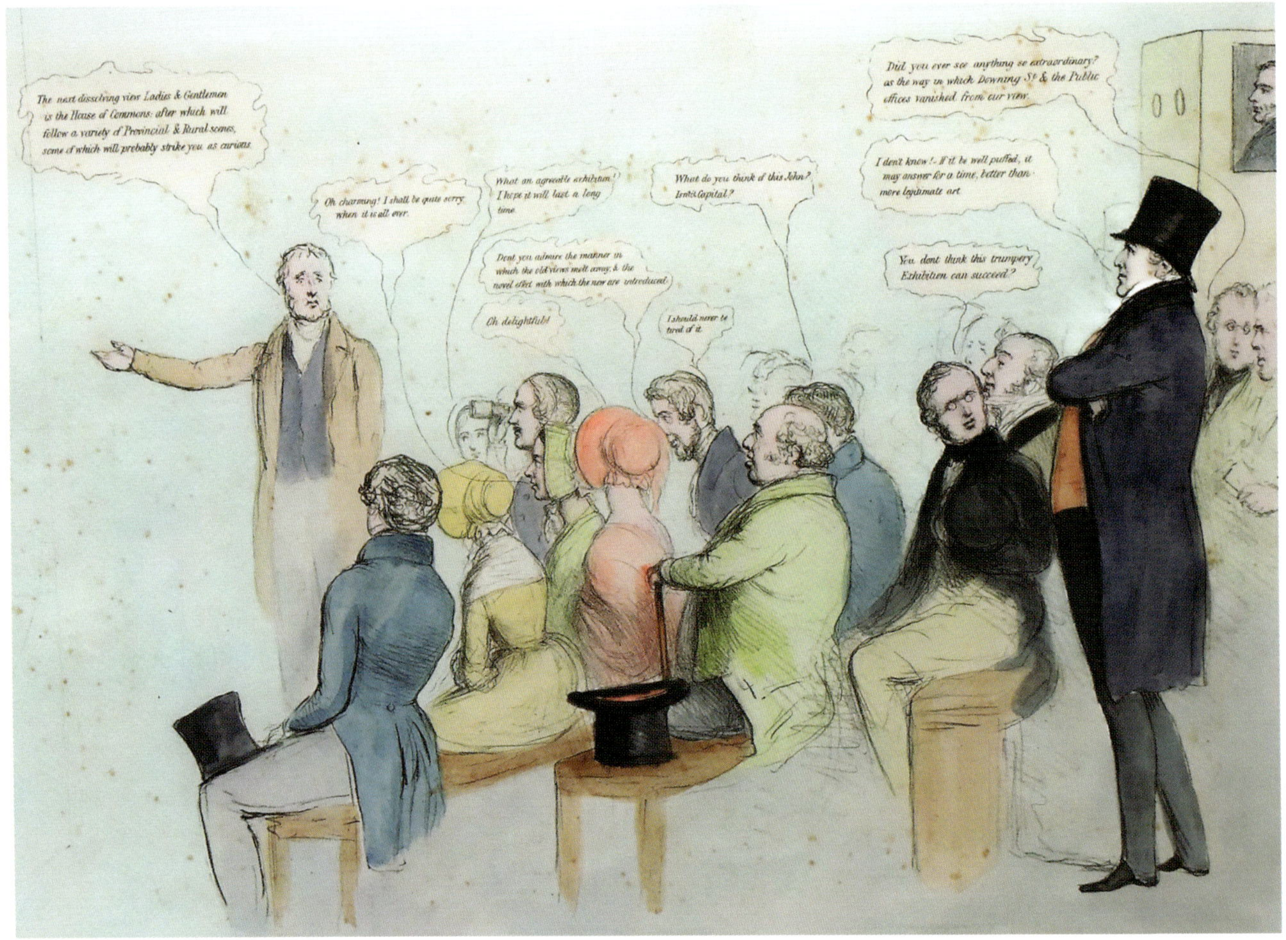

[86] ***No. 689, 'Dissolving Views' (published 1 June 1841)*** At a show of optical illusions, the master, standing at the left (Lord Melbourne), explaining about the views to a seated and standing audience (Prince Albert, Queen Victoria, Lord Normanby, John Bull, Daniel O'Connell, Lord Stanley, Henry Goulburn, Sir James Graham, standing Sir Robert Peel, Emerson Tennent, Horace Twiss); at the right, a man seen in a box producing the effects (Lord John Russell). The reference is the optical illusions commonly known by the name of dissolving views which were exhibited daily at the Royal Adelaide Gallery and the Polytechnic Institution. In this sketch, the master of the show is Lord Melbourne, and his coadjutor, whose head appears at the window of a small inclosure on the opposite side of the piece, where the machinery is employed to produce the effect, is Lord John Russell. The exhibition of the House of Commons among the dissolving views, alludes to the then intended dissolution of Parliament, and the provincial and rural scenes which are to succeed, refer to the ensuing general election; and the point of the sketch is the hope entertained by the Whigs that by a dissolution of Parliament they might cause their difficulties to vanish like the scenes in these popular exhibitions. The audience is composed of persons of various ranks and parties. Among those on the front bench are the Queen and Prince Albert, and immediately behind Her Majesty the person of Lord Normanby is discernible, in conversation with a lady in waiting (his wife was a lady of the Bedchamber). Conspicuous in the centre bench sits John Bull, in wide astonishment at the exhibition, and with no very friendly expression of countenance, although a person at his side, whose outline brings to mind the figure of Mr. O'Connell, endeavours to engage his admiration and applause. Behind these are a group of malcontents, Lord Stanley (in the spectacles), Sir James Graham, and Mr. Goulburn. The figure of Sir Robert Peel standing with his arms folded, is too striking to be mistaken, and behind him Mr. Emmerson Tennent, M.P. for Belfast, turns towards his sympathetic friend, Mr. Horace Twiss, and expresses his vexation at the disappearance of Downing Street and the public offices.

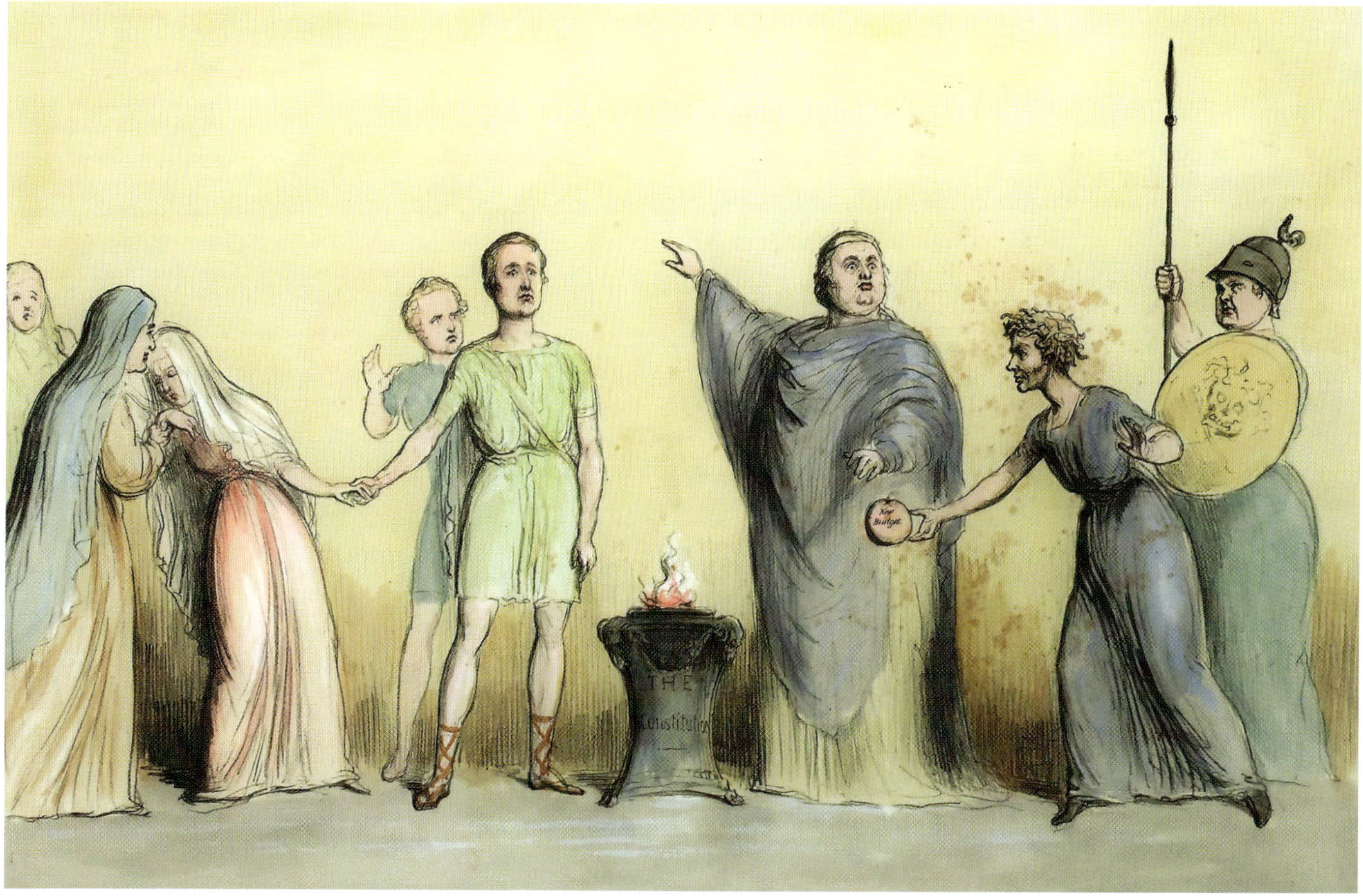

[87] ***No. 690, ''The Nuptials of <u>Peeleus</u> and Thetis interrupted by the Goddess of Discord' (published 10 June 1841)*** A Roman marriage-scene; at the centre, an altar with burning fire, lettered with 'The Constitution'; at the centre left, the bridegroom, in the character of Peleus (Sir Robert Peel), standing, holding the hand of the unwilling bride, in the character of Thetis (Queen Victoria), supported by a man dressed as a woman (Lord Melbourne); a man standing behind Peleus (Lord Stanley); the priest, John Bull, standing at the centre right, with his right arm raised, and his left hand above an apple lettered with 'New Budget', held by a man dressed as a woman, in the character of the goddess of discord (Lord John Russell); at the far right, a man dressed as a woman, in the character of Britannia (Daniel O'Connell), holding a shield and spear. According to Homer, Peleus courted Thetis but his pretensions were rejected, and the goddess even fled from him with the greatest abhorrence. Peleus, however, like all true lovers, became the more animated by her refusal, and when, after long perseverance, he had at length surprised and seized her and she found it impossible to escape from his grasp, she consented to marry him. At the celebration of the nuptials the goddess of Discord, who had not been invited, being irritated by this seeming neglect, threw a golden apple into the midst of the assembly of the gods with the inscription 'detur pulchriori'. The bridegroom Peleus is Sir Robert Peel, attended by Lord Stanley as bridesman—the bride Thetis is the Queen, and her unwilling acquiescence is apparent from her almost sinking into the arms of her attendant. John Bull officiates as the priest, and the union is about to be solemnized on the altar of the Constitution, when Lord John Russell, as the goddess of Discord, rushes in with his budget for a golden apple, for the purpose of exciting and agitating the country. It was just at the moment when the Conservative party appeared to have gained the ascendancy, both within and without the House of Commons, and when it was quite manifest that Ministers could neither go on with the existing House, nor prevent a still greater loss of support in the event of a dissolution, that the budget was brought forward, and it was proposed to remove the protection duties from Corn, Sugar, and Timber. Of course it was intended that the public should catch at the hope of a reduction in the price of those staple commodities, and be induced to restore their confidence to the Whigs, and thus break off the match about to be solemnized.

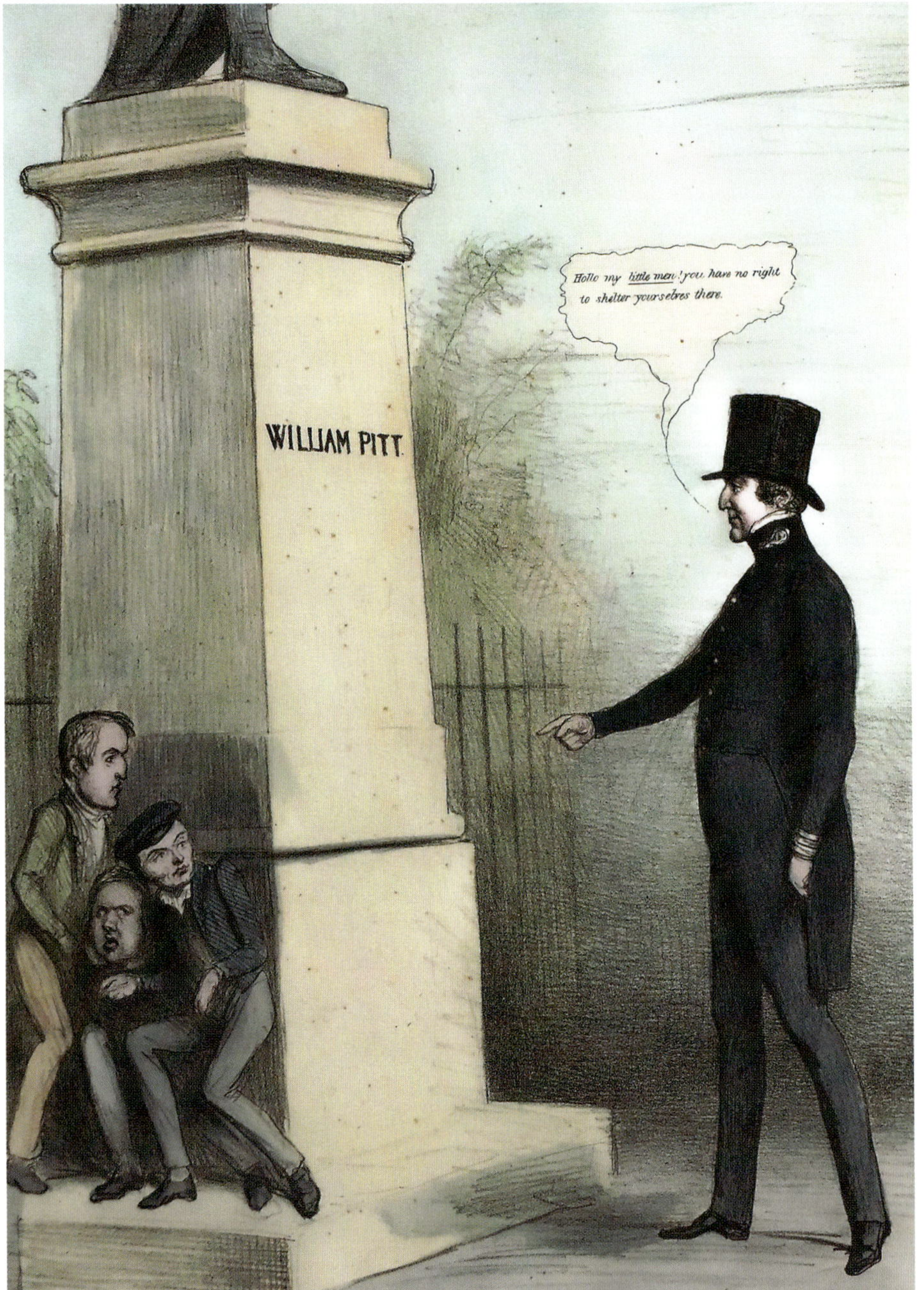

[88] ***No. 695, 'A Pit-iable Situation' (published 22 June 1841)*** Three boys crouching at left under a statue, lettered on the plinth 'WILLIAM PITT' (John Cam Hobhouse, Lord Morpeth and Lord John Russell), about to be driven from their shelter by a policeman, approaching from the right (Sir Robert Peel). The Whig Ministry, retaining their places and carrying on the Government of the country, after being repeatedly in a minority in the House of Commons, and justifying themselves by the example of Mr. Pitt, are happily represented (in the persons of Sir John Cam Hobhouse, Lord Morpeth, and Lord John Russell), as poor boys, houseless and penniless, sheltering themselves behind Mr. Pitt's statue in Hanover Square; and Sir Robert Peel, who in his replies to ministers denied the parallel between the two cases, and strove to show that the proceedings of ministers were not justifiable by any example whatever, is aptly represented as a policeman driving the miserable objects from their shelter to 'abide the pelting of the pitiless storm'.

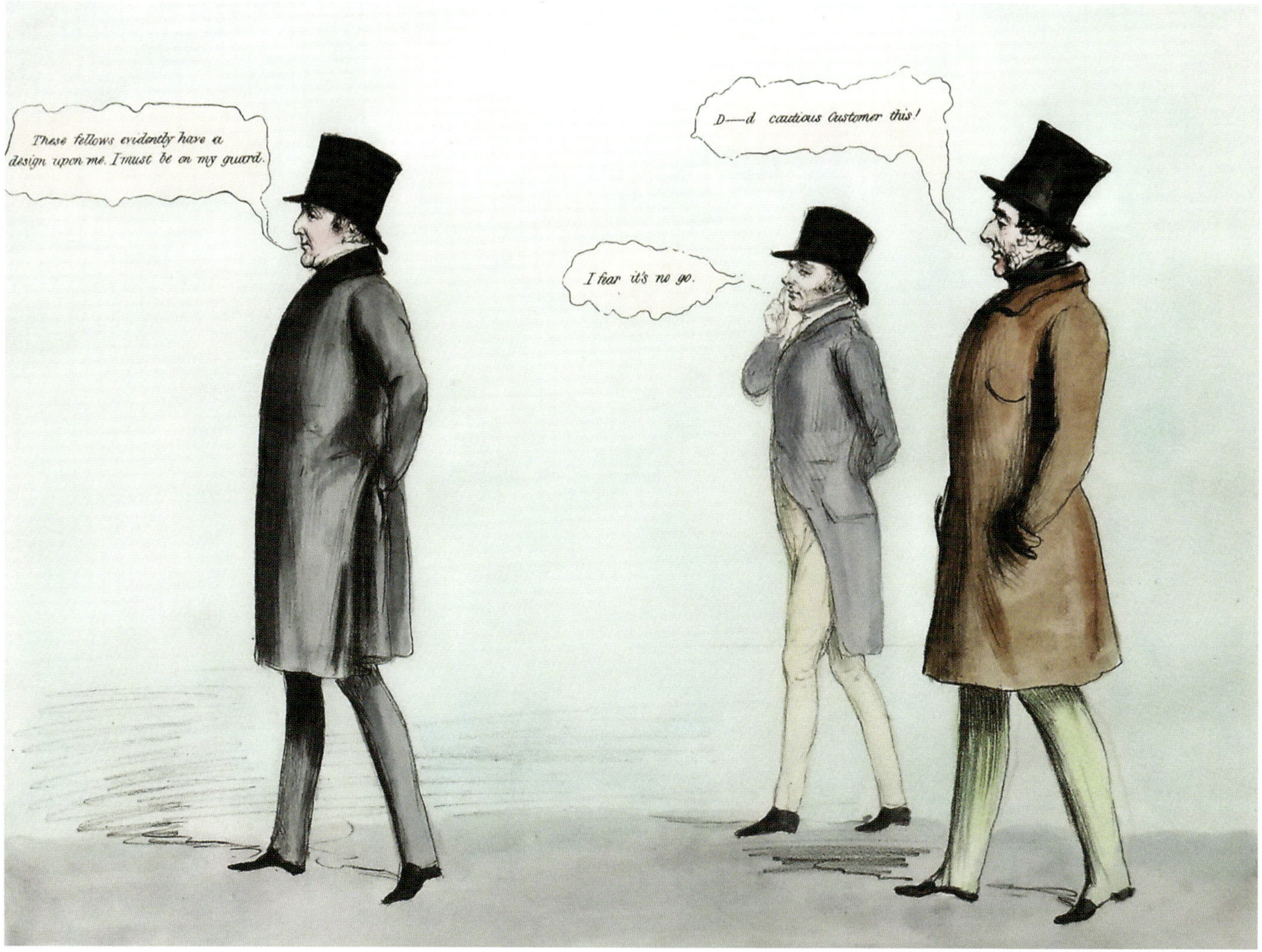

[89] ***No. 699, "'Take care of your Pockets" – "Beware of the Swell Mob!'" (published 12 Aug. 1841)*** A man at the left, walking in the street (Sir Robert Peel), with his left hand in the pocket of his coat; he is scared of two pickpockets, following him from the right (Lords John Russell and Melbourne). The tactics of the Tories, on the occasion of the Ministerial proposition to retrieve their financial losses by an alteration of the duties on corn, sugar, and timber, were to oppose the Ministry, without affording the slightest materials for guessing what line of policy they themselves would have substituted. The Ministers, on the other hand, seemed to consider it peculiarly unfair in their opponents to bestow such ruthless treatment on their proposal, without submitting some plan of their own, on which it would have been possible for Ministers and their friends to retaliate. Every speech from every supporter of the Government contained this appeal, either in the form of an expostulation, or a taunt. These attempts to extract from Sir Robert Peel his sentiments on the best plan of extricating the country from its financial difficulties, are playfully compared by 'H.B.' to the arts of the fraternity of pickpockets, two of whom, in the likeness of Lord Melbourne and Lord John Russell, are dogging the steps of Sir Robert Peel, with a view to relieve him of some of his property. Lord Melbourne fashionably dressed in a modern Taglioni coat, like a member of the swell-mob, is already aware that he has 'a cautious customer' to deal with, and Lord John Russell, with the same professional penetration acknowledges that it is 'No go'. The manner and look of Sir Robert Peel afford a pretty good intimation that he is not to be easily victimized.

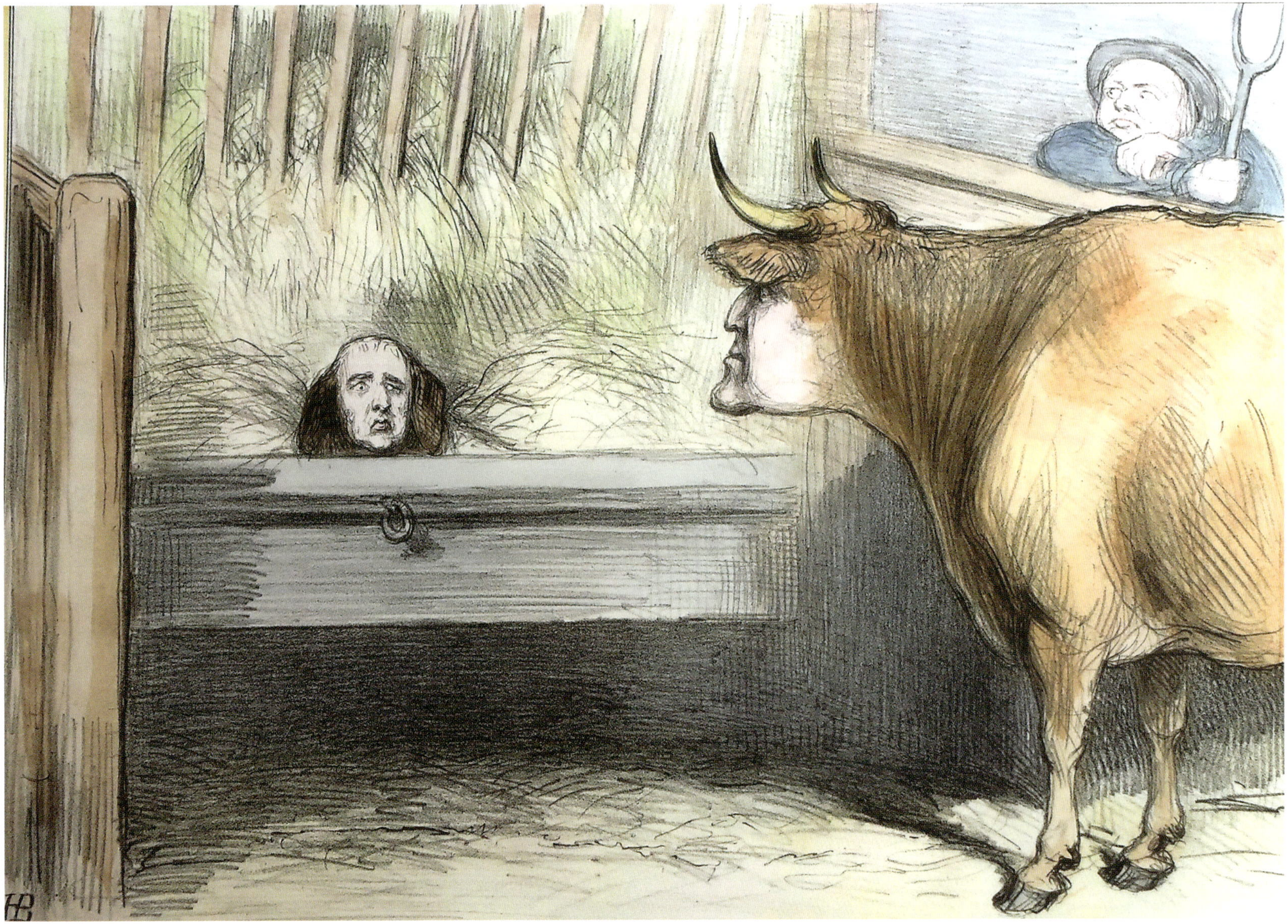

[90] ***No. 702, 'Illustration of The Dog in the Manger' (published 30 Aug. 1841)*** A dog with a man's face (Lord Melbourne) buried in hay in a manger, facing an ox with a man's head, staring at him from the right (Sir Robert Peel); John Bull standing at top right behind the partition with a fork in his left hand, looking in anger at the dog. The Dog in the Manger is Lord Melbourne, and the Ox, Sir Robert Peel. The sketch conveyed a rebuke to the premier on account of the reluctance of his party to surrender their places to the Tories when it was manifest that they were unable to retain them. The scowl with which John Bull is regarding the impotent attempts of the dog to prevent another from taking that which he himself is incapable of enjoying, indicates the unpopularity of the Whig party.

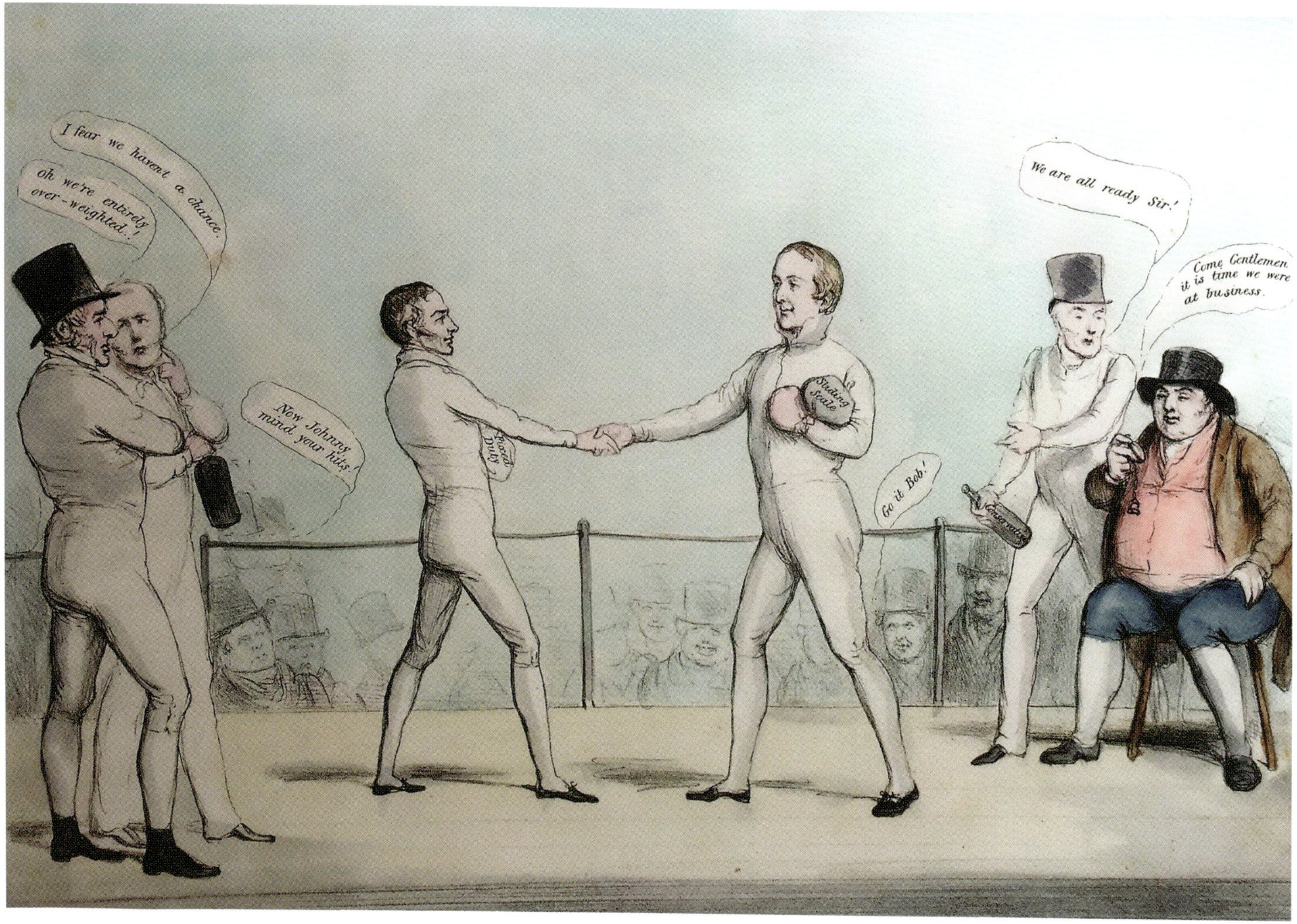

[91] ***No. 705, 'Beginning in good Old English Style' (published 13 Sep. 1841)*** In a boxing ring, two boxers shaking hands before their match; the one standing at centre left holding a glove lettered with 'Fixed Duty' (Lord John Russell), backed by two men standing at the far left, the second one holding a bottle lettered with 'Reform' (Lords Melbourne and Palmerston), and by men in the audience at the left (among them Daniel O'Connell); the boxer at the centre right holding a glove lettered with 'Sliding Scale' (Sir Robert Peel), backed by a man standing at the right, holding a bottle lettered with 'Conservative' (Duke of Wellington), and by men in the audience at the right (among them Lord Stanley); John Bull seated at the far right, acting as umpire. The battle to be fought was for the alteration of the Corn Laws, and it involved no less than the downfall of the Whig Administration. Lord John Russell's proposition was to change the sliding scale for a fixed duty of 8s. a quarter. If he succeeded the Ministry would stand; if he failed it must give way to the Conservatives. The combatants are going readily and steadily to the encounter. John Bull sits as umpire, to see fair play and decide controversial points. The Duke of Wellington waits on Sir Robert Peel, and Lord Palmerston, holding a bottle, on which is written 'Reform', attends on Lord John Russell. It was necessary to put his Lordship into the situation of his party's champion, the battle being a fiscal one, and therefore necessarily confined to the House of Commons; but Lord Melbourne, who stands by Lord Palmerston, is so much interested in the result, that he has mounted the stage, and is expressing to Lord Palmerston his fears that his man is over-weighted. Mr. O'Connell from among the crowd, on one side, encourages Lord John Russell, and Lord Stanley, on the other, calls out 'Go it Bob', to Sir Robert Peel.

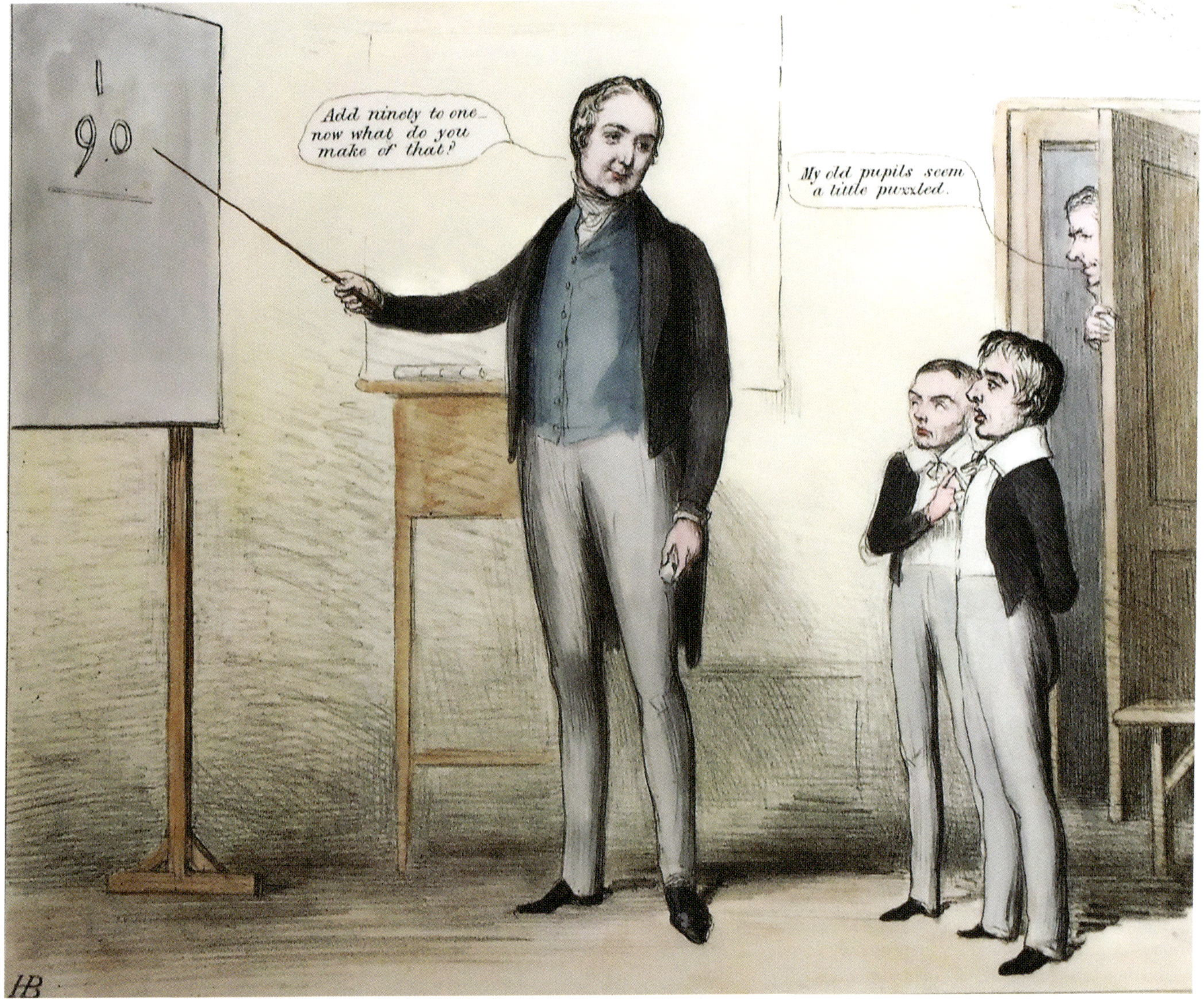

[92] ***No. 709, 'Simple Arithmetic – A Sum in Addition' (published 2 Oct. 1841)*** A schoolmaster, standing at centre (Sir Robert Peel), pointing at a board at left with a stick held in his right hand, asking two boys standing at the right (Lords Melbourne and John Russell), looking puzzled, to add one to ninety; a man looking in at the door at the far right (Lord Brougham) smiles at the slowness of his old pupils. The first shock sustained by the Whig Ministry was their being beaten by a majority of one, upon a motion of want of confidence. They then dissolved the parliament, and made an appeal to the country, and, upon the assembling of the new parliament, the opposition carried an amendment to the address by a majority of 91. In this sketch, Sir Robert Peel appears installed in his office as Prime Minister, astonishing his beaten adversaries, Lord Melbourne and Lord John Russell, by the sum in addition, which is chalked upon the board. Lord Brougham, the schoolmaster-general, and self-constituted tutor of the late Ministry, is looking in, not well pleased, to find his old pupils so sadly puzzled.

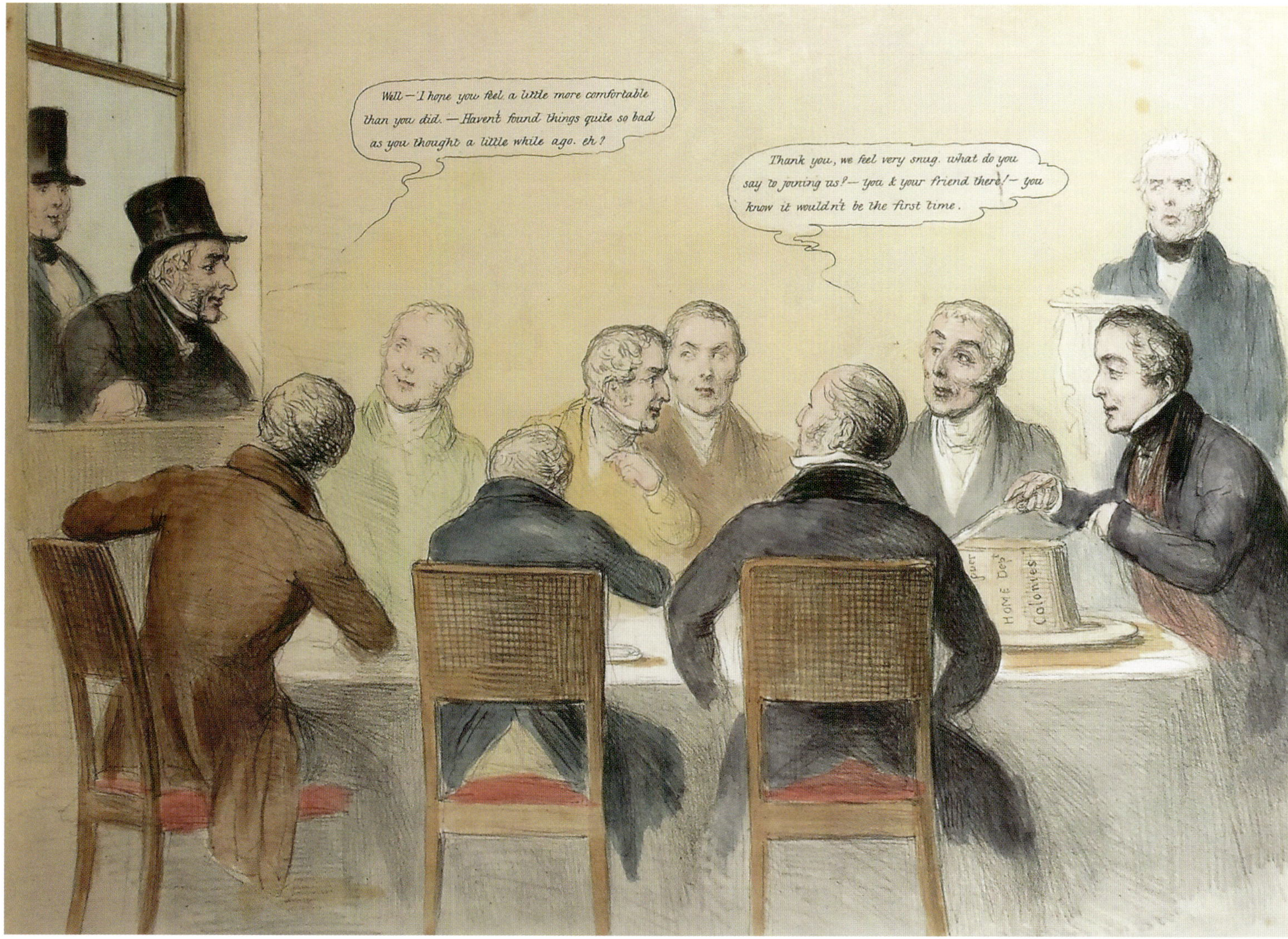

[93] ***No. 717, 'A Cabinet Pudding' (published 21 Feb. 1842)*** Two men at the left, looking through a window into a room (Lords Palmerston and Melbourne), where a group of men are seated around a table, about to cut up their 'cabinet pudding' (from left to right, Lords Haddington, Ripon, Wharncliffe, Stanley, Aberdeen, Sir James Graham, the Duke of Wellington, Sir Robert Peel); a waiter standing in the background at left, holding a tray (Horace Twiss). The principal members of the Tory Cabinet are here met, to participate in the enjoyment of the pudding, which the Premier has the agreeable task of carving for them. Lord Haddington, first Lord of the Admiralty, Lord Wharncliffe, Privy Seal, and Sir James Graham, Secretary for the Home Department, are sitting in the fore ground, with their backs to the spectator, and on the opposite side, next to Sir Robert Peel, who is carving the pudding, sits the Duke of Wellington, and beyond him are Lord Aberdeen, Foreign Secretary, Lord Stanley, Colonial Secretary, and Lord Ripon, President of the Board of Trade. The two persons looking in at the window are the ex-ministers, Lord Melbourne and Lord Palmerston. The patient individual officiating in the character of waiter is Mr. Horace Twiss.

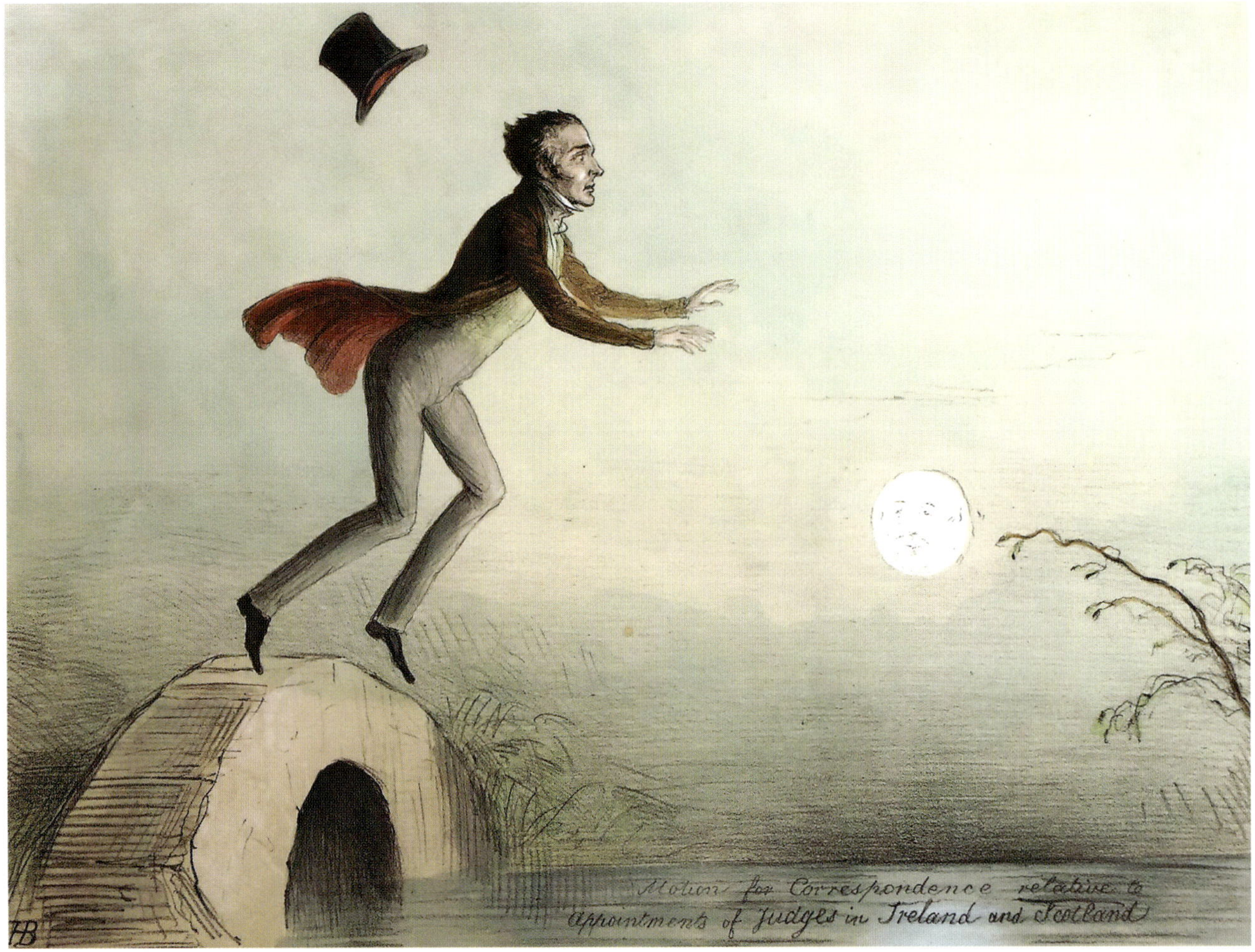

[94] ***No. 718, 'A Suicidal Plunge' (published 21 Feb. 1842)*** Exhibits Lord John Russell jumping off a very low bridge into a very small pond where it would be impossible that he should receive more than a mere splashing. The idea originated in a speech of Thomas Wakley, Coroner for Middlesex and M.P. for Finsbury, on Russell's motion for the production of papers relative to the resignation of the Lord President of the Court of Session in Scotland and the late Chief Justice of the Queen's Bench in Ireland. The object of the motion was to show that both had either retained their offices beyond the period when they had become incapacitated for the due discharge of their duties, or had prematurely applied for permission to retire; the motive being to throw the patronage of the appointment of their successors into the hands of the new Government. The charge against the government was, so far as related to Ireland, singularly unlucky, as it afforded them the opportunity of a counter argument with respect to the displacing of Lord Plunket from the office of Irish Lord Chancellor to make room for Lord Campbell. *The Times* reported Wakley's speech as follows, 'He was much puzzled to guess what the motive of the Noble Lord might have been, in bringing forward this motion, and having the habit, like others who were pressed for time, of looking over the notice paper, in order to dismiss those notices which were not likely to excite attention, in the house or give rise to dissensions which were of any interest to the public, some of which were mere nonsense and others mere fudge, and in order to mark those of a different character, it was curious enough that he should have marked the notice of the noble Lord "Suicide" (loud laughter) thinking that it might be one which would require his official interference'.Wakley's features are seen on the disk of the great luminary peering through the fog that hovers over the scene of the suicidal leap. Thus, whilst the Contents to the relevant volume of 'H.B.'s 'Political Sketches' indicates that Peel is a protagonist in this scene, it is – as the later key to the sketches makes clear – Wakley.

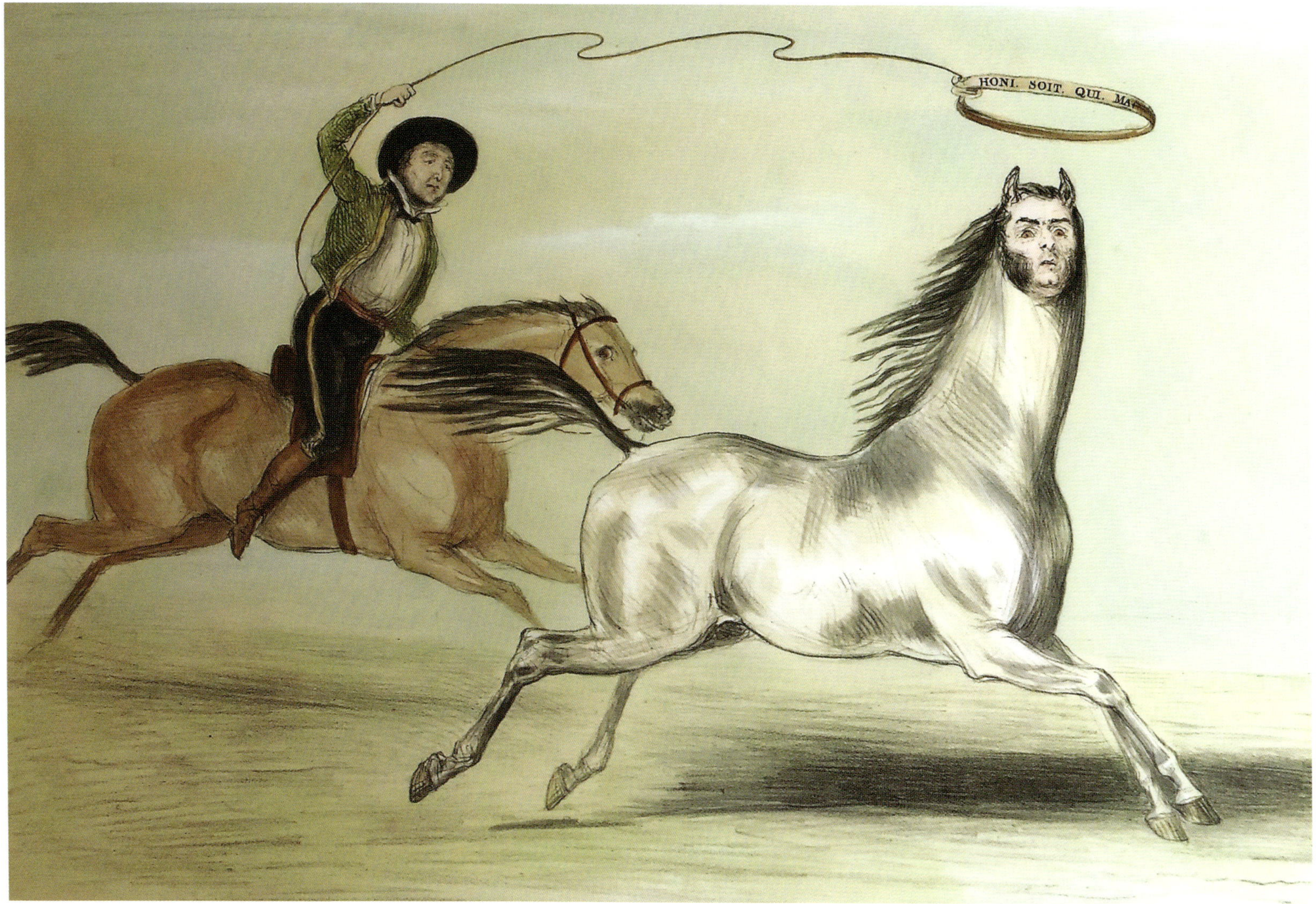

[95] ***No. 720, 'Throwing the Lasso' (published 21 Mar. 1842)*** A man riding a horse, from left towards right (Sir Robert Peel), throwing a lasso lettered with 'Honi. Soit. Qui. Ma[l]' at a horse with a man's face (Duke of Buckingham), galloping in foreground towards the right. The Duke of Buckingham was a member of the Tory Cabinet as originally formed, but resigned his office upon being out-voted on the question of the Corn Laws, in which Sir Robert Peel proposed to make some alterations prejudicial, as the Duke of Buckingham conceived, to the interest of the British Farmer. In taking this step, however, his Grace expressly stated, that although the difference of opinion between his late colleagues and himself, on the question of the Corn Laws, compelled him to separate from them, he approved of their policy in general, and should continue to give them his cordial support. Very shortly after this his Grace was honoured with the blue ribbon of the Garter, and it was supposed by many that his separation from the Peel Administration was temporary only, and that he would re-join them as soon as the Corn Question was settled. In this belief, 'H.B.' has sketched him as a runaway horse, pursued by Sir Robert Peel in the character of a South American Gaucho, who is endeavouring to catch him by a lasso, formed of the Garter.

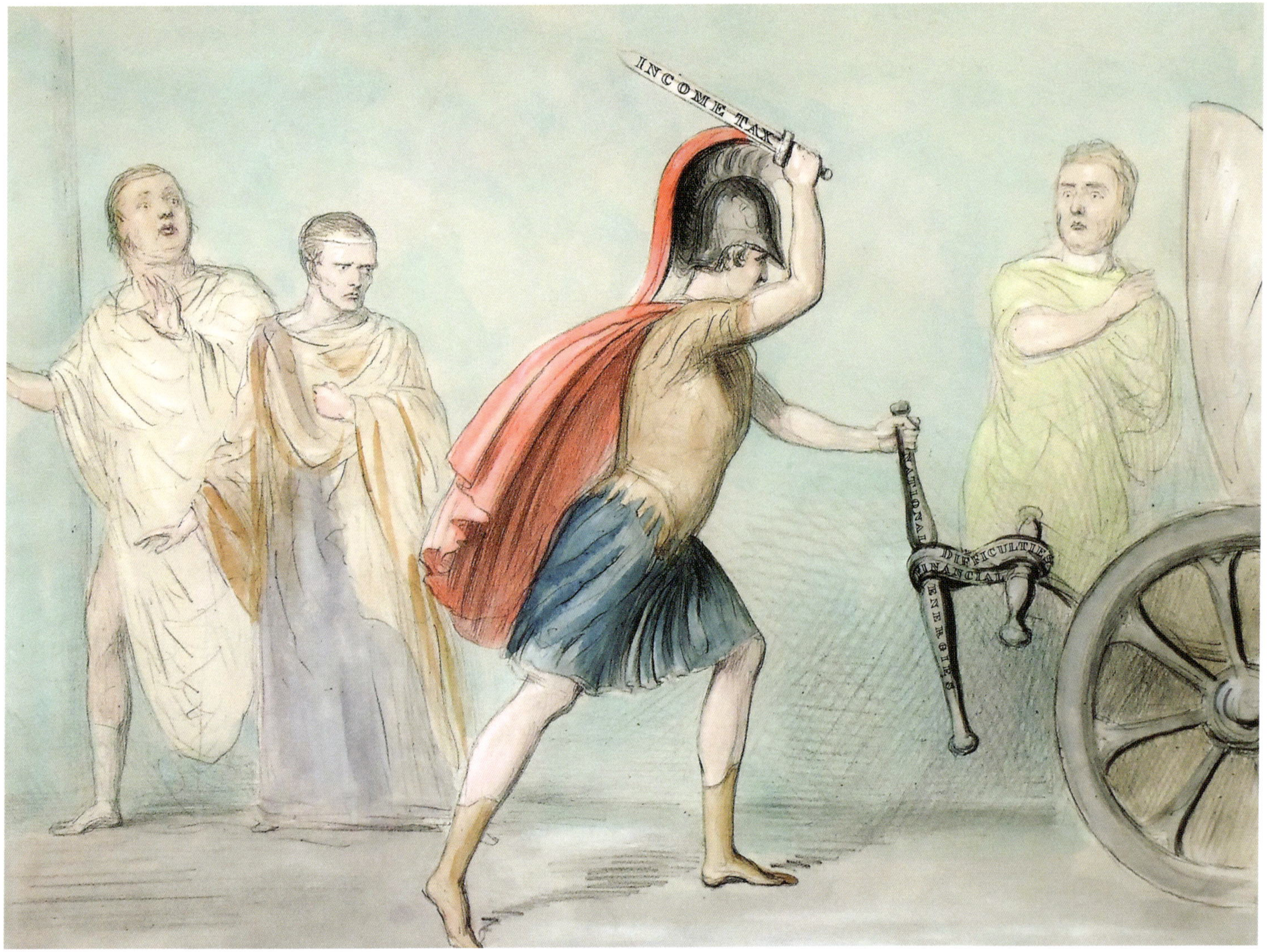

[96] ***No. 726, 'Cutting the Gordian Knot' (published 23 Apr. 1842)*** A scene with men dressed as Romans; a man standing at the centre, in the character of Alexander (Sir Robert Peel), holding a sword lettered with 'Income Tax' in his right hand, cutting a knot lettered with 'National Energies Financial Difficulties'; two men standing at the left (Francis Baring, Lord John Russell), and a man standing at the right (Lord Melbourne) looking on in astonishment. The financial difficulties of the country were the proximate cause of the change of Ministry and Sir Robert Peel, who had been courted in vain to afford some intimation of the means by which he would attempt to overcome these difficulties, his opponents thinking only of the Corn, Sugar, and Timber Duties, is represented in the character of Alexander cutting the Gordian Knot, by the imposition of the Income Tax, that should raise at once not only enough to bring up the Revenue to the level of the charge upon it, but enable him to take off some portion of the Customs Duties. Lord Melbourne in the back ground expresses surprise at the boldness of the attempt. Mr. Baring, on the extreme left, appears to be equally surprised, but Lord John Russell, not unequal to Sir Robert Peel in boldness, seems to be stung with vexation that it did not occur to him to deal with the difficulty after the same mode.

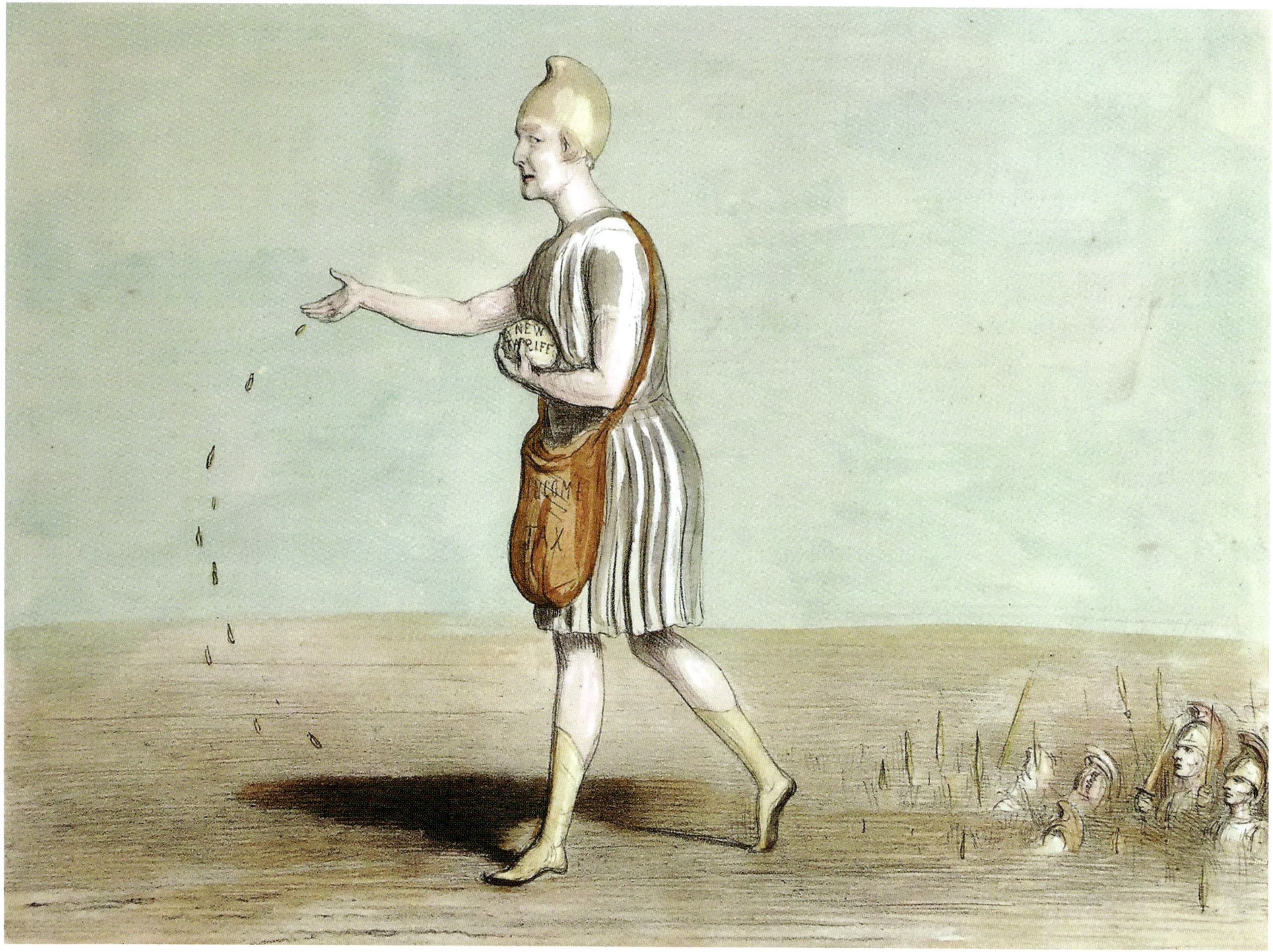

[97] ***No. 730, 'Jason Sowing the Dragon's Teeth' (published 3 May 1842)*** In a barren landscape, a man in the character of Jason (Sir Robert Peel), walking from right towards left, sowing dragon's teeth with his right hand, from a bag lettered with 'Income Tax', holding a stone lettered with 'New Tariff' in his left hand; at the bottom right, a group of soldiers, wearing helmets (among them Lords Melbourne and John Russell), emerging from the ground. Sir Robert Peel's task of overcoming the financial difficulties of the country is compared with that of Jason when he went in quest of the "Golden Fleece." The imposition of the Income Tax, in lieu of the Whig measure of a fixed duty on foreign corn, like the sowing of the dragon's teeth, raised up a certain number of enemies to the Ministerial plans, but the New Tariff, like the stone cast by Jason among the armed men, diverted their rage from himself and set them against each other. Among the armed men rising out of the ground, the heads of Lord Melbourne and Lord John Russell are distinctly visible.

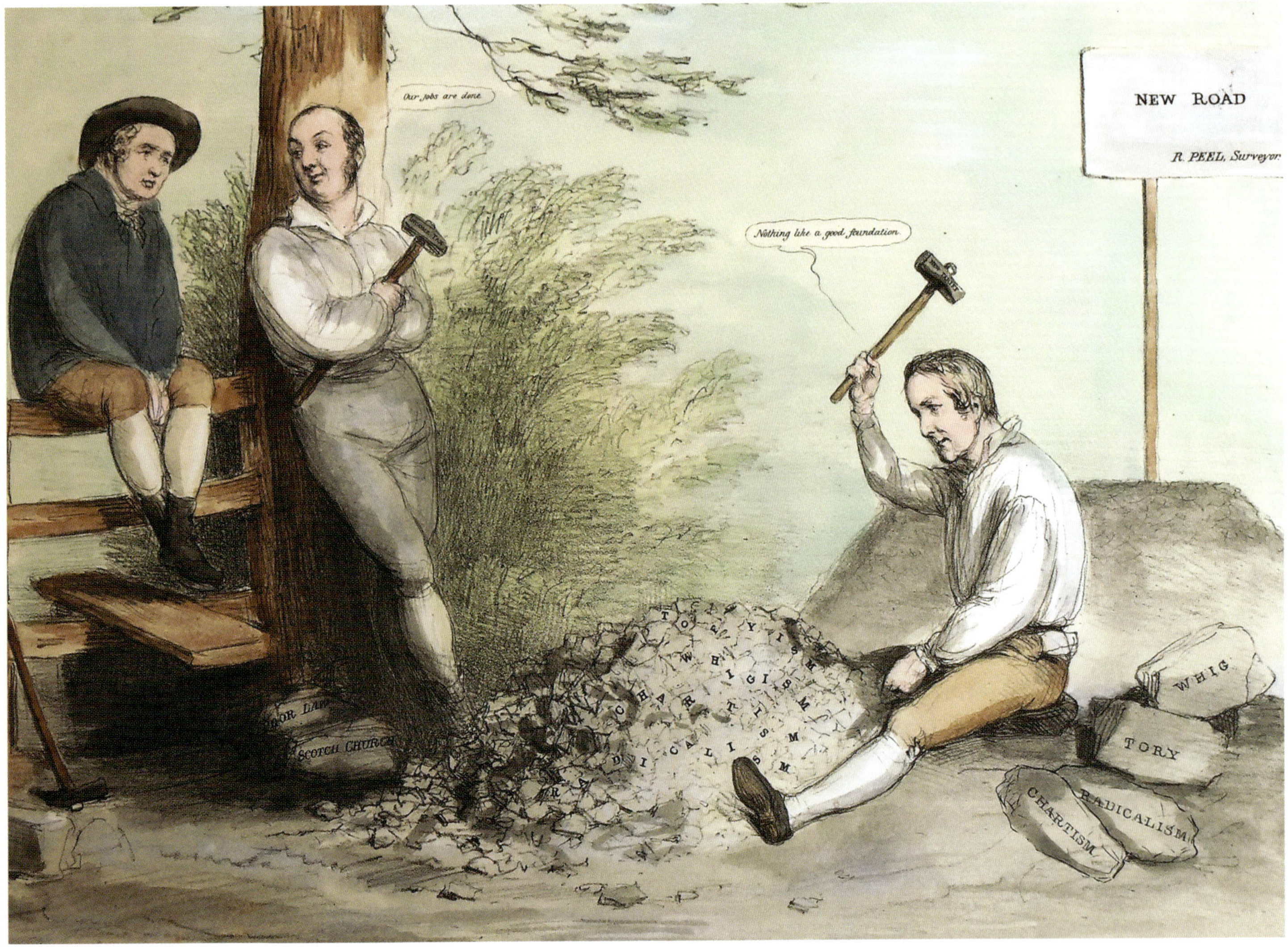

[98] ***No. 733, 'The Political McAdam' (published 23 June 1842)*** A man (based on the famous road construction expert John McAdam) seated on the ground at right, in profile to left (Sir Robert Peel), under a signpost lettered with 'New Road' and below 'Robert Peel, Surveyor', breaking stones lettered with names of various political parties and movements, with a hammer lettered with 'New Tariff'; at the left, two men standing by having nothing to do, one seated on a wooden gate (Lord Stanley), the other standing next to him, leaning against a tree, holding a hammer lettered with 'Income Tax'; stones at their feet are lettered with 'Poor Law' and Scotch Church'. Sir Robert Peel is drawn in the act of breaking up the party distinctions of Whig, Tory, Radical, and Chartist, and making a broad foundation for his own government; by a combination of the fragments. The task, however, is a laborious one, much more so (and, therefore, best suited to him as the Prime Minister) than that assigned to his colleagues, two of whom, Lord Stanley, and Sir James Graham, are resting after the accomplishment of their respective tasks. Lord Stanley sits cross-legged on the stile, after laying down his hammer, entitled [Canada] Corn-Bill, and Sir James Graham leans against a tree, having done his part of the work of the Income-Tax. At his feet lie two large unbroken lumps, marked Poor-Law and 'Scotch Church' both of which remained at that time intact, and were intended, as it appeared, to stand over for another session.

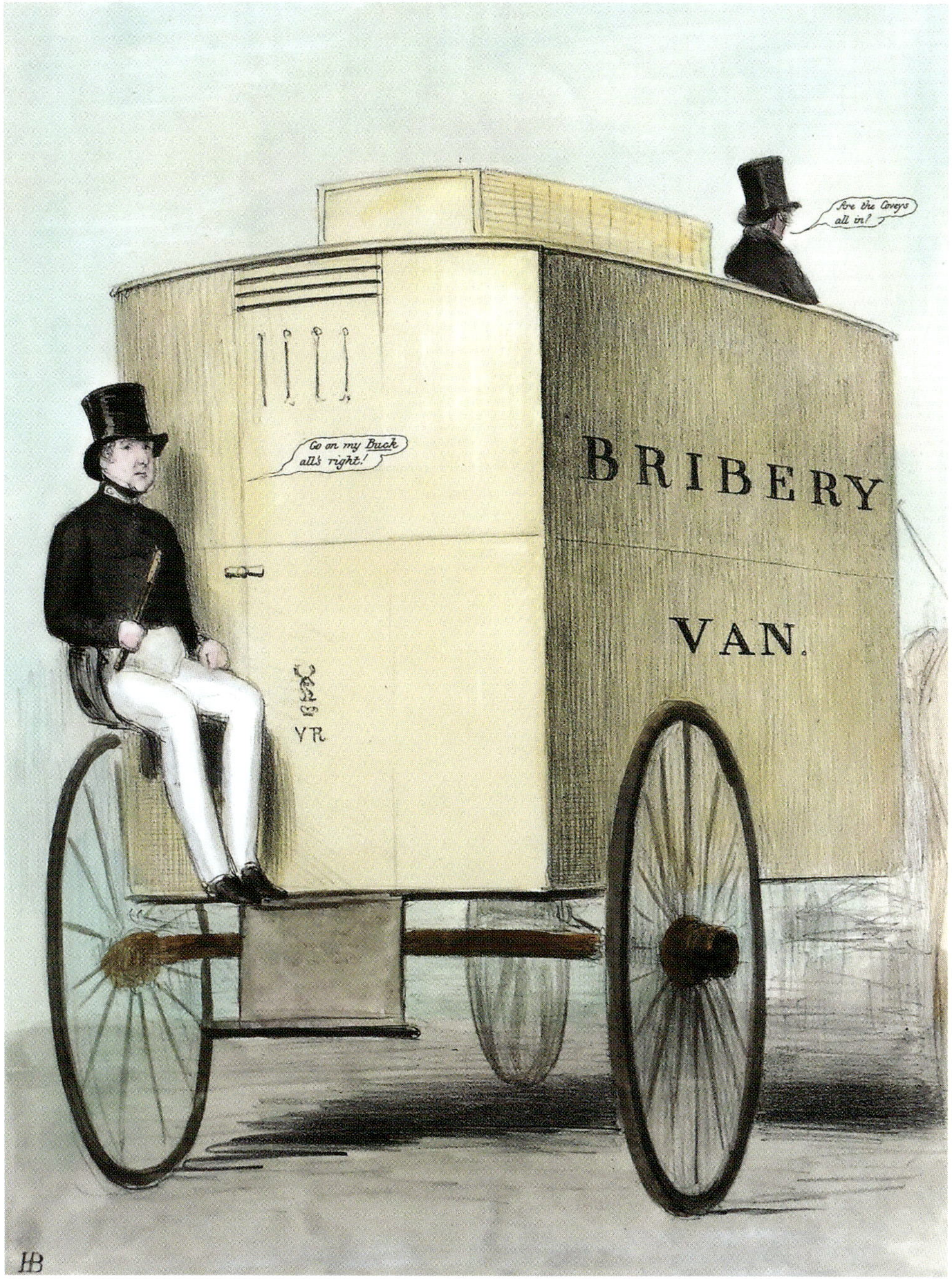

[99] ***No. 734, 'Curious Signs of the Times' (published 23 June 1842)*** A horse-drawn van lettered with 'Bribary [*sic*] Van.' on its side and 'V R' on its back, driven by a coachman towards right (John Arthur Roebuck), with a guard seated at the back (Sir Robert Peel). Mr. Roebuck is driving a carriage similar to that in which the Criminals are daily conveyed from the Police-offices to the Prisons and Houses of Correction. It is supposed to be filled with those Members of the House of Commons who had been guilty of the crime of bribery at elections. The office of assistant to the Honorable Member for Bath, is conferred on Sir Robert Peel, in compliment to the assistance which he lent to Mr. Roebuck, in his prosecution of the object of exposing bribery. Sir Robert Peel's cordiality in this affair was considered not a little extraordinary, and, as the sketch calls it, a curious sign of the Times.

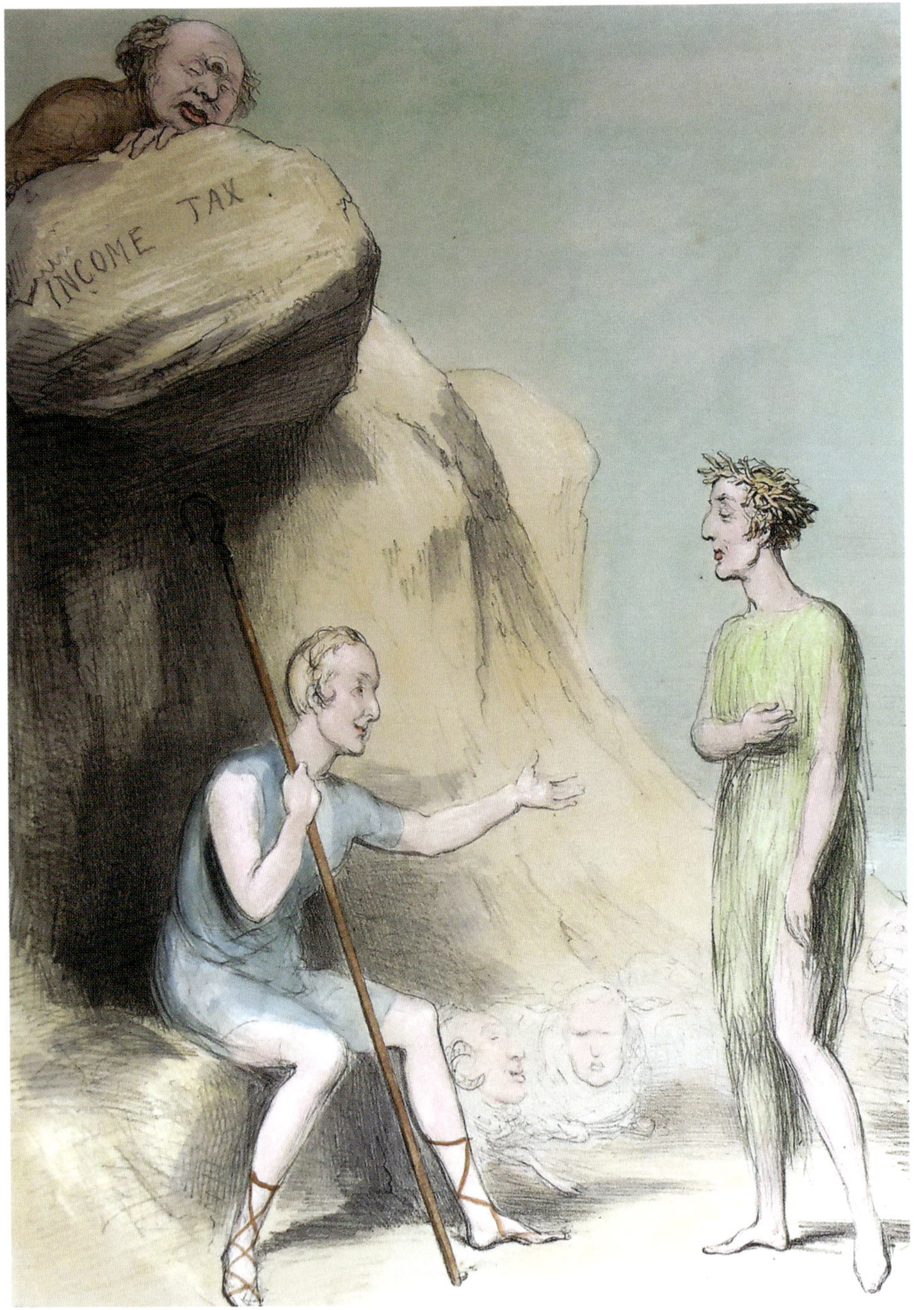

[100] ***No. 736, 'Acis and Galatea' (published 13 July 1842)*** Below the title: Acis: 'The Flocks shall leave the Mountains / The nymphs desert the fountains / Ere I desert my love'. Polyphemus [*sic*] 'Fury! Rage! Despair! / I cannot cannot bear!' A man as a shepherd, in the character of Acis (Sir Robert Peel), seated at the left on a rock, holding a crook in his right hand, his left arm outstretched towards a man dressed as a woman, in the character of Galatea (Duke of Wellington), standing at the right, wearing a wreath; at the top left, John Bull in the character of Polyphemus, preparing to hurl a huge stone inscribed 'INCOME TAX' on Acis's head; a flock of sheep with men's heads lying at centre and right. It was widely believed that, following his conversion to Catholic Emancipation in 1829, Sir Robert Peel was politically seduced by the Duke of Wellington, and had 'lost his character', as a public man. In this sketch the same popular idea is followed up with the variation of changing the sexes of the parties: a Galatea formed out of an old soldier of more than seventy, tempting to his ruin a shepherd of ripe age. John Bull as 'the Monster Polypheme' is about to crush Sir Robert Peel, with his own Income-Tax, while he, infatuated by his love, is unconscious of the fate that awaits him. The two sheep have the likenesses of Sir James Graham and Lord Stanley. In the eighteenth century, the story of the undying love between Acis and Galatea, and of the jealousy of the monstrous giant Polyphemus, which led him to murder Acis, was set to music by Handel.

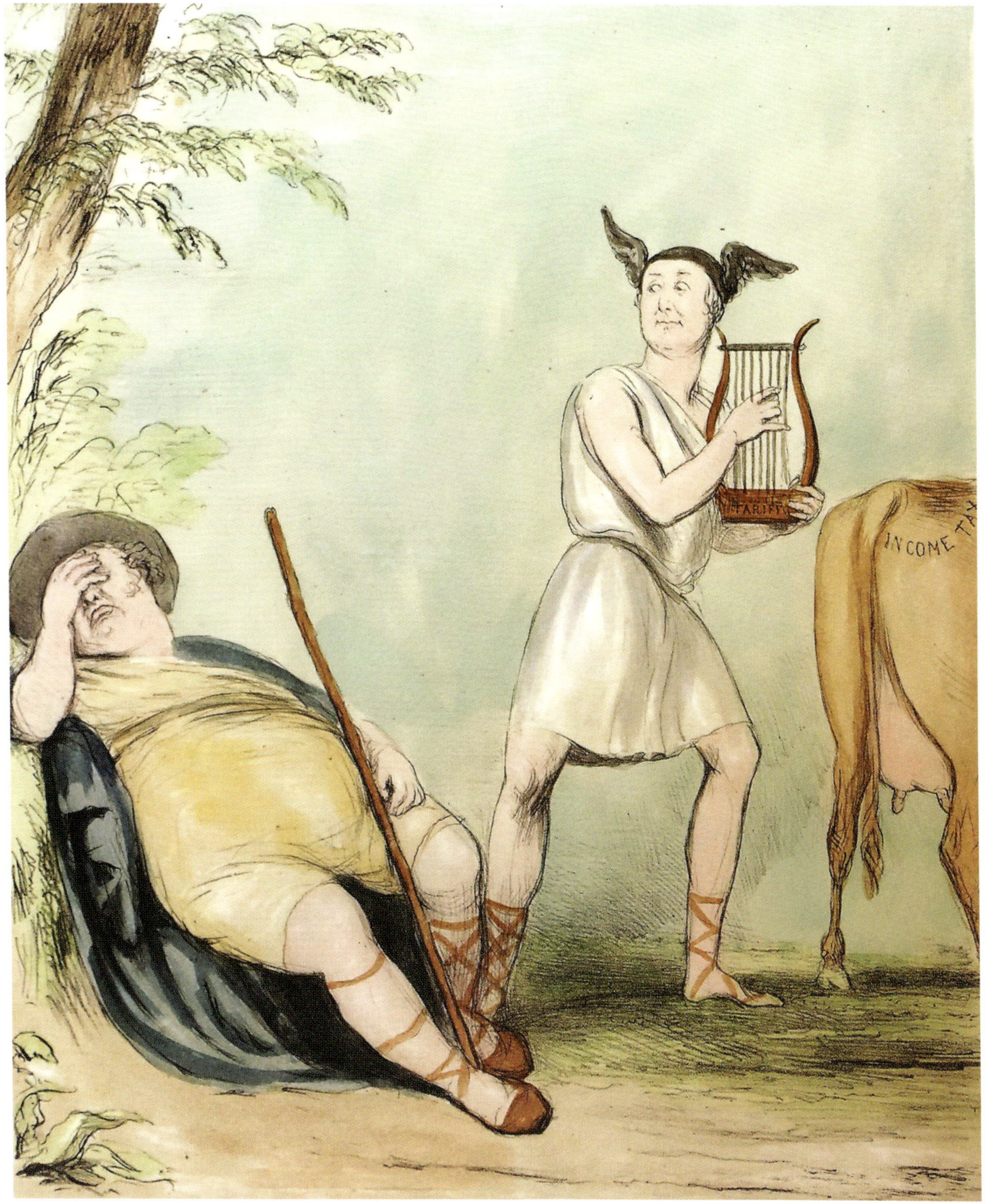

[101] ***No. 737, 'Mercury and Argus'*** Below the title: 'Having lulled Argus to sleep carries off the Beautiful Milch cow IO!' A man in the character of Mercury (Sir Robert Peel), standing at the right, holding a lyre lettered with 'Tariff', lulling John Bull, in the character of Argus, lying under a tree at the left, covering his eyes with his left hand, and carrying off a cow, in the character of Io, seen from behind at far right, lettered with 'Income Tax'. Sir Robert Peel fills the part of Mercury; he plays upon his instrument marked 'Tariff', or a new scale of reduced Custom Duties on foreign cattle, coffee, and various articles and things of daily use and consumption and charms the watchfulness of John Bull (Argus) who generally keeps all his eyes open upon matters that affect the pocket, and succeeds in carrying his Income-Tax, the beautiful cow, (Io – Heigh-oh!!) which, having been calculated to yield three millions and a half, and yielding in fact, more than five millions, has proved to be a good milch cow to the Exchequer.

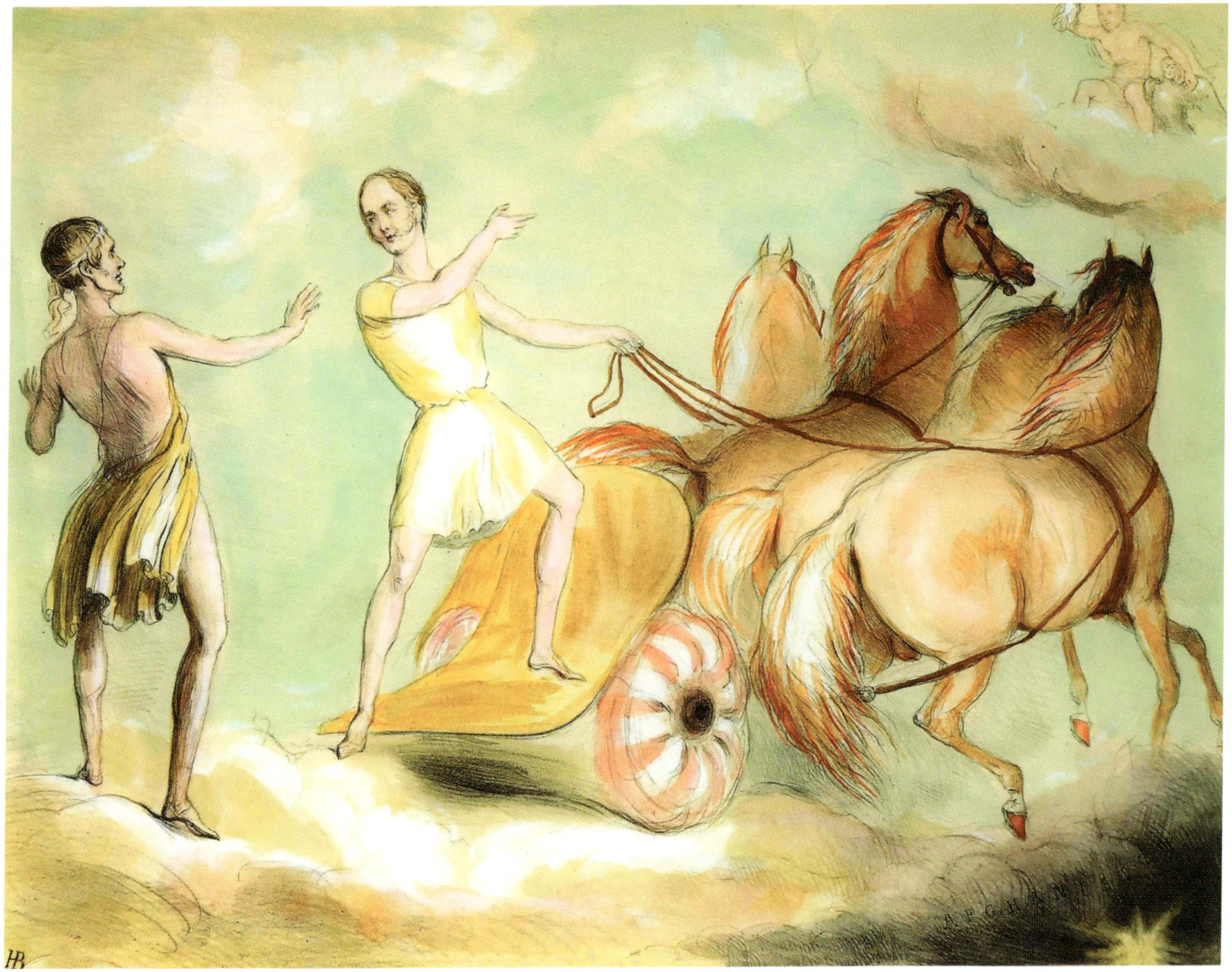

[102] ***No. 743, 'Phaeton taking the reins from Phoebus'*** In Greek myth, Phaeton attempted to ride the chariot of the sun but the horses knew that Phoebus was their true master and raced on regardless of him until they threw their rider and he perished in the river below – the moral being, 'Phaeton was full of pride, but he failed in a great undertaking'. On clouds in the sky, a man at the centre in the character of Phaeton (Lord Palmerston), standing on a chariot, holding the reins of four horses, taken over from a man standing at the left in the character of Phoebus (Lord John Russell); at the top right, a man in the character of Jupiter Tonans (Sir Robert Peel), holding thunderbolts, followed by an eagle with a man's head (the Duke of Wellington); clouds at the bottom right are lettered with 'Afghanistan'. This sketch refers to the lead taken by Lord Palmerston, in the place of Lord John Russell, in a general assault upon the administration of Sir Robert Peel at the close of the session of 1842. The war in Afghanistan formed the principal ground of attack. Palmerston's illustrious father (in politics), Lord John Russell, while yielding to the entreaties of 'his daring son to be permitted to take "a drive" at the enemy', expresses both in look and attitude, his admiration and his fears. The fatal issue of the trial is, however, seen in the distance. JUPITER TONANS, with his attendant eagle, in the likenesses of Sir Robert Peel and the Duke of Wellington, appear on high: the angry God is raising his avenging arm to launch a bolt that shall hurl the presumptuous driver from his seat, and at once terminate his experiment.

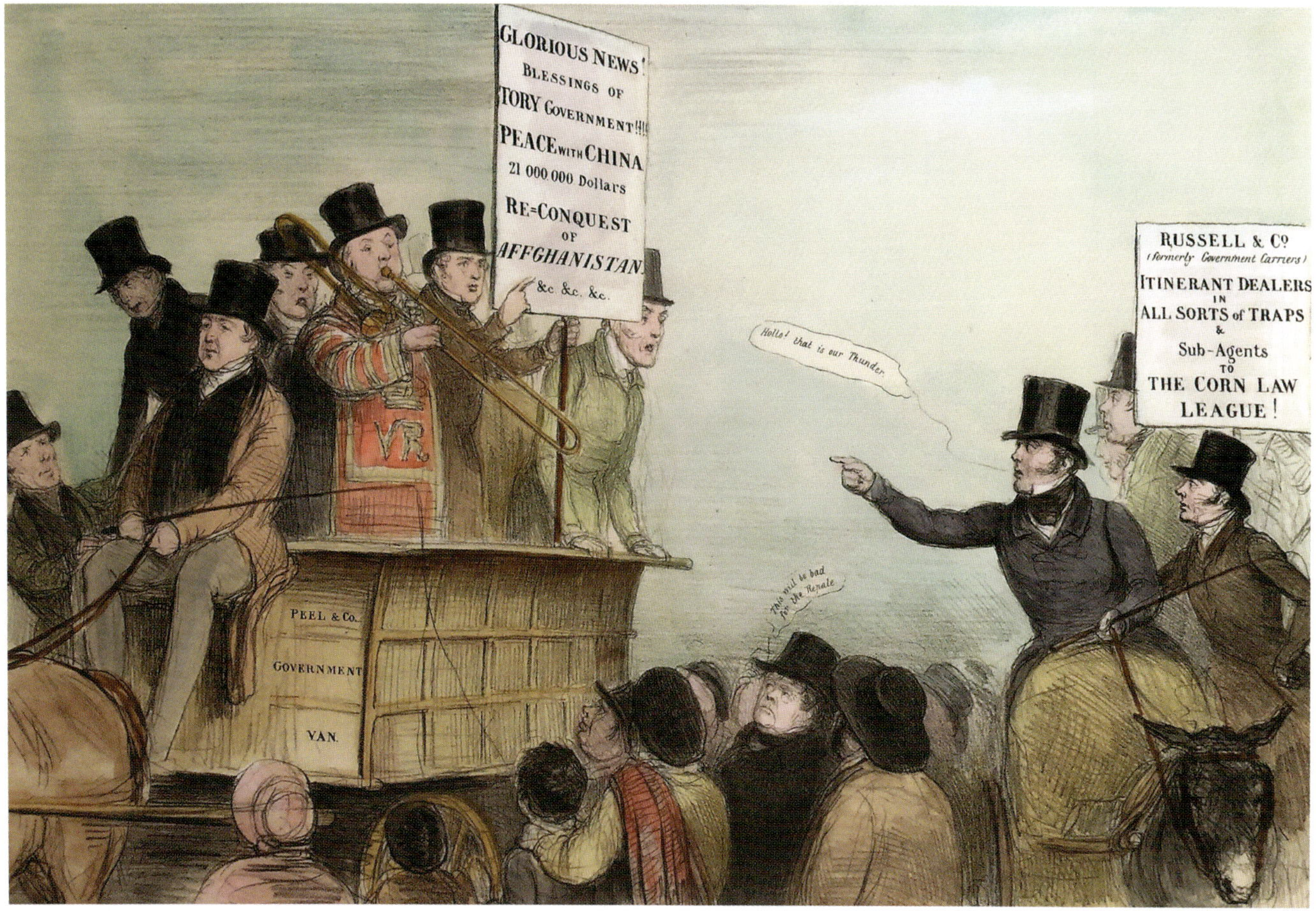

[103] ***No. 752, 'Curious Inns and Outs, or The Disputed Thunder'*** A horse-drawn cart at the left, driven by a man holding the reins in his left hand and a whip in his right hand (Sir Robert Peel); a man at left about to climb up (Lord Brougham); a group of men standing on the cart, one behind the coachman at left (Lord Lyndhurst), one blowing a trumpet (Sir James Graham), the one behind him blowing the French horn (Lord Aberdeen), another pointing to a placard lettered with 'Glorious news! [...] &c.', announcing peace to China and re-conquest of Afghanistan (Lord Stanley), and a man next to him at the right (the Duke of Wellington); they are watched by a crowd in the foreground (Daniel O'Connell at the centre); a cart drawn by a donkey passing by at the far right, with three men (Lord Palmerston, Francis Thornhill Baring, Lord John Russell), and a placard lettered with 'Russell & Co. [...] The Corn Law League!'. The Tories, Peel and Co. have here got possession of the Car of State, or Government Van, and are loudly advertising their goods. The very first incident that succeeded the change of Government, was the successful issue of the war in Afghanistan, the release of all the prisoners and the withdrawal of the troops. This being followed by a treaty with China, put the nation into pretty good humour with the new Government, and produced a corresponding degree of chagrin in the opposition party, who considered these results as the proper fruit of their policy, and not that of their successors. Hence the Ex-foreign Secretary, Lord Palmerston, sitting by the side of Lord John Russell, is represented in the act of claiming the authorship of the 'Thunder', which is pealing from the Government Van. Sir Robert Peel is the driver of the Van, and Sir James Graham close behind is sounding a trombone with great vehemence. Next to Sir James Graham stands Lord Stanley pointing to the placard, while the Duke of Wellington is staring with astonishment at the cool impudence of the Opposition in claiming the merit of these great events. Lord Brougham appears to be in the act of climbing up the Government Van, unassisted however by a single friendly hand, while the look and manner of Lord Lyndhurst appears to admonish him that no welcome awaits him. Lord Aberdeen, never in the front rank, but satisfied to be well employed, is blowing a horn behind Sir James Graham. Among the mob between the two factions, the broad face of Mr. O'Connell is seen, remarking that the good news for the Empire will be disadvantageous to his favourite plan for a repeal of the Union with Ireland.

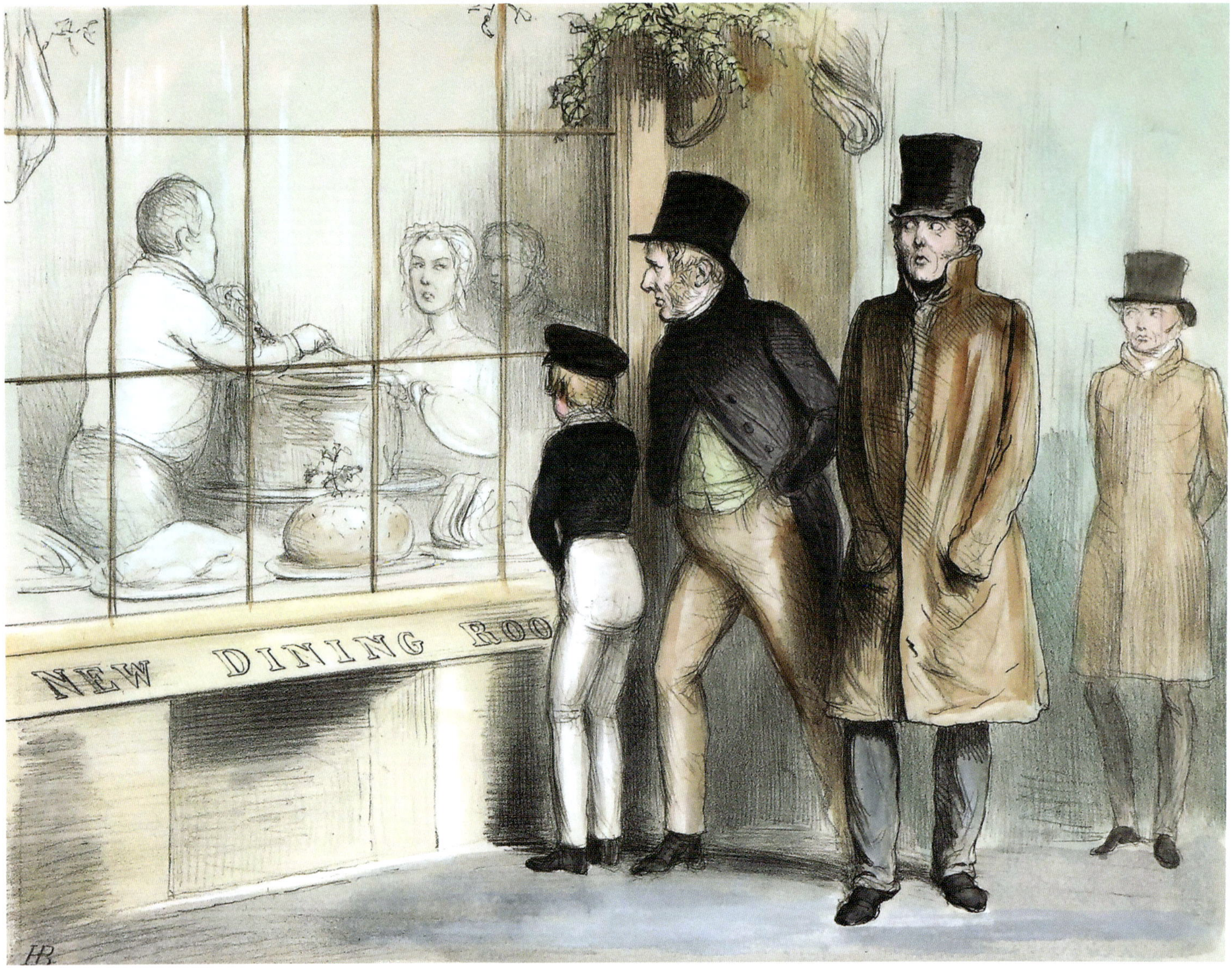

[104] ***No. 755, 'A Touching View of Some of the Inns and Outs of this World'*** Four men (Lords Morpeth, Melbourne, Palmerston and John Russell) standing at the right hungrily, by an eating-house, at the left, lettered with 'New Dining Roo[m]', inside which a man (Sir Robert Peel) is serving out helpings of soup to a man dressed as a woman, and a man (Lords Aberdeen and Lyndhurst). The complacent and comfortable figure of Sir Robert Peel, among the Ins, while dealing out the good things among his friends, is not better conceived than those of the Outs; namely, Lord Melbourne, who seems ready to rush forward and seize the dispensing ladle; Lord Palmerston, who, though he turns not his face, cannot prevent his eyes from rolling towards the solids; and Lord Morpeth, whose mouth, like that of any other big boy, waters for a piece of pudding; and Lord John Russell, who looks exceedingly melancholy in the back ground.

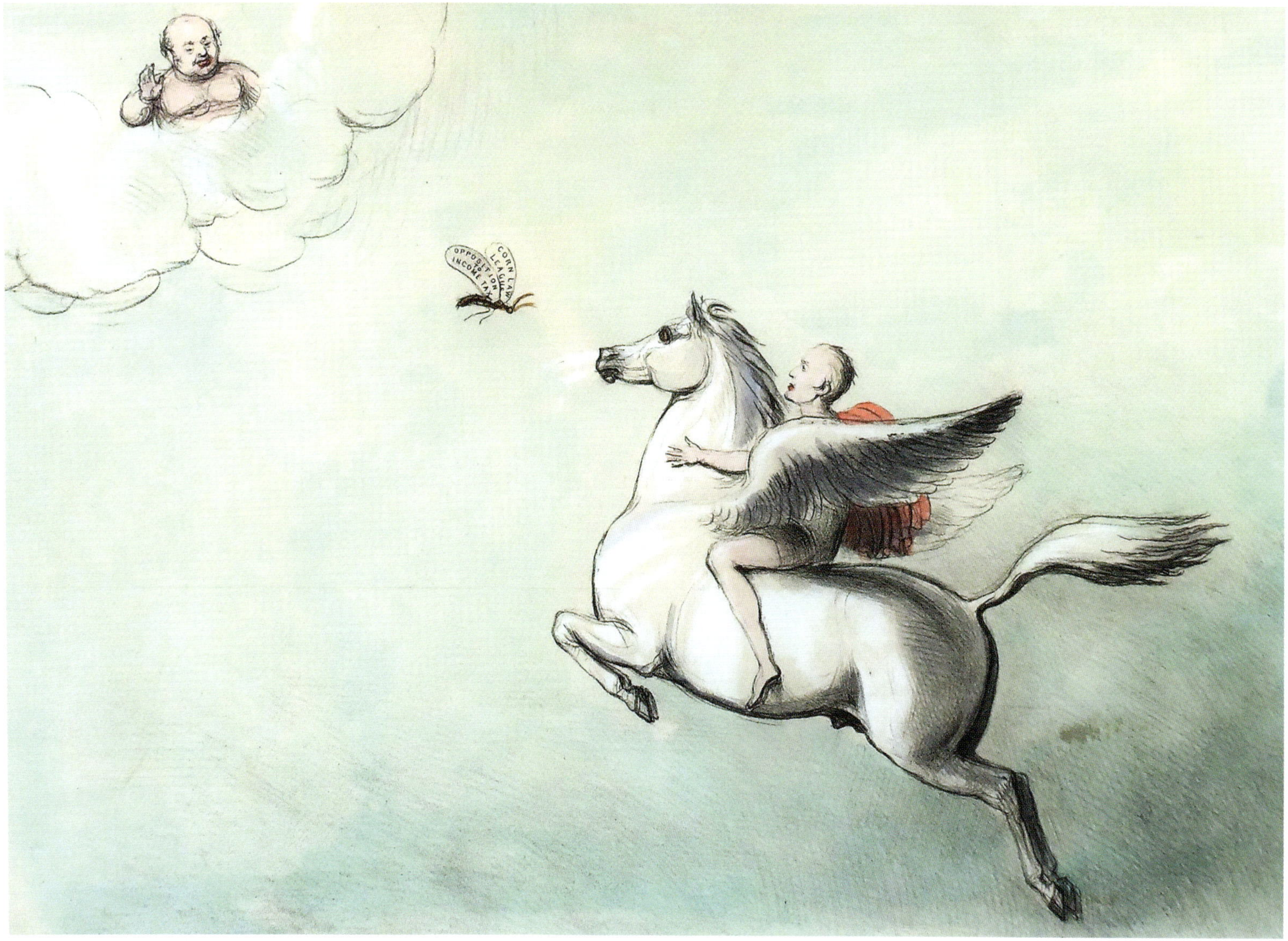

[105] ***No. 757, 'Bellerophon in Danger'*** Below the title: 'Attempting to fly to heaven upon Pegasus, Jupiter sent an insect which stung the horse & threw down the rider &c'. A man in the character of Bellerophon, the greatest hero and slayer of monsters (Sir Robert Peel), rides Pegasus, soaring towards the sun. Bellerophon thought his many victories entitled him to ascend to Mount Olympus, the home of the Gods. Jupiter, angered by this, sent a gad-fly to sting Bellerophon's horse and plunge him back to earth. Here, John Bull is in the character of Jupiter, appearing among clouds at the top left, sending an insect, its wings lettered with 'Corn Law League' and 'Opposition to Income Tax', to sting the horse and overthrow the rider. Sir Robert Peel, as Bellerophon riding on the Pegasus of political power, is attempting to gain the heaven of John Bull's good graces; but John has sent forth an insect winged with opposition to the Income Tax and the Corn Law League: a pestilent stinging creature that threatens to defeat the hopes of the aspiring Minister.

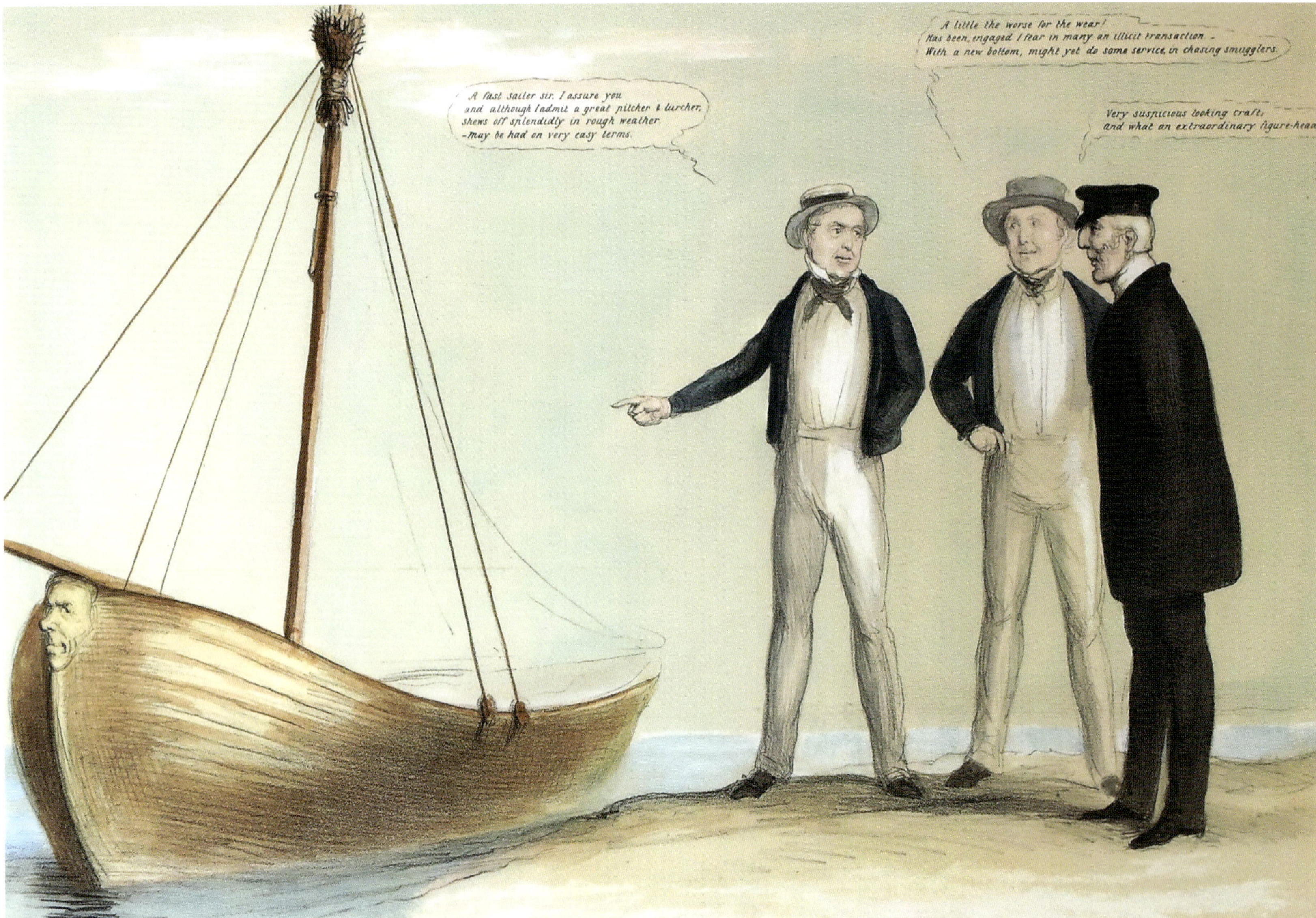

[106] ***No. 767, 'A Cutter for Sale, or A Br-----m at the mast head' (published 17 Mar. 1843)*** Three men standing on the seashore; the one at centre right (Lord Stanley) pointing at a cutter in the water at the left, with a man's head as figurehead (Lord Brougham), for sale on easy terms, to the other two (Sir Robert Peel and the Duke of Wellington). The broom at the mast head, is a well-known signal of a vessel being for sale: this cutter has not only a broom at the mast head, but a Brougham for the figure head, at the prow. In short it is Lord Brougham himself, who is represented as having cut all his old connexions with the Whigs, and being now on sale to the best bidder. The principal members of the Tory party are considering the question of purchasing the craft. Lord Stanley recommends it: Sir Robert Peel thinks it might be useful if newly bottomed. The Duke of Wellington seems to disapprove of the speculation.

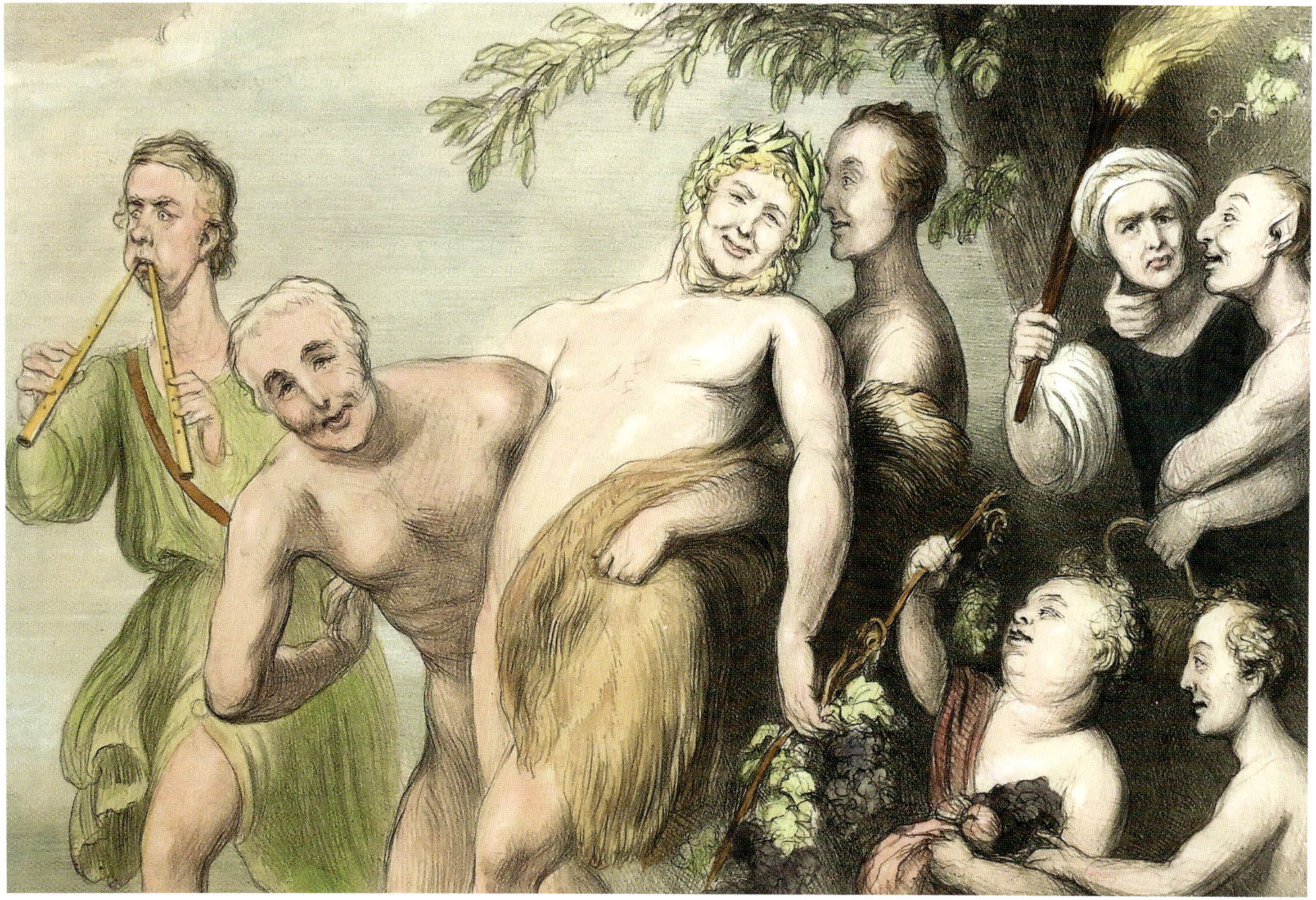

[107] ***No. 768, 'A Song of Triumph'*** Below the title: 'Very freely taken from the celebrated picture by Rubens in the possession of a Cabinet Minister'. A parody of Rubens's 'Triumph of Silenus' (1616–1617) (which Peel owned); a man in the character of Silenus (Lord Ellenborough), at the centre, led by two men (the Duke of Wellington at the left, Sir Robert Peel at the right) in a triumphal procession; at the far left, a man playing double pipes (Lord Brougham); at the far right in the background, a man holding up a torch (Lord Stanley) and a figure with pointed ears (Sir James Graham); in the foreground at the right, two young boys (the one at the far right James Emerson Tennent). The Duke of Wellington defended Lord Ellenborough's conduct as Governor General of India (1842–1844) against the Marquess of Lansdowne, and others who ridiculed or censured him after he was recalled in June 1844. 'H.B.' caught up Wellington's expression 'The Song of Triumph', and adapted to his purpose the well-known picture of Bacchus and his followers, by Rubens. The first figure is that of Lord Brougham, to whom, in compliment to his oratorical powers, is given the office of grand piper to the group. His double-pipe is an allusion to his equivocal principles, now Radical, now Conservative. The principal figure, clothed in a lion's skin and crowned, not exactly like Bacchus with ivy, but with bays, is that of Lord Ellenborough led by the Duke of Wellington and supported by Sir Robert Peel. The droll figure of Sir James Graham, with an asinine expression of countenance and strangely elongated ears, clasping with foolish fondness the figure of Lord Stanley, is not without meaning. The fat boy represents no one in particular; the figure in the corner is Mr. Emmerson Tennant, Secretary to the India Board.

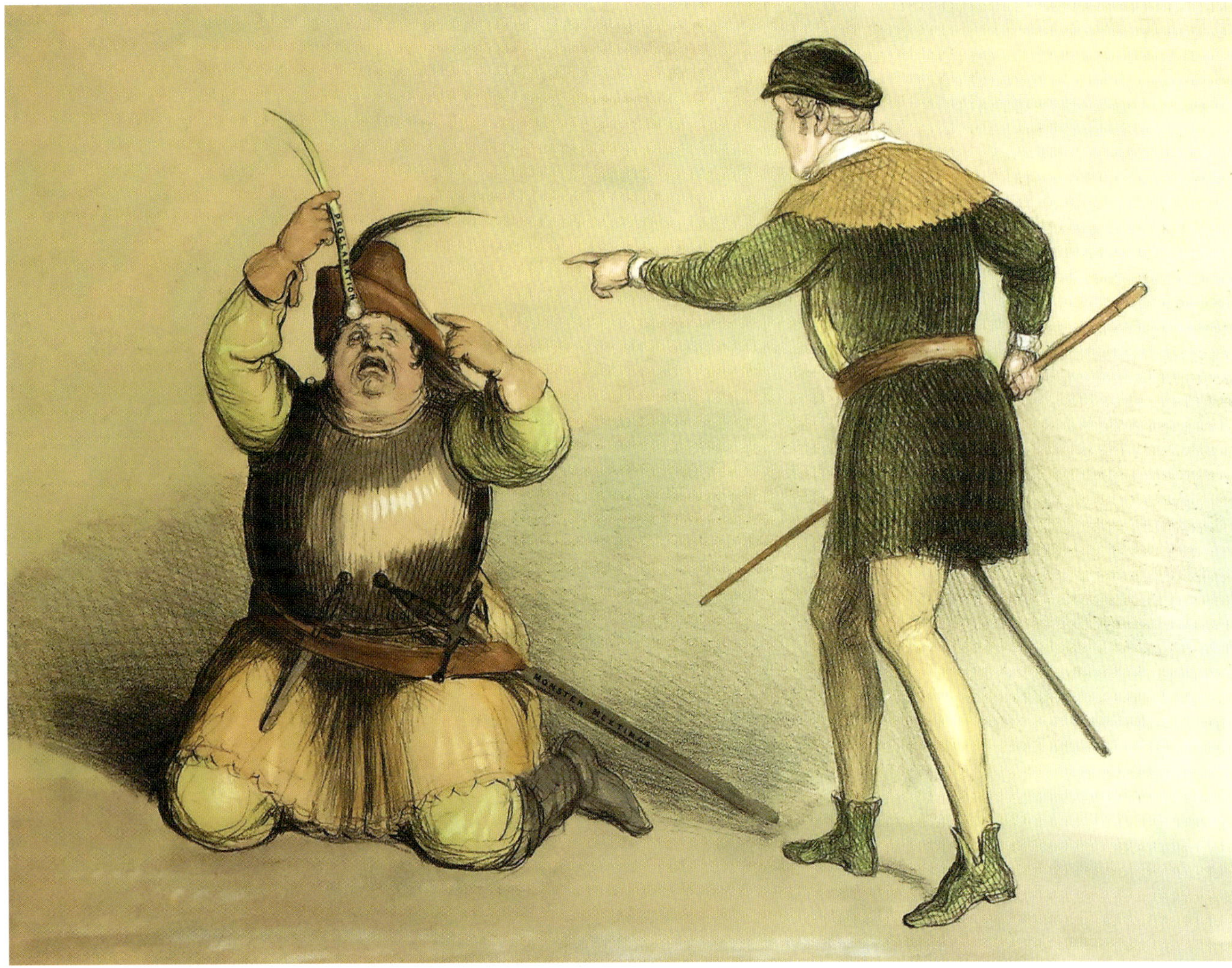

[108] ***No. 786, 'Swallowing the Leek' (published 25 Oct. 1843)*** Below the title: 'Pistol – Must I bite? Fluellen – Yes certainly, and out of doubt, and out of question too, and ambiguities'. Inspired by Shakespeare's 'Henry V' (1599) (Act V, Scene I). A man in the character of Fluellen (Sir Robert Peel), standing at the right, forcing a terrified man, in the character of Pistol (Daniel O'Connell), kneeling on the ground at the left, wearing a sword lettered with 'Monster meetings', to swallow a leek lettered with 'Proclamation', held up in his right hand. One repeal meeting in Ireland followed another so rapidly without interruption, and each more numerous than the last, that it seemed as if Government were paralyzed, and the Repealers grew bolder and bolder in proportion to the forbearance of the authorities, until they openly defied all control. At length a meeting was announced to be held at Clontarf, and the directions given by the Repeal Agitators to those who should attend the meeting, appearing to the Government to warrant an interference, a proclamation was issued by the Lord-Lieutenant (Earl de Grey), forbidding the meeting. Upon this, the Repeal Association met, and issued orders to their followers that the proclamation should be obeyed, and the intention of assembling at Clontarf abandoned. After the bold defiance offered to Government by Mr. O'Connell and his followers, their submission to the Government proclamation appeared rather small, and afforded a fair ground for comparing O'Connell to ancient Pistol, when compelled by Captain Fluellen to eat the leek with which he had wantonly insulted the courageous Welshman. Fluellen is Sir Robert Peel as the representative of the Government.

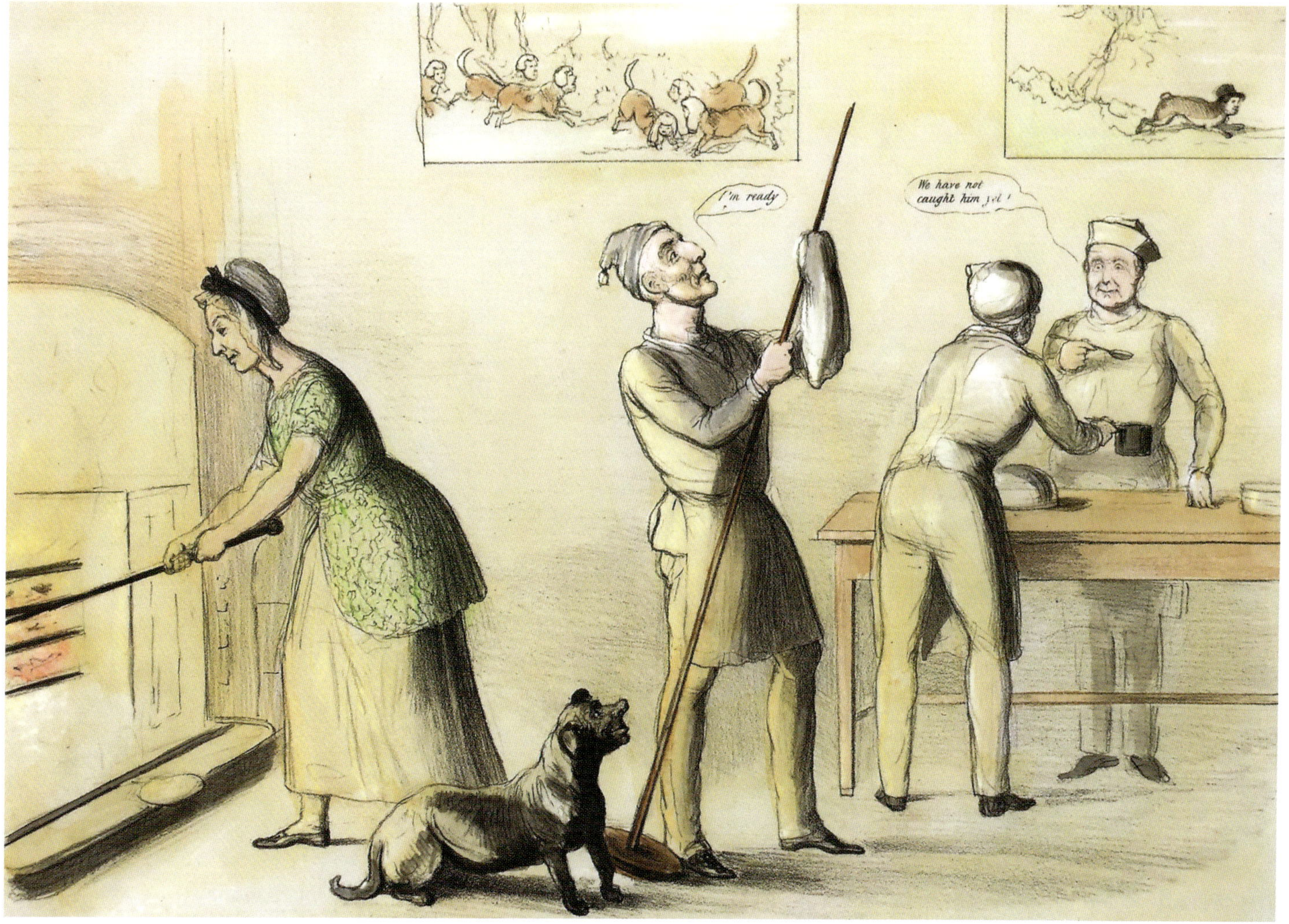

[109] ***No. 791, 'First Catch your Hare' (published 26 Dec. 1843)*** A woman dressed as a man (Sir James Graham), holding a poker in the fire of a stove at the left; a man standing at the centre, holding a long pole, saying he is ready (the Duke of Wellington); a dog with a man's head standing at his feet, looking up at him (Lord Brougham); two men tasting food at a table at the right (Lord Stanley and Sir Robert Peel), the one at the far right suggesting that the game has not been caught yet; on the wall behind him, a picture of a running hare, with a man's head, wearing a hat (Daniel O'Connell), and another picture at the centre, showing hunting dogs with men's heads, wearing wigs, trying to follow the scent of game. The Tory Ministers are here represented, preparing to give Mr. O'Connell a dressing, but inasmuch as at the date of this sketch Mr. O'Connell had not been convicted, 'H.B.' gives them the advice, with which Hannah Glasse in her *The Art of Cookery* (1747) commences her directions for dressing a hare – 'First catch your hare'. The Duke of Wellington, as head cook, is preparing the spit to be passed through the body of the hare, with true professional coolness and precision. Sir James Graham is stirring up the fire, Lord Stanley presents a little stew-pan filled with sauce, for Sir Robert Peel to judge of its piquancy, but Sir Robert, always a plain matter-of-fact man, suggests that the game is not yet caught. Lord Brougham is degraded to the character of a humble turnspit, waiting at the heels of the head cook. The pictures on the wall, are two belonging to a series called the Chase. No. 1 exhibits the hounds 'Finding', No. 2 the hare just starting from his place of shelter: a cunning old jack hare he is, and well used to doubling (Dublin).

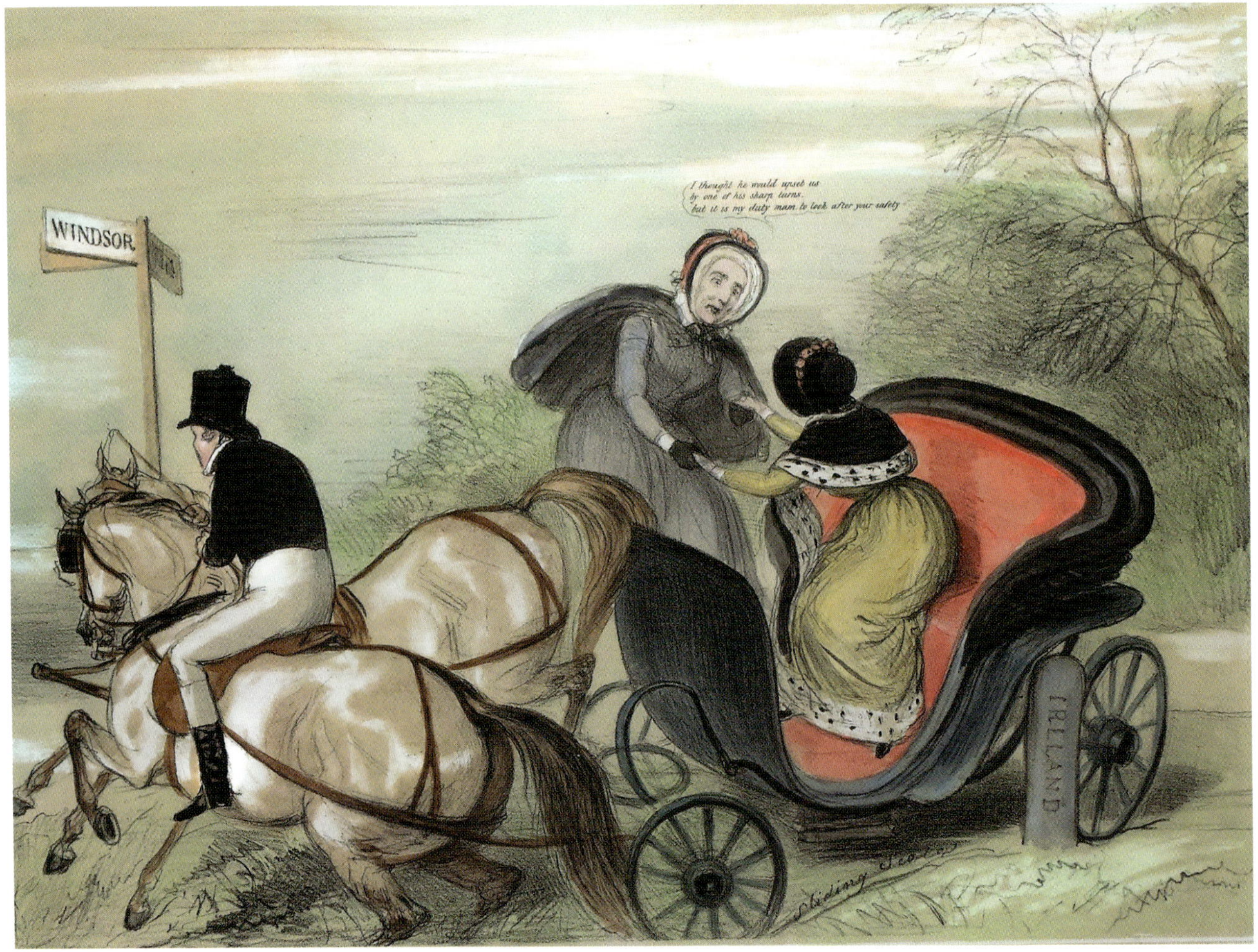

[110] ***No. 794, 'Late Threatened Upset near Windsor' (published 18 Jan. 1844)*** A coach drawn by two horses, one ridden by a postilion (Sir Robert Peel), sliding into a ditch at a road sign lettered with 'Windsor', on a road lettered with 'Sliding Scale', and colliding with a post lettered with 'Ireland'; the passenger, a woman wearing ermine-trimmed robes (Queen Victoria), is rescued by a man dressed as a woman (Duke of Wellington). The following paragraph appeared in the morning papers a short time previously to the date of this sketch. 'Windsor, Friday, 5th January, 1844. – A slight accident, which happily proved of no consequence, happened to Her Majesty, who was being driven in a pony carriage, with the Marchioness of Douro. The postilion took too short a turn from one road into another, and the left wheel of the carriage went into a broad ditch, which threw the carriage against the hedge. Her Majesty and Lady Douro were speedily rescued from their unpleasant position, and returned to the castle in a pony car, driven by Colonel Arbuthnot, which was kindly given up by a lady who was driving close by, and His Royal Highness Prince Albert accompanied the car on horseback. We are gratified to learn that Her Majesty has not experienced any inconvenience from the accident'. 'H.B.' has turned this accident into a pleasant comic fiction. The postilion is the Prime-Minister, Sir Robert Peel, and the turn too-sharply made, is an illusion to a change of commercial policy, which it was rumoured Sir Robert Peel was about to make, and which would have not only been exceedingly 'sharp', but so much so, as to have endangered the Ministry, and probably occasioned its overthrow. The sliding-scale of Corn Duties, is the path from which the carriage is making the sharp turn; but this is not the only mischance, the postilion has brought the vehicle into collision with the post inscribed Ireland – a collision that cannot fail to give both the carriage and the royal personage within it a very serious and violent shock. The place of the Marchioness of Douro, who afforded such timely assistance to Her Majesty, is filled by her father-in-law, the Duke of Wellington.

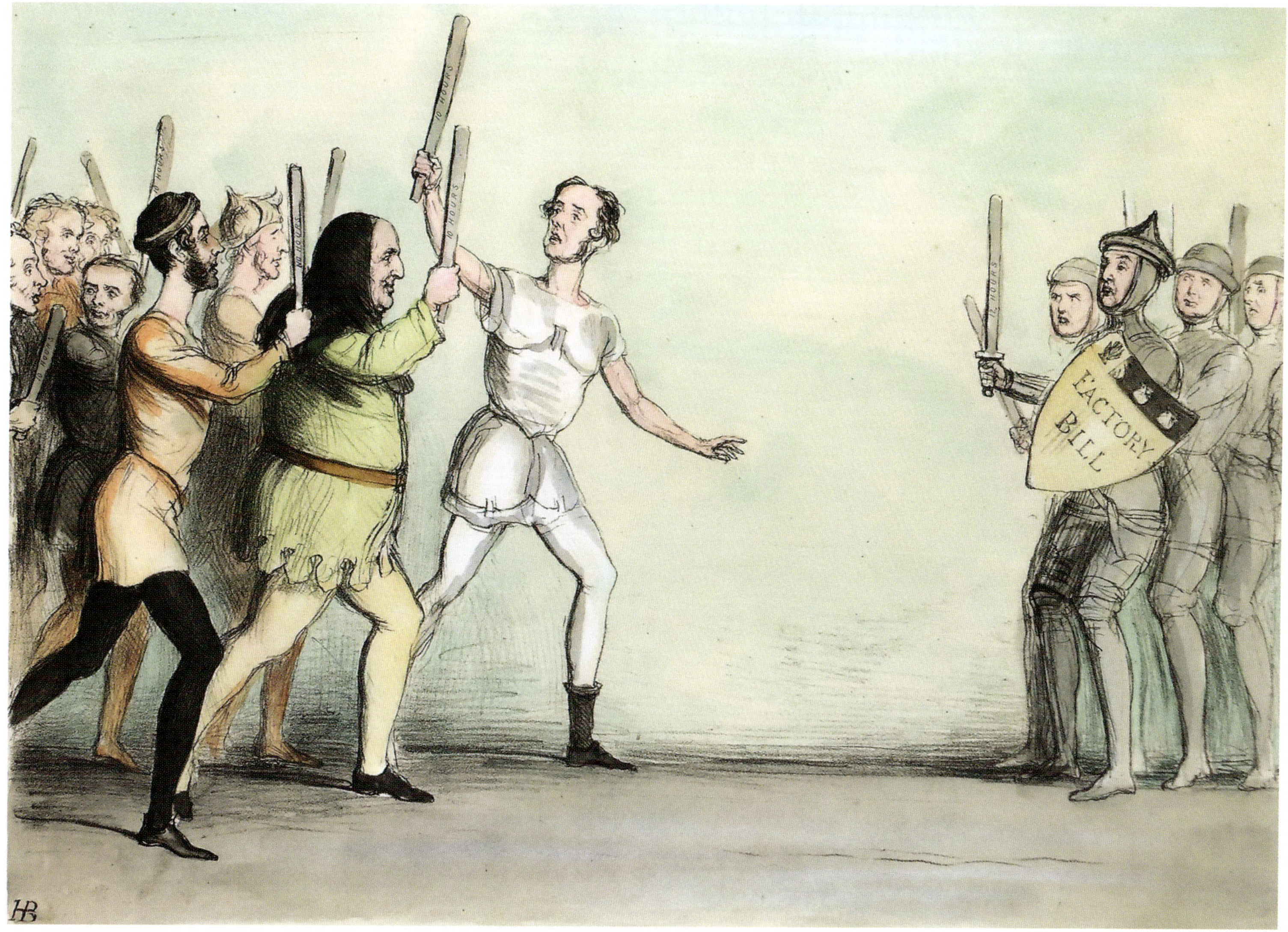

[111] ***No. 801, 'Jack Cade's Insurrection' (published Apr. 1844)*** A man in the character of Jack Cade (Lord Ashley), at centre, holding a stick lettered with '10 hours', leading his supporters (from left to right, Lord Howick, Charles Buller, Lord Cochrane, Lord John Russell, Thomas Slingsby Duncombe, Lord Sandon, Sir Robert Inglis) against a group of men standing at the right, their leader holding a sword lettered with '12 hours', and a shield lettered with 'Factory Bill' (Sir James Graham; next to him, Lord Stanley, and behind at the right, Sir Robert Peel and Henry Goulburn). The sketch illustrates the division in the Conservative party created by the campaign for a factory working day of ten hours (on the part of humanitarian and Evangelical reformers such as Ashley) against the government proposal of a twelve hour day. The proposals led to severe disruption amongst the Conservative backbenchers and hostile divisions in the House of Commons which threatened the future of Peel's government. Only the threat of resignation forced the issue and the rebel vote in favour of ten hours was reversed in consequence. Here Ashley (the future Earl of Shaftesbury of 'Eros' fame) is represented as Jack Cade, who led a revolt against Henry VI's government in 1450.

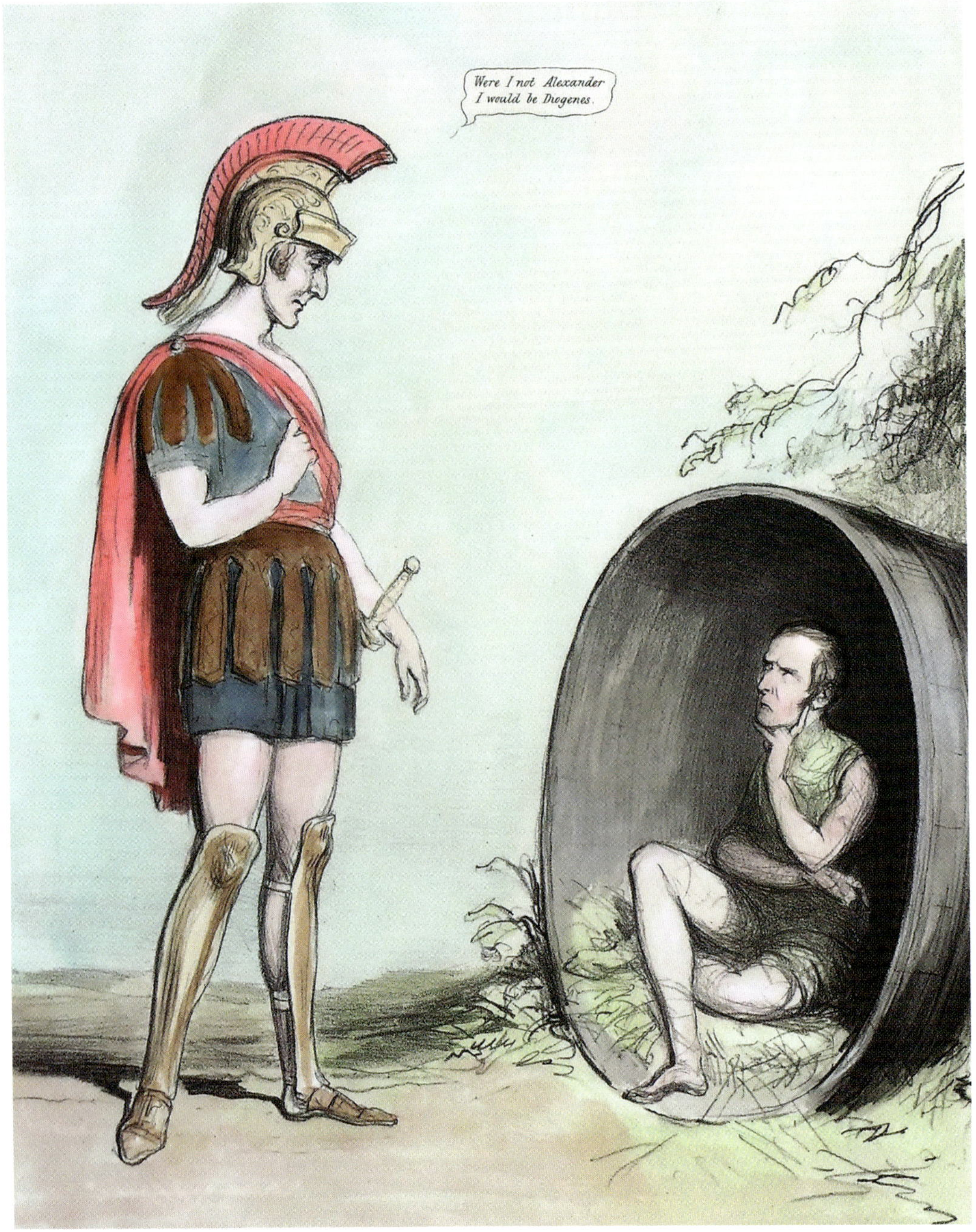

[112] ***No. 803, 'Alexander and Diogenes' (published 14 May 1844)*** A man in the character of Alexander (Sir Robert Peel), standing at left, looking with admiration at a man in the character of Diogenes (Mr Roebuck, M.P. for Bath), seated in a tub at the right. In April 1844 Roebuck, after having previously criticised the Home Secretary Sir James Graham, defended him against various charges. For his pains, Roebuck was denounced by George Smythe as the 'Diogenes of Bath' whose actions were always contradictory. The classical reference is to the purportedly brief meeting between Alexander the Great and Diogenes in which the former told the latter, 'if I were not Alexander, I should wish to be Diogenes', to which Diogenes replied 'if I were not Diogenes, I should also wish to be Diogenes'.

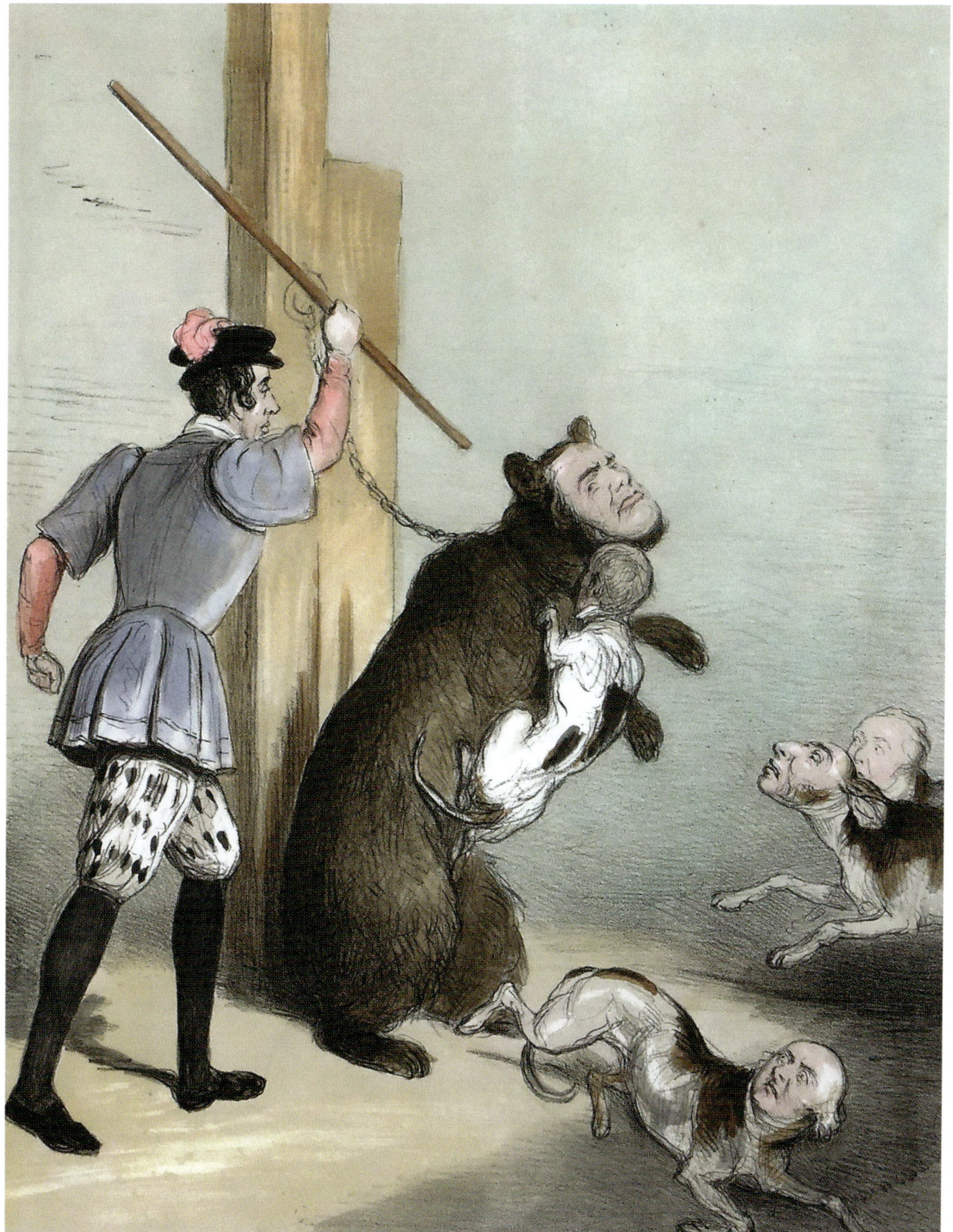

[113] ***No. 806, 'Bear Baiting, Or Old English Pastimes Revived. Dedicated to Young England'*** A bear with a man's face (William Busfeild Ferrand), at centre, chained to a pole, attacked from the left by a man with a stick (Benjamin Disraeli), and by dogs with men's heads, one jumping at his throat (John Arthur Roebuck), two running towards him and one running away in foreground towards the right (James Weir Hogg, Sir James Graham, Sir Robert Peel). Sir James Graham's factory legislation was opposed with spirit by William Busfeild Ferrand, the M.P. for Knaresborough. At a meeting in Leeds, Ferrand accused the Home Secretary of having used his power to induce an assistant Poor Law Commissioner (Charles Mott, d.1851) to make a false report for the purpose of crushing him. Roebuck brought this charge to the notice of the House of Commons and called upon Ferrand to state distinctly to what minister and what member he referred. This led to a series of violent recriminations in the House of Commons which brought in members of the 'Young England' group of M.Ps, notably Disraeli and George Smythe. The Young Englanders supported the revival of old English pastimes as a means of alleviating the miserable condition of the industrial poor. One such ancient pastime, bear-baiting, is invoked by 'H.B.' to show Ferrand as the bear goaded on by his detractors.

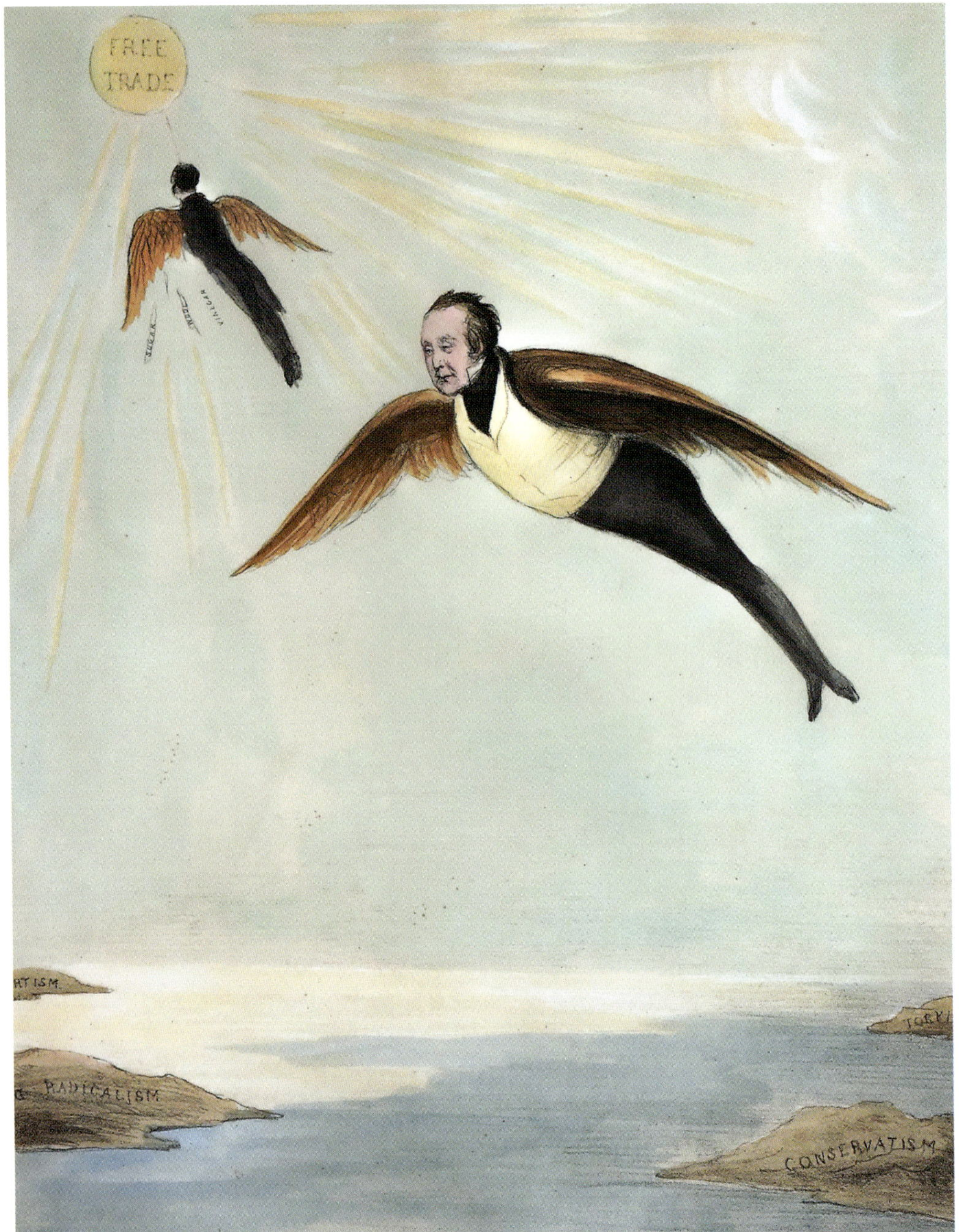

[114] ***No. 809, 'The Flight of Daedalus and Icarus! Illustrated under a new aspect' (published 1 July 1844)*** Two men with wings, one in the character of Icarus, at left (William Ewart Gladstone), the other in the character of Daedalus, at centre (Sir Robert Peel), flying over the sea above islands lettered with 'Chartism', 'Whig Radicalism', 'Toryism' and 'Conservatism', towards the sun, lettered with 'Free Trade'; Icarus getting too close to the sun, losing feathers lettered with 'Sugar', 'Wool' and 'Vinegar' from his wings. A satire on the position of Gladstone as Vice-President of the Board of Trade. Having originally been disheartened by his appointment to the office ('I have been sent to govern packages' he confided), Gladstone became an enthusiast for the new doctrines of 'Free Trade' which hallmarked the government's economic and fiscal policy. In 1842, Gladstone had rashly offered his resignation when the Corn Law measure did no go as far as he would have wished. 'H.B.'s satire calls to mind the mythological story of Daedalus and his son Icarus who, flying too close to the sun with wings held together with wax, the wax melted, the wings gave way and he fell into the sea and drowned.

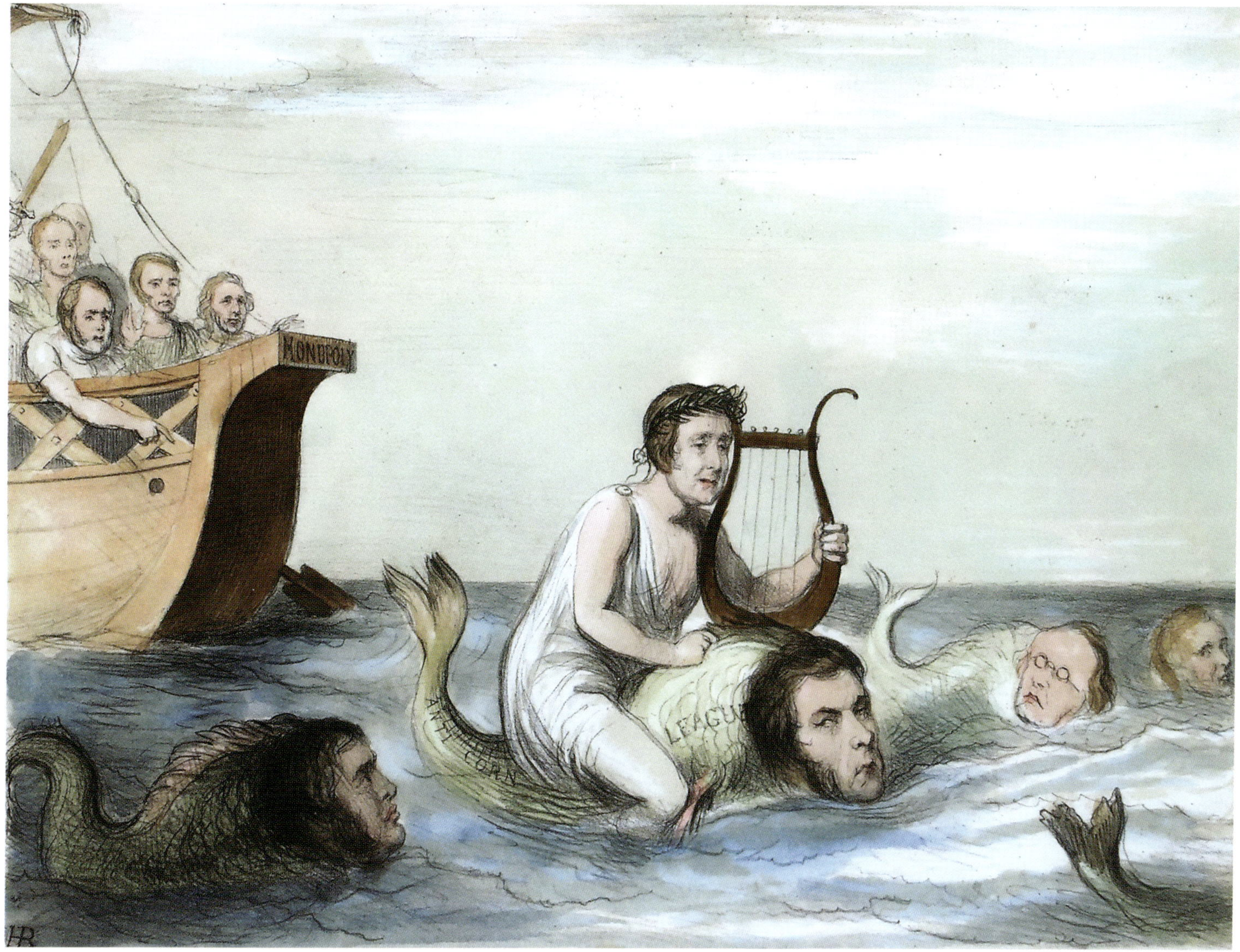

[115] ***No. 811, 'Arion Saved by the Dolphins' (published 1 July 1844)*** A man in the character of Arion (John Bright), playing the lyre, seated on a dolphin with a man's head, at the centre, lettered with 'Anti Corn League' (Richard Cobden), surrounded by other large fish with men's heads (among them Sir Robert Peel, James Weir Hogg), watched by a group of men from a ship at the left, lettered with 'Monopoly' (among them Lords John Russell, Palmerston and Howick). The sketch recalls the mythical story of Arion, who was hunted by pirates and given the choice of suicide (with a proper burial on land) or being thrown into the sea. Arion pleaded to sing one last song, after which he threw himself into the sea, but his song attracted the dolphins, one of whom saved his life by transporting him to Poseidon. Bright and Cobden, the leaders of the Anti-Corn Law League are here satirized as Arion and the Dolphin, menaced by the pirates of 'Monopoly' and the ambivalent other large fish (Peel and Hogg, the M.P. for Beverley) who were prepared to leave Bright to the mercies of his opponents in the House of Commons.

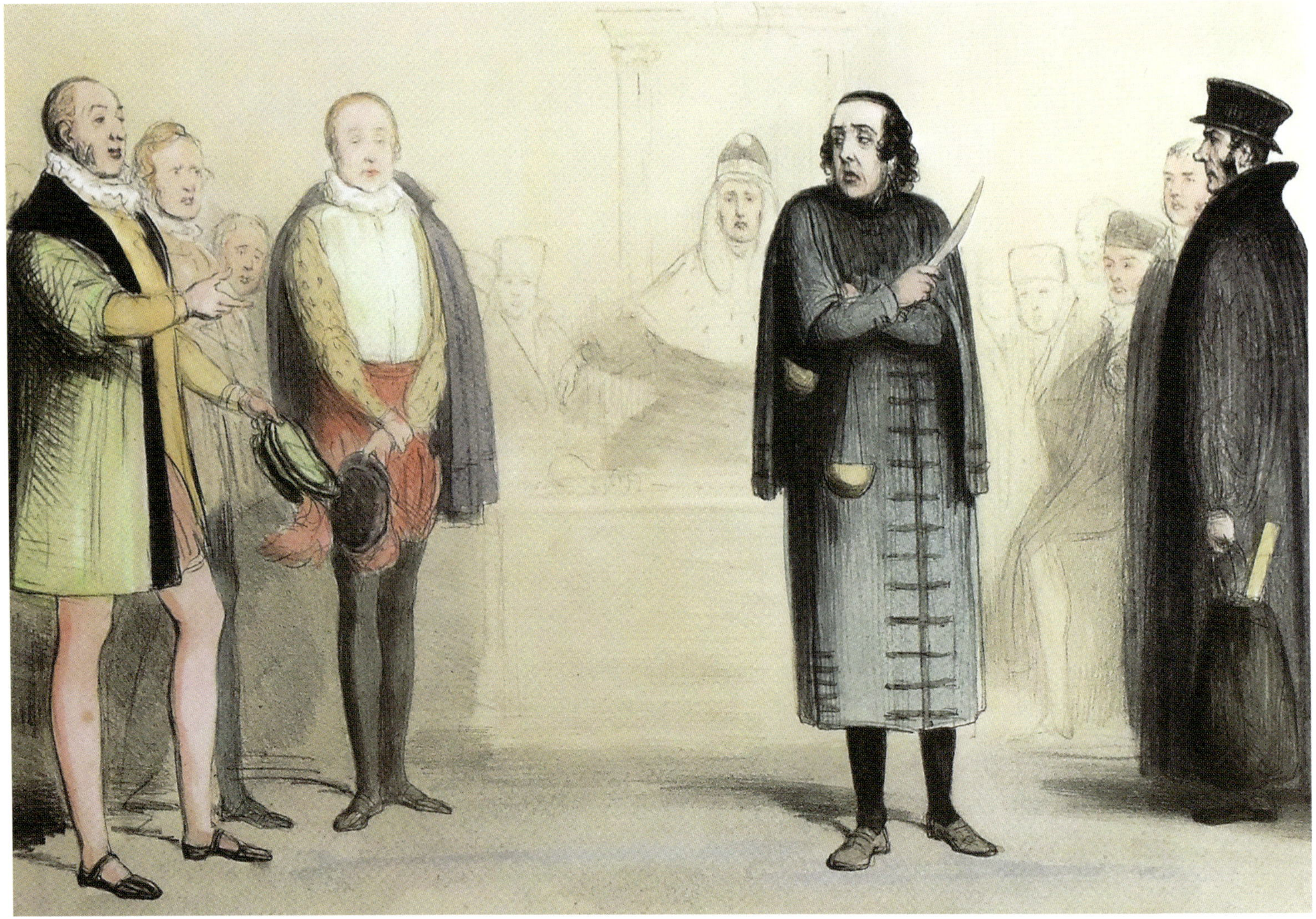

[116] ***No. 812, 'A Scene from Shakespeare' (published 8 August 1844)*** Below the title: 'Duke – Shylock, the world thinks and I think so too / That thou but lead'st this fashion of thy malice / To the last hour of act; and then tis thought / Thoult shew thy mercy & remorse, more strange / Than is thy strange apparent cruelty. Shylock – So can I give no reason nor I will not / More than a lodged hate & a certain loathing I bear Antonio, that I follow thus / A losing suit against him'. A scene from Shakespeare's 'The Merchant of Venice' (c.1596–1598) (Act IV, Scene I, lines 16–21, 59–62); at the left, a man in the character of the Duke of Venice (Sir James Graham), addressing a man in the character of Shylock, standing at the centre, holding a dagger (Benjamin Disraeli), watched by a group of men (second from left Lord Stanley, next to him Sir Robert Peel, in the background wearing a wig Charles Shaw-Lefevre, at the right Richard Cobden). A satire on the emergence of Disraeli as a Conservative critic of the front-bench, notably through attacks on Peel and Sir James Graham (the Home Secretary). Using the character of Shylock was a common means of satirising Disraeli, who had memorably denounced the Whigs, during the 1830s, as a 'Venetian Oligarchy'.

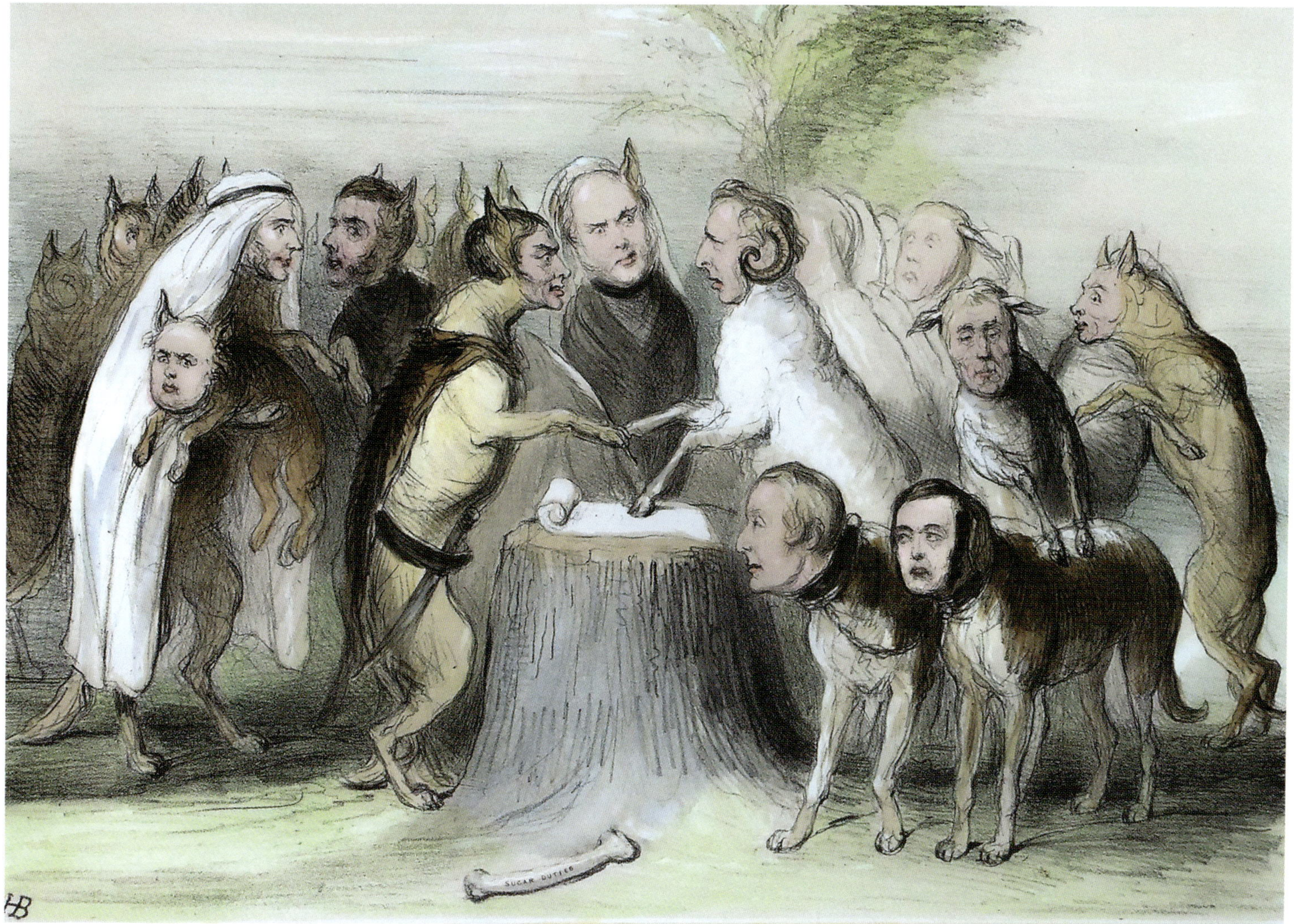

[117] ***No. 813, 'The Treaty between the Sheep and the Wolves. After 'Les Loups et les Brebis' of Granville' (published 8 August 1844)*** J J Grandville was the pseudonym of Jean Gérard Grandville a French caricaturist. A scene with animals with men's heads; the wolves, standing at the left (from left, Henry Labouchere, holding Richard Lalor Shiel as a cub, Thomas Slingsby Duncombe, Lord John Russell, Lord Palmerston) making a pact with the sheep, standing at the right (Lord Sandon, Sir Howard Douglas), their leaders signing a treaty on a tree stump at the centre, against the dogs, standing in foreground at the right (Sir Robert Peel, William Ewart Gladstone); a bone, lettered with 'Sugar Duties', is lying on the ground at the centre in foreground. The notion of an alliance of convenience between traditional enemies is here used to represent the divisions created by the government's proposed modification to the Sugar Duties in 1844. The government planned to reduce the tariff on foreign sugar grown by free labour from 63s per hundredweight to 34s plus 5 per cent, while leaving the duty on colonial sugar unchanged at 25s 3d. An amendment proposing that the tariff differential between colonial and foreign sugar should be widened by reducing the duty on colonial sugar to 20s attracted the support of many Whig and Radical M.P.s as well as 62 Conservative M.P.s and the government lost the vote by 20. Peel denounced the amendment and used the threat of resignation to get his way and rescind the vote.

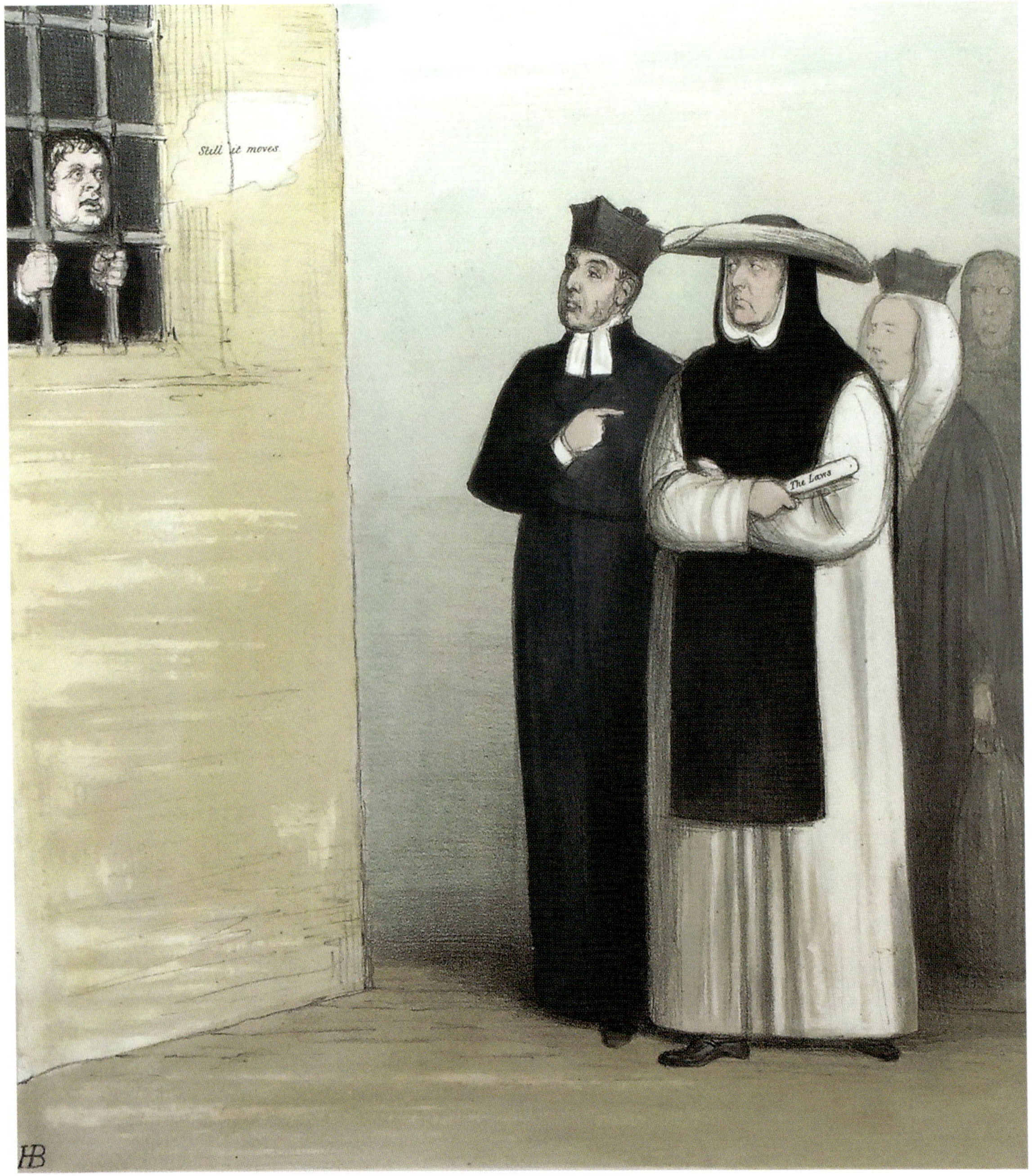

[118] ***No. 816, 'An Irish version of Galileo and the Inquisition' (published 8 Aug. 1844)*** Below the title: 'e pur si muove' ['and yet it moves']. A man in the character of Galileo, in prison (Daniel O'Connell), holding onto the bars of the window, at the left, addressing a group of men representing the Inquisition, standing in front of the building at right (Sir James Graham, Sir Robert Peel, Thomas Berry Cusack Smith, Lord Brougham). Galileo was brought to the attention of the Inquisition in 1611 for his Copernican views which placed the sun (rather than the earth) at the centre of the universe. The analogy here is with O'Connell's trial before the House of Lords which commenced on 13 January 1844. O'Connell and his co-defendants were found guilty of conspiring to intimidate the Queen's subjects and to overawe both Houses of Parliament, sentenced to a fine and twelve months' imprisonment. An appeal was mounted, on the basis of irregularities in the trial, and on 4 Sept. 1844, the Law Lords voted 3–2 to reverse the judgement. Thomas Cusack Smith was the Attorney General.

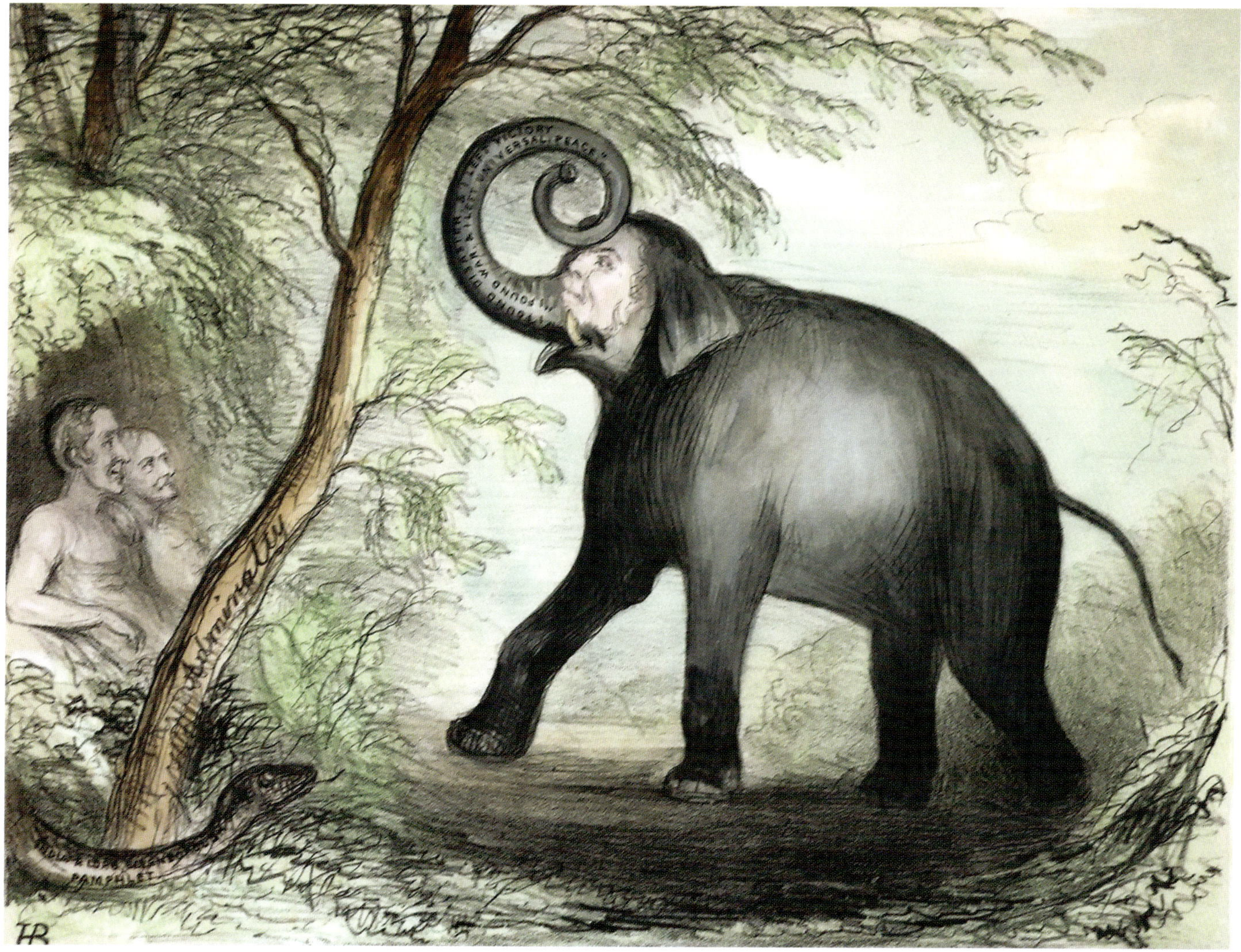

[119] ***No. 824, 'A wild elephant <u>trumpeting</u>, or A Scene from <u>Paradise Lost</u>!' (published 28 Dec. 1844)*** Below the title: 'The unwieldy elephant / To make them mirth, used all his might, and wreathed / His lithe proboscis' (Book IV) (1667–1674). In woodland, an elephant with a man's face (Lord Ellenborough), standing at centre, his trunk lettered with '"I found disaster, & I left victory" and "I found war & I left universal peace"', turning towards two men seated at the left (at the far left Sir Robert Peel) under a tree lettered with 'Admiralty'; on the ground in bottom left corner, a snake lettered with 'India & Lord Ellenborough Pamphlet,' watching the elephant. A Whig pamphlet attacking Ellenborough's Indian administration, for which he had been recalled by the Directors of the East India Company in 1844, was published in 1845 under the title 'India & Lord Ellenborough'. According to a report in *The Spectator* (30 Nov. 1844 p.8), Ellenborough had responded to an address congratulating him on his successes in India as follows: 'Undoubtedly, great changes took place in our position in India while I administered the government. I found disaster, and I left victory. I found war, and I left universal peace; from which has already resulted a great extension of our commerce with the East, necessarily bringing with it some improvement in the general condition of the people. But not to me be ascribed the merit of these happy events'. Ellenborough subsequently re-entered Peel's government as First Lord of the Admiralty.

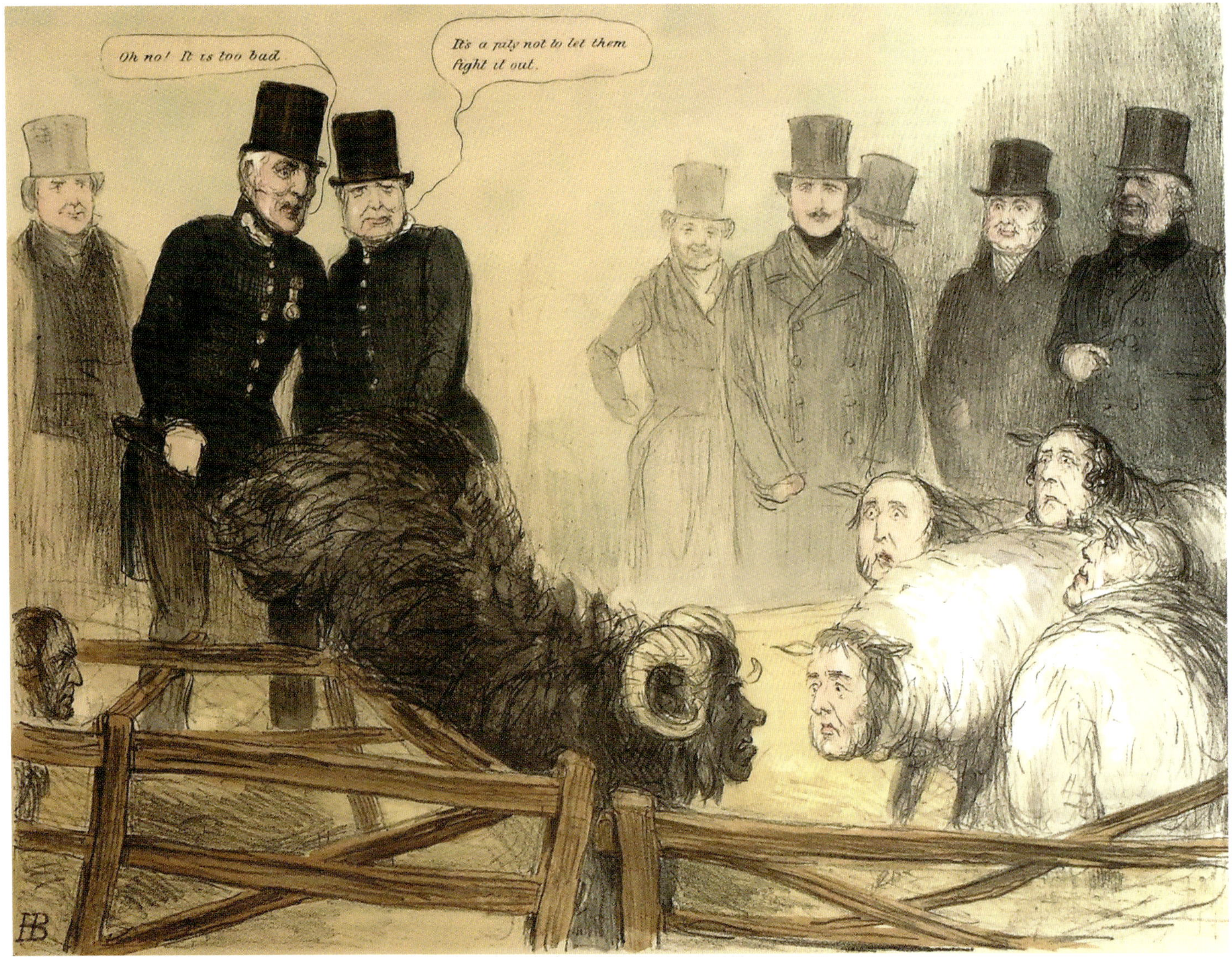

[120] ***No. 825, 'Christmas Show' (published 28 Dec. 1844).*** Below the title: 'A paragraph has been going the round of the papers about a curious conflict at the late show, between a Black Porker, and Prince Albert's pigs, in the adjoining pen, to quell which required the united efforts of several of the Police. It is presumed that there must be some mistake in the story, and that it relates to a furious attack made some time ago by a BLACK SHEEP upon some of the QUEEN'S LAMBS'. Scene involving sheep with men's heads; two policemen (the Duke of Wellington and Lord Lyndhurst) holding the back-legs of a black ram at the centre (Lord Brougham), watched in the pen by a black sheep or dog at the left, a group of white sheep at the right (Lords Melbourne, Campbell, Normanby, Duncannon), and a group of men, standing in the background (from left, Sir Robert Peel, an unidentified man, Prince Albert, Lord Spencer and the Duke of Cambridge). The sketch references the continuing disputes between Brougham and his former Whig colleagues.

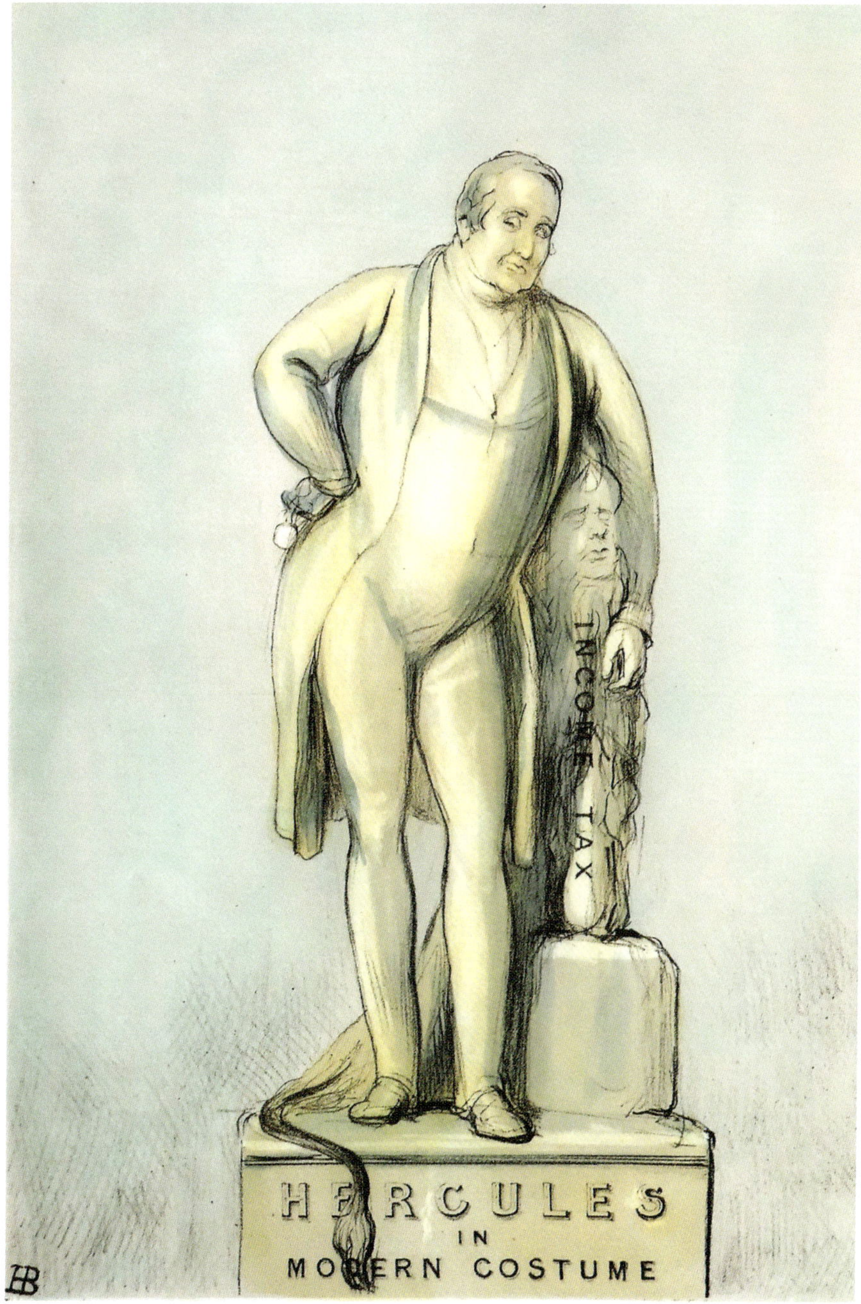

[121] ***No. 827, Hercules in Modern Costume' (published 5 Mar. 1845)*** Sculpture of a man in the character of Hercules (Sir Robert Peel), on a plinth, resting on his club lettered with 'Income Tax', covered with a lion's skin with outlines of a man's face (Daniel O'Connell). Hercules, the son of Zeus, was renowned for wearing a lion-skin costume and wielding a club.

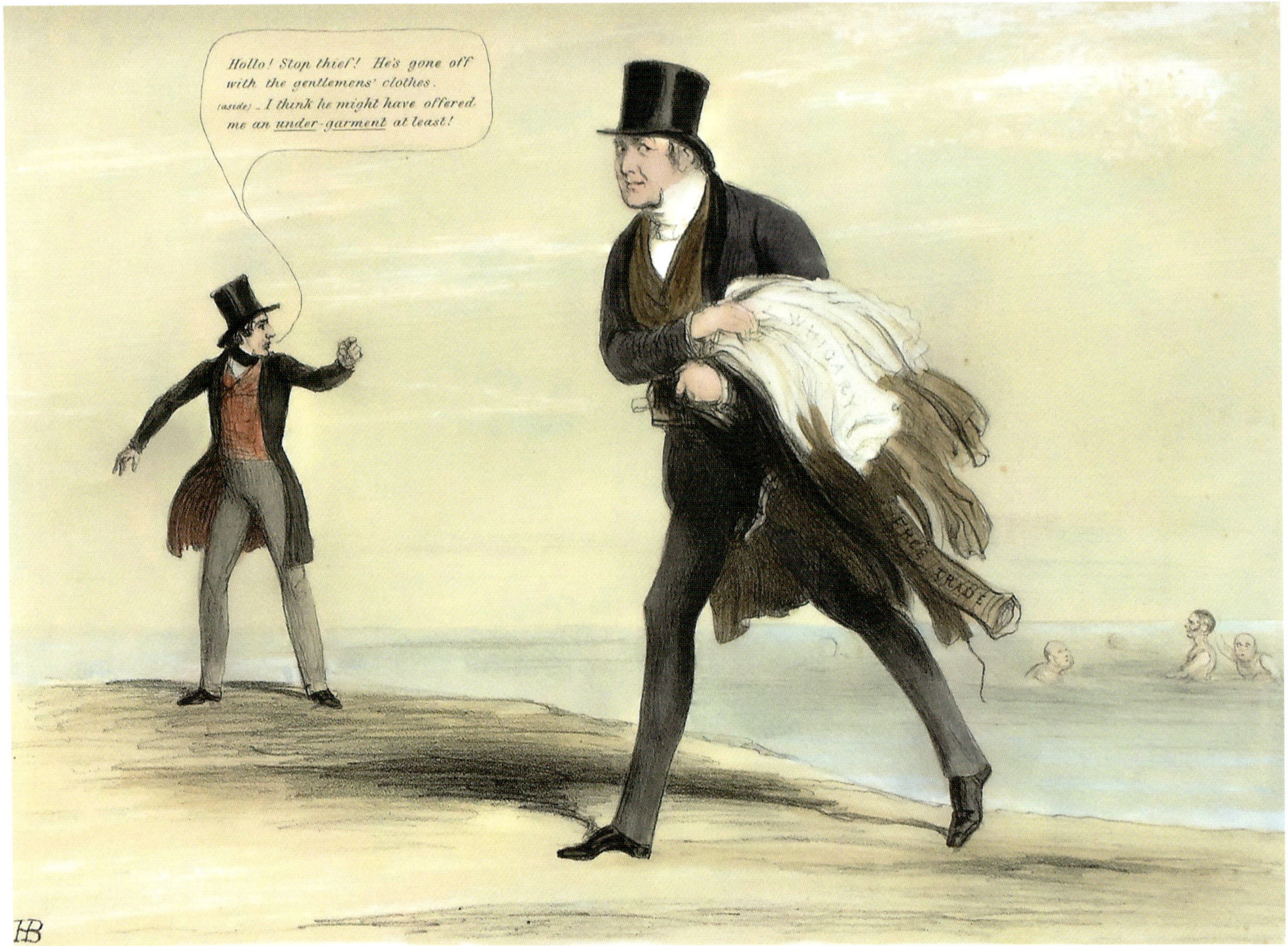

[122] ***No. 829, 'A Genteel version of the vulgar saying "Set a Thief to Catch a Thief" (published 24 Mar. 1845)*** Two men on the seashore, the one standing in background at the left (Benjamin Disraeli) shouting to a group of men swimming in the sea at the right (among them Lords Palmerston and John Russell) to help stop a thief (Sir Robert Peel), walking towards left at the centre foreground, carrying clothes lettered with 'Whigary' and 'Free trade'. A satire on Peel's perceived burglary of Whig policies and conversion to Free Trade; Disraeli famously castigated Peel as the 'burglar of others' intellect' who 'traded on the ideas and intelligence of others' but the allusion here is to his recent observation that 'the Right Honorable gentleman caught the Whigs bathing and walked away with their clothes'. The implication of 'H.B.'s satire is that Disraeli is himself a 'thief' who has helped the opposition by unmasking Peel.

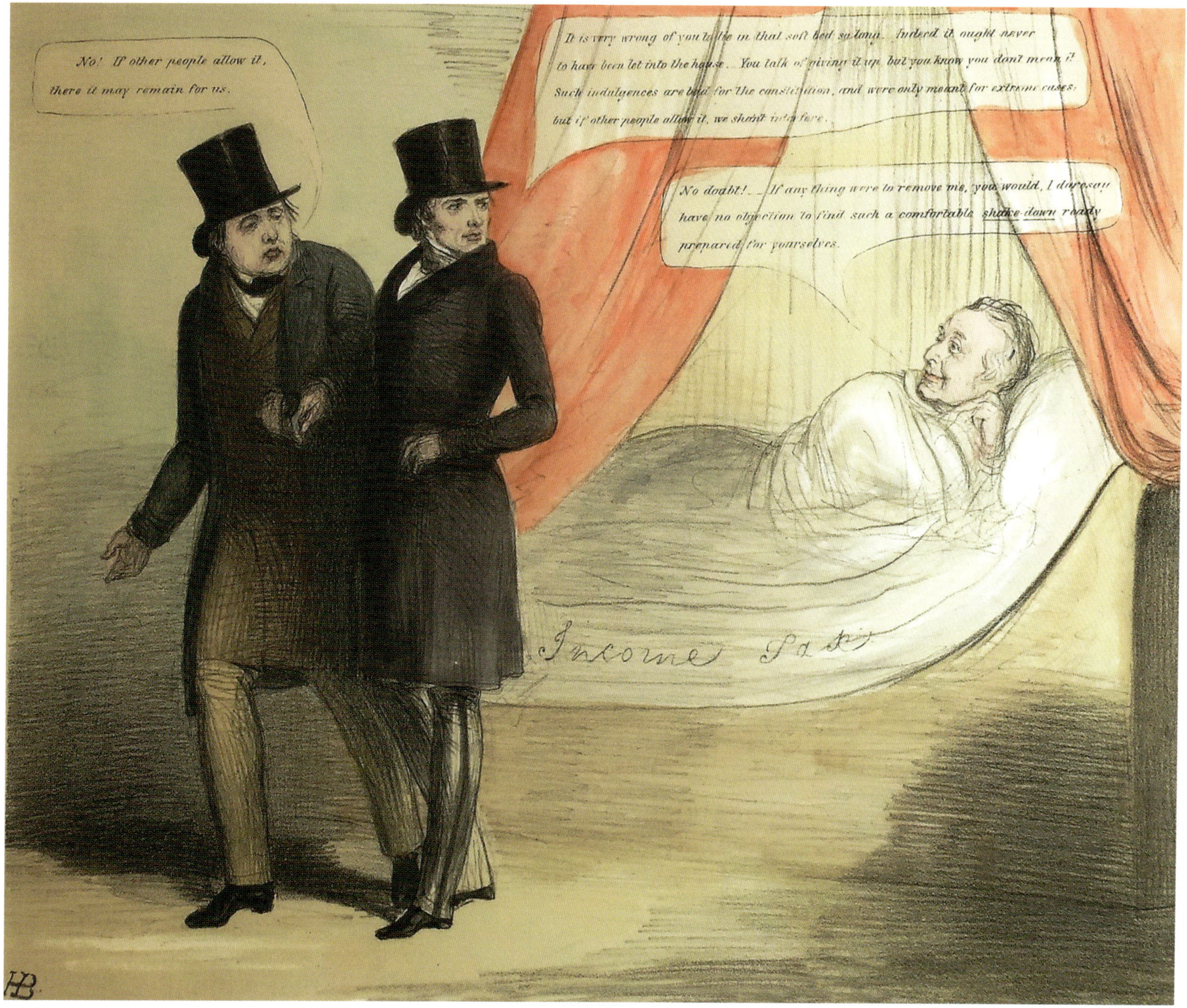

[123] ***No. 830, 'Small Insinuations' (published 5 Apr. 1845)*** A man lying at the right on a bed lettered with 'Income Tax', engaged in conversation with two men, walking away towards left (Francis Thornhill Baring and Lord John Russell). A satirical representation of the extension of the Income Tax beyond its original 'temporary' three-year period. Baring was one of the family of bankers whose financial house was a mainstay of English financial policy in the nineteenth century.

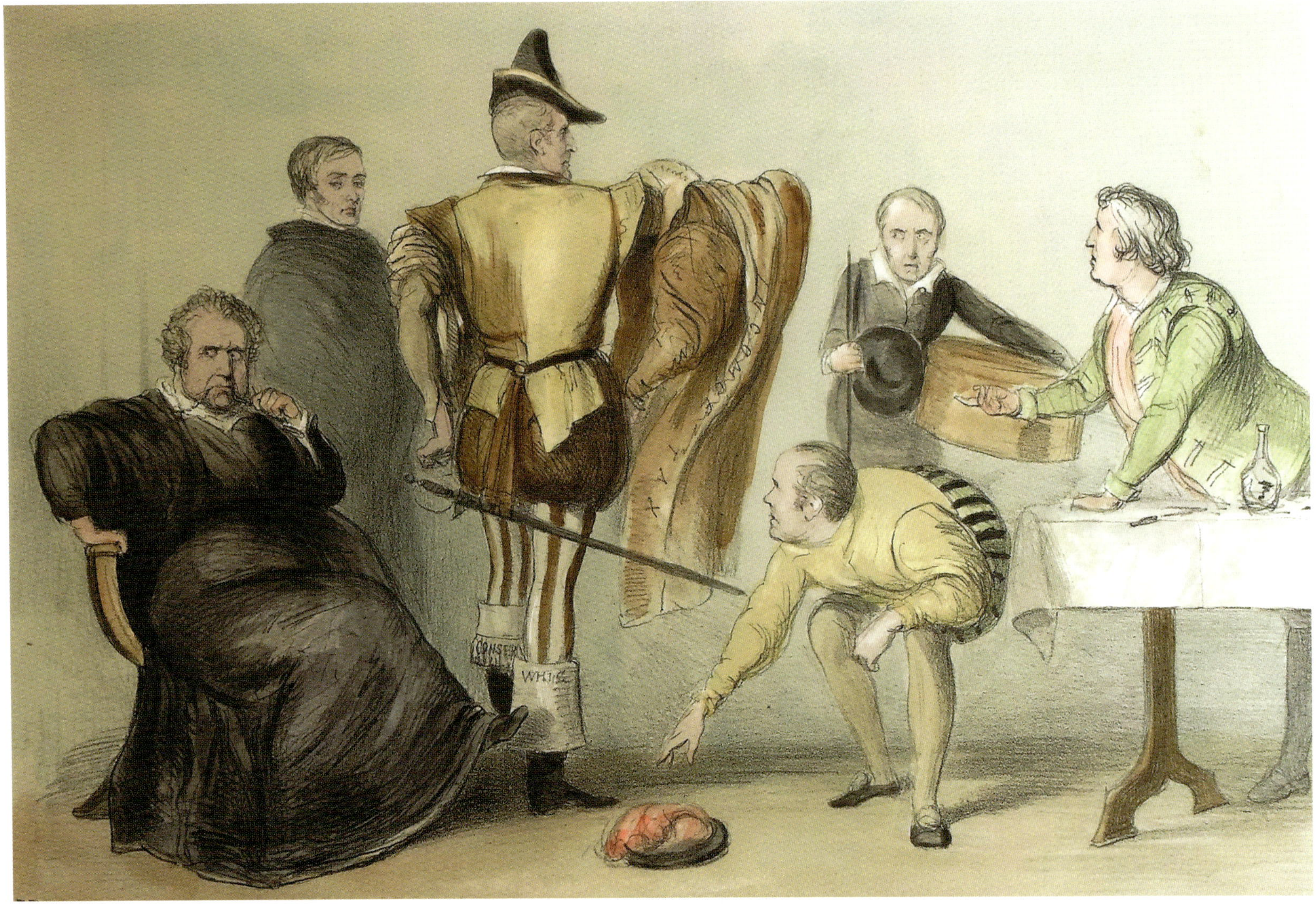

[124] ***No. 833, 'Catherine and Petruchio – Designed by Mr D'I------, And retouched by Lord J R----ll (after Mr Leslie's admired picture)' (published 15 Apr. 1845)*** A parody of Charles Robert Leslie's painting (1832), based on Act IV, Scene 1 of Shakespeare's 'The Taming of the Shrew' (c.1590–1592). The story of Catherine and Petruchio is here translated to the relationship between Peel and Joseph Hume (the inveterate opponent of government financial waste). A man in the character of Petruchio (Sir Robert Peel), standing at the centre left, his boots lettered with 'Conserv' and 'Whig', rejecting the cap and gown, lettered with 'Income Tax', brought by the Haberdashers, at the right (Mr Borthwick, John Arthur Roebuck, Thomas Wakley) for a man dressed as a woman, in the character of Catherine (Joseph Hume), seated in an armchair at the left; standing behind her, a man in the character of Hortensio (Lord John Russell) looks on with interest. Peel, like Petruchio, is attempting to teach Hume submission to his measures in the manner laid down by Shakespeare in the scene: 'This is a way to kill a wife with kindness / And thus I'll curb her mad and headstrong humour / He that knows better how to tame a shrew / Now let him speak: 'tis charity to show'.

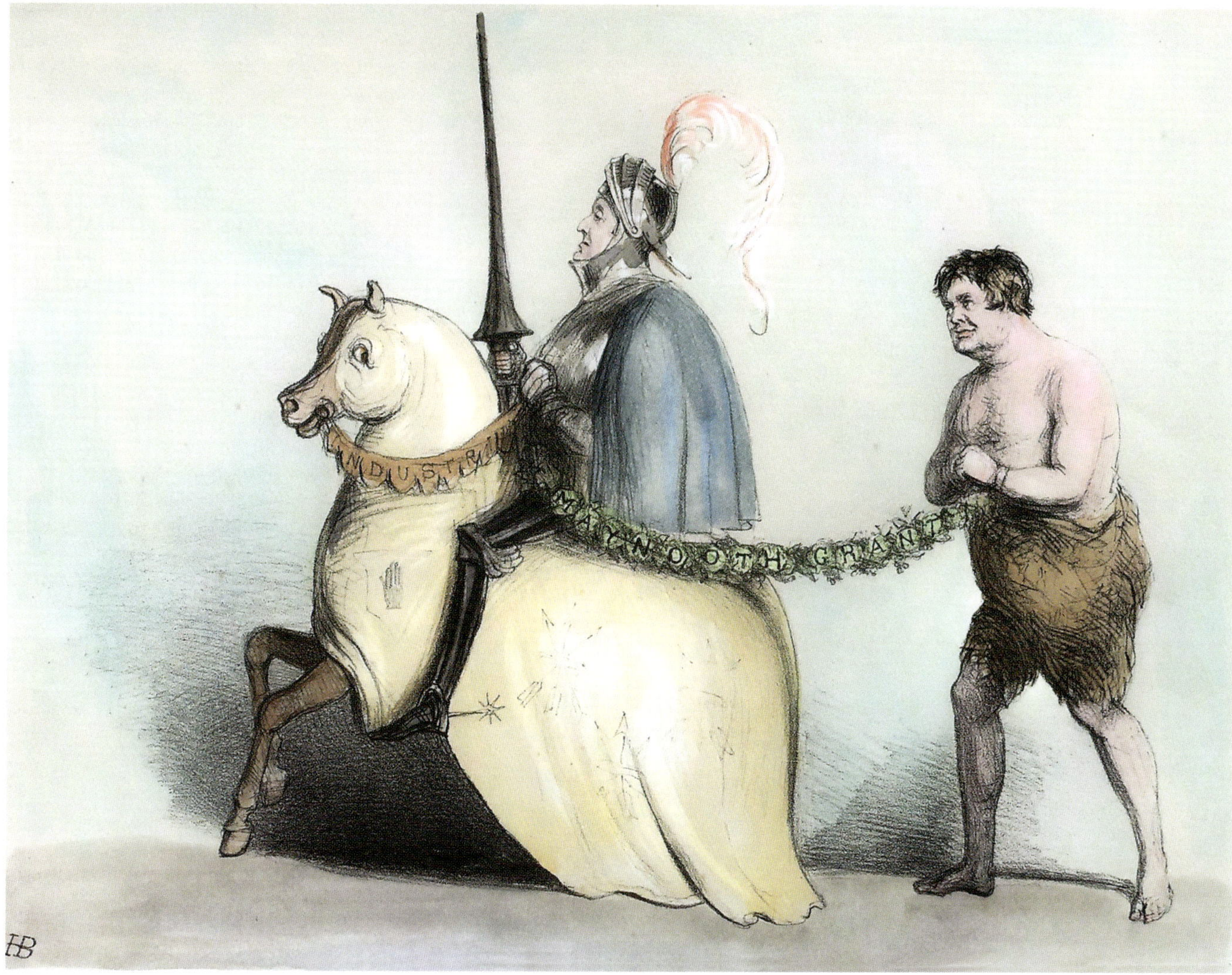

[125] ***No. 834, 'Valentine and Orson' (published 15 Apr. 1845)*** Parody of the medieval romance in which twin brothers are abandoned as infants in the wood and brought up in contrasting circumstances – Valentine as a knight at court, Orson as a wild man of the woods who is eventually tamed by Valentine. Here the parody is used to illustrate the change in Peel's policy towards Ireland, with more conciliatory measures designed to undermine O'Connell's support amongst the Catholic priesthood and laity. A man in the character of Valentine (Sir Robert Peel), on horseback at centre, the bridle lettered with 'Industri', leading a half-naked man, in the character of Orson (Daniel O'Connell), in a posy chain, lettered with 'Maynooth Grant'. The 1845 parliamentary session was dominated by Peel's proposal to triple the annual government grant (initiated in 1795) to the Catholic training seminary at Maynooth in Ireland, from £8,000 (the level set in 1809) to to £26,000, making it part of the Consolidated Fund (and therefore no longer subject to an annual vote) and providing a grant for building repairs of £30,000. The intention was to improve the conditions of Catholic priests in Ireland, from whom the Repeal movement gained so much support. The measure split Peel's Conservative followers in the House of Commons, with 159–147 voting for the second reading and 149–148 voting against the final Bill. The measure only passed with the support of the opposition.

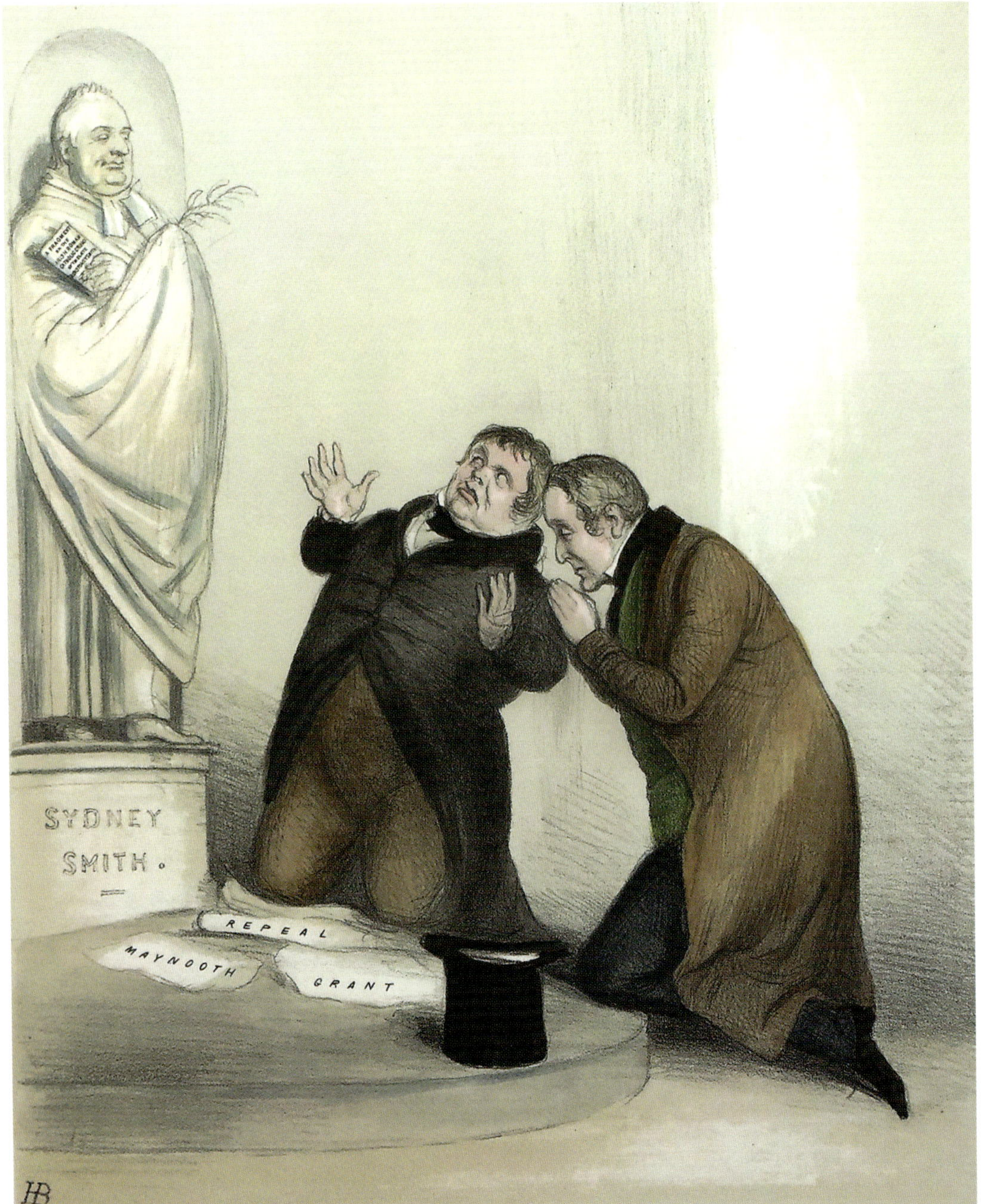

[126] ***No. 835, 'Two Penitents Kneeling at the Same Shrine' (published 23 Apr. 1845)*** Two men, one at the centre (Daniel O'Connell), the other at the right, kneeling on a step, with papers in front of them lettered with 'Repeal', 'Maynooth' and 'Grant', before a statue of a priest at the left, lettered with 'Sydney Smith' on the plinth (Reverend Sydney Smith), holding a book lettered with 'A fragment of the Irish [...]' in his left hand. *The Spectator* of 5 Apr. 1845 p.15 explains the context for this illustration: 'In addition to all that is passing on the question of religious temporalities, the present week has been enriched by a "Fragment on the Irish Roman Catholic Church", from the dying hand of Sydney Smith; which his executors have properly given to the world. From a prefixed list of "private memoranda of subjects intended to have been introduced in the pamphlet," we catch a glimpse of the manner in which the author prepared his matter, and the fullness with which he would have treated his subject had life been spared to him: one significant jotting of "a head," as yet untouched— "England should cast off its connexion with the Irish Church" — shows the length to which he himself was prepared to go'. The newspaper concluded by observing that 'while all around were changing, he and the Duke of Newcastle, political antipodes, alone stood on their old spot'. Smith, a noted churchman, wit and pamphleteer, who died in February 1845 at the age of 74, had vigorously supported Catholic Emancipation.

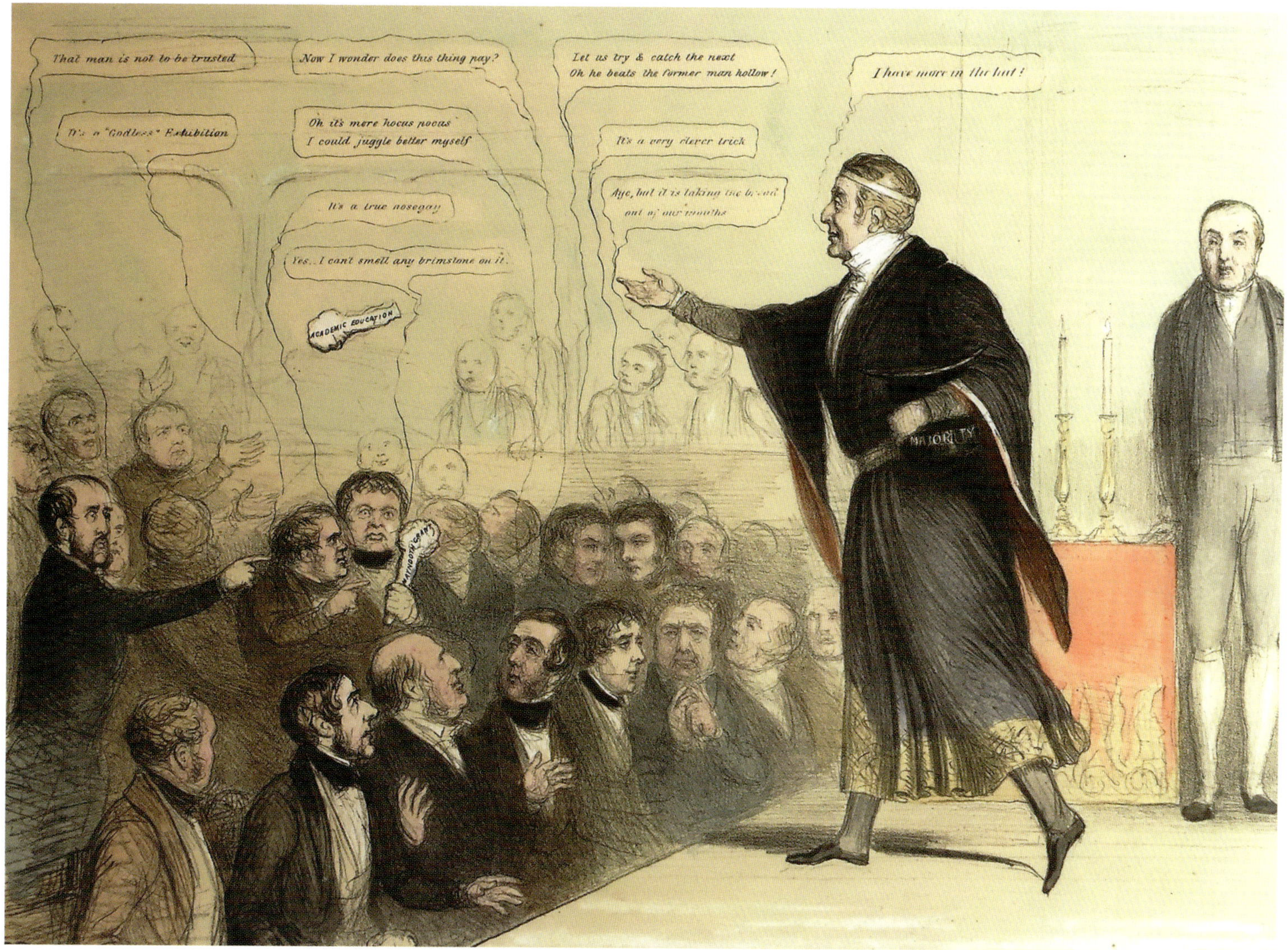

[127] ***No. 837, 'Soirées Mysterieuses – Wonderful performance at St Stephen's Theatre' (published 12 June 1845)*** A man acting as a conjuror (Sir Robert Peel), standing on a stage at the right, producing two bouquets, lettered with 'Academic Education' and 'Maynooth Grant', from his hat, throwing them to the audience, to their surprise, admiration, and distrust (among them, from left to right, Thomas Wyse, Joseph Hume, Colonel Sibthorp, Richard Lalor Shiel, Daniel O'Connell, Lords John Russell, Palmerston and Ashley, Sir Robert Inglis, Thomas Slingsby Duncombe and Benjamin Disraeli); a man standing on the stage at the far right (Sir James Graham) is looking on. In addition to the controversy concerning the Maynooth Grant, Peel's government was embroiled in the battle to pass a Provincial Academic Colleges act for Ireland, creating the three Queen's Colleges (to be enshrined within one institution, on the model of the University of London). The institution was to be secular, with no religious tests for students or members of the faculty. Graham introduced the measure to the Commons, which gained support from the likes of Wyse but was denounced as a 'gigantic scheme of godless education' by Colonel Sibthorp. The term 'godless colleges' gained currency as a result. The Commons met in the ancient chapel of St Stephen's, until the fire of 1834.

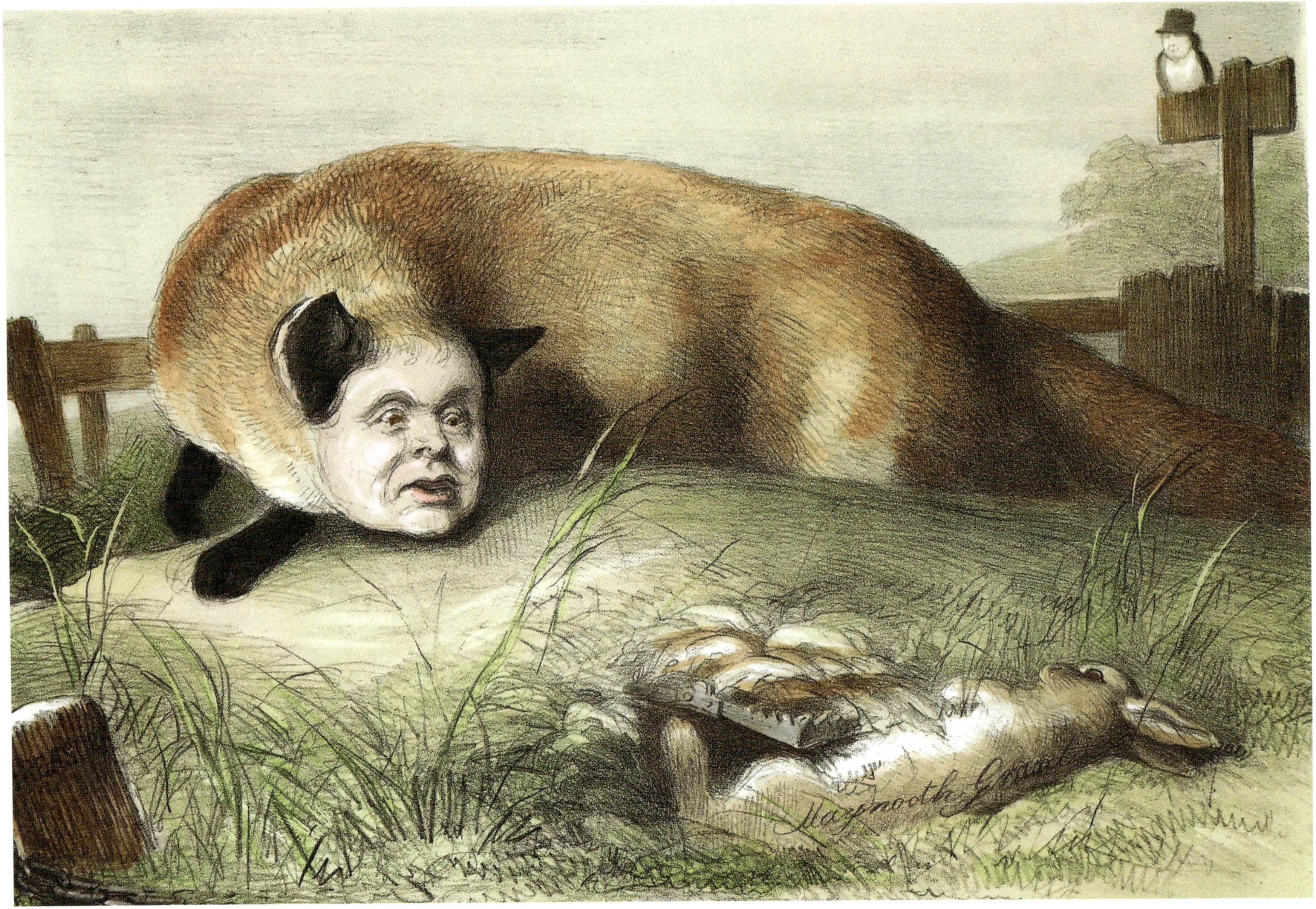

[128] ***No. 845, 'Not Caught yet – After E Landseer's admired picture' (published 22 Dec. 1845)*** A parody of Edwin Landseer's latest painting; a fox with a man's head (Daniel O'Connell) avoiding a trap, baited with a dead hare lettered with 'Maynooth Grant', chained to a stone at the left, lettered with 'Treasury'; a bird with a man's head (Sir Robert Peel), wearing a top hat, seated on a wooden pole at right, looking on. A commentary on the perception that Peel's conciliatory policies towards Ireland were motivated (in part) by a desire to trap O'Connell and nullify his influence over the Catholics.

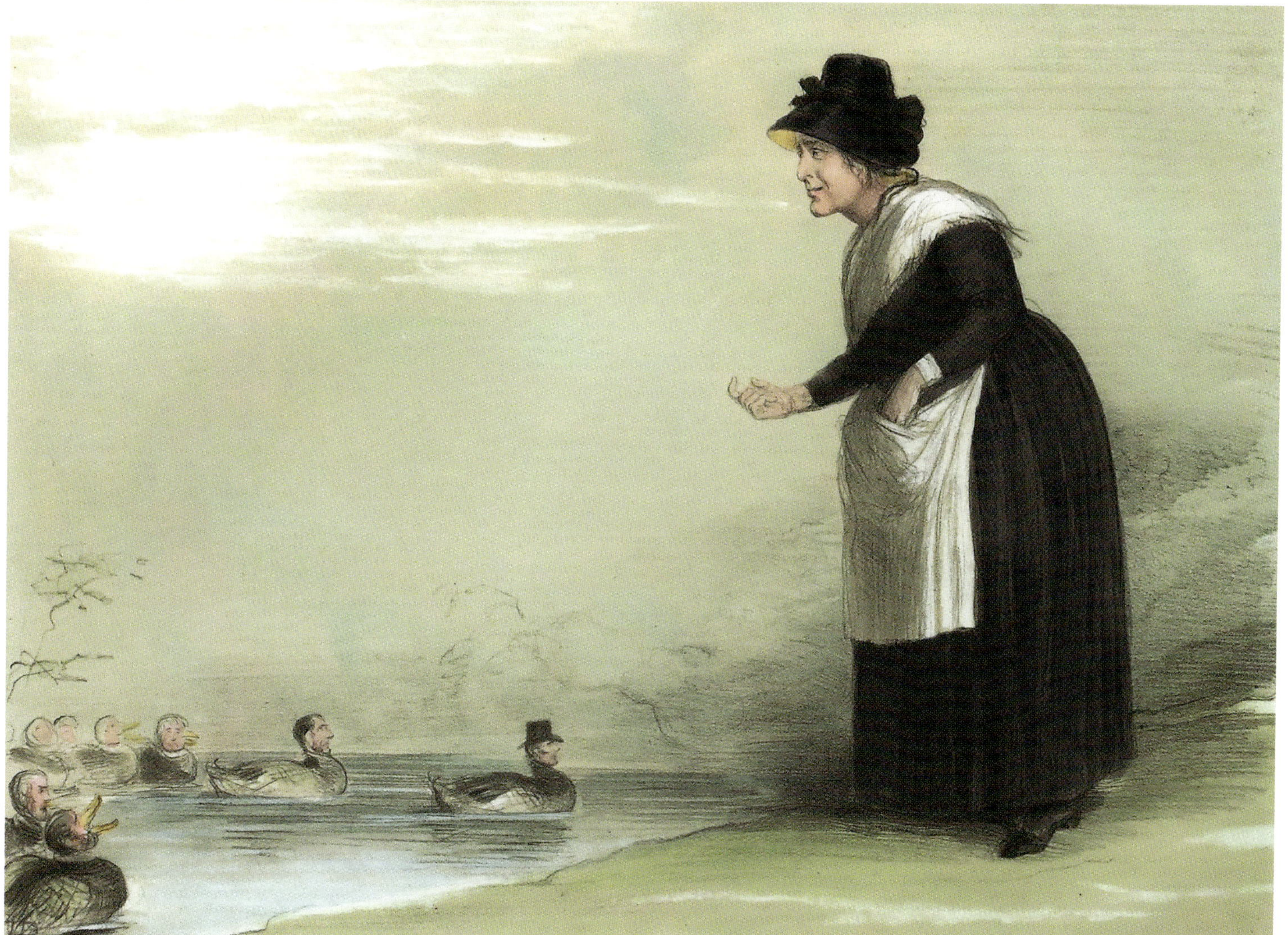

[129] ***No. 846, 'Dilly – Dilly – Come and be Killed' (published 22 Dec. 1845)*** Below the title: 'Mrs Bond she came out to the Pond in a rage / With her pockets full of onions, & her aprons full of sage / Dilly, dilly, come & be killed &c'. Inspired by the nursery rhyme 'Mrs Bond'. A man dressed as a woman (Sir Robert Peel), standing on a bank at the right, with her left hand in the pocket of her apron, calling a group of ducks with men's heads, swimming towards her from left (among them, from left to right, Duke of Richmond, Duke of Buckingham, Lord Ashley, Bickham Escott). A satire on the emerging crisis created by the potato famine in Ireland and the future of the Corn Laws. The Duke of Richmond (a former member of Stanley's 'Derby Dilly' group in the mid-1830s) had become President of the newly-founded Central Agricultural Protection Society in February 1844. This so-called 'Anti-League' (opposed to the Anti-Corn Law League) was designed to maintain support for agricultural protection; the Duke of Buckingham was its Vice-President. Lord Ashley would go on to support Peel's conversion to the Repeal of the Corn Laws, voluntarily offering himself for re-election by his constituents; Bickham Escott was the M.P. for Winchester (1841–1847).

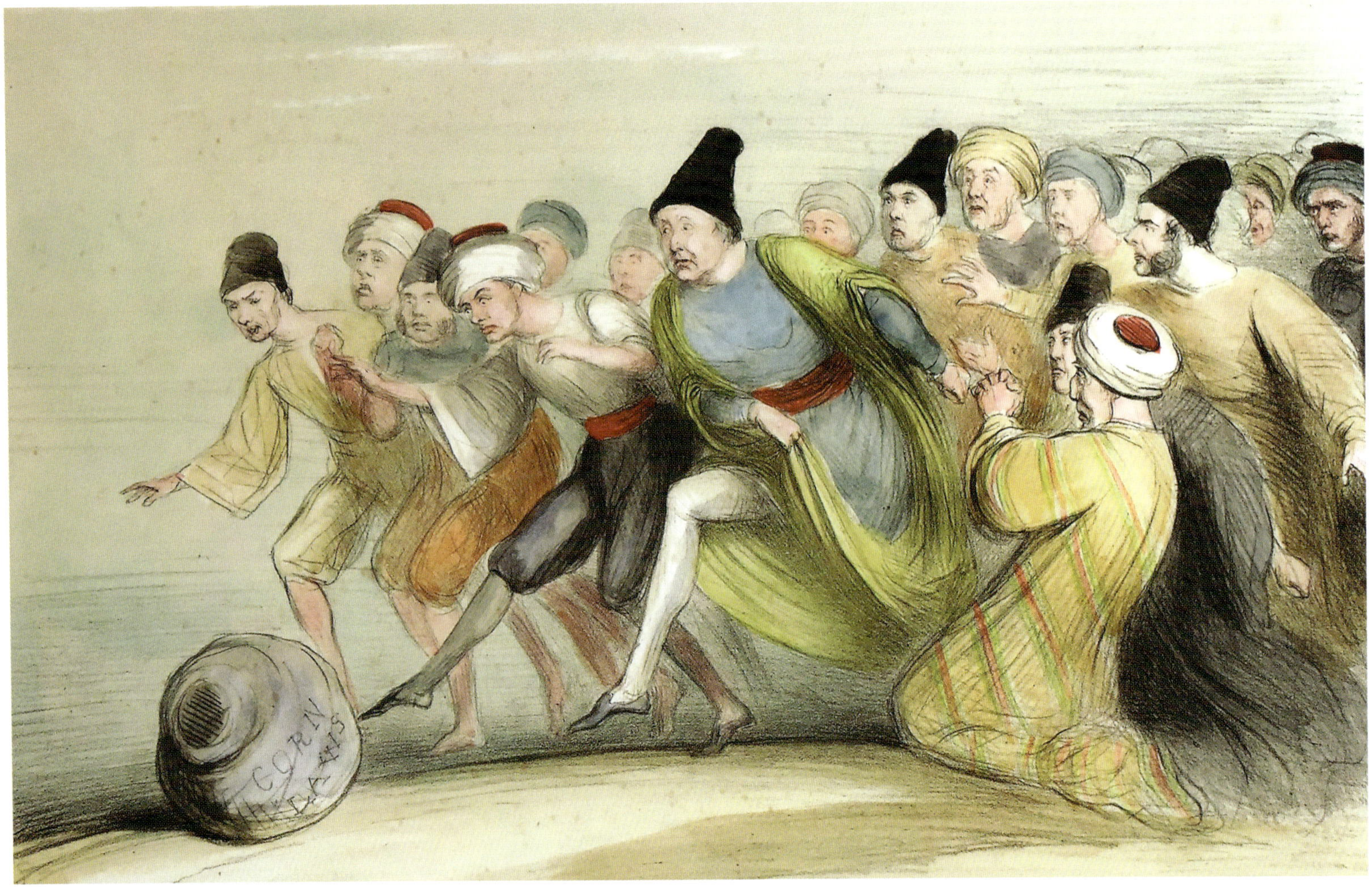

[130] ***No. 847, 'A Scene from Vathek (Realised)' (published 22 Dec. 1845)*** Below the title: 'The Caliph, more furious than the rest gave as many kicks as he could. His zeal caused him to receive many kicks intended for the ball. Mozamhabad and two or three viziers...wishing to prevent the Caliph from making a show of himself, threw themselves on their knees to stop him, but he jumped over their heads and continued on his course'. A group of men wearing oriental costumes and turbans kicking a ball lettered with 'Corn Laws', seen rolling at the left; the Caliph (fourth from the left, Sir Robert Peel) more furious than the rest, kicking hardest (others kicking, from left to right, Richard Cobden, Lord Morpeth, John Bright, Lord Aberdeen, Sir James Graham, Henry Goulburn, the Duke of Buckingham and the Duke of Richmond); a man, in the character of Mozamhabad (the Duke of Wellington) and his companion (Lord Stanley) kneeling in the foreground at the right, trying to stop the Caliph, without success. Stanley had been raised to the House of Lords in his father's lifetime in 1844, effectively acting as second-in-command to the Duke of Wellington. Both Wellington and Stanley were amongst those who doubted the wisdom of Peel's policy on the Corn Laws. Peel's inability to secure a united cabinet behind his policy was the reason why he offered his resignation to Queen Victoria in December 1845. Here, Wellington and Stanley's attempts to restrain Peel from joining those opposed to the Corn Laws is represented as a scene from William Beckford's 'History of the Caliph Vathek' (usually known simply as 'Vathek' or 'An Arabian Tale'), first published in English in 1786. The 'Scene' relates to Vathek's confrontation with the merchant Giaour, after which Giaour is transformed into a ball which Vathek compels everyone to kick.

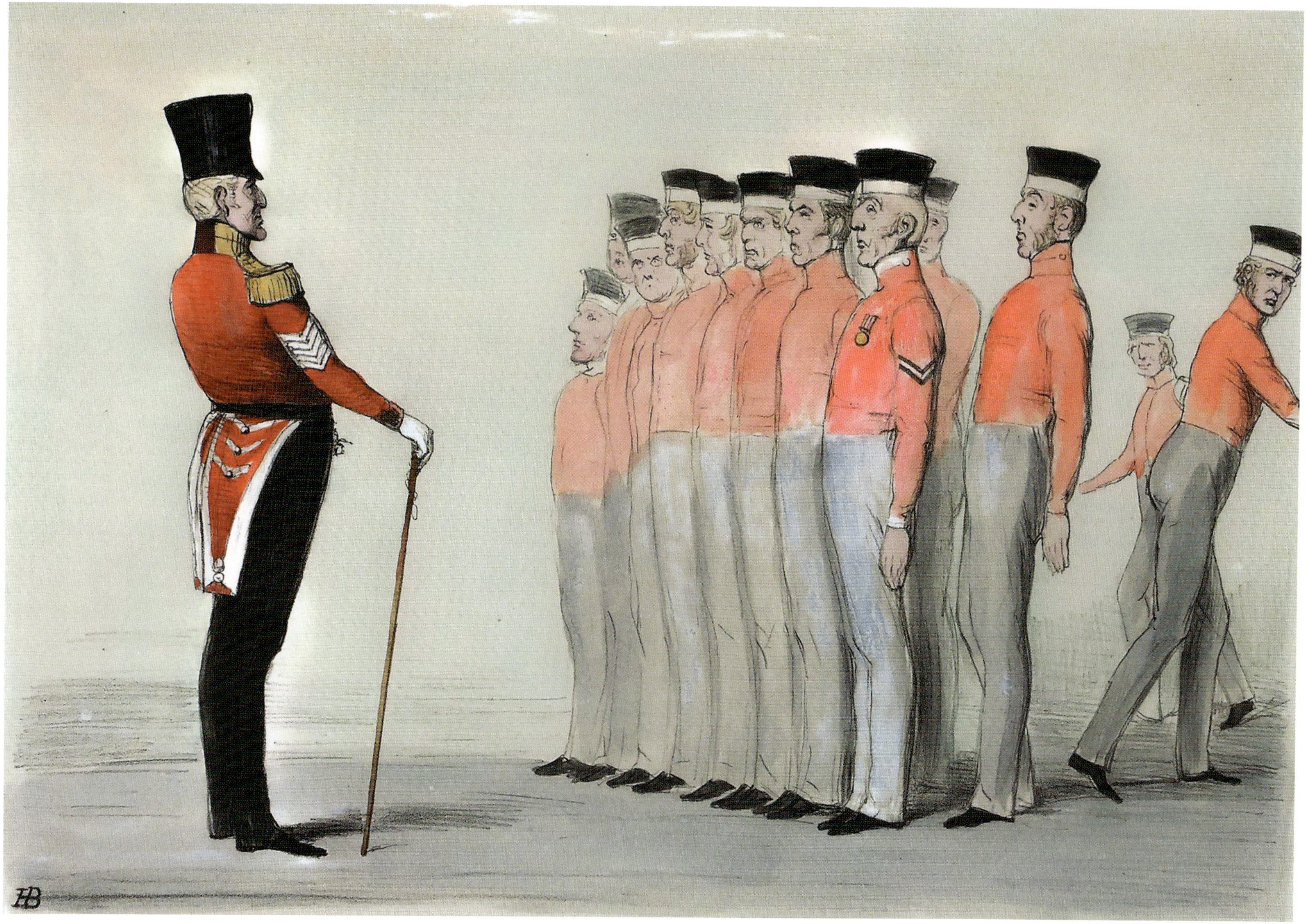

[131] ***No. 851, 'The Drill – 'Dismiss' – 'As you were' (steady there in the rear rank)' (published 18 Jan. 1846)*** A man dressed in military uniform, wearing a top hat (Sir Robert Peel), standing at the left in profile to the right, drilling his squad (from left to right, Lord Somerset, three unidentified men, Henry Goulburn, Lords Lyndhurst and Aberdeen, the Duke of Wellington and Lord Ellenborough); a man at the far right (Lord Stanley) disobeys the second order, walking away towards right. After Lord John Russell's abortive attempt to form an alternative ministry, pledged to repeal, Peel returned as Prime Minister. Wellington agreed to serve in the interests of the Queen's government but Stanley refused, walking away from 'the drill' represented here by 'H.B.'

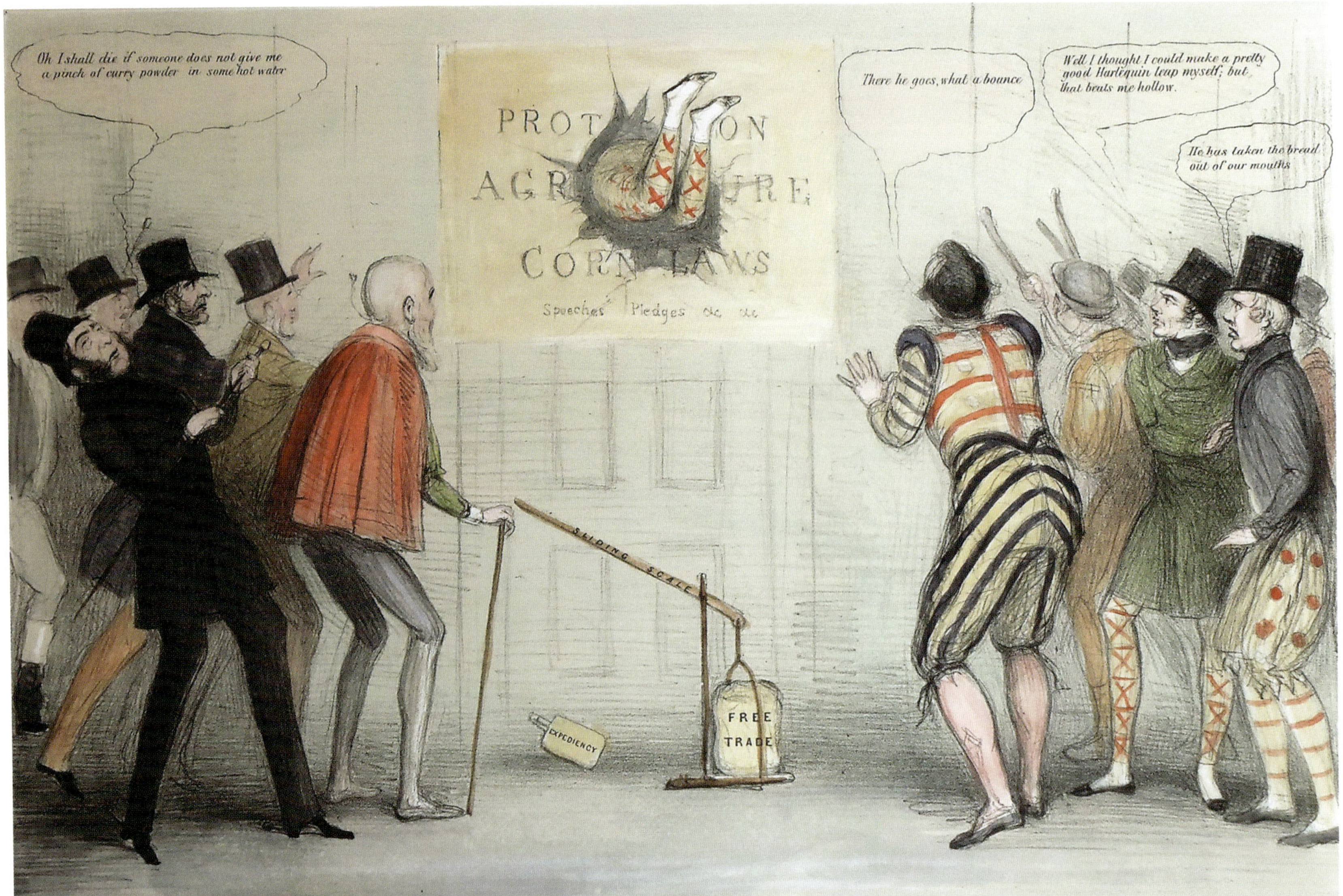

[132] ***No. 852, 'Christmas Pantomime (No. 2) – Extraordinary Harlequin Leap' (published 18 Jan. 1846)*** Harlequin (Sir Robert Peel) jumping head first through a screen at centre, lettered with 'PROT[...]ON AGR[ICULT]URE CORN LAWS Speeches Pledges &c &c', while Pantaloon (Duke of Wellington), at the centre left, and the Clown (Sir James Graham), at the centre right, look on in admiration, two men at the far right (Lords John Russell and Morpeth) in envy, a man at the left in a fainting fit of horror (the Duke of Norfolk), and two men behind him in astonishment (the Dukes of Buckingham and Richmond); at the centre on the floor, scales lettered with 'Sliding Scale', an object underneath with 'Expediency', and a sack with 'Free Trade'. The political crisis engendered by the Repeal of the Corn Laws coincided with the Christmas festivities and the pantomime season. 'H.B.' employs this understandable conceit to render the political changes of the period in a comic form. The Harlequinade is the part of the pantomime where the Harlequin and Clown (or Pantaloon) play the principal parts.

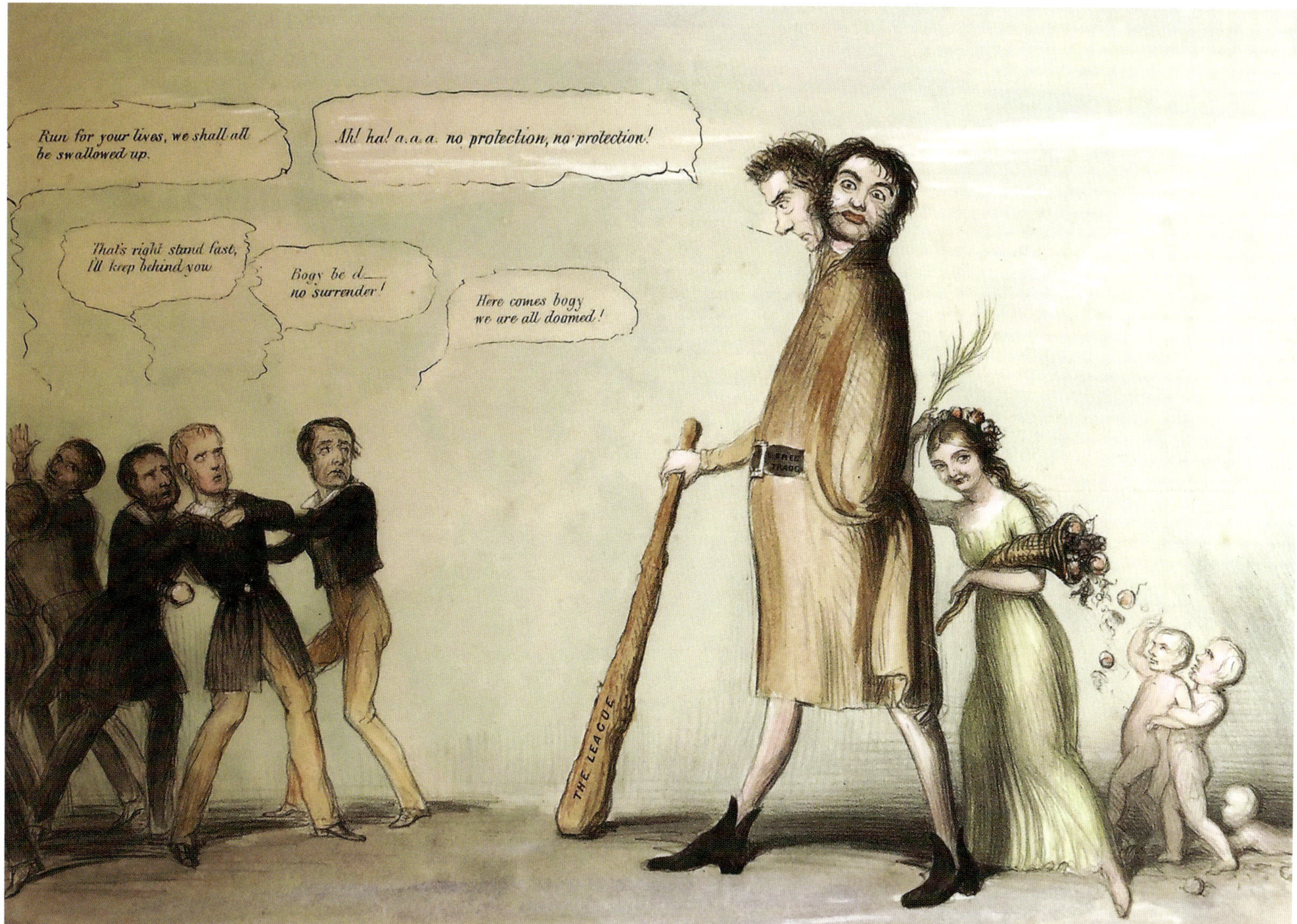

[133] ***No. 853, 'Bogy's Coming – An Allegory for the Nursery' (published 22 Jan. 1846)*** A man with two heads (Richard Cobden and John Bright), walking towards the centre from the centre right, wearing a belt lettered with 'Free Trade', holding a club lettered with 'The League', followed by a young girl carrying a cornucopia, and two naked infants (Lords John Russell and Morpeth); a group of men fleeing at the far left (looking back, the Duke of Buckingham), but one man is willing to confront him, with one of his companions hiding behind his back (Duke of Richmond), and the other trying to escape (Sir Robert Peel); a baby lying on the floor at the far right. In classical mythology, the infant Zeus was protected from his devouring father Cronus by a number of divine attendants. The unstoppable momentum of the League's campaign for Free Trade is seen here marching towards its 'prey', challenged only by Richmond (who became the leading opponent of the measure in the House of Lords). Lord Morpeth (heir to the Earl of Carlisle) had announced his conversion to Repeal at the end of November 1845.

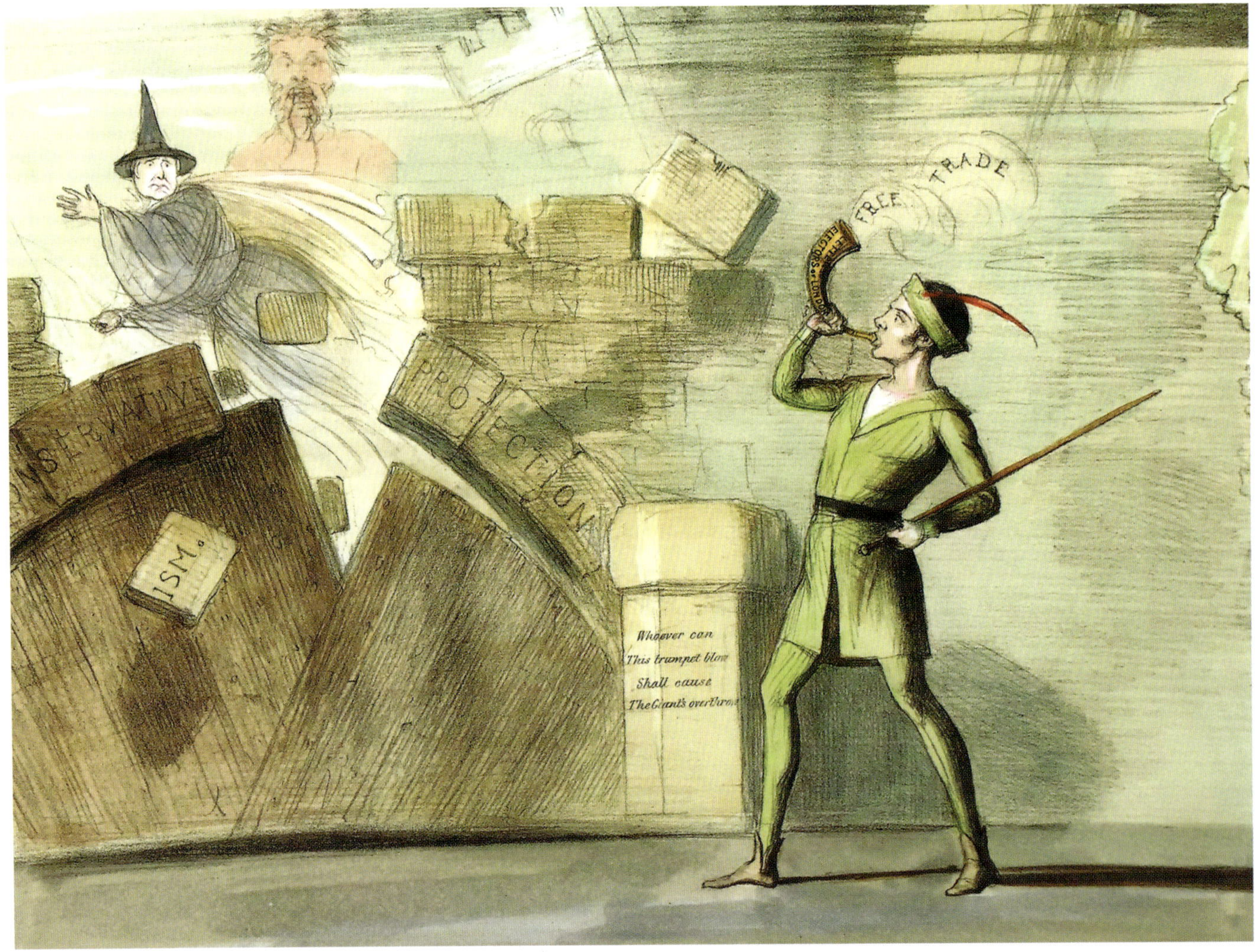

[134] ***No. 854, 'Jack the Giant Killer' (published 2 Feb. 1846)*** Below the title: 'He seized the trumpet, & blew a loud blast, which made the Castle fall to pieces & fly away like Smoke! The Giant knowing that his wicked cause was at an end, Stood biting his thumb, & the magician was carried off in a whirlwind!'. A man in the character of Jack (Lord John Russell), standing at the right, blowing a horn lettered with 'Letter to the Electors of London', the sound-waves lettered with 'Free Trade', in front of a castle, at the left, lettered with 'Conservative Protection', falling to pieces; a man in the character of the magician (Sir Robert Peel), fleeing the castle at the left; a man in the character of the giant, standing behind him, biting his thumb. The tale of 'Jack the Giant Killer' first appeared in print in 1711 and its message of a plucky young man slaying giants achieved a resonance with subsequent writers and satirists. 'H.B.'s illustration relates to the part of the tale where Jack blows a horn to awaken the giant from its slumbers. Lord John (or 'Jack') Russell issued a 'Letter to the Electors of the City of London' on 22 Nov. 1845 announcing his conversion to Repeal in the following terms: 'I confess that on the general subject my views have in the course of twenty years undergone a great alteration. I used to be of opinion that corn was an exception to the general rules of political economy; but observation and experience have convinced me that we ought to abstain from all interference with the supply of food'. The letter, issued from Edinburgh (and known as Russell's 'Edinburgh Letter') complicated Peel's position at a time when he was trying to unify his cabinet behind his own policy; however, it also provided a possible alternative government if Peel's attempt failed.

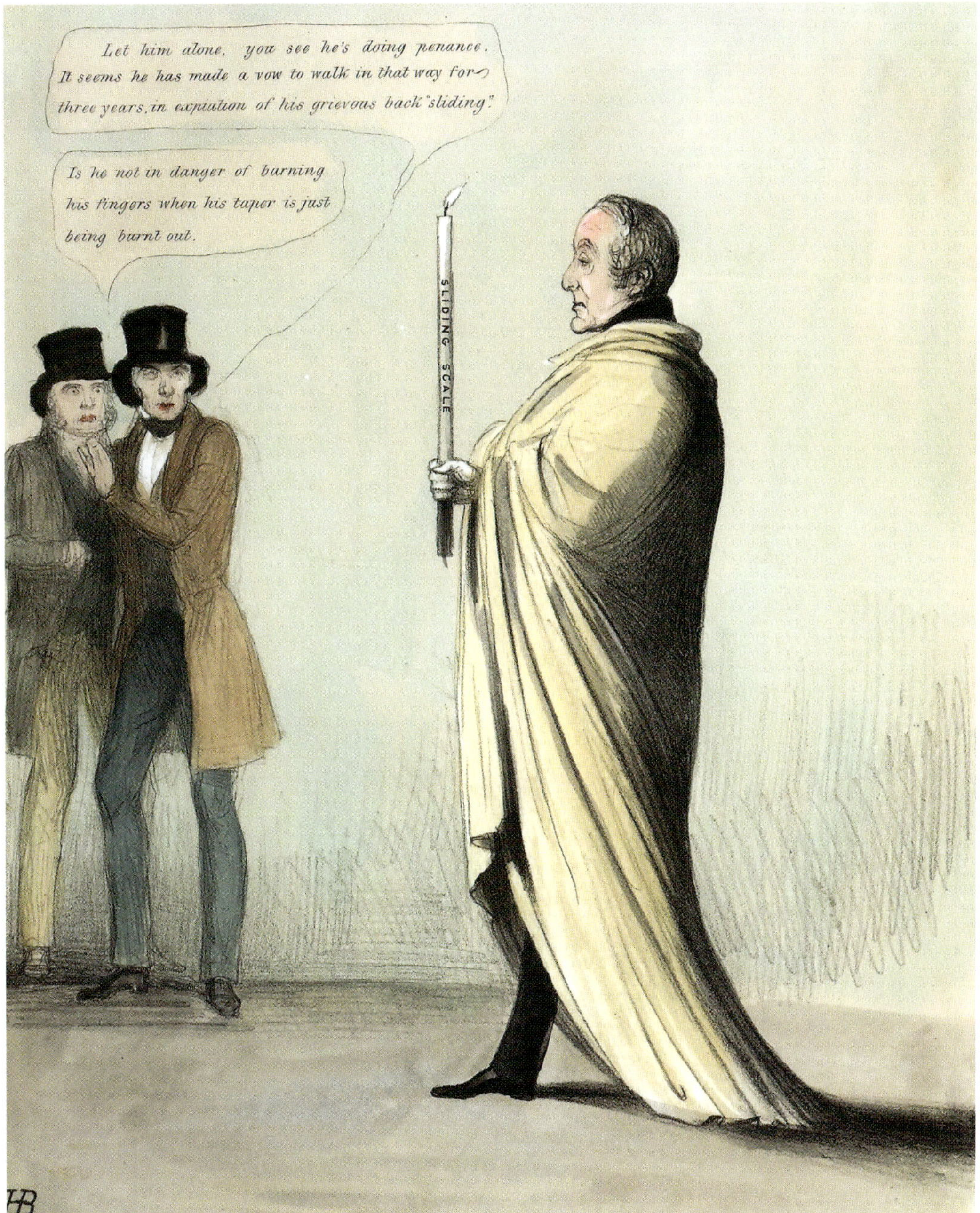

[135] ***No. 855, 'Doing Penance' (published 6 Feb. 1846)*** A man at the centre, in profile to the left, holding a candle lettered with 'Sliding Scale' in his right hand (Sir Robert Peel), walking towards the left, watched by two men in background at the left (John Bright and Richard Cobden). Peel's 1842 Corn Law legislation had been predicated on the basis of a sliding scale of duties, with the import duty on foreign corn descending as domestic prices rose. Critics of Peel's conversion to full repeal, in 1845–1846, argued that he had not tried his own 1842 act sufficiently before deciding to abandon it. Doing penance was a traditional public act of atonement in the Christian church, often undertaken in a white sheet and with a white wand in hand.

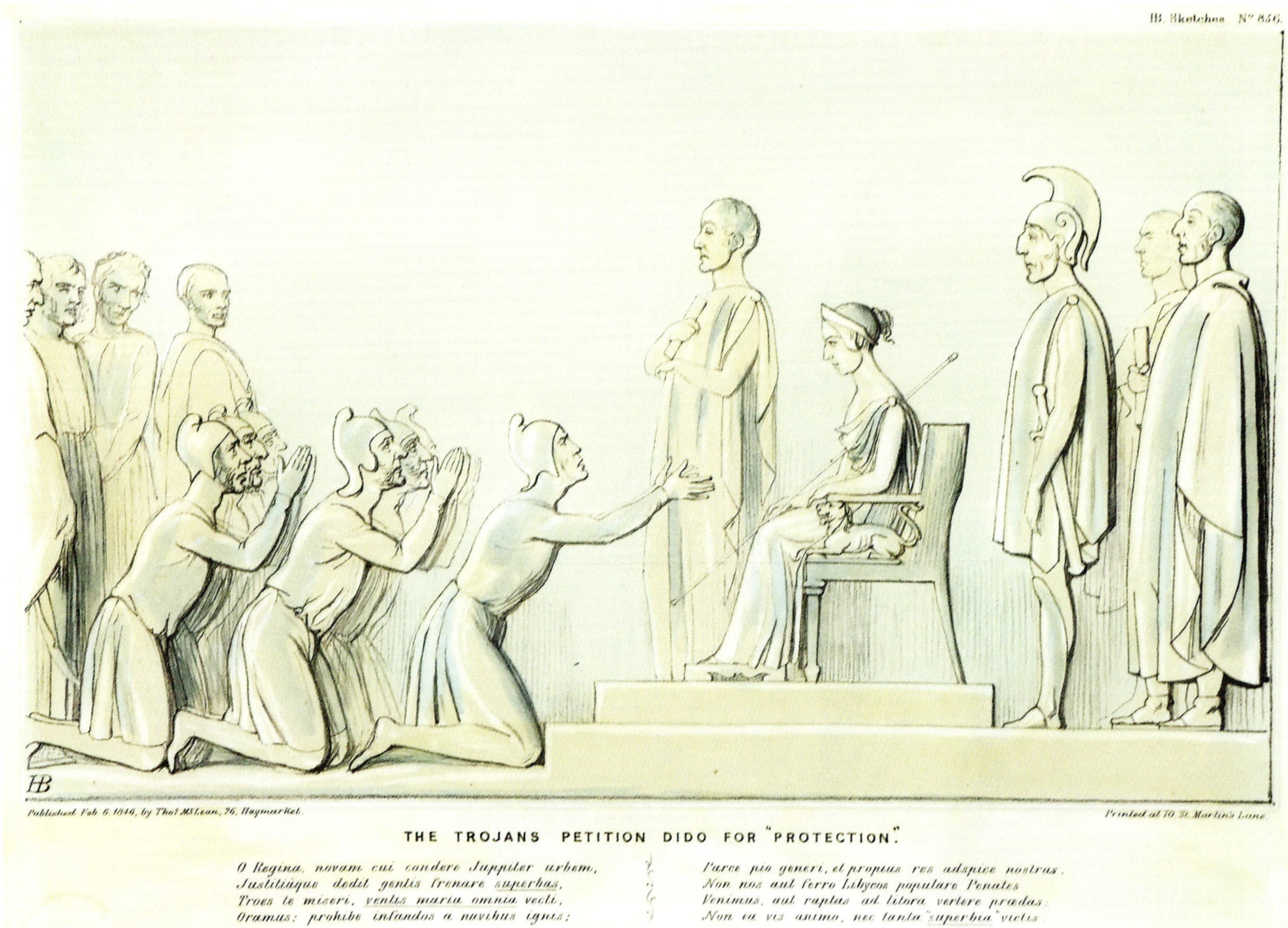

[136] ***No. 856, 'The Trojans Petition Dido for Protection' (published 6 Feb. 1846)*** A group of men acting as Trojans, kneeling at the left, petitioning (among them, from left to right, the Dukes of Newcastle, Beaufort, Buckingham, Norfolk and Richmond), in front of stairs leading to a platform, where a woman is seated on a throne (Queen Victoria); three men standing around the throne (behind at the centre right, Sir Robert Peel, at the far right, the Duke of Wellington, Lord Aberdeen and Sir James Graham); a group of men standing at the left (John Bright, Richard Cobden, Lord John Russell) frowning upon the supplicants. The scene is inspired by Virgil's *Aeneid,* in which Dido (the Queen of Carthage), is petitioned for relief by the Trojans. At the beginning of 1846, a number of 'Protectionist' peers, including Richmond, claimed the traditional aristocratic right of a personal audience with the monarch to plead the case for agricultural protection.

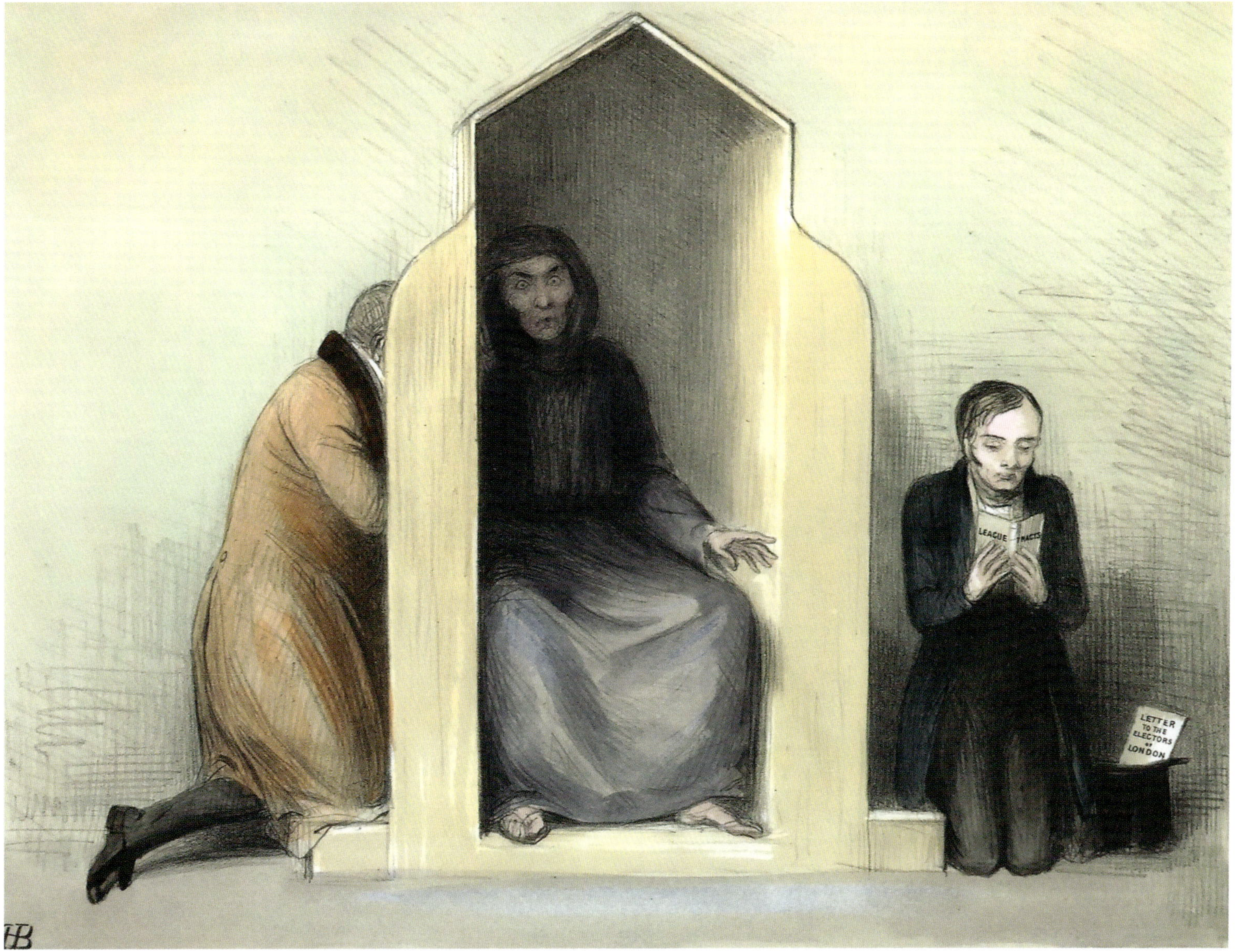

[137] ***No. 857, 'The Confessional' (published 6 Feb. 1846)*** A man kneeling in a confession box at the left, his face hidden (Sir Robert Peel); the confessioner (Richard Cobden) seated at the centre to the front, listening with a horrified expression on his face; a man kneeling at the right, reading a book lettered with 'League Tracts'; next to him at the right, a top hat lying on the floor with a paper in it lettered with 'Letter to the Electors of London'. A reinforcement of recent 'H.B.' sketches on the theme of Peel's conversion to Repeal and the arguments of Richard Cobden and the Anti-Corn Law League. The top hat and reference to the 'Letter' indicates Lord John Russell.

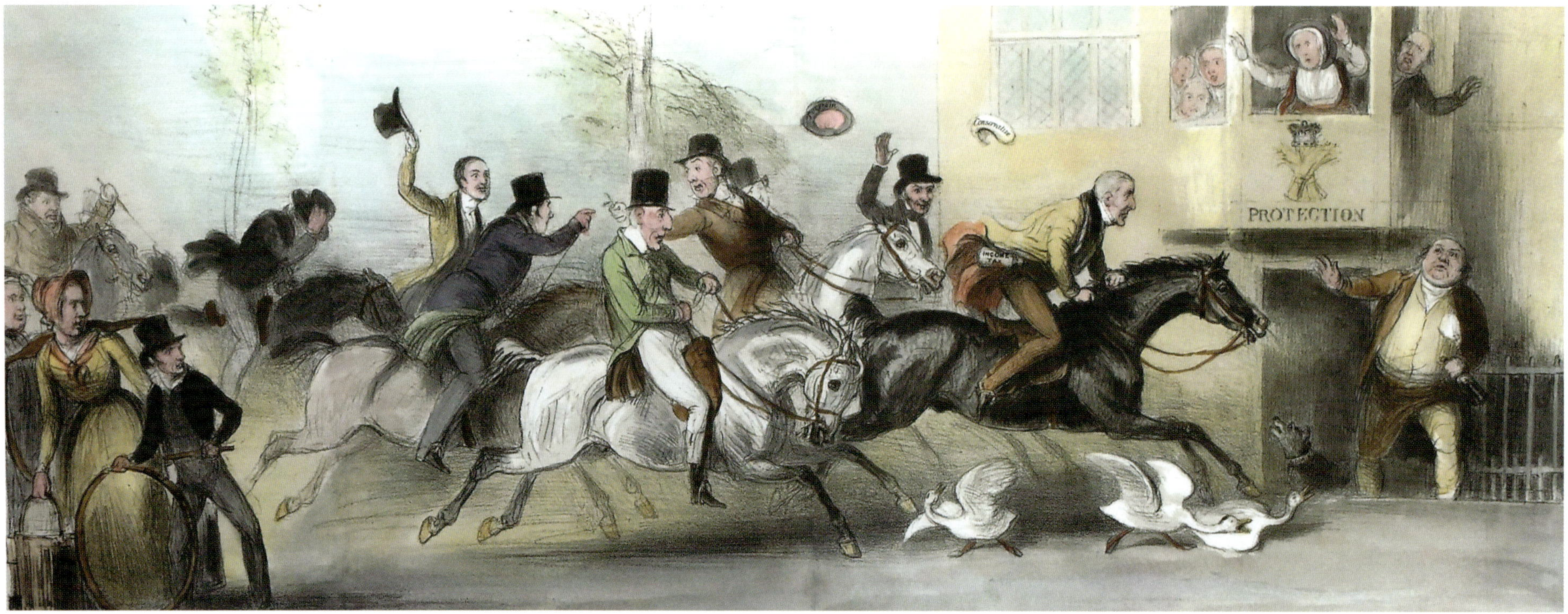

[138] ***No. 858 & 859, 'New Version of John Gilpin after Stothard' (published 2 Mar. 1846)*** Cowper's comic poem was the inspiration for a painting by Thomas Stothard (d. 1834). 'H.B.' here parodies this; a man in the character of Gilpin (Sir Robert Peel) riding headlong, among geese on the road, passes the 'Protection' inn, followed by other riders (Richard Cobden, Henry Goulburn, Sir James Graham, the Duke of Wellington, Lord Aberdeen, Sidney Herbert, John Bright and Daniel O'Connell), riding past a building lettered with 'Protection' on the balcony, from where a group of people are trying to stop them (the Duke of Richmond dressed as a woman, next to him at the right, Sir Robert Inglis); John Bull, the inn-keeper, standing at the far right, with a dog, holding a bottle in his left hand, holding up his right hand and calling to stop them; at the far left, a man (Alexander Baring), a man dressed as a woman (Lord Morpeth) and a man holding a hoop lettered with 'Free Trade' (Lord John Russell), looking on. 'H.B.' satirises Peel's head-long drive after Repeal, intimating its unpopularity with 'John Bull' (the embodiment of British public opinion) as well as the leading 'Protectionists' ranged against him.

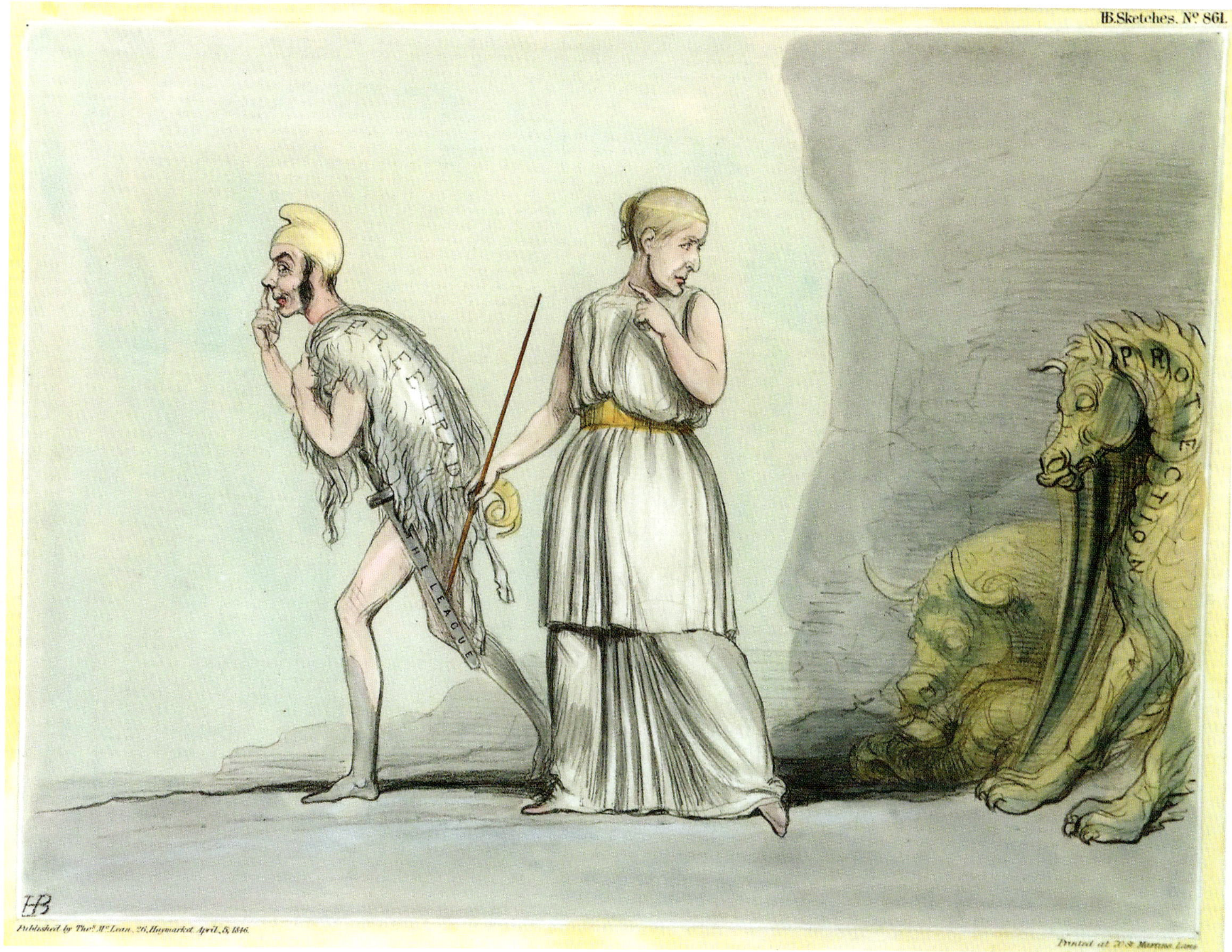

[139] ***No. 861, 'Jason, aided by Medea, carries off the Golden Fleece' (published 5 Apr. 1846)*** A man in the character of Jason (Richard Cobden), wearing a sword lettered with 'The League', walking towards the left, carrying off the Golden Fleece, lettered with 'Free Trade', on his back, aided by a man dressed as a woman, in the character of Medea (Sir Robert Peel), standing behind him at the centre; at the right, the dragon, lettered with 'Protection', is asleep. In Greek legend, Medea (the sorceress) was the wife of Jason, who enabled him to complete his tasks. His final task was to overcome the dragon which guarded the Golden Fleece. With the assistance of a potion supplied by Medea, Jason was able to accomplish his aim. 'H.B.' uses the conceit to suggest that Peel's conversion and subsequent promotion of a Repeal Bill through the House of Commons is the means of overcoming 'Protection' in order to achieve Cobden's aim of 'Free Trade'.

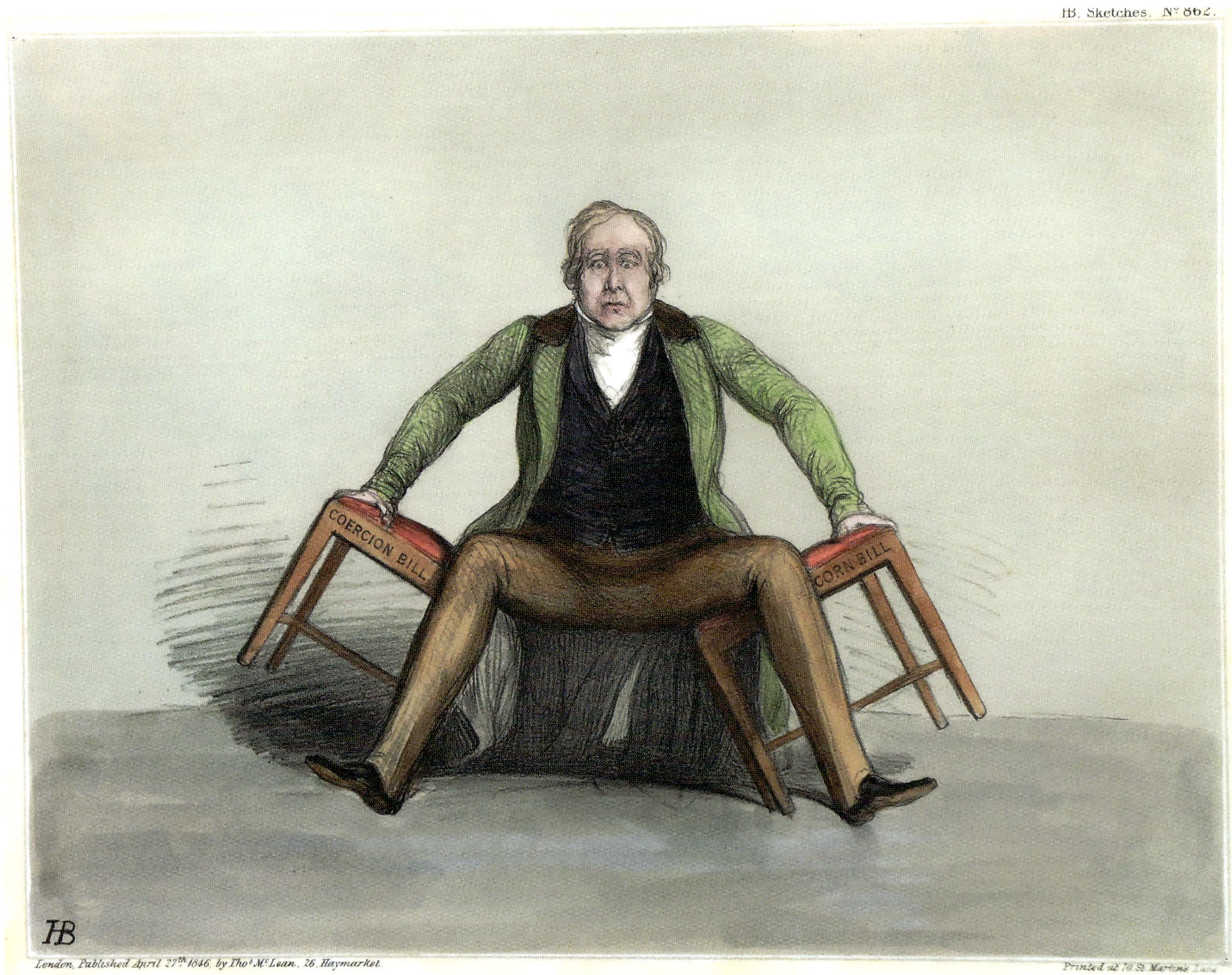

[140] ***No. 862, 'A Dangerous Situation' (published 27 Apr. 1846)*** A man at the centre (Sir Robert Peel) falling on the floor between two stools, the one held in his right hand lettered with 'Coercion Bill', the other held in his left hand lettered with 'Corn Bill'. A combination of Whigs, Radicals and Protectionists, gathered in what the Duke of Wellington famously described as a 'blackguard combination', defeated Peel's ministry on 25 June 1846 on its Irish Coercion Bill by 292–219. Earlier in the evening, the Repeal of the Corn Laws had passed the House of Commons. Defeat on the Coercion Bill had been widely foretold, not least by Wellington himself. 'H.B.' here shows the precarious nature of Peel's position, as he seeks to carry both measures. In reality, Peel failed to 'fall between two stools' in that he succeeded in securing the larger measure of Repeal.

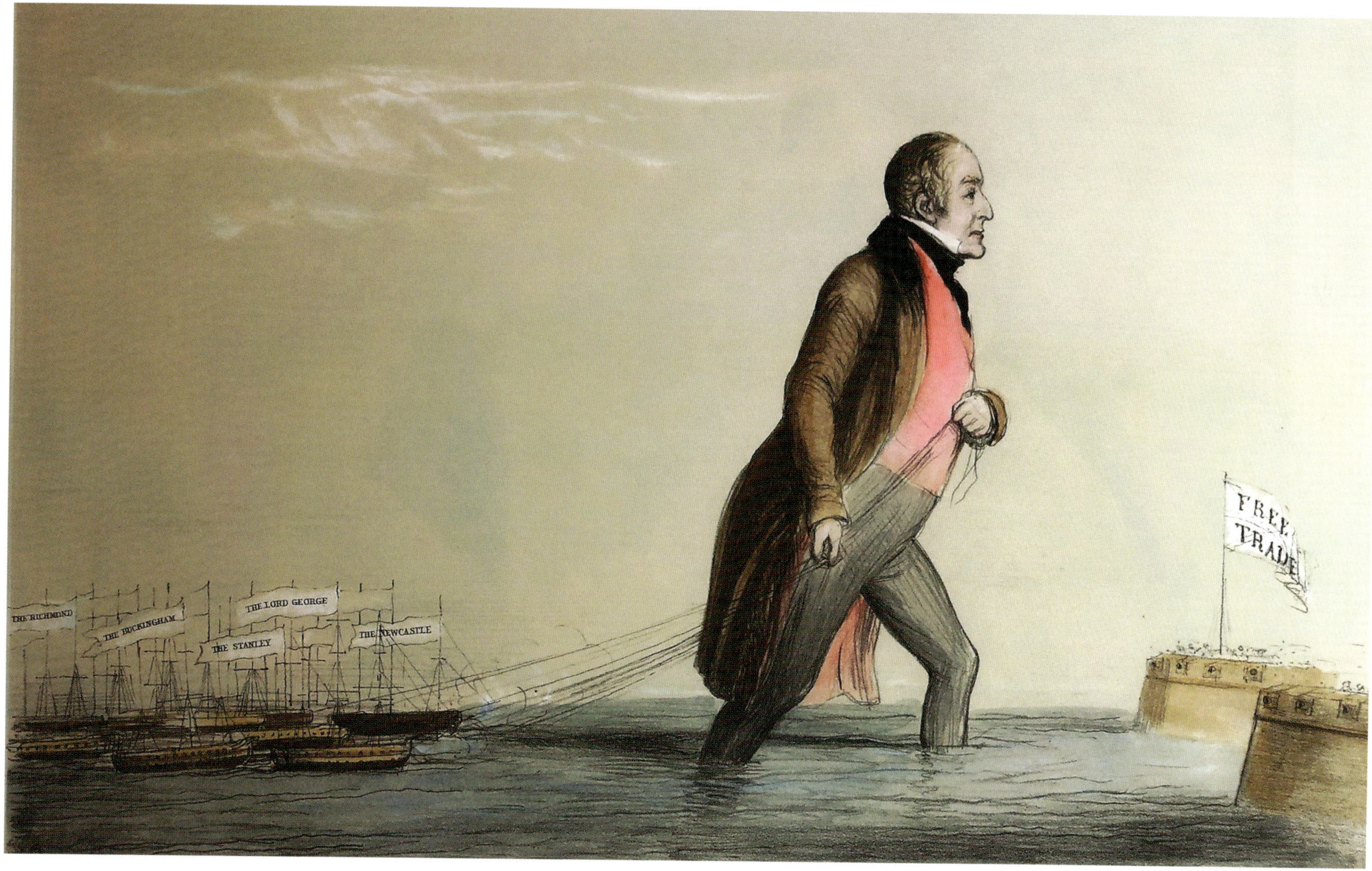

[141] ***No. 865, 'Gulliver Capturing the Enemy's Fleet' (published 29 May 1846)*** A man in the character of Gulliver (Sir Robert Peel), at the centre right, walking in the sea towards a fort at right, its flag lettered with 'Free Trade', pulling after him on threads a group of sailing ships, lettered on their flags with 'The Newcastle', 'The Lord George', 'The Stanley', 'The Buckingham' and 'The Richmond'. A conceit drawn from Jonathan Swift's *Gulliver's Travels* (1726) in which Lemuel Gulliver captures the Blefuscudian fleet by wading out into the water and dragging it ashore: 'putting off my coat, shoes, and stockings, [I] walked into the sea, in my leathern jerkin, about half an hour before high water. I waded with what haste I could, and swam in the middle about thirty yards, till I felt ground. I arrived at the fleet in less than half an hour. The enemy was so frightened when they saw me, that they leaped out of their ships, and swam to shore, where there could not be fewer than thirty thousand souls. I then took my tackling, and, fastening a hook to the hole at the prow of each, I tied all the cords together at the end. While I was thus employed, the enemy discharged several thousand arrows, many of which stuck in my hands and face, and, besides the excessive smart, gave me much disturbance in my work' (Part I, Chapter V). The fleet carries the names of noted Protectionists including the Duke of Newcastle and Lord George Bentinck. The 3rd reading of the Repeal bill passed the House of Commons on 15 May 1846 by 327–229 (majority 98).

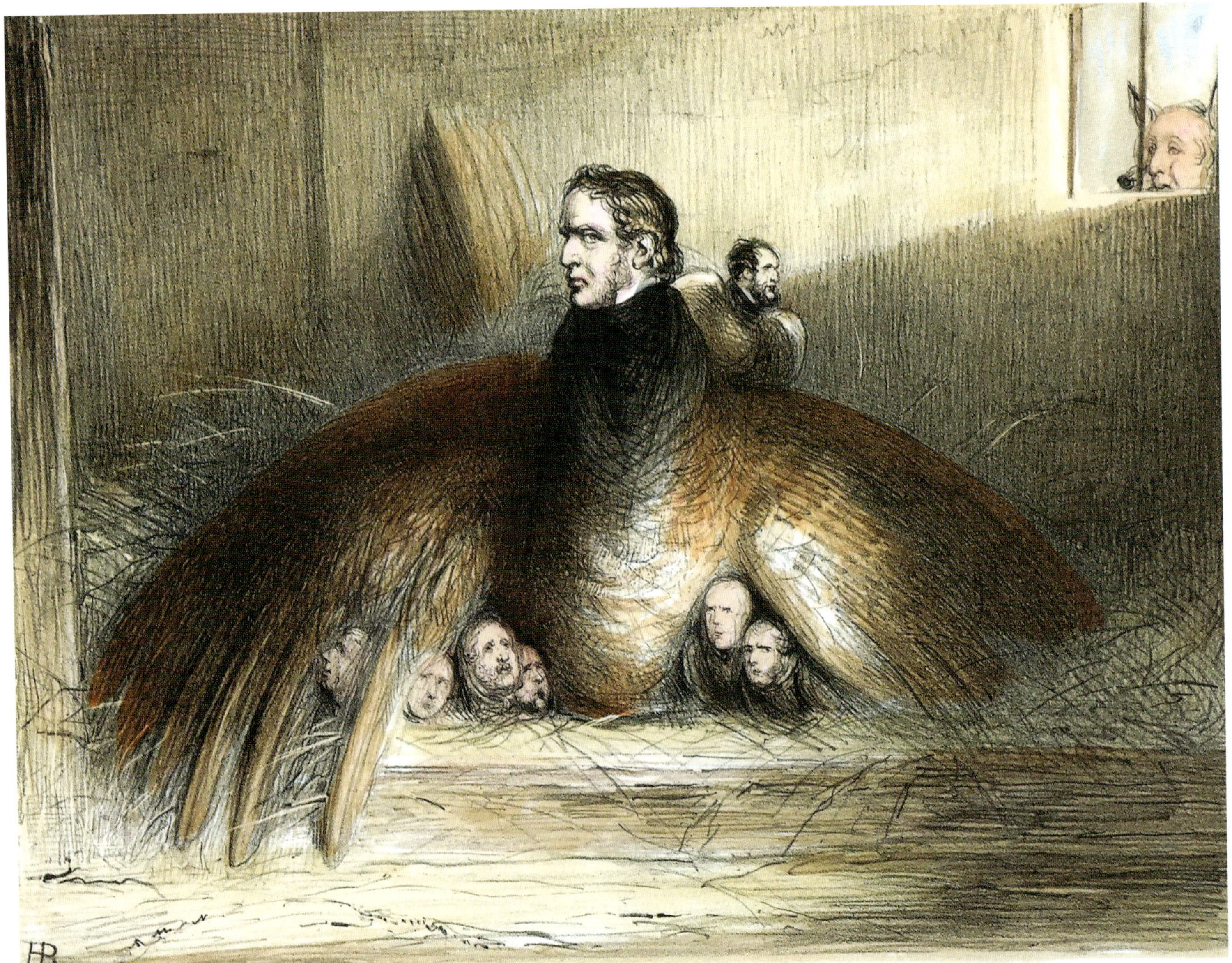

[142] ***No. 867, 'Protection' (published 26 June 1846)*** Below the title: 'A Hen & Chickens of an extraordinary Game breed, not to be found in any work on Ornithology'. Inside a farm-building, a hen with a man's head (Lord Stanley), lying on straw, with chicks with men's heads (politicians) under its wings and on its back; an animal with a man's head (Sir Robert Peel) looking in through a window at top right. Richmond and other landowners perform the role of chickens. Stanley formally assumed leadership of the post-Peel Conservative party in July 1846, having had his way smoothed by the Duke of Wellington in the House of Lords. Peel, however, remained a continuing presence in British politics during the next four years.

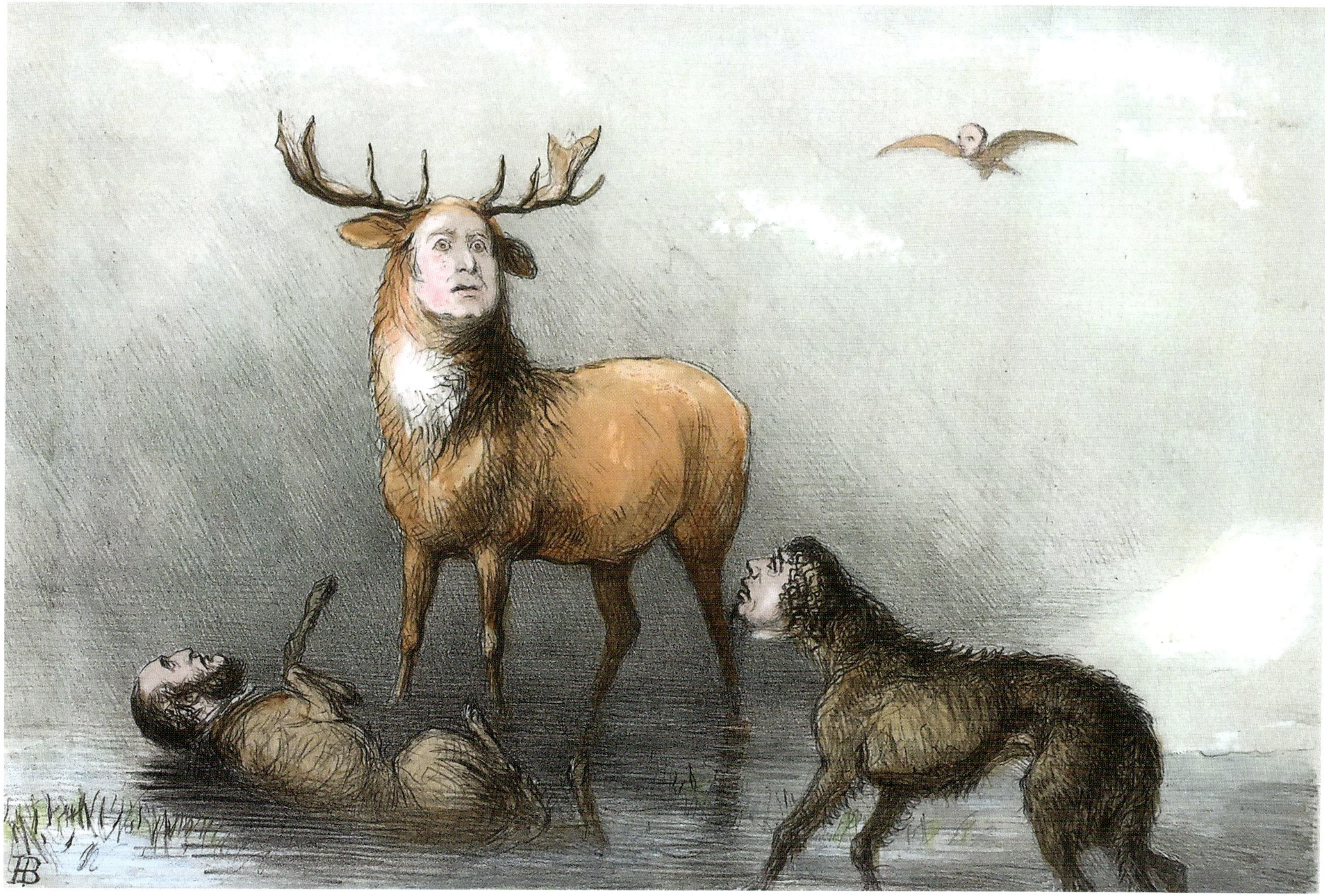

[143] ***No. 868, 'Stag at Bay – Suggested by the Beautiful Picture of Edwin Landseer R.A. Esq. exhibited at the Royal Academy 1846'*** A parody of Landseer's painting, the animals have men's heads; a stag (Sir Robert Peel) standing at the centre, with a frightened expression; two wolves, one lying on his back at the left (Lord George Bentinck), the other standing at the right (Benjamin Disraeli), looking up at the stag; a bird approaching from the sky at the right. The notion of an encircling doom around Peel, in terms of the attacks of his principal opponents in the House of Commons, is here rendered in the form of Landseer's painting of a hunted stag. Lord George Bentinck, a younger son of the Duke of Portland, emerged from backbench obscurity in the parliamentary session of 1846 to become Peel's most consistent and vitriolic opponent. In partnership with Benjamin Disraeli, the two men went on to lead the Protectionists in the Commons after Peel's fall from power.

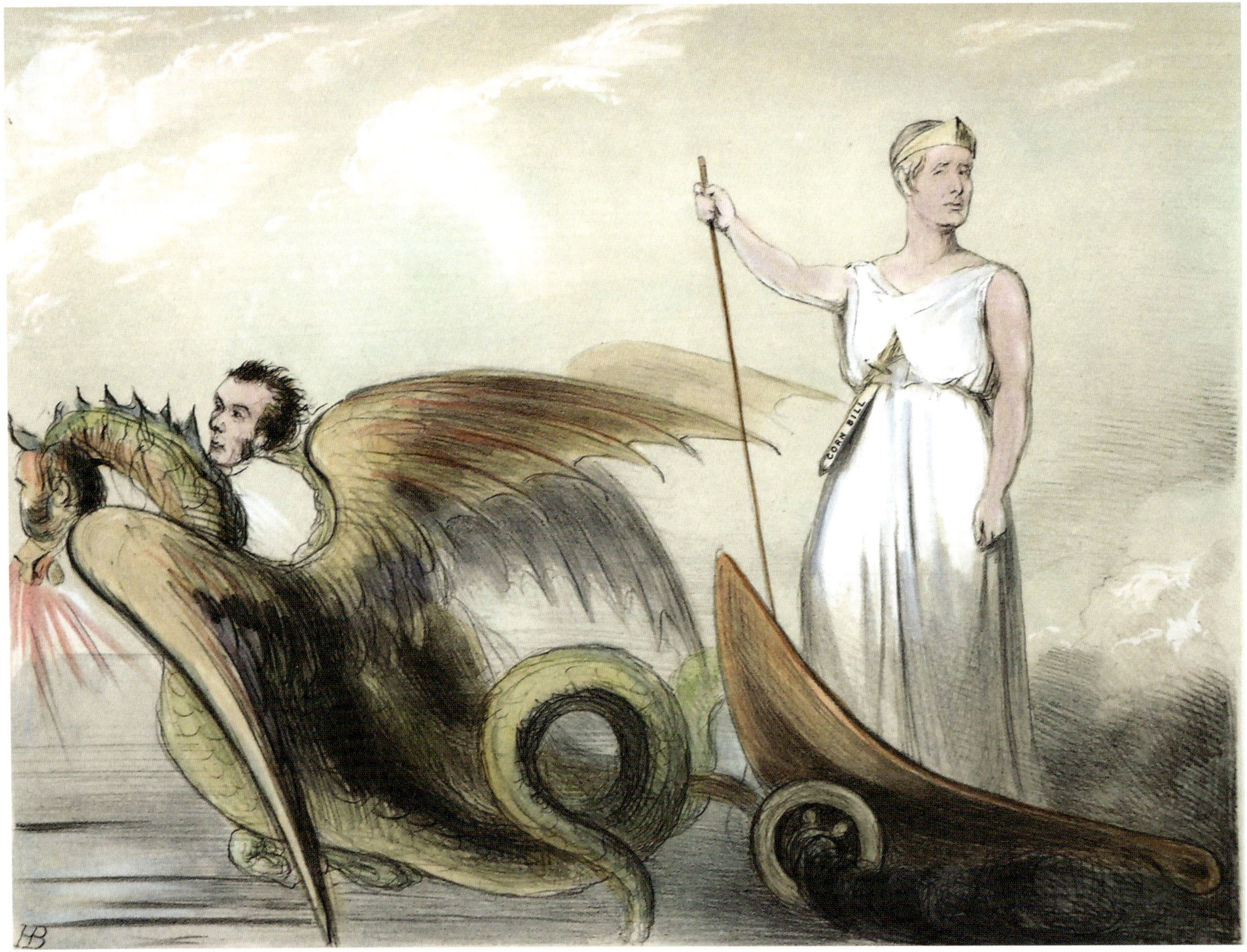

[144] ***No. 870, 'Medea' (published 18 July 1846)*** Below the title: 'Having destroyed her children vanishes through the air, upon a chariot drawn by winged dragons'. A man dressed as a woman, in the character of Medea (Sir Robert Peel), wearing a dagger lettered with 'Corn Bill' on 'her' belt, standing at the right on a chariot drawn by two dragons (John Bright and Richard Cobden) from the right towards the left. In classical legend, the sorceress Medea killed two of her sons with a dagger. She escaped by flying to Athens in a golden chariot driven by dragons sent by her grandfather (Helios, god of the Sun). The sketch references Peel's resignation speech as Prime Minister, on Monday 29 June 1846, in which he praised Cobden's part in the passage of Repeal, whilst condemning his own 'Protectionist' followers.

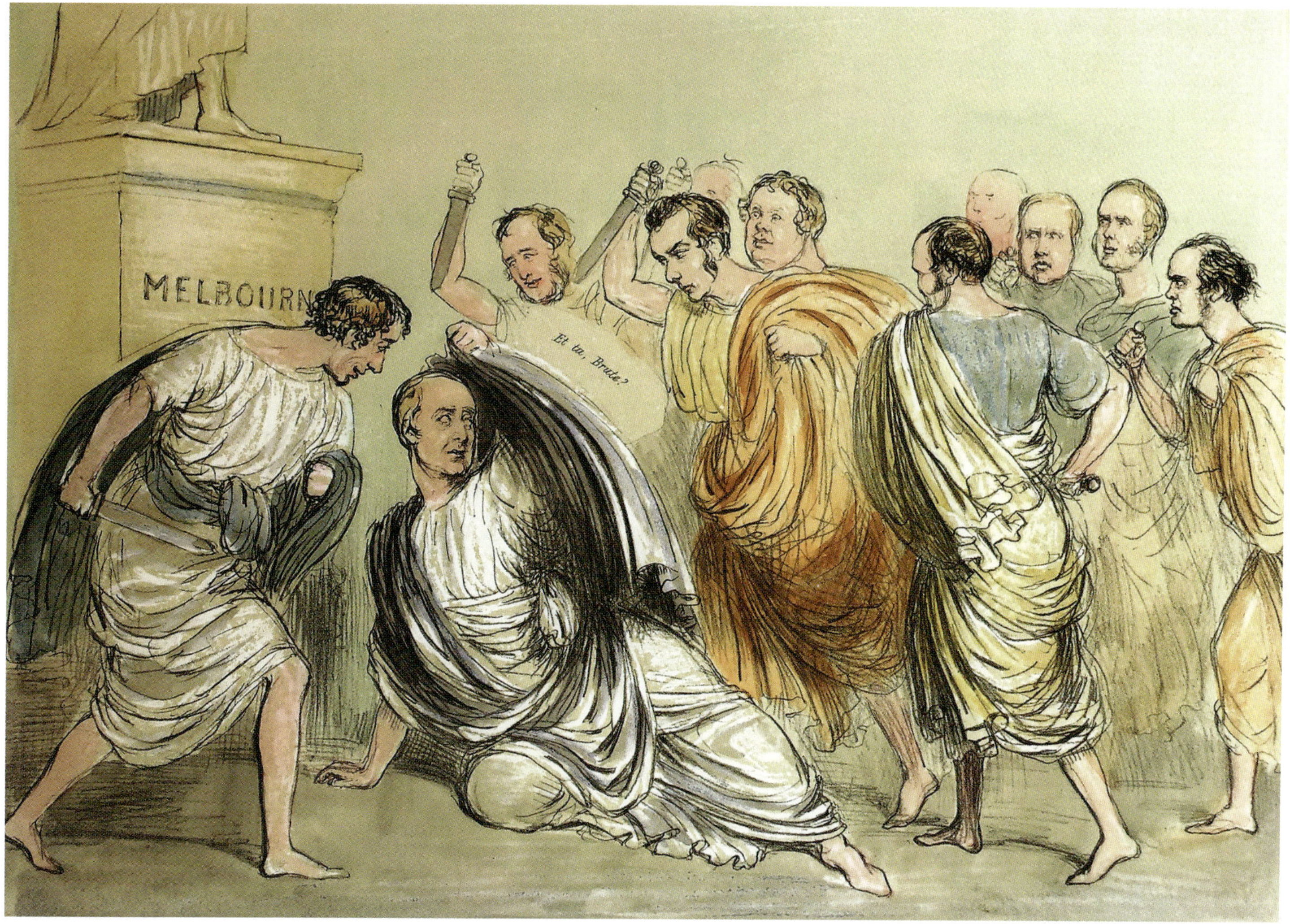

[145] ***No. 872, 'The Fall of Caesar' (published 18 July 1846)*** A man in the character of Julius Caesar (Sir Robert Peel), falling in the foreground at the centre at the base of a sculpture, at the left, its plinth lettered with 'MELBOURN[E]', struck by a group of men, holding daggers (from left to right, Benjamin Disraeli, Lord George Bentinck, Richard Cobden, Daniel O'Connell, Lords John Russell, Morpeth and Palmerston and Richard Lalor Shiel). Peel is saying to Cobden, 'Et tu, Brute'. A conceit based on the well-known fall of Caesar at the hands of his own followers. Extra piquancy is rendered by the fact that Peel falls at the base of the statue of Melbourne, whose government Peel had helped to displace in 1841 after it proposed a fixed moderate duty on corn in place of agricultural protection. The sketch records the fall of Peel's government on 25 June 1846. At Manchester, on 15 Jan. 1846, Cobden had stated his position with respect to the political parties: I am anxious, not merely that we should all of us understand each other on this question, but that we should be considered as occupying as independent and isolated a position as we did at the first moment of the formation of this League. We have nothing to do with Whigs or Tories; we are stronger than either of them; and if we stick to our principles, we can, if necessary, beat both. And I hope we perfectly understand now, that we have not, in the advocacy of this great question, a single object in view but that which we have honestly avowed from the beginning. Our opponents may charge us with designs to do other things. No, gentlemen, I have never encouraged that…It will be enough if the League accomplishes the triumph of the principle we have before us'.

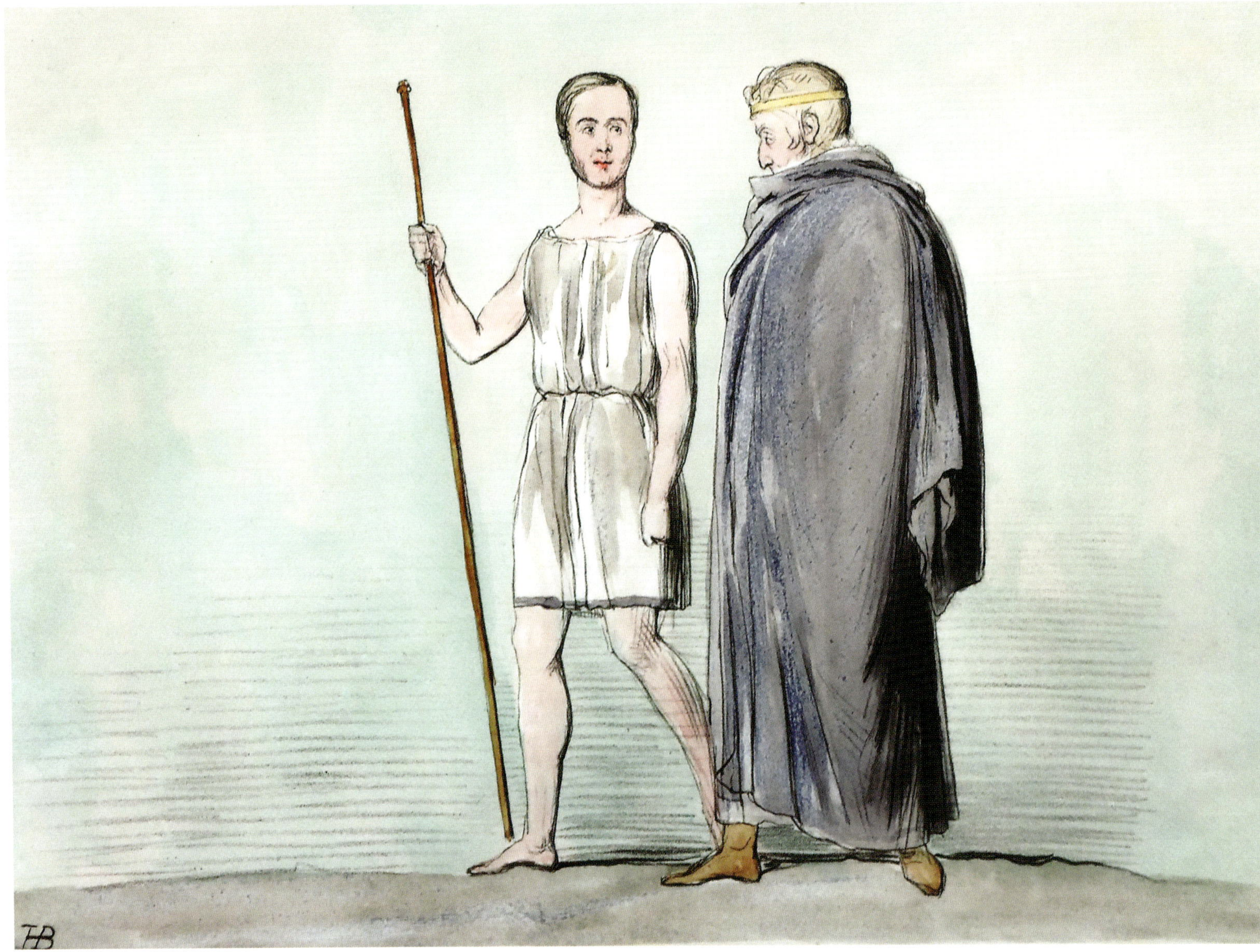

[146] ***No. 882, 'Telemachus and Mentor' (published Mar. 1847)*** A man in the character of Telemachus, at the centre (Lord Lincoln), holding a staff in his right hand, walking with a man in the character of Mentor, at the centre right (Sir Robert Peel). In Homer's 'Odyssey', Mentor was left in charge of Telemachus by Odysseus, who was Telemachus's father. 'H.B.' is unlikely to have been praising the Duke of Newcastle (Lord Lincoln's father) as Odysseus, but Lincoln himself was known to be extremely close to Peel on personal and political grounds. In many respects, Lincoln offered a possible future leader for the Peelites. As a Mentor, Peel is imparting wisdom and knowledge to his young charge.

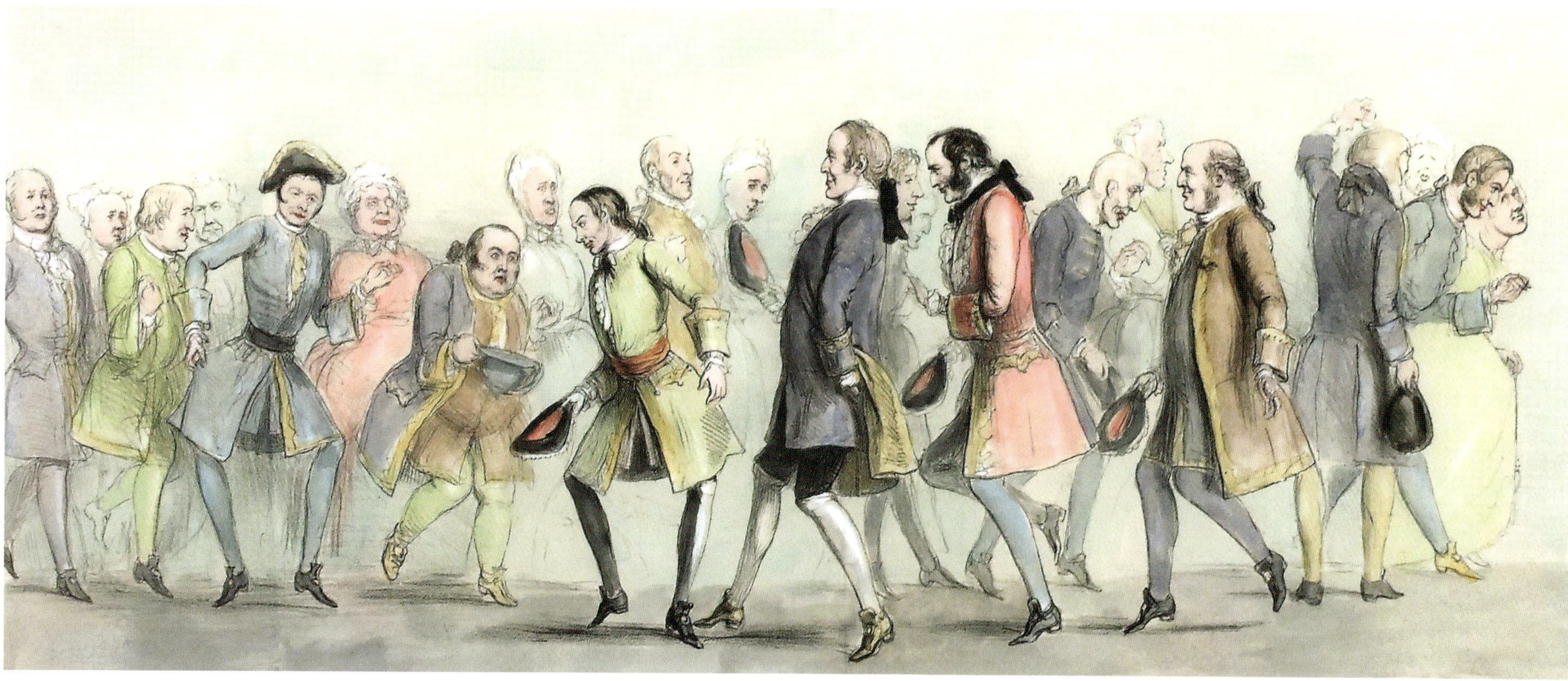

[147] ***No. 888, 'A Fancy Ball – "Sir Roger de Coverley" – In appropriate costume' (published 26 Feb. 1847)*** A group of men, and men dressed as a woman, dancing (from left to right, Lord Palmerston, Peter Borthwick, Sir John Cam Hobhouse, Joseph Hume, the Duke of Rutland, Sir Frederick Trench, George Hudson, Colonel Sibthorp, Lord John Russell, Sir James Graham, Thomas Duncombe, Sir Robert Peel, Benjamin Disraeli, John Arthur Roebuck, Lord George Bentinck, the Duke of Wellington, Lord Brougham, Sir Robert Inglis, Lord Cottenham, Charles Shaw-Lefevre, Lord Lincoln and Lord Morpeth). An assorted cast of politicians of all shades of opinion engage in the popular past-time of dancing the 'Sir Roger de Coverley'. Sir Roger was a fictitious character in *The Spectator* magazine (1711) where he was used to represent an English country gentleman who was 'rather beloved than esteemed'. A dance of the same name (mimicking a hunted fox going in and out of cover) was first published in 1695. The conceit expresses the various political machinations which occurred in the confused state of parliamentary politics following the Repeal of the Corn Laws.

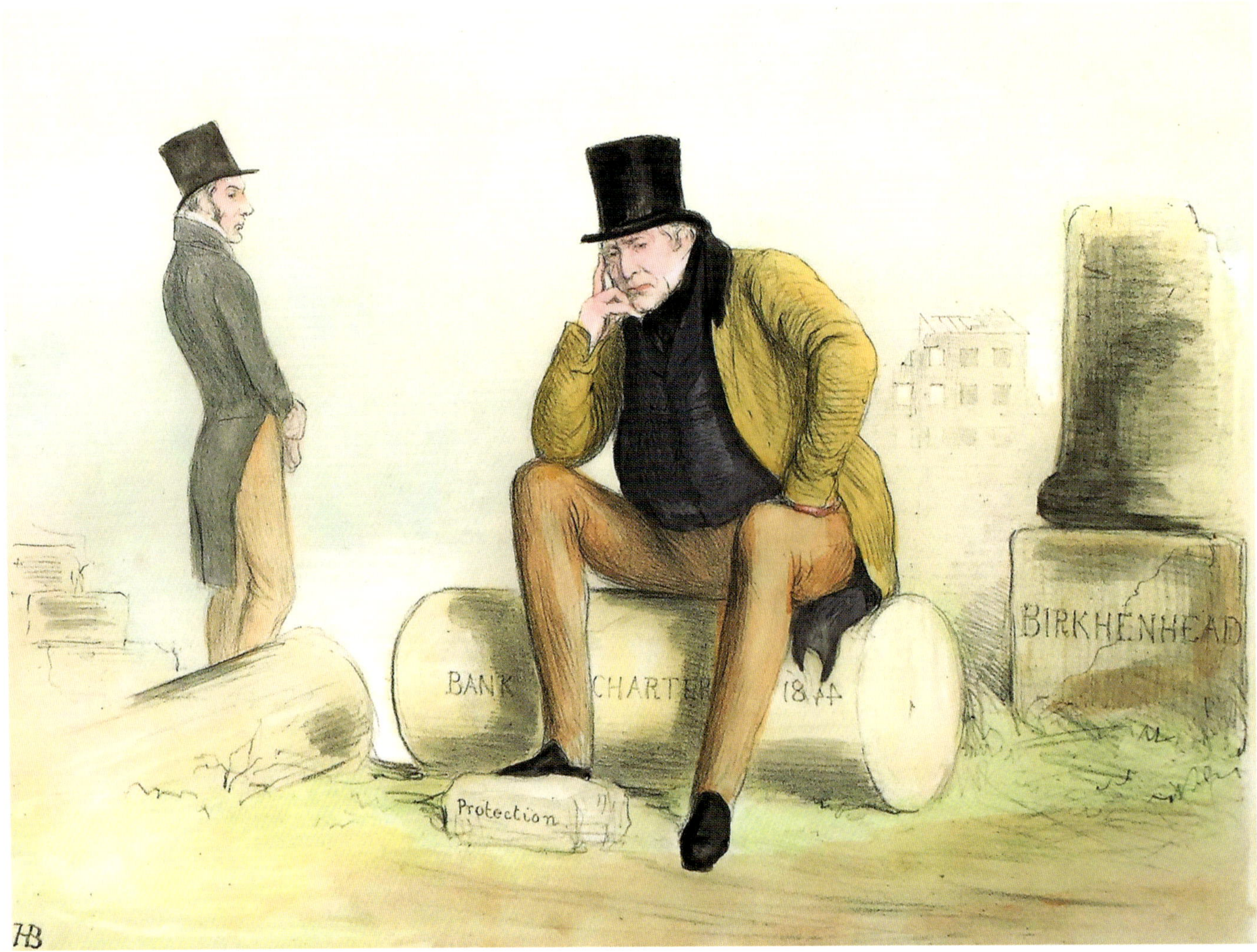

[148] ***No. 890, 'A Study for a Caius Marius sitting amidst the Ruins of Carthage' (published 10 Nov. 1847)*** Below the title: 'Rather a serious subject. Napoleon was in the habit of comparing England to Carthage'. This sketch is inspired by a famous early-nineteenth century painting by John Vanderlyn which was exhibited in Paris and won the Napoleon gold medal. A man (Sir Robert Peel) seated amidst ruins at the centre in a thinking pose on a broken horizontal column lettered with 'Bank Charter 1844', his right foot on a piece of stone lettered with 'Protection'; next to him at the right, a broken upright column, its base lettered with 'Birkenhead'; another man (Richard Cobden) standing at the left, looking on. The year 1847 saw a major challenge to Peel's Bank Charter Act of 1844, which imposed severe restrictions on the issue of paper currency. Peel regarded it as one of his greatest legislative achievements but the financial and banking crisis which occurred that year, together with the continuing recriminations about the Repeal of the Corn Laws, made Peel a controversial figure and his policies the subject of intense and hostile debate. *The Spectator* of 16 Oct. 1847 p.8 notes Peel's visit to Merseyside: 'Subsequently he crossed over to Birkenhead, in the Medina mail-steamer, and spent some time viewing the Docks, Park, and buildings'. The docks (then in course of development) were managed by the Birkenhead Dock Company until the financial crisis of 1847. Caius Marius was consul of Rome seven times (returning from exile to take control for the last time). 'H.B.'s sketch draws a parallel with Peel's current exile from political office whilst suggesting that, like his Roman forebear, a return to rule might not be entirely out of the question.

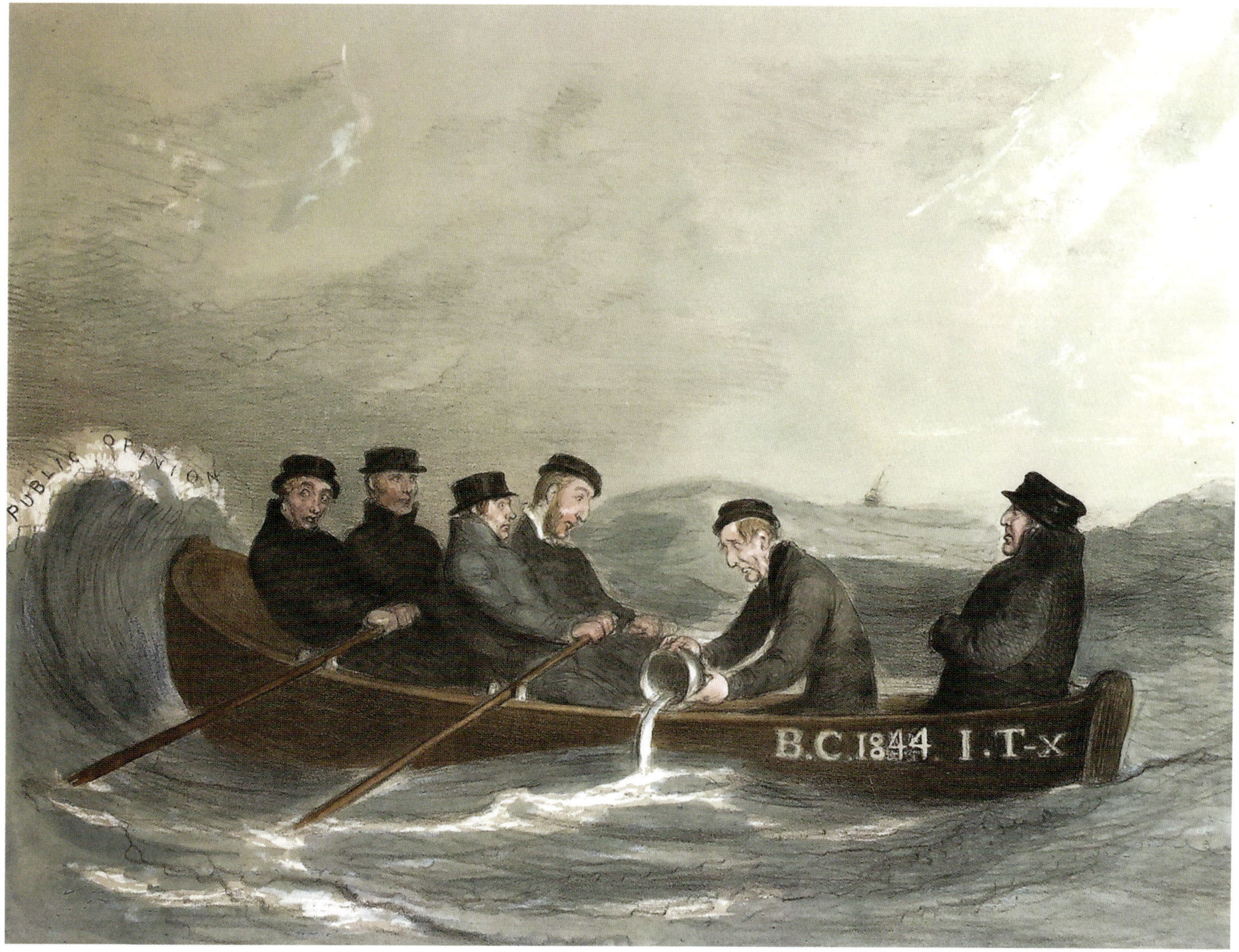

[149] ***No. 895, 'Rowing in the same Boat – Something wrong at bottom, – weather rather squally' (published 21 Mar. 1848)*** Six men at sea in a rowing boat lettered with ' B.C.1844 I.T-x', in stormy weather, on a wave behind at the left lettered with 'Public opinion', four rowing (from the left, Earl Grey, Sir George Grey, Lord John Russell, an unidentified man), one bailing water out of the boat (either Goulburn or Sir Charles Wood), and one seated at the far right (Sir Robert Peel). The Whig government of Lord John Russell proposed a 2% addition to the Income Tax and maintained Peel's Bank Charter Act of 1844 in spite of a major financial and banking crisis during 1847. Peel remained an informal adviser to Charles Wood, the Whig Chancellor of the Exchequer (Henry Goulburn had fulfilled this office in Peel's ministry). A satire on the proximity of the Whigs and Peelites over matters of financial and commercial policy during the 1846–1852 government. Peel died on Tuesday 2 July 1850 as a result of injuries from a riding accident on 29 June; Doyle discontinued his 'Political Sketches' in 1851; a year later, a Whig-Peelite government was formed under the premiership of Lord Aberdeen. As *The Times* commented at the time, 'in one sense, we are all Peelites'.

INDEX TO THE CATALOGUE

Direct references to Peel are excluded, as he features in all but two of the 'Political Sketches'.